And the War Came

. . . But the Government at Washington, denying our right to self-government, refused even to listen to any proposals for a peaceful separation. Nothing was then left to us but to prepare for war.—JEFFERSON DAVIS' INAUGURAL ADDRESS, FEBRUARY 22, 1862.

. . . Both parties deprecated war, but one of them would make war rather than let the nation survive, and the other would accept war rather than let it perish, and the war came.—ABRAHAM LINCOLN'S SECOND INAUGURAL ADDRESS, MARCH 4, 1865.

MAJOR ROBERT ANDERSON
(From a photograph in the National Archives)

And the War Came

~~~~~~

THE NORTH
AND THE
SECESSION CRISIS
1860-1861

~~~~~~

by Kenneth M. Stampp

LOUISIANA STATE UNIVERSITY PRESS

To
Katherine Mitchell
Stampp

Preface

MUCH CAN BE learned about the general nature of the
American sectional conflict from a study of the northern reaction to southern secession during the five months between
the election of Lincoln and the attack upon Fort Sumter. During
this brief and dramatic period all the sharp issues which had divided the sections for a generation were telescoped and intensified
in such a way as to bring on a tragic climax. In the end, the overwhelming majority of Northerners accepted this crisis as the final
test of power between them and their southern rivals. In the end,
they were ready to have Federal laws enforced in the South and
to risk the consequences.

It has not been my purpose to undertake what appears to me
the fruitless and impossible task of proving or disproving that the
Civil War was inevitable. Instead I have been concerned with
the problem of *why* the war came, especially why Northerners
were unwilling to acquiesce in disunion. To me the conclusion
seems inescapable that this conflict was the product of deep and
fundamental causes and that most of the compromise proposals
were essentially superficial. There was no basis for sectional harmony as long as Negro slavery survived and as long as Northerners
used their overwhelming political power in Congress to advance
their special interests at the expense of the South. Since the dominant groups on neither side were willing to yield on these points,
separation was the last hope for a peaceful settlement. Why the
southern attempt to apply this solution did not produce peace
between North and South will be the major theme of this book.

While assuming sole responsibility for errors of fact and interpretation, I owe much to those who have advised and assisted me
in the preparation of this study. I am deeply grateful to Richard
N. Current of Mills College and to Richard Hofstadter of Columbia University for their painstaking criticisms of both the style
and contents of the entire manuscript. I am also indebted to Frank

Freidel of the University of Illinois; to Wesley M. Gewehr of the University of Maryland; to Fred H. Harrington and William B. Hesseltine of the University of Wisconsin; to John D. Hicks of the University of California; and to T. Harry Williams of Louisiana State University.

The staffs of the various libraries I have visited were uniformly generous in making available their research materials. I have a special obligation to the Institute of Social Sciences at the University of California for providing funds for microfilming and typists. The editorial staff of the Louisiana State University Press have improved the manuscript considerably by their careful editing.

Parts of Chapters X and XIII appeared in an article entitled "Lincoln and the Strategy of Defense in the Crisis of 1861," in the *Journal of Southern History*, XI (1945), 297–323. The editor has graciously permitted me to republish portions of this material.

I must also thank my wife for much valuable assistance, and especially for the title of the book, which she found in Lincoln's second inaugural address.

Berkeley, California
September, 1949

KENNETH M. STAMPP

Preface to the Paperback Edition

T HE L OUISIANA paperback edition of this book is unchanged from the original edition published in 1950. This does not mean that it is written exactly as it would be were I to write it now. Indeed, in every chapter I would like to delete some passages, add others, and rewrite many more. I cannot say with certainty that the book I would write would be better—only that in some respects it would be different. The revisions resulting from the opening of new sources would be few; those from new insights and changed perspectives, many. I would, for example, give greater emphasis to the ideologies of nationalism, democracy, and antislavery as forces encouraging Northerners to demand the preservation of the Union. Though still unsure that civil war was at all times the inevitable consequence of a generation of sectional conflict—the South, after all, *might* have given up slavery; the North *might* have given up the Union—I am now more skeptical that during the months of the secession crisis there were viable alternatives to force.

From the perspective of 1970, I could hardly write a book such as this without devoting at least part of a chapter to secession as it was viewed by articulate northern free Negroes. Frederick Douglass, the most distinguished Negro abolitionist, in a series of editorials written for his newspaper, *Douglass' Monthly*, analyzed the issues with a relentless logic seldom found in other quarters. He had no doubt that it was slavery that "disturbs, divides and threatens to bring on civil war, and to break up and ruin the country. . . . Slavery is a disease, and its abolition in every part of the land is essential to the future quiet and security of the country." When South Carolina passed her ordinance of secession, Douglass called upon the federal government to use its power to preserve the Union. If, however, the choice were between compromise and disunion, "if the North is to foreswear the exercise of all rights incompatible with the safety and perpetuity of slavery . . . then . . . let the Union perish, and perish forever." Lincoln's pledge, in his Inaugural Address, not to interfere with slavery and to enforce the Fugitive Slave Law, Douglass found appalling. Such a pledge was "wholly discreditable to the head and heart of Mr. Lincoln," and put him "upon the same moral level" with slaveholders. Douglass wrote with great bitterness about "the prevailing contempt for the rights of all persons of African descent"—"our much hated variety of the human family."[1]

Nor could one study the secession crisis from our present perspective without a close and detailed analysis of northern racial attitudes. In the light of what has been written on this subject since the publication of this book, my brief reference to it on page 251 seems less than adequate. Winthrop D. Jordan, in *White Over Black: American Attitudes Toward the Negro, 1550-1812* (Chapel Hill, 1968), probes and analyzes the sources of white racism, and he makes it abundantly clear that this has been a central theme not only of southern but of American history. Leon F. Litwack, *North of Slavery: The Negro in the Free States, 1790-1860* (Chicago, 1961), documents the workings of race prejudice in the laws and customs of the northern states. Eugene H. Berwanger, *The Frontier Against Slavery: Western Anti-Negro Prejudice and the Slavery Extension Controversy* (Urbana, 1967), demonstrates that Negrophobia was a significant reason for antebellum northern opposition to slavery expansion. Many Free Soilers of the 1840's and Republicans of the 1850's gave evidence of being not so much anti-slavery as anti-Negro and anti-southern. V. Jacque Voegeli, *Free but Not Equal: The Midwest and the Negro During the Civil War* (Chicago, 1967), and Forrest G.

---

[1] These editorials are reprinted in Philip S. Foner (ed.), *The Life and Writings of Frederick Douglass* (New York, 1952), III, 57-85. See also James M. McPherson, *The Negro's Civil War: How American Negroes Felt and Acted During the War for the Union* (New York, 1965), 3-18.

Wood, *Black Scare: The Racist Response to Emancipation and Reconstruction* (Berkeley, 1968), trace the theme of Negrophobia through the war years and emphasize the hysterical fear that emancipation would produce a mass migration of free Negroes from the southern to the northern states. Even some of the Radical Republicans and political abolitionists were infected with the virus of racism and found association with Negroes on terms of equality impossible. They made it clear that a Northerner could be at once anti-slavery and anti-Negro.

Thus to understand the northern response to southern secession, one must recognize that the racial attitudes of the great majority of Northerners were not much different from those of Southerners. It is doubtful that many Northerners put concern for the black man high on the list of reasons why the Union had to be preserved. Free-state Democratic politicians, seeking a compromise with the South, demagogically exploited northern race feeling in order to discredit the Republicans. As they had done in the 1850's, Democrats constantly referred to their political foes as "Black Republicans," "nigger-lovers," "wooly heads," and "amalgamationists" who, by opposing a sectional compromise, subordinated the interests of the white man to those of the black. Responding to this attack, Republicans assured northern voters that their program was designed to protect *white* farmers and laborers from the aggressions of the Slave Power. It was an unedifying debate.

Nevertheless, after taking account of Negrophobia among rank-and-file Republicans, something more must be said about racial attitudes within their party. In the first place, national Republican leaders did not ordinarily take the initiative in appealing to race prejudice. When, during the secession crisis, Republicans explained their opposition to compromise in terms of the interests of white men, they were usually reacting to the demagoguery of the Democrats who accused them of undue concern for blacks. If race prejudice was evident among both Republicans and Democrats, there was still a qualitative difference. The average northern Republican, compared to the average northern Democrat, seemed to be a little more relaxed about race—a little less hysterical about the threat of a black invasion, somewhat less hostile to civil and political rights for Negroes.[2] In fact, I am convinced that during the 1850's differences in racial attitudes helped to determine northern political affiliations.

Moreover, there was a significant element in the Republican party that really did have strong moral feelings about slavery; and some among the party's political abolitionists—men such as Charles Sumner and George W. Julian—even showed concern for the free Negro and strove to win equality for him. Whatever their limitations (no doubt they were guilty of paternalism), these Radical Republicans showed far greater racial tolerance than other white Americans of their day. During the secession crisis some of them did seem to think that the time had come to strike a blow at slavery as well as at the Slave Power. In short, to be realistic about northern Negrophobia is not to deny altogether the reality of the moral crusade against slavery, or that this crusade was one reason among many for the northern determination to preserve the Union.

No doubt every writer would like to clarify those passages of his book which he thinks reviewers have misunderstood. I was rather startled to find, in Thomas J. Pressly, *Americans Interpret Their Civil War* (Princeton, 1954), pages 288-91, this book described as "fundamentally in accord with the 'revisionist' tradition." In Civil War historiography revisionism is associated with the notion that the war lacked fundamental causes, that it grew out of a series of artificial crises precipitated by a "blundering generation" of irresponsible politicians and agitators, and that it was therefore "needless." The revisionists believe that nothing was at stake of such great importance that it could not have been settled by mutual concessions; and, accordingly, they make compromisers such as John J. Crittenden and Stephen A. Douglas the heroes of their age.

According to Pressly, *And the War Came* manifests its re-

[2] During the 1860's, several northern states controlled by Republicans voted against extending the franchise to Negroes. But in each case a substantial minority supported Negro suffrage, and it is reasonable to assume that nearly all of the favorable votes were cast by Republicans.

visionist approach by taking the position that "a peaceful solution was worth any sacrifice," that peace "could have been and should have been preserved." I do not believe that this book takes such a position. It does suggest that "peace at any price" was one alternative among several open to political leaders, but it observes that "by the common standards of statesmanship" such a policy was not acceptable. To see the tragedy of war— of the failure to find a peaceful way to solve a problem such as slavery—is not to contend that war could have been and should have been avoided.

As further evidence of this book's revisionist tone, Pressly quotes three passages to show that its "principal basis" is the idea that "the most logical and reasonable policy" for the North to follow would have been acquiescence in peaceful disunion. First, in the preface, I state that my prime concern is to discover "why Northerners were unwilling to acquiesce in disunion." Second, again in the preface, I observe that since neither section would yield on certain crucial issues, "separation was the last hope for a peaceful settlement. Why the southern attempt to apply this solution did not produce peace between North and South will be the major theme of this book." Third, on page 205, I declare that there is no simple explanation of "why Northerners believed that the formation of a southern Confederacy would have been such a terrible disaster." Each of these passages attempts to define the basic problem that this book tries to solve. Pressly, by finding in them an endorsement of peaceful secession, draws an inference that, in my opinion, is totally unwarranted.[3]

Though refusing to deal with the thorny problem of inevitability, this book takes the position that the Civil War was the result of fundamental sectional differences, and that the compromise movement was superficial and in some respects fraudulent. This position is in conflict with a basic assumption of revisionist historians. If Pressly had found in my interpreta-

---

[3] To support his case, Pressly also observes that this book was reviewed favorably by two revisionist historians. But it was criticized by other revisionists, and reviewed favorably by some historians who are decidedly not revisionists.

tions a large measure of the economic determinism identified with the historian Charles A. Beard, he would have been much nearer the mark; and it is this aspect of the book that I would modify most of all. The closing paragraph of the last chapter, which Pressly attributes to revisionist disappointment with the outcome of the war, reflects far more the influence of Beard and Marx, some of whose ideas were part of the intellectual baggage I carried with me out of the 1930's.

In addition to examining the northern reaction to secession, this book takes part in a debate among several historians over Lincoln's role in the critical months between his election as President and the outbreak of war. The debate began during the war itself, but Charles W. Ramsdell introduced it to modern scholarship in 1937 with his article "Lincoln and Fort Sumter." According to Ramsdell, Lincoln cynically maneuvered the Confederates into firing on Fort Sumter, because he believed that a war was necessary to save not only the Union but his administration and the Republican party. Three years later, James G. Randall replied to Ramsdell in an article, "When War Came in 1861," which holds that Lincoln's policy was at all times peaceful, and that his Sumter strategy was designed to minimize the danger of war.[4] David M. Potter amplifies Randall's argument in his book *Lincoln and His Party in the Secession Crisis* (New Haven, 1942). Lincoln's policy, Potter argues, was based on a common northern belief that Unionism was still strong in the South and that a pro-Union reaction was bound to come. His aim, therefore, was to avoid further irritation of the South and thus to provide both time and the best possible conditions for southern Unionists to regain control. Potter, like Randall, believes that Lincoln was still trying to maintain the peace at the time of the crisis at Fort Sumter, that he tried to relieve the fort in the manner least likely to provoke a hostile Confederate response. Therefore, he concludes, the Confederate attack on Sumter was a defeat, not a victory, for Lincoln's policy.

My own interpretation of Lincoln's strategy is developed in Chapters X and XIII, and these are the chapters that I would be

[4] These articles are listed in my bibliography.

least inclined to revise. The little new evidence that has turned up since 1950 has not altered my belief that by January, 1861, Lincoln had lost faith in a southern Unionist reaction and had come to the conclusion that he might have to use force to preserve the Union. I do not think that he ever intended deliberately to provoke a war, but I do think that his Sumter policy revealed his willingness to risk one for the sake of the Union if the responsibility for aggression could be placed upon the South. In a recent book, *Lincoln and the First Shot* (New York, 1963), Richard N. Current examines all the evidence with meticulous care and, by a different route, reaches conclusions similar in most essential respects to my own.

In a new preface for the paperback edition of his book (1962), Professor Potter continues the debate and asks whether Lincoln, given his determination to save the Union, could "have followed any more peaceable course than he did" with reference to Fort Sumter. After all, he gave the Governor of South Carolina advance notice that the relief expedition was coming, and he assured the Governor that his aim was to supply the fort with provisions only. Historians who attribute to him a coercive policy must "name a less provocative course that he might have followed," or they are guilty "of arguing that a man may pursue a course which offers the maximum possibility of peace and may at the same time be open to the accusation of scheming to bring about war."[5] Indeed, Potter contends that Lincoln, to preserve peace and encourage southern Unionism, was even ready, under certain contingencies, to evacuate Fort Sumter.

In response to this challenge I would argue that, except for the important consideration of northern public opinion, it mattered little whether Lincoln attempted to supply Sumter in the least provocative or the most provocative way, because, as he well knew, *any* attempt was bound to open hostilities. Moreover, I do not think that Lincoln's Sumter policy was in fact the least provocative course he might have followed. For ex-

[5] I should emphasize again that, unlike Ramsdell, neither Current nor I accuse Lincoln of scheming to bring on a war.

ample, before sending a relief expedition, he might have directed
Major Anderson to try to obtain the needed supplies in Charleston. South Carolina authorities might well have refused such a
request (though they permitted Anderson to purchase fresh
meats and vegetables in the Charleston market), but the request
was never made. As to the course Lincoln did follow, while
he assured the Governor of South Carolina that the relief
expedition would land provisions only, he also hinted that an
attempt (with notice) to land "men, arms, or ammunition"
might be made at some future time. A Sumter policy designed
to minimize provocation would hardly have suggested such a
possibility at that critical juncture. Nevertheless, I will certainly
concede that Lincoln satisfied the vast majority of Northerners
that he was merely trying to feed a starving garrison and that
his purpose was entirely peaceful.

An important question in this debate is whether Lincoln
actually considered evacuating Fort Sumter as a matter of
deliberate political policy. In my opinion, the sources indicate
that Lincoln did, in early March, consider evacuation as a possible *military necessity*, but that he always viewed it, under all
circumstances, as a potential disaster for the Union cause. I do
not believe that he ever thought of the evacuation of Sumter as
a possibly desirable political strategy; and I do not believe that
the evidence supports Potter's contention that Lincoln would
have ordered evacuation if he had achieved the reinforcement
of Fort Pickens before a certain crucial date. It is not to accuse
Lincoln of deliberately starting a war to argue, as I do, that
the Confederate attack on Sumter was a triumph, not a defeat,
for his policy. His ultimate goal, after all, was to preserve the
Union, not to preserve the peace. Moreover, it was Jefferson
Davis, not Lincoln, who made the final decision to open
hostilities.[6]

In his new preface, Professor Potter also discusses the subject of compromise in a most searching and thoughtful way.

[6] For a continuation of this debate, see the essay by Professor Potter,
"Why the Republicans Rejected Both Compromise and Secession," and
my comments on his essay in George H. Knoles (ed.), *The Crisis of
the Union, 1860-1861* (Baton Rouge, 1965), 90-113.

He suggests that the Crittenden Resolutions "represented a possible basis for compromise" and "a possible alternative to war in 1861." He concedes that these proposals would not have settled anything and would have preserved the peace only temporarily. But that is the way peace is always preserved, and it at least has the merit of being better than war. The advantages of such a tenuous, finite peace, he agrees, must be weighed against what was accomplished by the war: the preservation of the Union and the emancipation of four million slaves. Potter does not doubt that these gains were immense, but he is staggered by the price. He notes that one soldier was killed for every six slaves who were freed and for every ten white Southerners who were held in the Union, and he concludes: "A person is entitled to wonder whether the Southerners could not have been held and the slaves could not have been freed at a smaller per-capita cost."

This is an interesting question, but Potter provides only half an answer. The adoption of the Crittenden Resolutions, he believes, might well have restored the Union without war, but he has nothing to suggest about alternative ways of freeing the slaves. Indeed, the purpose of the Crittenden Resolutions was to extend and perpetuate slavery. Whether it was worth the life of one man to give freedom to six others (and their descendants) is a moral problem that no man can answer for another. Twenty years after writing the decidedly negative last paragraph of this book, which emphasizes the cost in human misery and the incompleteness of Negro emancipation, Potter's question arouses in me a rather different response. It is that by 1860 white Americans had tolerated more than two hundred years of black slavery and still had discovered no peaceful way to abolish it. Therefore, a person is also entitled to ask how many more generations of black men should have been forced to endure life in bondage in order to avoid its costly and violent end.

K.M.S.

Berkeley, California
January, 1970

Contents

I

The Roots of the Crisis

SIR, DISGUISE the fact as you will, there is an enmity between the northern and southern people that is deep and
enduring, and you never can eradicate it—never!" Alfred Iverson
of Georgia, accomplished fire-eating orator, was addressing his
senatorial colleagues a month after the election of Abraham Lincoln. Recasting ominous phrases which had become trite to the
Americans of 1860, Iverson looked squarely at the Republicans in
the Senate chamber: "You sit upon your side, silent and gloomy;
we sit upon ours with knit brows and portentous scowls. . . .
We are enemies as much as if we were hostile States. I believe that
the northern people hate the South worse than ever the English
people hated France; and I can tell my brethren over there that
there is no love lost upon the part of the South." [1]

Perhaps, in his eagerness to carry the South out of the Union,
Senator Iverson overstated his case. Yet there was much truth in
what he said. The hostility between northern Republicans and
southern Democrats in Congress, which he so eloquently described, was a fact. Real enmity existed between a host of Yankees
and countless sons of Dixie; even moderate men, North and South,
looked upon the rival section with suspicion. There were numerous
apostles of "irrepressible conflict," besides Senator Iverson himself. Abolitionists, fire-eating politicians, and malignantly partisan editors had long been preparing the secession crisis now at
hand.

The propaganda of northern and southern agitators is often
considered one of the prime causes of the American Civil War.
William Lloyd Garrison, Horace Greeley, and Wendell Phillips,

---

[1] *Congressional Globe*, 36 Cong., 2 Sess., 12. Hereinafter, unless otherwise
stated, all references to the *Globe* will be to this session.

it is said, exaggerated the barbarities of slavery and the cruelties of slave masters; William L. Yancey, Robert Barnwell Rhett, and Edmund Ruffin misrepresented the North and maligned its citizens. In both sections propagandists distorted public opinion and so, it is argued, eventually brought on disunion and war.

There is an element of truth in this view. Before a bloody war could be waged, there had to be a systematic molding of mental attitudes. But this was not the whole story. Beneath all the propaganda there was the fact of Negro slavery.[2] Without the "peculiar institution" there could have been no proslavery or antislavery agitators, no division on the issue (whether real or fictitious) of the extension of slave territory. The northern attack on slavery was a logical product of nineteenth-century liberal capitalism. The southern defense of slavery—by planters deeply concerned about both their profits and their capital investment—was just as understandable.

Enmeshed with slavery were other economic differences which contributed to sectional hate. The South was a static, agrarian, debtor section, tied to an economy of staple crops. The North was a dynamic, commercialized, industrializing, creditor section. The South was exploited and the North was the exploiter. Spokesmen for the two sections could never agree upon the wisdom of protective tariffs, navigation acts, shipping and fishing subsidies, national banks, or Federal appropriations for internal improvements. These matters, together with slavery, were always back of the tirades of the agitators. And these matters, rather than the tirades, were at the roots of things. Without them there could have been no sectional agitation and no civil war. Between North and South there did exist a profound and irrepressible clash of material interests.

All this did not make a civil war necessary or inevitable. Actually the question of "inevitability" is not within the historian's province, for it is something that can never be solved by research. It should be left to the philosopher. But William H. Seward, the author of the phrase "irrepressible conflict," himself vigorously

[2] For an evaluation of the slavery issue in the sectional conflict see Dwight L. Dumond, *Antislavery Origins of the Civil War in the United States* (Ann Arbor, 1939).

denied the inevitability of war when the final crisis came. Social and economic differences need not always be referred to battle-fields. The Civil War was no more necessary or inevitable than any other war. Neither was it any less so. Unfortunately the issues were the sort that often produce hatreds that, in turn, drive men to mortal combat. Some wars have grown out of less serious causes.

One should not deal too harshly with the men who failed to prevent war in 1861. It is unfair to judge them by more than the common standards of statesmanship. There was nothing unique about the problem they faced, nor about the way they elected to "solve" it. The statesmen of 1861 were thinking in terms of "national interest." Unless the concept of "national interest" is re-evaluated, their decision, their choice of war rather than peace, must be accepted as just and right.

The politicians did have an alternative. They might have agreed that the price of war was too high, that a peaceful solution was worth any sacrifice. Southerners might have yielded to northern political supremacy and prepared to see their "peculiar institution" go sooner or later. Northerners might have agreed to southern independence. From either decision sectional leaders would have gained a fame unique in the history of statesmanship. The choice they actually made was the usual one. It was nevertheless tragic.

2

The economic development of the United States, from the very beginning, had the effect of variously strengthening or weakening the national loyalties of its citizens. Public men who lived through this development found their views changing as the interests of their sections changed. It was hard for politicians to keep up an appearance of consistency. Actually they had to entertain extremely flexible opinions regarding the comparative merits of nationalism and state rights. A man could begin his public life by glorifying the grand destiny of the nation and close it by "calculating the value of the Union." Or he might reverse the process. The political philosophy prevailing in a state or section at a given time would depend upon the current policies of the Federal government and upon the advantages or injuries which important economic groups seemed at the moment to derive from those policies.[3]

So it was from the start. Federalist merchants under the benevolence of Hamilton began as nationalists, and Republican farmers under the leadership of Jefferson began as state-rights men, who even flirted with nullification in the Kentucky and Virginia Resolutions. A few years later, when the South and West were in power, New England Federalists toyed with secession schemes while Jeffersonians were outdoing Hamilton in augmenting the powers of Congress. When Daniel Webster and Josiah Quincy, of Massachusetts, took refuge in the Constitution, it was John C. Calhoun of South Carolina who sneered at their crabbed sophistries, while the Richmond *Enquirer* screamed "Treason!" [4] Two decades afterward, when South Carolina under a reformed Calhoun sought to nullify a tariff close to the hearts of New England manufacturers, it was Webster's turn to take national grounds and warn solemnly of the perils of disunion.

In the 1830's and after, the state-rights concept was the dogma of the South, and national doctrines were entrenched in the North; but there were always qualifications and exceptions. Thirteen northern members of Congress signed a declaration that the annexation of Texas would justify a dissolution of the Union.[5] A coterie of Garrisonian abolitionists openly advocated separation from the slaveholders. Various northern states found enough virtue in state rights to justify their personal-liberty laws, which in a sense nullified a Federal law, the fugitive-slave act of 1850. Defying the United States Supreme Court, the Wisconsin legislature resolved that the Federal government was not the final judge of the powers delegated to it. Rather, "as in all other cases of compact among parties having no common judge, each has an equal right

---

[3] For an excellent, brief discussion of the state-rights issue in American History see Arthur M. Schlesinger, *New Viewpoints in American History* (New York, 1922), 220–44.

[4] Richmond *Enquirer*, quoted in Charles A. and Mary R. Beard, *The Rise of American Civilization* (New York, 1927), I, 428.

[5] William B. Hesseltine, *The South in American History* (New York, 1943), 250.

to judge for itself as well of infractions as of the mode and measure of redress." [6] That may have been the Calhoun gospel, but Southerners howled in protest when a northern state applied it to northern ends. Likewise, Southerners disregarded Calhoun's strictures upon judicial usurpation when the Supreme Court, in the Dred Scott decision, favored southern interests by opening all the territories to slavery.

These, perhaps, were mere aberrations. In the North, where population and economic and political power were growing fast, most statesmen became champions of the Union. In the South, where economic development was lagging, politicians came more and more to espouse defensive doctrines of localism.[7] As early as the 1820's a faction of South Carolinians looked to secession as their only recourse against northern encroachments. Thereafter Southerners repeatedly threatened to secede. They did so after the Mexican War when sectional leaders were debating the question of slavery expansion into the newly acquired territories. By the Compromise of 1850 the politicians set up a new equilibrium, but it was a precarious one. Within a few years they found the balance again upset, following the passage of the Kansas-Nebraska Act and the formation of the Republican party, a strictly sectional organization. During the presidential campaign of 1856 southern politicians repeatedly warned that a "Black" Republican victory would mean immediate dissolution of the Union.[8] During the next four years this cry became a commonplace of southern rhetoric.

Giving an ear to this cry, northern nationalists warned of the consequences of disunion. Daniel Webster insisted that the Union could never be dissolved without bloodshed. Henry Clay, during the Senate debates in 1850, replied to a secessionist from Georgia by avowing his readiness to try the strength of the nation, to ascertain "whether we have a government or not." "Nor, sir," he said, "am I to be alarmed or dissuaded from any such course by

[6] Dwight L. Dumond, *The Secession Movement, 1860–1861* (New York, 1931), 5 n.

[7] Jesse T. Carpenter, *The South as a Conscious Minority, 1789–1861* (New York, 1930).

[8] David M. Potter, *Lincoln and His Party in the Secession Crisis* (New Haven, 1942), 1–3.

intimations of the spilling of blood." [9] Nine years later Edward
Bates, the venerable St. Louis Whig, recorded his conviction that
control of the lower Mississippi River would never be surrendered
to a foreign power. Southerners needed to know that this was "a
fighting question, and not fit to be debated." [10]

After the execution of John Brown for treason against Virginia,
Senator Zachariah Chandler of Michigan drew from Brown's
fate a lesson for the South. He wanted that episode to go on the
records as a "warning to traitors" from any section: ". . . dare
to raise your impious hands against this Government, against our
Constitution and laws and you hang." [11] And in the same month
Abraham Lincoln, speaking at Leavenworth, Kansas, echoed those
sentiments: "So, if constitutionally we elect a president, and therefore you undertake to destroy the Union, it will be our duty to
deal with you as old John Brown was dealt with. We can only
do our duty." [12]

Americans had become accustomed to threats and counter-
threats when the presidential election of 1860 got under way.
Political sophisticates could hardly have been surprised when
southern newspapers and orators once more raised the old cry of
impending disunion.

3

The visions of politicians facing defeat at the ballot boxes are
generally etched in black. In October, 1860, the Democratic New
York *Herald* saw a fearful "spirit of violence and unreason . . .
abroad in the land." Southern fire-eaters talked of fighting to
preserve their rights. Youthful supporters of Lincoln, the "Wide-
Awakes," engaged in military drills with "simulated muskets and
lances, real cannon, [and] a regular battle cry." The *Herald*'s
editor, James Gordon Bennett, believed these demonstrations were
"but the thunder mutterings of the coming tempest." [13] But editor

[9] *Congressional Globe*, 31 Cong., 1 Sess., 1486.
[10] Howard K. Beale (ed.), *The Diary of Edward Bates, 1859–1866*, in American Historical Association, *Annual Report*, 1930, IV (Washington, 1933), 20.
[11] *Congressional Globe*, 36 Cong., 1 Sess., 34.
[12] New York *Evening Post*, October 31, 1860.
[13] New York *Herald*, October 6, 1860.

Bennett might well have had some inward doubts about the accuracy of his melancholy forecast. He would have had doubts if his thinking had harmonized with that of the majority of Northerners.

True, the southern threats that disunion would be the consequence of a Republican victory were more widespread and serious than ever before. The legislatures of South Carolina, Alabama, and Mississippi were actually taking preliminary steps toward secession.[14] In the North nearly every Democratic or Constitutional Union newspaper printed generous excerpts from the letters, speeches, and editorials emanating from the South.[15] A pro-Douglas paper thought the people should see the peril from "the unanimous tone of the Southern press; the plain business-like statements, . . . showing the utter impossibility of the South's remaining in the Union should our National Government pass under the control of Black Republican fanatics." [16]

After Republicans swept the October state elections in Pennsylvania, Ohio, and Indiana, the other parties redoubled their prophecies of approaching doom. "Fanaticism and treachery have triumphed," wailed a Douglas partisan. "The 'irrepressible conflict' of Seward and Lincoln has commenced. No human foresight can see the end." [17] Another Democrat foresaw "State after State declaring its independence . . . panic and confusion on all sides . . . banks suspending, business men failing, commerce languishing, industry starving." [18] A New York opponent of the Republicans feared the prosperity of Wall Street merchants was hanging in the balance, for with the South out of the Union, "New York ceases to be the Empire State, this city becomes no more a great national metropolis." [19]

Some of this was doubtless written in good faith, but much of it

---

[14] Potter, *Lincoln and His Party in the Secession Crisis*, 3–9; Dwight L. Dumond, *Southern Editorials on Secession* (New York, 1931); Ollinger Crenshaw, *The Slave States in the Presidential Election of 1860* (Baltimore, 1945).

[15] New York *Herald*, October 3, 11, 23, 24, 27, 1860; New York *Journal of Commerce*, October 23, 30; November 3, 1860; Boston *Daily Courier*, October 25, 1860.

[16] New York *Leader*, October 13, 1860.

[17] Indianapolis *Indiana Daily State Sentinel*, October 10, 1860.

[18] Providence *Daily Post*, October 31, 1860.

[19] New York *Herald*, October 18, 25; November 4, 1860.

was probably considered by its authors as a legitimate election-eering device. Most Republicans dismissed it all as scaremonger-ing, and the secession flurry in the South as a colossal game of bluff.[20] *"Who's afraid,"* mocked Seward. *"Nobody's afraid; no-body can be bought."* [21] The simple fact was that the disunion alarm had been sounded so often that only a few were willing to heed it any longer. To Republicans it was "the last desperate re-sort of the pro-slavery democracy," "the idlest gossip imaginable," "too absurd either for discussion or ridicule," an "effort to bully the people out of their choice." [22] Quoting strong Union senti-ments from the southern press, Republicans found abundant evi-dence that the small clique of secessionists would be put down by the people at home. The sooner this "game" ceased to be profitable, "the sooner shall we be delivered from these periodical soundings of the Disunion gong." [23]

How, indeed, could the South survive without the Union when it was more vital to her than it was to the North? How could her stormy politicians live without the rich plums of Federal patron-age? The Providence *Journal* was sure that if the Union survived "as long as the applicants for office in any southern State exceed the whole number at the disposal of the President in all the States," it would be perpetual.[24] Some Republicans went so far as to promise the beginning of a new era of good feeling after the inauguration of Lincoln. His wise and conservative policies would benefit all sections, and "we venture to predict a time of actual repose and peace . . . quite unheard of for the last ten years." [25]

[20] Lawrence T. Lowery, *Northern Opinion of Approaching Secession, Oc-tober, 1859–November, 1860* (Northampton, Mass., 1918), 247-49; Potter, *Lin-coln and His Party in the Secession Crisis*, 9-19.

[21] New York *Daily Tribune*, December 4, 1860.

[22] *Ibid.*, October 12, 22, 1860; Philadelphia *Public Ledger*, October 31, 1860; Bangor *Daily Whig and Courier*, October 30, 1860.

[23] New York *Times*, October 10, 1860; New York *Evening Post*, October 20, 1860; New York *World*, October 19, 1860; Philadelphia *North American and United States Gazette*, October 20; November 3, 1860; Boston *Daily Journal*, October 26, 1860; Springfield (Mass.) *Daily Republican*, October 31, 1860.

[24] Providence *Daily Journal*, October 16, 1860; New York *Daily Tribune*, October 22, 1860; Philadelphia *North American and United States Gazette*, October 6, 1860.

[25] Philadelphia *North American and United States Gazette*, October 6, 19, 1860; *Morning Courier and New-York Enquirer*, October 11, 1860.

It was clearly in the interest of Republicans to minimize the danger from the South.

There was reason, then, to doubt the entire sincerity of northern Democrats and Bell men who seemed so pessimistic. But there was also reason to doubt the complete sincerity of Republicans who wore, some of them almost gaily, an air of optimism. While giving calm assurances that the South was only bluffing, Republican papers sometimes issued stern and disquieting appeals to the northern people to see the issue through, to try at last the "policy of courage and firmness." They said that Lincoln deserved to be elected simply "to have this question of disunion . . . settled . . . [and] to see the matter tested and decided." [26] Among the propertied classes there were, according to the independent New York *World*, some who were ready "to let worst come to worst, so that now and finally there may be an end of this quadrennial disunion clamor." [27] Was it not time, asked others, to find out whether the constitutional election of a President would provide sufficient cause for dissolving the Union? [28]

By their nervous impatience to face the issue, some Republican editors and politicians revealed their uncertainty as to its outcome. Conversely, the majority of eastern merchants, whose prosperity hinged upon the southern trade, revealed their uncertainty by a fear of risking the test. Partly for this reason they were overwhelmingly opposed to Lincoln's election.[29] Right after the Republican victories in October, a panic occurred on the New York stock exchange, railroad shares and southern state bonds declined rapidly, and credit became stringent.[30] Evidently the men of Wall Street anticipated a political crisis, and the parties opposing Lincoln exploited their terror to the utmost.

Republicans, however, were ready with their own explanations

[26] Boston *Daily Advertiser*, October 9, 1860; Providence *Daily Journal*, October 31, 1860.

[27] New York *World*, November 1, 1860.

[28] Philadelphia *North American and United States Gazette*, November 2, 1860; Providence *Daily Journal*, November 5, 1860.

[29] Philip S. Foner, *Business & Slavery: The New York Merchants & the Irrepressible Conflict* (Chapel Hill, 1941), 169–207.

[30] See files of New York *Herald* for October, 1860; *Morning Courier and New-York Enquirer*, November 1, 1860.

of the panic. They said it stemmed from a mixture of cowardice and conspiracy. The "Dry Goods party," the "dear old ladies" who marketed their "patriotism in packages," were once more bending the knee to their southern masters and letting themselves be bullied and frightened.[31] In an editorial entitled "Wanted—A First-Rate Panic!" the New York *Times* developed the thesis that the whole thing was a fraud, the last desperate effort to defeat Lincoln.[32] The New York *World* asserted that the fall of stocks was "a purely fictitious operation, conducted in pursuance of an atrocious plot concocted by leading political and financial gamblers." [33] A few eastern businessmen, feeling that the scare campaign had gone too far, ultimately supported the Republicans.[34] But most businessmen were too preoccupied with the dangers of the immediate future to be able to appreciate the more remote economic possibilities of a Republican victory.

The merchants' fears increased when some of Lincoln's followers gave renewed warnings that, once in power, the Republicans would resist with force any attempt at secession. Some of the bolder spirits openly, defiantly, challenged the secessionists to proceed at their own peril. Carl Schurz, the fiery German-American orator, told Southerners that the Yankees would "fight now, if need be." "There is a great column of Germans and Scandinavians," Schurz said, "who can handle a musket, who stand ready to aid them." [35] At a Brooklyn rally late in October one Republican spokesman vowed that if Lincoln were not inaugurated the following March, 200,000 Wide-Awakes would "know the reason why." Another speaker, Senator Benjamin F. Wade of Ohio, added gruffly that secessionists would find "a sleeping lion in their path." [36] The day before the election William Curtis Noyes informed a gathering of New York merchants that seceders would

[31] New York *Evening Post*, October 9, 1860; New York *Daily Tribune*, October 5, 9, 12, 17, 1860.

[32] New York *Times*, October 10, 1860.

[33] New York *World*, October 27, 31, 1860. See also New York *Evening Post*, October 24, 26, 1860; New York *Daily Tribune*, October 26, 1860; Boston *Evening Transcript*, October 27, 1860.

[34] New York *Daily Tribune*, October 29, 1860; *Morning Courier and New-York Enquirer*, November 2, 3, 5, 6, 1860; New York *Evening Post*, November 6, 1860; Foner, *Business & Slavery*, 169–207.

[35] *Daily Boston Traveller*, October 22, 1860.

[36] New York *Herald*, October 30, 1860.

"share the fate of all traitors." [37] Meanwhile the New York *Evening Post*, finding lessons in history, recounted President Washington's suppression of the Whiskey Rebellion and President Jackson's forceful handling of the nullification crisis. There was no reason now for treating rebels any differently, said the *Evening Post*; President Buchanan, like his illustrious predecessors, should do his duty and execute the laws.[38] There were enough expressions of this kind to prompt the New York *World* to caution against any further irritation of the South.[39]

To be sure, these belligerent sentiments were often combined with expressions of doubt that there would be need for drastic action. They nevertheless reflect a certain apprehensiveness. Though the majority in all parties doubted that the South was in earnest, some were not quite sure, and a few credited their senses and expected the worst. As usual, one could not always determine a man's beliefs by the things he said in public—nor even by the things he wrote in private.

All this pre-election talk of secession and force indicated that the elements of a crisis were already present. The Republicans, with their sectional platform, threatened to upset the balance of power which had prevailed between the two sections for a generation. Inevitably this would challenge the South to seek some new security for its peculiar interests, perhaps through political independence. If the North found its own interests endangered thereby, it would have the choice of a political retreat or direct intervention to prevent secession. The latter alternative would force the South in turn to choose between surrender and resistance. And, finally, if Southerners elected a trial of strength, the verdict ultimately would go to the side with superior physical and human resources.

This was neither the first nor the last time that two peoples were driven to hostilities by essentially similar forces. On this as on other occasions disaster resulted not because the leaders on either side failed to show greater wisdom after the crisis was upon them. Disaster came because these men accepted as God-

[37] *Morning Courier and New-York Enquirer*, November 6, 1860.
[38] New York *Evening Post*, October 20, 31, 1860.
[39] New York *World*, October 22, 1860.

given the social institutions and political standards which gen-
erated and shaped the forces making for war. The five months
following Lincoln's election were to show that, once released,
these forces became too powerful for human resistance.

II

The Search for Remedies

IN NOVEMBER 1860 the Republicans won but a narrow and limited victory at the polls. They failed to get control of either branch of Congress. Their presidential candidate, Lincoln, while gaining a clear majority in the free states, received in the country as a whole almost a million fewer votes than his three opponents. In this dubious triumph the Chicago *Tribune* saw "only another incentive for continuing the revolution which has begun." [1] Another Republican organ found some consolation in the fact that the country had been spared the transfer of the presidential contest to the House of Representatives, "which might have threatened the stability of the government." [2] Now, presumably, the people could settle down for a quadrennium of relative quiet.

Politicians in the Deep South, however, thought otherwise. In response to Lincoln's election they quickly prepared to carry their states out of the Union. Within a few weeks South Carolina's senators had resigned, seven states had called conventions to consider secession, specially appointed commissioners had begun to advance and co-ordinate the general withdrawal, and such prominent Southerners as Howell Cobb, Secretary of the Treasury, and Robert Toombs, Senator from Georgia, had publicly declared for immediate southern action. Fire-eaters sketched vivid pictures of coming northern aggressions upon southern rights. Newspapers predicted the early formation of a new Confederacy.[3] These activities in the South made interesting copy, and the northern press gave them much space.

But the majority of Yankees who read these reports in Novem-

---

[1] Chicago *Daily Tribune*, November 8, 1860.
[2] Boston *Evening Transcript*, November 7, 1860.
[3] Dumond, *Secession Movement*, 113 ff.; *id., Southern Editorials on Secession*, 221 ff.

ber were little more impressed than they had been by southern
bluster during the recent campaign. "As to disunion," wrote William Cullen Bryant, "nobody but silly people expect it will happen." [4] A friend of Charles Sumner's rejoiced that "the gasconading Slave drivers" would "find it necessary to eat their own
words." [5] Senator Wade knew that Southerners would "howl and
rave, like so many devils, tormented before their time," but believed it was "all a humbug" and meant nothing.[6] Other Republican leaders such as Seward, Sumner, Charles Francis Adams, and
Edward Bates found no reason to disagree.[7] In Springfield, Illinois,
the President-elect received the news from the South with "equanimity," for "he could not in his heart believe that the South
designed the overthrow of the Government." [8] Neither could the
Republican press; as late as December 13 the New York *Evening
Post* still doubted that "the secession of a single state—even of
South Carolina" would actually be accomplished.[9]

Some Democrats showed no greater perspicacity in their initial
reactions to the southern movement. A pro-Douglas paper in New
York declared, "The Disunion furor will have blown pretty well
over, long before the 4th day of next March. It will be a fizzle
on a grand scale. . . ." [10] The pro-Breckinridge Boston *Post*
thought the South was talking much but would do little.[11] Even

[4] William Cullen Bryant to his brother, November 29, 1860, Bryant Papers,
New York Public Library.

[5] C. S. Henry to Charles Sumner, November 12, 1860, Sumner Papers, Widener
Library, Harvard University.

[6] Benjamin F. Wade to Lyman Trumbull, November 14, 1860, Trumbull
Papers, Library of Congress. See also F. Dainese to *id.*, November 9, 1860, *ibid.*;
Henry W. Bellows to Cyrus A. Bartol, November 7, 1860, Bellows Papers,
Massachusetts Historical Society.

[7] Charles Francis Adams, Jr., *Charles Francis Adams, 1835-1915, An Autobiography* (Boston, 1916), 69-70; Beale (ed.), *Diary of Edward Bates*, 157-58.

[8] New York *Herald* ("Springfield Correspondence"), November 22, 1860;
Donn Piatt, *Memories of the Men Who Saved the Union* (New York, 1887),
33-34; Paul M. Angle (ed.), *Herndon's Life of Lincoln: The History and Personal Recollections of Abraham Lincoln as Originally Written by William H.
Herndon and Jesse W. Weik* (New York, 1930), 382.

[9] For similar expressions see Boston *Daily Journal*, November 7, 10, 12, 19,
1860; *Daily Boston Traveller*, November 10, 12, 19, 1860; Boston *Evening Transcript*, November 13, 1860; Springfield (Mass.) *Daily Republican*, November 9,
10, 12, 17, 19, 24, 1860; Worcester (Mass.) *Daily Spy*, November 9, 14, 15, 20, 1860.

[10] New York *Leader*, November 10, 1860. See also Boston *Herald*, November
26, 1860; Philadelphia *Press* (letter from "Occasional"), November 11, 1860.

[11] Boston *Post*, November 13, 1860.

President Buchanan was at first inclined to doubt that the South was in earnest.[12] Well might the Springfield *Republican* tell the secessionists that they "would feel mortified" if they knew how indifferent the masses of the people of the free states were. "All the startling reports that come from the South fail to waken a conviction that there is anything real or permanent in the whole thing." [13]

The majority of Democratic spokesmen professed to believe that Southerners meant what they said. But the Republicans tried to make it appear that the Democrats, too, really had their doubts. Secession, said the Republicans, was only a rumor, a Democratic effort to frighten the northern people and discredit and disorganize the Republicans by forcing them to abandon their principles. Only for that purpose did Democrats wail dismally about impending national ruin and beg Lincoln to arrest the crisis by renouncing his party's platform.[14] How, indeed, could Republicans give assurances to the South when their newspapers were not read there? Rather, it was for those who had misrepresented the Republicans to retract their lies, to "acknowledge their slanders . . . , assuring their southern friends that these were but electioneering falsehoods manufactured to frighten voters." [15]

These skeptics were equally cavalier in dismissing the business panic which grew in intensity after the election. There was no denying that stocks were falling, that wheat prices were dropping sharply, that a bank crisis was taking shape, or that factories were curtailing operations and discharging mechanics. Nor could they ignore the increasing number of bankrupt merchants. The New York *Times* had to confess that the panic feeling "appeared to run as wild as in some of the blackest days of 1857." [16] Nevertheless, it

[12] Samuel W. Crawford, *The Genesis of the Civil War, The Story of Sumter* (New York, 1887), 22.

[13] Springfield (Mass.) *Daily Republican*, November 16, 1860.

[14] During November, Democratic and Constitutional Union papers were filled with appeals to Lincoln to repudiate the radicals and proclaim a conservative policy. See, for example, New York *Herald*, November 11, 1860; Philadelphia *Morning Pennsylvanian*, November 10, 15, 1860.

[15] Springfield (Mass.) *Daily Republican*, November 14, 1860; New York *Daily Tribune*, November 10, 1860; New York *Evening Post*, November 10, 1860; *Morning Courier and New-York Enquirer*, November 13, 1860.

[16] New York *Times*, November 14, 1860. The progress of the panic can be traced in the "Financial and Commercial" columns, and in many special reports

was still possible to describe the disturbance as temporary, or explain it as the result of an effort of political panic makers to wreck the Republican party.[17] At least it was comforting to know that the chief sufferers were those tricksters who had engineered the crisis in the first place.[18]

2

But suppose there was substance to the disunion reports; suppose an effort would actually be made to separate the slave states from the free. Many in the minority who had expected such a move from the start, and others who gradually came around to that opinion, still could see no cause for serious concern. Was it not true that Douglas and Bell had polled more southern votes than Breckinridge, that important newspapers were favoring the Union, and that influential politicians like Alexander H. Stephens were fighting the disunionists at home? Was it not logical to assume that, given sufficient time, the excitement would subside and the Unionists gain control? Certainly the Republican press found abundant evidence that separation was not popular with the southern masses. A typical conclusion was that, while secession might be attempted, "sane men of the South" would soon "take care of the thing, and prevent the Hotspurs from absolutely ruining that section." [19] The New York *Times* thought it likely that the whole movement would "resolve itself into a convention of the Southern States," and in such a gathering the Union would be "safe." [20] That, it was recalled, had been the outcome of another crisis a decade before.

From this smug and comforting diagnosis of the malady there emerged a simple remedy. It was particularly popular during the first six weeks after the election, although some had faith in it al-

and editorials in the New York *Herald* for November and December, 1860. See also Foner, *Business & Slavery*, 208–23.

[17] Henry W. Bellows to his son, November 14, 1860, Bellows Papers; New York *Daily Tribune*, November 14, 20, 1860; New York *World* (Commercial Column), November 8, 1860.

[18] Boston *Daily Advertiser*, November 17, 1860; Springfield (Mass.) *Daily Republican*, November 13, 1860.

[19] Bangor *Daily Whig and Courier*, November 10, 1860.

[20] New York *Times*, November 13, 1860.

most to the end. According to this prescription there was nothing for the North to do but remain calm, avoid any word or act that would produce further irritation, wait for the South to regain its senses, and encourage the growth of the inevitable Unionist reaction. In other words, the case required a "Fabian policy" of "masterly inactivity." The Boston *Advertiser* defined the formula:

> Never was there a case which seemed to call more obviously for a "masterly inactivity." . . . It rests with the Union-loving men of the South itself to hold their section to its duty. In this work their strength must not be paralyzed either by threats of external force, or by irritating comments. . . . But if left to deal with the matter in their own way, the real Union men of the South have, as we believe, both the will and the ability to grapple with the danger, to take advantage of the reaction which . . . will soon set in, and to defeat finally and forever the attempt to draw from its fidelity to the Constitution even a single State of the South.[21]

Accordingly, great numbers of Northerners started out to save the Union by sitting tight, regarding the South with cool indifference, and letting the "Heathen" rage.[22] Moderate Republican papers sniffed auspicious omens in the winds from the South. Correspondents of Salmon P. Chase assured him that the secessionists would "be put down by the sober second thought of the people of that region without any help from the North."[23] "If we give the disunionists . . . rope enough to hang themselves," wrote Carl Schurz, "they will perform that necessary and praiseworthy task with their own hands."[24]

That Lincoln also shared this early hope for the triumph of the southern Unionists was evident from the few lines he wrote for insertion in Senator Lyman Trumbull's speech at Springfield on November 20. The secessionists, thought Lincoln, were in "hot haste" to leave the Union at once, for they saw that they would

[21] Boston *Daily Advertiser*, November 12, 1860.

[22] Philadelphia *Press*, November 15, 1860; New York *Evening Post*, December 7, 1860.

[23] T. R. Stanley to Salmon P. Chase, November 13, 1860; Luther B. Bruen to *id.*, November 13, 1860, Chase Papers, Library of Congress.

[24] Joseph Schafer (ed.), *Intimate Letters of Carl Schurz, 1841–1869* (Madison, Wis., 1928), 232; Frederic Bancroft (ed.), *Speeches, Correspondence, and Political Papers of Carl Schurz* (New York, 1913), I, 164.

be unable to misrepresent the Republican party to their people much longer. Fortunately the current military preparations in the South would "enable the people the more easily to suppress any [secessionist] uprising there. . . ." [25] President Buchanan, too, looked expectantly to this solution. "Time is a great conservative power," he reminded Congress. "Let us pause at this momentous point and afford the people, both North and South, an opportunity for reflection." [26]

Of all the northern politicians who put their faith in this remedy, none adhered to it with more persistence or administered it with greater shrewdness than Senator Seward of New York. His peculiar genius was perfectly suited to the intricate maneuvering that such a formula involved. While many others had spontaneously adopted this strategy, it was Seward's great influence in party councils that gave it significance, and his political adroitness that kept this hope alive so long. Aided by Thurlow Weed, his crafty political manager, he gathered key men about him and secured their endorsements of his nostrum. Important party leaders such as Charles Francis Adams and newspapers such as the Boston *Advertiser* and Henry J. Raymond's New York *Times* fell under his spell.[27] Weed, pursuing the same end, became "the busiest politician in the country. He carries a legislature in his pantaloons pocket, he influences a President, moulds a Secretary, and 'sews up' dozens of editors at one and the same time." [28]

To some it came as a shock to hear the apostle of the "higher

[25] Gilbert A. Tracy (ed.), *Uncollected Letters of Abraham Lincoln* (Boston, 1917), 168–69; Horace White, *Life of Lyman Trumbull* (New York, 1913), 109–10.

[26] John Bassett Moore (ed.), *The Works of James Buchanan* (Philadelphia, 1908–1911), XI, 97.

[27] The best account of Seward's course during the secession crisis is in Potter, *Lincoln and His Party in the Secession Crisis.* See also Frederic Bancroft, *Life of William H. Seward* (New York, 1900), II, 26–38; Henry Adams, "The Secession Winter, 1860–61," Massachusetts Historical Society, *Proceedings*, XLIII (1910), 678–85; Adams, *Autobiography*, 105–107; Thurlow Weed Barnes (ed.), *Memoir of Thurlow Weed* (Boston, 1884), 307–308; Charles Francis Adams to Richard H. Dana, Jr., February 9, 1861, Dana Papers, Massachusetts Historical Society; Seward to Hamilton Fish, December 11, 1860, Fish Papers, Library of Congress. Henry Adams also traced the development of Seward's policy in an excellent set of letters from Washington to the Boston *Daily Advertiser.* See especially his letters in the issues of December 10, 1860, and February 2, 1861.

[28] Boston *Post*, April 3, 1861. See also Weed to Trumbull, November 21, 1860, Trumbull Papers.

law," the prophet of the "irrepressible conflict," speak so serenely and address the South with such tolerance and affection. But there need have been no shock. In actual fact Seward was never an abolitionist as was Sumner nor a political radical as was Chase. His occasional flings at the South had been sufficient to hold the support of antislavery Whigs but never went far enough to alienate completely the conservative business interests of New York. He never supported the Free-Soil party and was slow to desert the Whigs for the Republicans. Always he managed to maintain cordial relations with numerous southern Whigs, some of whom he now found useful in the development of his crisis strategy.[29] With all his hostility to slavery, the Boston *Post* now shrewdly observed, "it is far from his purpose to prosecute the 'irrepressible conflict' to the extremity of breaking up the government which he aims to control, and producing a revolution which would annihilate the Union and his party together." [30]

So Seward moved among the politicians, puffing cheerfully at his cigar and breathing confidence and kindly sentiments. Shortly after the election he urged upon his Auburn friends and neighbors a spirit of "magnanimity . . . [of] moderation in triumph," in order to defeat the secessionists "by our patience, our gentleness, our affection toward them." [31] Arriving in Washington for the opening of Congress, he freely stated that there was nothing which need cause great alarm. He was "chipper as a lark," swearing "by yea and by nay that everything was going on admirably," as Henry Adams said after dining with him.[32] He jovially assured the solid men of the New England Society of New York that secession was growing weaker. "I believe," he said, "that . . . if you only give it time, sixty days more suns will give you a more cheerful atmosphere." [33] To the very last, almost alone, Seward

---

[29] Bancroft, *Seward*, II, 7, 19.   [30] Boston *Post*, December 29, 1860.

[31] George E. Baker (ed.), *The Works of William H. Seward* (Boston, 1853–1884), IV, 115–16.

[32] Worthington C. Ford (ed.), *Letters of Henry Adams (1858–1891)* (Boston, 1930), 62–63. See also New York *Evening Post* ("Washington Correspondence"), December 4, 1860.

[33] Speech at the Astor House, December 22, 1860, printed in New York *Evening Post*, *Herald*, and *Times*, December 24, 1860. A revised version of this speech which omits this optimistic prediction appears in Baker (ed.), *Works of Seward*, IV, 644–50.

kept his hopes bright,[34] while state after state seceded and the seceders set up a government of their own. Only the guns of Sumter were able to silence the optimism in his voice.[35]

Though his program was destined to failure, Seward played a glorious role until the tragic end. He vindicated his claim to the Republican presidential nomination in 1860. Recovering slowly from his bitter disappointment, he found himself again in the months of crisis. While the President-elect sat silently in Springfield, Seward assumed the task of saving his party and the country from ruin. He got public attention with every movement he made; he, it was generally conceded, was the real party leader, the "premier" of the incoming administration. "It seems to me that if I am absent only three days," he wrote his wife with disarming sincerity, "this Administration, the Congress, and the District would fall into consternation and despair." All parties "cast themselves upon me." [36]

Early in March young Henry Adams titillated the Seward ego with a tribute to his masterful performance. Adams told how Republicans had gone to him "in despair to say that something must be done. . . . And he did save us. For two months he has swayed the whole nation." [37] But it was only a respite, not salvation, that Seward had achieved. At best he deserved a large measure of credit for preserving the peace until the inauguration of Lincoln.

In retrospect there is no escaping the fact that the disingenuous device of saving the country by doing essentially nothing—by waiting for a pro-Union reaction—was doomed from the start. Underlying it were two fatal misconceptions: first, an overestimation of the southern-Unionist strength, and second, a failure to understand that in the South Unionism meant one thing, in the North another.[38] Southern Unionism did not mean unconditional opposition to secession, for that was a negligible quantity in the majority of slave states. Among Northerners these errors were

[34] Ford (ed.), *Letters of Henry Adams,* 87; Frederick W. Seward, *Seward at Washington, as Senator and Secretary of State* (New York, 1891), II, 505.
[35] As late as April 10, 1861, Seward was still explaining and defending his strategy to Charles Francis Adams. Baker (ed.), *Works of Seward,* V, 205.
[36] Seward, *Seward at Washington,* II, 496–97; New York *Evening Post* ("Washington Correspondence"), December 4, 1860.
[37] Boston *Daily Advertiser* ("Washington Correspondence"), March 7, 1861.
[38] Potter, *Lincoln and His Party in the Secession Crisis,* esp. 374–75.

widespread in the first days of the crisis. Seward and some others continued to harbor them to the end, but growing numbers began as early as December to doubt whether disunion would be suppressed by Southerners alone. A few occasionally returned to this idea; the majority sought other and more positive remedies.

3

On December 11, Hamilton Fish of New York, man of property, conservative Whig-Republican, and intimate associate of wealthy business interests, observed the change in attitudes that was occurring. He was impressed by the prevailing anxiety which resulted from the disarrangement of business and the depreciation of values. Republican politicians, he believed, were simply "whistling to keep their courage up." Fish noted an increasing desire among Republican merchants to grant further concessions to the South. "It cannot be doubted that a great change has taken place," he said. "It cannot be denied that these men are now turning to, (if not upon,) their friends & calling upon them to save them." Democrats and Constitutional Unionists had already come out overwhelmingly for compromise, and now an effort was being made to unite conservative Republicans with these groups.[39]

Here was an early sign of a widening realization that the secession movement had reached serious proportions. With another Union crisis taking shape, a vast element in the North grasped almost automatically for the time-tested remedy of compromise. Perhaps the issue could be evaded once again by "reasonable and honorable" concessions. By December a great variety of schemes for sectional adjustment had found sponsors among politicians and editors. Generally they were focused around proposals to give additional guarantees to slavery in the form of a constitutional amendment, to repeal personal-liberty laws, to compensate Southerners for the loss of fugitive slaves, to admit New Mexico as a slave state, or to extend the Missouri Compromise line to California. While Democrats assumed the prime role of "Union-

[39] Fish to William P. Fessenden, December 11, 1860, Fessenden Papers, Library of Congress. The Douglas Papers in the University of Chicago Library indicate that Democrats were overwhelmingly in favor of some form of compromise.

savers," a minority of Republicans was ready ultimately to support moderate concessions—"adjustment without dishonor." [40]

A smaller faction of Republicans, however, appeared to favor a more drastic remedy. Whether or not there was a legal right of secession, they argued, it would be best for the national health to remove the infected part, to let the disloyal slave states secede in peace. Horace Greeley's New York *Tribune* was unquestionably the most influential exponent of this course. But it was by no means the only important Republican paper that seemed to look upon it with favor. The Philadelphia *Public Ledger*, Boston *Traveller*, Springfield *Republican*, *Ohio State Journal*, Indianapolis *Journal*, Cincinnati *Commercial*, Chicago *Tribune*, and a score of others at one time or another echoed Greeley's sentiments. "If she [South Carolina] will," said the Chicago *Tribune*, "let her go, and like a limb lopped from a healthy trunk, wilt and rot where she falls." [41] Northern Democrats howled that these quacks would kill the patient with their radical cure.

But Greeley's solution was a fraud from the start. He was ready to let the South depart in peace only so long as some doubt remained of its desire to go, and so long as there was danger of Republicans abandoning their principles. Moreover, from the very beginning he placed so many qualifications on the process as to render it absolutely meaningless.[42] And almost every other advocate of this course was guilty of the same deception.

Peaceful secession as envisioned by these northern nationalists hardly fitted the pattern of the state-rights concept. It was not a matter to be initiated and consummated by a single state upon its own terms. "I have no appetite for blood," wrote a correspondent of Senator Wade's, "& will not say that in a proper way, I will not consent to let the South go, provided it shall appear that in the Cotton States there is a very general determination to break

[40] See Chapter VIII.   [41] Chicago *Daily Tribune*, October 11, 1860.
[42] See especially New York *Daily Tribune* issues of November 2, 9, 16, 19, 26, 30; December 3, 8, 24, 1860; January 14, 1861. See also Greeley to Lincoln, December 22, 1860, Lincoln Papers, Library of Congress; David M. Potter, "Horace Greeley and Peaceable Secession," *Journal of Southern History*, VII (1941), 145–59; Ralph R. Fahrney, *Horace Greeley and the Tribune in the Civil War* (Cedar Rapids, 1936), 38–74; James H. Wilson, *Life of Charles A. Dana* (New York, 1907), 160–66. For a different interpretation see Jeter A. Isely, *Horace Greeley and the Republican Party* (Princeton, 1947), 304–12.

up the Union." But, this writer hastened to add, "I do not think that feeling exists outside of South Carolina, to the extent of unanimity that I would require." In other words, the seceders must first satisfy northern skeptics that the secession movement had sufficient popular support.[43]

Next, Southerners must make formal application for permission to secede. The request could be submitted to Congress, which in turn could refer it directly to the people, or to a national convention for approval. Until such consent had been granted, "the Government must maintain its authority even in South Carolina, and punish if assailed." [44] Finally, should separation ultimately be approved, a constitutional amendment would still be required to make it legal.[45]

Meanwhile the South must wait quietly until the Federal government and the northern people had time for careful deliberation. A constituent of Representative E. B. Washburne of Illinois explained the proper procedure: "Hold still, entirely still, . . . neither threaten or coax, and 'let 'em wiggle' and if secession has sense and discretion enough (which I doubt) to avoid overt act of treason, and rebellion, and can get their case fairly before the nation by proper means, and in a proper spirit, and wish to form a separate government, if the thing should be found practible [sic] and mutualy [sic] benificial [sic] let them go." [46] Or, as another advocate of peaceful secession put it, "*The first thing* to be done is to execute the laws. *The second* to decide whether the States shall be allowed to secede—& if so, on what terms." [47]

Secession, then, must be slow and painless, a product of negotiation which would respect the authority of the Federal government

[43] C. Delano to Benjamin F. Wade, December 21, 1860, Wade Papers, Library of Congress. This was a qualification that Greeley invariably made. See New York *Daily Tribune*, November 26, 1860.

[44] Indianapolis *Daily Journal*, January 3, 1861; New York *Daily Tribune*, November 26, 1860; Springfield (Mass.) *Daily Republican*, November 10, 15, 22; December 3, 1860; Cincinnati *Daily Commercial*, January 31; February 1, 2, 5, 1861; George H. Porter, *Ohio Politics during the Civil War Period* (New York, 1911), 50–51.

[45] New York *Times*, November 15, 16, 1860; New York *World*, December 8, 1860.

[46] Nath Vose to E. B. Washburne, December 15, 1860, E. B. Washburne Papers, Library of Congress.

[47] James Freeman Clarke to Sumner, December 8, 1860, Sumner Papers.

and protect the interests of the nonseceding states. Accordingly, the Philadelphia *Public Ledger* would have demanded that the seceders "make such terms as shall render those States which do not secede no worse off in point of security by the separation." This would require that all guns on the shores of the Mississippi be dismantled, that New Orleans be made a free city under a joint protectorate, and that the Federal government retain possession of such vital positions as Key West and Pensacola.[48] Others believed that strategic considerations would probably make it impossible to permit Florida and Louisiana to secede.[49]

It was but a short step from this position to the next. Peaceful separation was impossible because Southerners themselves were attempting it illegally through violence. "The rebellious states . . . insist upon treating the Constitution as a nullity," indignantly complained the *World*. "The great law-abiding North will not give way to it." [50] Representative Charles H. Van Wyck of New York raised the same objection: "I desire not to preserve this Union at the point of the bayonet; but we do not mean to be driven from it by force. If you desire a peaceful secession, why do you not seek it? . . . But when you forcibly seize the federal property, and then fire upon its flag, you should not sit down and picture the horrors of civil war." [51] The New York *Tribune* finally escaped through the same wide opening: "That we no longer advocate acquiescence in the demands of the seceding States is because the nature and tone of these demands have altogether changed. Instead of asking for a peaceable and legal separation, the seceding States . . . have resorted to violence; . . . and now stand defiantly in the attitude of traitors and rebels." [52]

Thus the circle was complete. Peaceful secession was desirable, but it must be on northern terms and in accordance with a rigid formula. Since the South rejected both the terms and the formula, there could be no peaceful secession. Greeley's deception seemed

---

[48] Philadelphia *Public Ledger*, March 9, 1861; Boston *Daily Journal* (letter of "G.A.C."), February 13, 1861.
[49] Chicago *Daily Tribune*, November 10, 1860; New York *Daily Tribune*, December 8, 1860.
[50] New York *World*, April 10, 1861.   [51] *Congressional Globe*, 631.
[52] New York *Daily Tribune*, February 2, 1861.

to be motivated chiefly by his implacable hostility to any form of compromise. A few adopted his position in good faith but added the nullifying qualifications as they slowly appreciated the serious complications which would result from disunion.

In any event, except for a handful of Garrisonian abolitionists and extreme prosouthern Democrats, the scheme of peaceful separation had nearly evaporated by the end of December. Greeley's *Tribune* ultimately confessed: "The right of secession has been almost universally denied at the North, . . . and but a very small proportion of the Northern people have been willing to acknowledge that the bonds of our Union were utterly broken. . . ." [53] In December, Greeley wrote in a private letter to Lincoln that Southerners would "have to be made to behave themselves." [54] Thereafter the *Tribune*'s columns contained a confusing mixture of empty talk about qualified peaceful disunion and increasingly violent demands for the enforcement of the laws and the suppression of rebellion. By a devious route Greeley, like so many others, finally arrived in the camp of the proponents of force.

4

Military coercion, as a remedy for disunion, had its advocates from the start. At first some of those who spoke belligerently may have had suspicions—perhaps, more accurately, hopes—that the crisis would blow over. Whether or not their warlike tone was conceived merely as a counterbluff, the important fact was that ultimately the bluff (if such it was) was called.

Even before the election of 1860 some in the minority who believed the South in earnest had warned that the North would resist secession. Now, as the weeks passed and the illusions began to fall away, those who had originally talked of force were finding new recruits. As early as November the New York *Herald* noted deploringly that numerous Republican journals were "using violent,

[53] *Ibid.*, March 19, 1861.
[54] John G. Nicolay and John Hay, *Abraham Lincoln, A History* (New York, 1890), III, 258; Greeley to Lincoln, December 22, 1860, Lincoln Papers.

defiant and exasperating language toward the Southern States, as if they were anxious to precipitate disunion and civil war upon the country." [55]

One of the editors the *Herald* doubtless had in mind was James Watson Webb, whose New York *Courier and Enquirer* was reputedly Seward's "Wall Street organ." But "Chevalier" Webb, long famous for his contentiousness and for his vitriolic pen, had no faith in the Senator's gentle moderation toward the South. He began at once to boast of the North's military power and vowed that "no disruption of . . . this nation . . . could be accomplished without . . . terrible penalties upon the rebellious population engaged in the effort." [56]

Scores of newspapers quickly agreed with the Boston *Transcript*'s pronouncement, "Secession, when it is manifested in act, must be met at once by the full power of the government. . . ." [57] The Indianapolis *American*, while admitting that it expressed a minority view for the present, boldly said, "*Our voice is for war! If it be bloody, fierce and devastating, be it so.*" [58] But few surpassed in violence the radical "Long John" Wentworth's Chicago *Democrat:* "You [Southerners] have sworn that if we dared to elect such a man [as Lincoln] you would dissolve the Union. We have elected him, and now we want you to try your little game of secession. Do it, if you dare! . . . But every man of you who attempts to subvert this Union, which we prize so dearly, will be hung as high as Haman. We will have no fooling about this matter. By the eternal! the Union must be preserved." [59]

Many of these journals did not speak consistently and exclusively for military coercion. Editorial consistency was never one of the virtues of the northern press during the secession crisis. A Greeley could advocate qualified peaceful secession and force, a Webb compromise and force, simultaneously, often in different

---

[55] New York *Herald*, November 22; December 11, 1860.

[56] *Morning Courier and New-York Enquirer*, November 12, 23, 1860.

[57] Boston *Evening Transcript*, November 12, 1860; New York *Evening Post*, November 9, 1860; Trenton *Daily State Gazette and Republican*, November 10, 1860; Madison *Wisconsin Daily State Journal*, November 10, 1860.

[58] Indianapolis *Indiana American*, November 21, 1860.

[59] Chicago *Daily Democrat*, quoted in Providence *Daily Post*, December 11, 1860.

columns of the same issue.[60] Others fluctuated from one remedy to another as conditions changed.

There is abundant evidence that the war press had a substantial popular following even in the days immediately succeeding the election. A Syracuse correspondent reported many of the farmers and townspeople of upstate New York "ready and willing for a fight" if the South desired one.[61] On November 14 the Republican Central Committee of New York City resolved: "There is the power and the will to defend the Constitution with forbearance but without faltering." [62] At a victory celebration in Boston's Music Hall, Charles W. Slack told the Lincoln Wide-Awakes that they might have a further duty to discharge. It might be necessary to go to the aid of the new commander in chief and carry him "triumphantly . . . to the head of the government." Senator Henry Wilson added his vow, "We intend to stand by the Constitution—(Applause.) by the Union at any and every hazzard [sic] come what may. (Great applause.)" [63] And Carl Schurz assured a Republican gathering in Milwaukee that if Southerners tried to prevent the inauguration of Lincoln "the traitors would find justice swift, and the indignation of an outraged people inexorable." If need be, "we can rally hundreds of thousands of armed men at the tap of the drum. . . ." [64]

The correspondence of Republican politicians was peppered with similar sentiments from colleagues and constituents. "Tell Mr. Lincoln that little Boone [county] can be relied on for 500 Wide Awakes, well armed and equipped," wrote an Illinois man to Senator Trumbull.[65] A correspondent reminded Chase: Lincoln "must *enforce the laws of the U. States against all rebellion;*—no matter what are the consequences." [66] A friend advised Representative John Sherman, "If five or six of the Petted Slave States does Secede we may spend a few milions [sic] to whip them into their

[60] In the case of the *Tribune* the inconsistencies were due in part to the fact that editor Charles A. Dana never sympathized with Greeley's peculiar views on peaceful secession. Dana always favored coercion. Wilson, *Life of Dana,* 160–66.
[61] New York *Herald* ("Syracuse Correspondence"), November 11, 1860.
[62] New York *Daily Tribune,* November 15, 1860.
[63] Boston *Daily Journal,* November 10, 1860.
[64] Milwaukee *Daily Sentinel,* November 20, 1860.
[65] J. W. Whitney to Trumbull, November 19, 1860, Trumbull Papers.
[66] E. D. Mansfield to Chase, November 26, 1860, Chase Papers.

propper [*sic*] place. . . ." [67] Congressman Oris S. Ferry of Connecticut advised Gideon Welles that ten years of civil war would be preferable to a division of the Union.[68] And Edward Bates recorded in his diary a fear that the "dangerous game" of the secessionists might lead to open rebellion. "If they *will* push it to that dread extremity, the Government . . . will no doubt, find it wise policy to make the war as sharp and prompt as possible. . . ." [69]

With some, as Bates's opinion indicated, it was less a matter of *advocating* the use of force than of entertaining the fatalistic conviction that disunion, if it actually came, placed an inescapable duty upon the government to coerce the secessionists into submission. The President-elect gave early evidence of belonging to this group. Even while he still doubted that Southerners would actually secede, Lincoln was saying, "I must run the machine as I find it." [70] In December he became more explicit: "The very existence of a general and national government implies the legal power, right and duty of maintaining its own integrity. . . . It is the duty of a President to execute the laws and maintain the existing government." [71] The New York *Times* presented one of the best reflections of this state of mind: "If South Carolina is determined upon secession, she should make the plunge with her eyes open. She must face all the consequences,—and *among them all, the most unquestionable is War*. Not that we wish it,—not that thousands and tens of thousands of good men among us would not weep the bitterest tears they ever shed in their lives, over so dismal, so dreadful a prospect. But there is no possibility of escaping it. We cannot permit secession if we would." [72]

A demand for "preparedness" was still another variation of the force doctrine. The secession crisis produced its share of innocents who spoke of national mobilization as the road to peace and

---

[67] J. F. Smith to John Sherman, December 10, 1860, Sherman Papers, Library of Congress.

[68] O. S. Ferry to Gideon Welles, December 11, 1860, Welles Papers, Library of Congress.   [69] Beale (ed.), *Diary of Edward Bates*, 157–58, 167 n.

[70] Piatt, *Memories of the Men Who Saved the Union*, 33–34.

[71] Nicolay and Hay, *Lincoln*, III, 247–48. See also Lincoln to Weed, December 17, 1860, in John G. Nicolay and John Hay (eds.), *Complete Works of Abraham Lincoln* (New York, 1905), VI, 82.

[72] New York *Times*, December 1, 10, 1860.

safety. The way to avoid civil war was to prepare for it, to provide overwhelming military and naval power so that secession would cease to be a holiday affair. "You have only to put the Government in a position to make itself respected," affirmed Senator Trumbull, "and it will command respect." [73] The Chicago *Tribune* reminded Northerners that secessionists were, after all, only men. As long as they believed that they could plot against the government with impunity, they would go on with their conspiracy. But if they perceived the danger of punishment for treason, "thousands of the rampant bullies . . . would become as mild as so many sucking doves. . . ." [74]

With the government adequately prepared, if worst came to worst "a little show of force" entailing a minimum of bloodshed would suffice to crush the southern rebellion. This was a common belief: "The national government may have to *show* its teeth, but it is not at all likely that it will have to *use* them." [75] Or, at most, the government would require no greater measure of compulsion than "half a dozen naval vessels . . . [to] blockade southern ports." [76] In short, with proper preparedness, the process of suppressing a southern rebellion would be as simple as "putting down an ordinary fireman's riot in Philadelphia, or a plug ugly muss in Baltimore." Hence it was a misuse of language to speak of "war" as a possible consequence of existing difficulties. The crisis could result in nothing more serious than "the hanging of a score or two of the fools" who had "plotted their own certain destruction." [77]

Preparedness advocates overlooked the fact that their measures, rather than overawing the disunionists, more likely would drive them to similar military exertions. Every Yankee regiment would have its southern counterpart. The psychology of fear would eliminate the last vestiges of caution in the South. The adversaries would come to grips sooner, but the consequences would be no less bloody. No remedy for secession could have been more insidious than this.

[73] *Congressional Globe*, 1380–83.   [74] Chicago *Daily Tribune*, April 8, 1861.
[75] New York *Daily Tribune* ("Washington Correspondence"), December 18, 1860.
[76] Springfield (Mass.) *Daily Republican*, November 19, 1860.
[77] Chicago *Daily Tribune*, January 9, 1861.

But whether it was a matter of mobilization to frighten the South, or coercion as the sad but inescapable result of disunion, or force as a desirable remedy in itself, the use of military power had emerged as a distinct and likely course. A vigorous minority championed it openly. Many more concealed a similar purpose behind a camouflage of legalistic technicalities derived from a careful combing of the Constitution.

III

Exercises in Constitutional Logic

I N NORTHERN thinking during the secession crisis, there was
a good deal of wavering and inconsistency; there was also
much vagueness and confusion in the use of words. A person un-
acquainted with the science of semantics would have perceived
only a few simple ways in which the North might have dealt with
the proceedings of the secessionists. If Southerners were in earnest,
the North could (1) compromise, (2) recognize their independence, or (3) use force against them.

But semanticists would have demanded a more precise use of the
English language. You speak of compromise, they would have
said, but how do you define the word *compromise?* What do you
mean by *peaceful secession?* Are you not, perhaps, speaking of
a process which might better be called a *revolution?* Moreover,
if you suggest the use of military force, would you *coerce* a
sovereign state? Or do you simply advocate the *enforcement of
the laws?* Finally, if war should be the consequence, would you
be able to distinguish between acts of *aggression* and acts of *defense?* Unfortunately, few Americans of 1860–1861 were aware
of the problem of semantics.

Since the realities of the crisis were too terrible to be faced
head on, the few obvious solutions needed to have their nakedness
covered with philosophic rationalizations and decorated with
seductive words. Self-deception was a prerequisite for action.
Men could perform distasteful tasks only if they could find the
right language to conceal, even from themselves, what they actually were doing. As one shrewd observer said, "Men like to
have method in their madness, and like to carry . . . a pointed
abstraction more dearly than a pointed pike. . . ." [1] Another

[1] *Harper's New Monthly Magazine* ("Editor's Table"), XXII (March, 1861),
554.

contemporary observed that Northerners were like a council of physicians "wrangling with each other over abstract dogmas respecting life and health, whilst their patient was struggling in the agonies of death before them!" [2] Painful cures seemed to require the ingenious sedative of soothing phrases.

The semantic difficulty began, of course, with conflicting interpretations of the Union and the Constitution. By 1860 southern dialecticians had perfected the compact theory which entitled each sovereign state to separate from the rest of the states at its own discretion. The states were older than the Union; in ratifying the Constitution none had surrendered its sovereignty; each retained the right to resume its original independent position. Secession was an orderly legal process. It had been undertaken only after repeated flagrant violations of southern rights. [3]

Northern nationalists, however, found in the Constitution and in the arguments of Marshall and Webster abundant ground for denying the principle of state sovereignty and the legality of secession. When they ratified the Constitution, the states had ceded part of their sovereignty. In its own sphere, in the exercise of its delegated powers, the Federal government became supreme. [4] It was established "not by the States in their sovereign capacity, but emphatically as the preamble declared, 'by the people of the United States.' " The "supreme law of the land" clause and various judicial decisions showed that any state law which violated the Federal Constitution was null and void. An ordinance of secession would be void, because the Constitution provided for a permanent Union. "It makes provision for coming in, but none at all for going out. . . . If we had meant to reserve the right of secession to each State, of course it would have been necessary to insert a clause defining the right, and providing for a settlement with the remaining parties." [5]

[2] William H. Russell, *My Diary North and South* (Boston, 1863), 15.

[3] Carpenter, *South as a Conscious Minority*, 194–220; Dumond, *Secession Movement*, 120–21.

[4] John A. Dix to Horatio King, November 22, 1860, quoted in Horatio King, *Turning on the Light: A Dispassionate Survey of President Buchanan's Administration, from 1860 to Its Close* (Philadelphia, 1895), 26.

[5] Providence *Daily Post*, November 13, 19, 1860; New York *Times*, November 10, 1860; Philadelphia *Press*, January 1, 1861; Philadelphia *North American and United States Gazette*, November 20, 1860; Madison *Wisconsin Daily State Journal*, December 21, 1860.

There were other constitutional checks upon the states which, according to northern nationalists, rendered legal secession impossible. All state officers, obliged to take an oath to support the Constitution, were bound by their Federal allegiance. States were prohibited from entering into agreements with each other, or from keeping troops or ships of war in time of peace, without the consent of Congress. Each state was guaranteed a republican form of government—if a state could legally secede, it could then set up a monarchy just as easily as a republic.[6]

"It follows from these views," concluded Lincoln, "that no State upon its own mere motion can lawfully get out of the Union; that resolves and ordinances to that effect are legally void. . . . I therefore consider that, in view of the Constitution and the laws, the Union is unbroken." [7] And with few exceptions the northern people agreed with Lincoln. Though many may have favored compromise and hoped to avoid war, the masses of Republicans and Democrats shared the belief that the Union was perpetual. That was the most profoundly important conviction of nearly every Northerner during the crisis.

The Union was not the same thing to Northerners and Southerners. The words of the Constitution had fundamentally different meanings in the two sections. By 1860 each had formulated political concepts which suited its peculiar interests and had developed legal rationalizations which justified its particular course. There were inconsistencies and oversights, but these were irrelevant. The thing that counted was not absolute truth but what was *believed* to be true. And in 1860 Northerners stood almost solidly for the nationalist position insofar as it confirmed the perpetuity of the Union.

2

Assuming secession to be a completely illegal procedure, it followed, as Lincoln again phrased it for the North, that such

---

[6] New York *World*, February 11, 1861; New York *Daily Tribune*, February 16, 1861. For the significant contribution of Professor Francis Lieber, of Columbia College, to the nationalist argument see Frank Freidel, *Francis Lieber: Nineteenth-Century Liberal* (Baton Rouge, 1947), 301–305.

[7] Nicolay and Hay (eds.), *Works of Lincoln*, VI, 169–85.

action would be "insurrectionary or revolutionary, according to circumstances." [8] To be precise, what Southerners were attempting was not peaceful secession but a political revolution. They were seeking to resist and nullify the authority of the Federal government and to raise a rebellion. Such a definition of their action grated on the sensitive ears of most conservative Southerners, but a few were willing to admit its essential accuracy. Alfred Iverson, for example, confessed to the Senate that the Constitution did not give a state the right to secede. "I rather agree [he said] . . . that the secession of a State is an act of revolution." It was that right which he rose to defend.[9]

The right of revolution—the right of a people to "alter or abolish" a government which they regarded as oppressive—should have had no strange ring to these sons of 1776. But somehow, respectable Northerners were chilled to the marrow by the very sound of the word "revolution." It called to their minds visions of anarchy, violence—and an alarming depreciation of property values. In the immortal Declaration of Independence itself they found salvation. Jefferson had not betrayed them! For had he not said: "Prudence, indeed, will dictate that Governments long established should not be changed for light and transient causes . . ."? [10] The prudent heirs of Revolutionary fathers had found new virtue in Jefferson's sometimes disturbing document.

They found that the seceders lacked the required "prudence," which alone could justify their action. The Southerners' fatal error was "plunging into revolution prematurely—without any just ground" and without exhausting legal means of obtaining a redress of alleged grievances.[11] There was no "right of revolution at *pleasure*," explained the Philadelphia *Public Ledger*. "The reason given must be sufficient to justify it. The burden of proof lies on those who make the assertion of wrong, and the wrong must be clearly proved in the face of the whole world." [12]

Needless to say, few Northerners could see in southern complaints any real excuse for rebellion against existing political in-

[8] *Ibid.*   [9] *Congressional Globe*, 10–11.
[10] See, for example, Philadelphia *Press*, January 10, 1861.
[11] M. W. Jacobus to Joseph Holt, November 27, 1860, Holt Papers, Library of Congress.
[12] Philadelphia *Public Ledger*, December 28, 1860.

stitutions. The Philadelphia *Press* found no justification for "the destruction of a free and liberal Government, against which few or no serious objections can be urged, which is guilty of no real tyranny." It doubted whether there was ever "a revolution commenced on more trifling and trivial grounds" than that which the "conspirators" in the seceding states had inaugurated.[13] At least, added Governor Austin Blair of Michigan, "it ought to be a revolution *against*, and not in favor of oppression." [14] Thus evolved a concept which might be termed "the right of revolution by consent."

Others proposed an alternative theory of "orderly and constitutional revolution." According to them, the Founding Fathers had erected democratic political machinery which rendered unnecessary the use of violence. Political change could be achieved peacefully by constitutional amendments or at the ballot boxes "without confusion and without fighting." [15] Representative John A. Gurley of Ohio saw no need "for rebellion against a Government where the people themselves make and control it." Violent revolution against a despotism was proper, "but not against our Government, where each man is himself a ruler." [16] The conservative Boston *Transcript* found the chief virtue of the Constitution in the opportunity it afforded for revolution by "peaceful and legal means." Its framers ". . . made revolution compatible with law, by providing for frequent elections under the Constitution, and for amendments to the Constitution itself. . . . Revolutions, which in other countries dissolve society into anarchy, [and] give a vast shock to all property and industry, . . . the founders of our government thought they had contrived the means of accomplishing without the sacrifice of a single element of order and without the shedding of a single drop of blood." [17] In other words, the revolution of 1787 had eliminated the need for a repetition of the violence of 1776.

At least a few Northerners went the whole distance and flatly

[13] Philadelphia *Press*, April 13, 1861.

[14] Message to the Michigan legislature, January 3, 1861, quoted in Detroit *Free Press*, January 4, 1861.

[15] Providence *Daily Post*, December 4, 1860; New York *Journal of Commerce*, December 6, 1860.

[16] *Congressional Globe*, 417. [17] Boston *Evening Transcript*, January 14, 1861.

repudiated the Jeffersonian doctrine. They contended that the American people in adopting the Constitution had "remitted their abstract right of revolution." [18] One Pennsylvanian discovered that few revolutions had been for good causes. Rather, "in most instances where the public peace has been disturbed, the offenders were disorderly, turbulent, ambitious, and lawless—not patriotic—spirits." Indeed the right of revolution was a "pernicious error." [19] Another defender of social order, deploring the current tendency toward anarchy, feared that "a world of infidelity" had "crept into our notions of government." The idea that "governments derive their just powers from the consent of the governed" was only partly true. ". . . but there is an authority high above all that, which challenges our consent and obedience to established government. . . . Law, order, government are written upon the face of the whole universe. . . . It is this consideration alone which can clothe the civil magistrate with adequate dignity, and invest his sword with adequate terrors. He is authorized to lift that sword over the heads of those who resist his authority, and in the name of the God of heaven to bring it down upon their necks. . . ." [20] Southerners, then, were engaged in an utterly causeless rebellion against the best political institutions on earth.

But suppose that Southerners did have a fundamental right to rebel against Federal authority, and for causes which need satisfy themselves alone. Even on this basis the nationalists felt that they were not without a logical remedy. For the extralegal "right" of revolution did not imply that a government must *voluntarily* abdicate its power to a disaffected faction. An insurrection meant violence, and the revolting party must "take her chance in a martial contest." It was a duty of established government to attempt to suppress rebellion when it occurred.[21] This obligation would be invoked by "the instinct of self-preservation," if by nothing else.[22] Revolutionists must therefore proceed at their own peril.

[18] Philadelphia *Press,* May 8, 1861.   [19] *Ibid.,* January 10; May 8, 1861.

[20] Speech of John Y. Smith in the Wisconsin Assembly chamber, quoted in Madison *Wisconsin Daily State Journal,* April 5, 1861.

[21] Boston *Evening Transcript,* November 9, 10, 1860; Philadelphia *Public Ledger,* November 12, 1860; Providence *Daily Journal,* November 14, 1860; Providence *Daily Post,* November 19, 1860.

[22] Philadelphia *Press* (letter from "Occasional"), December 27, 1860.

Speculation about the legal position of insurrectionary states did not wait until the stormy debates of Reconstruction. Active interest in that problem developed even before the outbreak of war. During the secession crisis most theorists seemed to accept the position subsequently advanced by Lincoln: that the seceded states simply required the formation of loyal governments to be restored to their proper relationship with the rest of the Union.

But the viewpoint of Reconstruction radicals also found occasional exponents in this early period. There was no little irony in the fact that Andrew Johnson himself presented one of the first expressions of the "state suicide" theory. In a speech of December 19, Senator Johnson argued that a disloyal state would revert to the condition of a territory.[23] The Philadelphia *Press* asked whether the government had not "acquired three new Territories by the rebellious acts of Mississippi, Alabama, and Florida," and whether the President should not have the right to appoint a governor and other officers for each of them.[24]

Most Northerners came not only to deny the constitutional right of secession but also to identify the southern movement with rebellion against legal authority. Yankees were about to enjoy political power, and they reasoned accordingly, their ideas conforming to their interests.

3

Proceeding in devious ways, those who spoke the language of force reached at last the crux of their problem. Having refused to admit that Southerners had either a legal right to secede or cause for rebellion, these Northerners could build a case for armed intervention. In simple terms this meant the use of military and naval power to suppress rebellious combinations of the southern people and punish their leaders. But the coercionists refused to describe the alternative of war in such direct language. At this point the verbal hairsplitters had their say.

[23] *Congressional Globe*, 138–39.
[24] Philadelphia *Press*, January 17, 1861; New York *Evening Post*, January 11; February 2, 1861; New York *Daily Tribune*, February 5, 1861; Trenton *Daily State Gazette and Republican*, January 18, 1861; Boston *Daily Journal*, January 15, 1861.

At once they presented a baffling conundrum which drove most Northerners a little mad during the crisis months. There were, it appeared, two distinct ways in which military force could be applied: first, by coercing the southern states; second, by merely enforcing Federal laws. Upon a correct choice between these supposed alternatives would hinge the constitutional right of re- sorting to force. An incredible amount of mental anguish went into the clarification of that subtle point.

Each of these two concepts had a precise definition. *Coercion* was the invasion or subjugation of a state, the effort to force its people to send representatives to Congress, or to make them en- joy the benefits of Federal courts and postal services against their will. *Enforcement of the laws* was simply the collection of duties on imports, the administration of commercial regulations, and the holding of Federal property. In the end the great majority of Northerners agreed that it was not coercion but the enforcement of the laws which they desired—the first was unconstitutional and a bloody business; the second was only an inescapable duty of Federal authorities. *Coercion of states* was a phrase forbidden in the best circles of the disciples of force. *Enforcement of the laws,* a phrase that had a reassuring aura of respectability and legality, was widely used instead.

A truly phenomenal number of newspapers, letter writers, and politicians, Democratic and Republican, subscribed to this tenu- ous distinction. A Republican constituent of Trumbull professed that he "would not like coertion [*sic*]" but would "recommend force . . . in the protection of public property." [25] With an equally fine discrimination in the use of words a Buchanan Demo- crat informed Postmaster General Joseph Holt that he would shrink from coercing a state; "yet the Pres^t has the power to col- lect the Revenues & enforce the laws, and wo [*sic*] to those who shall resist. . . ." [26] The Boston *Advertiser* presented a viewpoint that became a commonplace among northern editors. It deplored "the confusion introduced by the use of the term 'coërcion.'"

. . . We know of no particular coërcion to be applied by the Government of the United States, except by enforcing its laws

[25] Richard Randee to Trumbull, January 29, 1861, Trumbull Papers.
[26] M. W. Jacobus to Holt, December 10, 1860, Holt Papers.

and the collection of its revenues. No power, however great, could compel the South Carolina Convention to rescind its ordinance, or her legislature to disown the Palmetto flag, or her citizens to cease to call themselves citizens of an independent State. . . . The general government can do no more than see that its laws are carried out; and we do not see that any exigency has arisen authorizing it to do any less than this. We may well enough admit that the government has not the power to make war upon any State, for it is not making war upon a State to execute the laws. . . .[27]

It was asserted that enforcement of Federal laws had no bearing upon states as political units. "Who, in the wide land, has talked of 'coercing *a State?*' " The laws operated upon individuals, not states. A state could not be rebellious or violate the laws; only individuals within a state could do so. These individuals, whether few or many, could be punished for resistance to national authority. Hence coercion of a state was a false issue raised by southern traitors and their abettors in the North.[28] "They are attempting to interpose the State as a shield to treason," argued Senator Preston King of New York. "The State cannot commit treason or fire a gun. . . . The constitution and laws of the United States are [enforced] directly upon persons who commit crimes against them, . . . and the State cannot interpose its authority to shield a citizen charged with an offense against a constitutional law of the United States. . . ." [29]

Indeed, said the friends of law enforcement, if the crisis raised the issue of coercion at all it was due to southern efforts to coerce the Federal government. "Nobody . . . proposes to subjugate or invade a seceding state," affirmed Representative John A. Mc-

[27] Boston *Daily Advertiser*, December 24, 1860. See also New York *Times*, December 13, 22, 1860; Springfield (Mass.) *Daily Republican*, February 9, 1861; Providence *Daily Post*, January 16; February 8, 1861; Philadelphia *Press*, January 5, 15, 1861; Columbus *Daily Ohio Statesman*, December 7, 1860; Columbus *Crisis*, January 31, 1861; Chicago *Daily Tribune*, January 9, 1861.

[28] Washington *Daily National Intelligencer*, December 18, 1860; Providence *Daily Journal*, November 26, 1860; Boston *Daily Advertiser*, December 29, 1860; New York *Herald*, December 28, 1860; New York *World*, December 11, 1860; Columbus *Daily Ohio Statesman*, December 22, 1860; Edgar Cowan to Simon Cameron, December 15, 1860, Cameron Papers, Library of Congress.

[29] Preston King to Dr. S. N. Sherman, December 17, 1860, quoted in New York *Herald*, December 31, 1860.

Clernand. "The true question is whether the United States Government will submit to the coercion of the seceding States. . . ." It was they who had armed themselves and had seized Federal property.[30] But when the government offered resistance, the disunionists had decided to "lift up their hands with holy horror, and talk about 'coercion.' " "Military preparations are wrong only when made by the government," concluded a northern editor, ironically. "Coercion is the prerogative of the secessionists alone." [31]

This theme of noncoercive law enforcement was played with numerous variations. Cassius Clay proposed simply to station revenue ships off southern ports to collect the duties on imports.[32] Others who opposed coercing the South favored the use of warships to blockade her ports or the repeal of the laws making them ports of entry. "It seems to me," wrote a friend of John Sherman, "that if South Carolina will not be pacified at all, that a very quiet way of dealing with her, will be to close *all* Post Offices, repeal all laws making any of her ports, Ports of Entry, hold the Forts and property of the Government, and *do nothing*. This keeps the parties in conflict from any point of attack. . . ." [33]

Here was, in effect, a significant application of Seward's formula of "masterly inactivity" as it was frequently interpreted. What it meant was that the Federal government, while it waited for the southern pro-Union reaction, was not to coerce or invade the South, but only preserve the *status quo* and "do nothing"! In other words, secession was to be tolerated for a time if the South violated no laws, if it refrained from "anything more than the adoption of empty resolves." [34] In the interim, however, Federal authority

---

[30] Peoria *Blade*, quoted in Chicago *Daily Tribune*, February 21, 1861. See also M. E. Hollister to Trumbull, January 18, 1861, Trumbull Papers.

[31] Providence *Daily Journal*, January 21, 1861; Springfield (Mass.) *Daily Republican*, January 1, 1861; New York *Evening Post*, January 18, 1861; Washington *Daily National Intelligencer*, February 11, 1861.

[32] Cassius Clay to John A. Andrew, February 18, 1861, Andrew Papers, Massachusetts Historical Society.

[33] Henry W. Elliot to Sherman, December 7, 1860, Sherman Papers. See also D. Solomon to James Buchanan, December 23, 1860, Buchanan Papers, Historical Society of Pennsylvania; New York *World*, January 17, 1861; Boston *Evening Transcript*, November 30, 1860; Philadelphia *Public Ledger*, December 3, 1860.

[34] Philadelphia *Press*, December 21, 1860; Madison *Wisconsin Daily State Journal*, December 18, 1860.

must be respected. If they conceded this much, the secessionists could be left to "resign as they please and declaim as they please for the time." [35]

This was rather whimsical reasoning. The preservation of the *status quo*, the enforcement of the laws, was a do-nothing policy! Disunionists would not be interfered with if they confined themselves to the adoption of ordinances of secession which did not mean actual separation. As soon as a seceding state should seek to act upon its independence, the program of "masterly inactivity" would break down. Then would follow the application of force, but still in its neat disguise of "law enforcement" rather than "coercion."

Of course, secessionists, regarding the dissolution of the Union as an accomplished fact, brushed aside these fine distinctions and branded any Federal intervention in the South as coercion. They left their own sophistries long enough to demolish such northern quibbles. If there was no power to coerce a seceded state, they held, there was no power to enforce national laws in it. "The most offensive form of coercion which could be adopted," said Senator Thomas L. Clingman of North Carolina, "would be the levying of tribute." [36] Representative William E. Simms of Kentucky accused Republicans of being "guilty of the moral cowardice of skulking the logical effect of . . . [their] policy." "If you mean war," he pleaded, "have the manliness to avow it." [37]

An occasional northern iconoclast did display a refreshing willingness to call things by their right names, to express what he desired in honest language. Representative James H. Campbell of Pennsylvania impatiently came to the point: "I care not what term may be applied to the preservation of the Union and the enforcement of the laws. If to do this means 'coercion,' then I am for coercion." [38] The Springfield *Republican*, as if to mock its own repeated vagaries, sneered at the "absurd attempt to distinguish between coercion and the enforcement of the laws.

[35] Philadelphia *North American and United States Gazette*, November 14, 1860; Springfield (Mass.) *Daily Republican*, February 26, 1861; Providence *Daily Journal*, November 16, 1860; James D. Ogden to John J. Crittenden, December 22, 1860, Crittenden Papers, Library of Congress; Augustus E. Noble to Fessenden, January 24, 1861, Fessenden Papers.
[36] *Congressional Globe*, 4.   [37] *Ibid.*, 1230.   [38] *Ibid.*, 911.

. . . To compel a rebellious state to observe the constitution and laws of the United States is coercion, and the enforcement of the laws against rebels without coercion is an impossibility." [39]

Indeed, argued a few, there was no point to this "mawkish sensibility" about coercion, for it was a daily practice of government. Lawbreakers were forever being coerced; a state was coerced when its laws were disallowed by Federal courts. The trouble was that the normally peaceful functioning of democratic processes had obscured from public attention "the compulsory powers of governments." [40] Senator Douglas, while pleading for compromise, had no patience for those who denied a government's right of coercion. "Sir," he said, "the word government means coercion. . . . Coercion is the vital principle upon which all Governments rest. . . . Hence I do not subscribe to all this doctrine that coercion is not to be used in a free Government." [41] In the same spirit, James Russell Lowell fastened the charge of verbal trickery upon the South: "The country is weary of being cheated with plays upon words. . . . Rebellion smells no sweeter because it is called Secession, nor does Order lose its divine precedence in human affairs because a knave may nickname it Coercion. Secession means chaos, and Coercion the exercise of legitimate authority. You cannot dignify the one nor degrade the other by any verbal charlatanism." [42]

The New York *Times* also turned abruptly to plain talk, and the result was an almost fatal blow to the logic of the southern position. The seceders claimed to be independent of the United States, the *Times* remarked. "And now they cry out that there must be no coercion of States—even while they claim to be foreigners. They still claim, it seems, the same immunities granted by the Constitution to States, as if they were still loyal and true co-partners in the Government." [43] The *Times* had truly found a flaw in southern reasoning. For, alas, it was still legal for one na-

[39] Springfield (Mass.) *Daily Republican*, December 17, 1860.

[40] *Morning Courier and New-York Enquirer*, December 14, 1860; New York *Evening Post*, January 5, 1861; Boston *Evening Transcript*, January 14, 1861.

[41] *Congressional Globe*, Appendix, 40–41.

[42] [James Russell Lowell], "E Pluribus Unum," *Atlantic Monthly*, VII (January, 1861), 238. See also J. R. Swan to Sherman, December 17, 1860, Sherman Papers.

[43] New York *Times*, April 12, 1861.

tion to coerce another, even though the latter was sovereign and independent!

Such evidences of forthrightness, however, were mere aberrations from the norm. Most of the northern people cherished legal subtleties with great earnestness. Almost certainly they would have voted overwhelmingly against coercion or war and in favor of the enforcement of the laws. One observer reported: "If the men in the country who are opposed to coercion are asked if they are for enforcing the laws [they] say yes." [44] Looking back over the crisis months the New York *Tribune* still failed to penetrate the fatal weakness of this position. To the very end, it believed, the northern people were unwilling to do more than hold Federal property and collect the revenues. For they "shrank from anything that should precipitate civil war [!]" [45] Yet this strange choice was but a choice of words. Call it "coercion" or "law enforcement," the practical result in either case was precisely the same. The rebel soldier could derive cold comfort from the assertion that the Yankee bayonet was a symbol, not of coercion, but of law.

4

There still remained one last masterpiece of word juggling to be demonstrated by sectional leaders. This appeared in their development of the concepts of *aggression* and *defense*. To make sure, if war came, that the enemy was responsible for the first shedding of blood, to cast the enemy in the role of aggressor, was a psychological advantage that neither side could afford to ignore.

This task was simplified for both sides by the fact that each had its special definition of the word *aggression*. By the very nature of the case both sections could simultaneously disavow aggressive purposes and affirm an intention to remain strictly on the defensive. Yet, because of the lack of agreement upon the meaning of words, this was no guarantee that the peace would not be broken. To the secessionists the Union was in fact dissolved, and any Federal attempt to reinforce or recover the forts, or to collect the revenues in southern ports, was aggression. It would mean war.

[44] G. Trumbull to Lyman Trumbull, January 27, 1861, Trumbull Papers.
[45] New York *Daily Tribune*, May 2, 1861.

"Why, sir," rhetorically asked Senator Louis T. Wigfall of Texas, "if the President of the United States were to send a fleet to Liverpool, and attempt there to enforce the laws of the United States, and to collect revenues, and that flag were fired at, would anybody say that the British Government was responsible for the blood that might follow?" [46]

But the average Northerner found it no more difficult to pin the label of *aggressor* upon the disunionists. The opportunity sprang from the fact that the burden of direct action rested with the seceding states, which, after all, were seeking to disturb existing political relationships. They felt it necessary, in order to make their independence a reality, to seize government forts and to destroy other evidences of national authority. The Union government, simply trying to maintain the *status quo*, needed merely to preserve the various symbols of its power. As a result it could forswear aggressive designs upon the South and simulate a defensive pose.

More than that, given the common northern belief that the Union had not been and could not be dissolved, the general government was entitled to make a number of seemingly defensive moves. These apparently nonaggressive acts could include such normal Federal functions as collecting the revenues, holding national property, perhaps even reinforcing the forts or recovering those that might be seized. Such a course, it was widely felt, was far different from marching a hostile army into the South to overawe its citizens. And in northern eyes southern resistance would be pure aggression.

Shortly after the election this point of view appeared with remarkable spontaneity. A correspondent of Senator Wade's articulated the almost universal hope "that if blood must be shed that the Rebels should take the initiatory." [47] Another Republican believed that the first blows should be struck in "defending the property or enforcing the laws of the U.S. The traitors are anxious to make the U.S. the aggressors and woe to us if they succeed in doing so." [48] A Douglas Democrat advised the government not to act "unless some violent seizure . . . [should] be made of its

---

[46] *Congressional Globe*, 1439–46.
[47] P. Voris to Wade, December 23, 1860, Wade Papers.
[48] J. R. Swan to Sherman, December 17, 1860, Sherman Papers.

property or resistance be made to the execution of some lawful process." [49] "My doctrine," explained Senator John C. Ten Eyck of New Jersey, "means nothing else but this: self-defense, . . . and if the doctrine of self-defense . . . leads to blows and bloodshed, they must come and fall." [50]

The northern press was equally adept at explaining the defensive nature of the government's position. "The Republican policy," asserted the Springfield *Republican,* "will be to make no war upon the seceding states, to reject all propositions for secession, to hold them to the discharge of their constitutional duties, to collect the revenues in the southern ports, and calmly to await the result. There can be no war unless the seceders make war upon the general government." [51] The New York *Times* demonstrated that the "whole policy of the Government" was "*defensive.*" "It is not at all impossible that war may grow out of our present difficulties. But if so it will be because the South insists upon it, and commences it. The Federal Government has no war to wage." [52] After presenting a sizable list of southern acts of aggression, the Cincinnati *Commercial* concluded: The rebels are "directly and solely responsible for the war into which we are drifting." [53]

With these varying interpretations of aggression it was almost certain that if war came neither side would assume responsibility for the first blow. Both northern and southern leaders would make full use of the "defense" idea. It was this concept that destined the people of each section to play the dual role of hateful aggressors against the other and heroic defenders of their own sacred soil.

So the debate went on to the final climax. Subsequent events were to prove that loaded words were dangerous weapons. A well-turned phrase could be translated into an army of soldiers. And those soldiers would make the tragic discovery that a pointed abstraction might be as deadly as a pointed pike.

[49] J. O. Harrison to Holt, November 16, 1860, Holt Papers. See also M. W. Jacobus to *id.,* February 1, 1861, *ibid.;* G. M. Wharton to Buchanan, January 3, 1861, Buchanan Papers.

[50] *Congressional Globe,* 779. See also letter of John Sherman to the citizens of Philadelphia, Cincinnati *Daily Commercial,* January 2, 1861.

[51] Springfield (Mass.) *Daily Republican,* December 19, 1860.

[52] New York *Times,* January 9, 1861.

[53] Cincinnati *Daily Commercial,* April 15, 1861.

IV

A Doughface Chooses the Union

LINCOLN's election was the token of an approaching political revolution. Ideally, the new President should have been quickly installed in office, where he could at once shape his policies. But the country had to abide by the provisions of the Constitution. A discredited administration would remain in power until the fourth of March, a lameduck Congress would assemble in December, and the newly elected Congress would have to wait thirteen months for its first regular session. These requirements were frustrating in normal times; in a period of stress they could be disastrous.

So during the critical months of the secession crisis President Buchanan continued to face the responsibilities of his high office. They were terrifying responsibilities, and he believed they rightly belonged to his successor. During the last hundred days of his presidency he endured violent criticism and suffered great mental torture. He looked out upon a world that was fast becoming strange to him, upon a changing political order that no longer had a place for leaders of his type. No President had ever been in an unhappier predicament.

James Buchanan of Pennsylvania, then in his seventieth year, was ending a long career in public life. He had served as state legislator, congressman, and senator; as Secretary of State in James K. Polk's cabinet; and as minister to St. Petersburg and the Court of St. James. Seldom during his forty years of political experience had he shown signs of intellectual brilliance; rarely had he risen from the mediocre level of a party hack to the heights of statesmanship. Yet this much maligned "Old Public Functionary" was hardly the unmitigated villain that his political enemies made him out to be. Among his virtues were personal integrity, obstinate courage, and a high sense of duty. His special talent lay in the arts of diplomacy rather than in executive leadership. His caution and literal constitutionalism were often confused with personal weakness and moral cowardice. Actually he was guilty of neither.

Buchanan was the sort of politician that foes of the Slave Power called a "doughface," a northern man with southern principles. On the slavery question his public record was amoral. He expressed no indignation over Negro servitude, save as he frowned upon those who agitated the issue or would deprive the southern states of their right to maintain the institution as they chose. He readily accepted the Dred Scott decision, which permitted slaveholders to carry their property into the Federal territories. He tried to bring Kansas into the Union under the proslavery Lecompton Constitution. Closely tied to the southern wing of his party, he allowed such men as Howell Cobb of Georgia, Jefferson Davis of Mississippi, John Slidell of Louisiana, and Henry A. Wise of Virginia to dominate his administration. As his party split along sectional lines, "Old Buck" found himself siding with the South and waging relentless war upon the friends of Stephen A. Douglas.

Thus the President who first had to deal with the disunion movement believed in the essential validity of southern grievances. He abhorred Republicanism and its sectional appeal. He was out of touch with the main currents of northern opinion. He enjoyed little more popularity among northern Democrats than among Republicans; the handful of Buchanan Democrats in the North was a despised and repudiated political faction. Ideologically Buchanan had been exiled to the South.

What, then, was to be expected of this "doughface," this northern outcast, this ally of secessionists, when the Union was imperiled? Only that he would be the chief architect of national ruin, that he would climax his subservience to the South by abdicating the executive power to aid the cause of rebellion. The broken Union would then stand as a monument to the perfidy of James Buchanan!

Such at least was the forecast of a large segment of the northern press. Republican organs charged that this unfaithful public servant was "conniving at the treasonable projects" of the southern fire-eaters. His principal advisers were disunionists who led him about by the nose. "He is surrounded from morning till night by as dangerous a set of traitors as ever escaped the halter." [1] His administration was the nation's greatest peril, for treason would now be its "last revenge" against those who had beaten and disgraced it.[2]

Pro-Douglas papers were, if anything, even more scathing in their attacks upon Buchanan. They blamed him for party disruption and political defeat. Knowing that a Republican victory would mean disunion, he had sought deliberately to split the Democrats to make that result a certainty. "Indeed it may readily be charged that the whole game of secession originated in his Cabinet. . . . He is, in fact, completely in the possession of the enemies of the country. . . . His intimates are the very chiefs of the secession conspiracy. . . ." [3] Rarely did a contemporary Yankee see anything but evil in James Buchanan.

Yet, considering his southern sympathies, his state-rights proclivities, and his low reputation in the North, Buchanan's actual record in the secession crisis contains some significant surprises. Viewed retrospectively, his indictment falls rather flat. When the tug actually came, he quickly proved that he shared one basic concept with the nationalists: a deep belief in the perpetuity of the Union. In truth, southern secessionists miscalculated Buchanan's course almost as badly as northern Unionists.[4]

2

Having doubted that his southern friends would actually break up the Union, Buchanan received a severe blow when secession became a reality. How could his political allies, whose rights he had defended with such ardent loyalty, have the heart to place

---

[1] New York *Evening Post*, November 8, 9, 10, 12, 28, 1860.

[2] New York *Times*, November 7, 1860.

[3] Providence *Daily Post*, October 27, 1860; Philadelphia *Press* (letter from "Occasional"), December 7, 1860; Detroit *Free Press*, December 16, 1860.

[4] For defenses of Buchanan's course during the secession crisis see [James Buchanan], *Mr. Buchanan's Administration on the Eve of the Rebellion* (New York, 1866); King, *Turning on the Light;* George T. Curtis, *Life of James Buchanan* (New York, 1883), II, 297–506; Philip G. Auchampaugh, *James Buchanan and His Cabinet on the Eve of Secession* (Lancaster, Pa., 1926); Frank W. Klingberg, "James Buchanan and the Crisis of the Union," *Journal of Southern History,* IX (1943), 455–74.

him in such a compromising and painful position? [5] He might well have been dismayed by the bitter alternatives fate had placed before him. Since his remaining support was in the South, he hesitated to alienate the Southerners. If he did, he would become a politician without a party, a leader without a popular following. For at this late hour there was little chance that even by taking the firmest possible stand for the Union he could reconcile many of his northern foes.

Buchanan was getting conflicting advice from his party associates, and this made his problem still more troublesome. Various advocates or apologists for secession sought to exploit their personal or party ties with the President to control his course. Assistant Secretary of State William H. Trescott of South Carolina, an ardent disunionist, used all his influence to persuade the administration to let the South go unopposed.[6] Robert Barnwell Rhett warned Buchanan not to send any more troops to Charleston Harbor unless he wished to risk the shedding of blood.[7] Caleb Cushing of Massachusetts, one of the President's few supporters in New England, promptly placed upon the North entire responsibility for the crisis and denied that the government had power to hold states in the Union by force.[8] Judge George W. Woodward of Pennsylvania not only justified the South for seceding but even regretted that his state did not elect to go with her.[9] William M. Browne, editor of the Washington *Constitution*, recognized as Buchanan's special organ, was an outspoken secession sympathizer.

Other Buchanan Democrats, however, argued that it was one thing to defend southern rights but a far different matter to support or even acquiesce in disunion. They advised the President not to compromise himself. He should stand by the South only

[5] For a letter of sympathy from a leading secessionist see John Slidell to Buchanan, November 11, 1860, quoted in Auchampaugh, *Buchanan and His Cabinet*, 168.
[6] See, for example, William H. Trescott to Thomas F. Drayton, November 19, 1860, copy in Edwin M. Stanton Papers, Library of Congress.
[7] Robert Barnwell Rhett to Buchanan, November 24, 1860, Moore (ed.), *Works of Buchanan*, XI, 5. Original in Buchanan Papers.
[8] Claude M. Fuess, *The Life of Caleb Cushing* (New York, 1923), II, 269–74.
[9] George W. Woodward to Jeremiah S. Black, November 18, 1860, Black Papers, Library of Congress.

so long as Southerners were loyal to the Federal government, and he should purge his administration of secessionists. None strove more actively to push him into this position than Assistant Postmaster General Horatio King of Maine. As early as November 7, King expressed "indignation on learning that men holding office here under your administration, were parading the streets . . . with disunion cockades on their hats!" King begged Buchanan to remove them, to repudiate Browne's *Constitution*, and to place the government "squarely and unequivocally on the side of the Union!" [10] Not content with his own efforts, he solicited other friends of the administration to intervene for the same purpose.[11]

King received a promise of cordial co-operation from Postmaster John A. Dix of New York, a wealthy merchant with considerable political influence. Dix promptly advised the President to defend the Union, while he assured King that he too was displeased "at the encouragement given to the secessionists." He wished the government "quietly and firmly [to] maintain the central authority." [12] If, other administration Democrats warned, Buchanan "falls one hairs breadth below the Jackson line—if by silence he seems to abdicate the authority of the Government of the Union, his character in history is gone." [13]

While all these conflicting admonitions came over the desk of the troubled President, he also had before him the remarkable opinions of Lieutenant General Winfield Scott. Having long been close to Whig politicians, the blustery old general was hardly a friend of the Buchanan administration. Scott preferred to maintain his headquarters not in Washington but in New York, as he had done since the inauguration of Franklin Pierce. In New York he divided his time between nursing the physical infirmities of

[10] Horatio King to Buchanan, November 7, 1860, *ibid.*; *id.* to *id.*, November 25, 1860, quoted in King, *Turning on the Light*, 27; *id.* to Black, December 14, 1860, quoted in *ibid.*, 33–34.

[11] Horatio King to Franklin Pierce, November 21, 1860, Pierce Papers (photostats), Library of Congress; *id.* to John A. Dix, November 25, 27, 1860; *id.* to Nahum Capen, November 25, 1860, quoted in King, *Turning on the Light*, 27.

[12] Dix to King, November 27; December 19, 1860, quoted in King, *Turning on the Light*, 27, 35.

[13] William B. Reed to Black, December 1, 1860, Black Papers; M. W. Jacobus to Holt, November 27, 1860, Holt Papers.

senescence and guiding the small regular army through its laby-
rinths of incompetence and red tape. Though a Virginian by birth,
Scott had no sympathy for the southern secessionists. So, on
October 29, more than a week before the election, the general in
chief took it upon himself to send Buchanan his political and
military "Views."

The document was a piece of military impulsiveness and political ineptitude. In his turgid style Scott began by conceding
(in order "to save time") the right of secession but balanced
against it the government's "correlative right" to prevent a "gap
in the Union" through the separation of an "interior" state. This
Federal prerogative, he felt, would not apply to Texas or to any of
the Atlantic states south of the Potomac River, the secession of
which would create no such "gap." Rather than endure the horrors of civil war, Scott confessed he would prefer the formation
of four separate confederacies, and he even described their proper
boundaries. He inserted an added irrelevancy by stating that his
current political sympathies were with the Bell-Everett ticket,
but that he did not believe there was danger of Lincoln's violating
the Constitution.

The general in chief's military advice was not entirely consistent with his dissertation upon politics. He pointed to the danger
of rash acts by the secessionists, such as the seizure of Federal
property. As a precaution against such a *coup de main*, he recommended the immediate garrisoning of nine southern forts. Scott
observed, however, that there were available for this purpose only
five companies of regular troops. Finally, he suggested that the
government collect its revenues from these forts or from the
decks of ships of war. Thus the invasion of seceded states could
be avoided and time could be gained for the development of
measures of conciliation! "General Scott," he concluded, "is all
solicitude for the safety of the Union." [14]

The officious general's amateurish proposals had no effect upon
administration policy.[15] Scott's confused political ideas were no
less chimerical than those the President received from many hum-

[14] Moore (ed.), *Works of Buchanan*, XI, 301–304.

[15] Curtis, *Buchanan*, II, 301; Scott to Crittenden, November 12, 1860, quoted
in Mrs. Chapman Coleman, *Life of John J. Crittenden* (Philadelphia, 1871), II,
219.

bler sources. In addition, he asked Buchanan to reinforce southern forts before the election was decided, before a state convention had been called, before an ordinance of secession had been passed, and with admittedly inadequate forces. This might well have precipitated the very thing it was supposed to prevent. Scott asked Buchanan to beg the whole question, to assume in advance that Southerners would resist Federal laws. Inevitably such a course would have compromised national authorities and given moral strength to the secessionists.[16] Buchanan ignored the General's "Views" without the courtesy of an acknowledgment.

Although this document was not actually published until January, Scott immediately showed it to various acquaintances. He sent a copy to Lincoln, for which he received thanks in a brief and noncommittal note. Possibly this communication raised in the mind of the President-elect his first doubts about the judgment of the general in chief.[17] Nevertheless, the immediate outcome was damaging to Buchanan's prestige rather than to Scott's. It soon became general knowledge that Scott had urged the sending of reinforcements to southern forts and that the President had rejected the advice. Here was an additional opportunity for Buchanan's enemies to accuse him of cowardice and to insinuate that he was in league with traitors.[18] This would not be the last time that the "timid" Buchanan would serve as a foil for the "vigorous" Scott.

Meanwhile the disunion question was not long in forcing itself upon the attention of the President's cabinet. Since his official advisers came from both sections, Buchanan found here the same exasperating division of opinion. The discussions, beginning on November 9, dealt with such matters as the calling of a national

[16] Curtis, *Buchanan*, II, 297–305; [Buchanan], *Buchanan's Administration*, 99–107; Auchampaugh, *Buchanan and His Cabinet*, 63–64; James Ford Rhodes, *History of the United States from the Compromise of 1850 to the Final Restoration of Home Rule at the South in 1877* (New York, 1896–1919), III, 125–38; Nicolay and Hay, *Lincoln*, II, 339 ff. For a summary of General Scott's career during the crisis see Charles W. Elliott, *Winfield Scott, the Soldier and the Man* (New York, 1937), 675–96.

[17] Nicolay and Hay (eds.), *Works of Lincoln*, VI, 68; Elliott, *Scott*, 687–88.

[18] New York *Times*, December 13, 15, 18, 1860. Scott's letter to Buchanan was published in Washington *Daily National Intelligencer*, January 18, 1861. For the subsequent controversy between Buchanan and Scott in the columns of this paper see Moore (ed.), *Works of Buchanan*, XI, 279–307, 310–17, 321–23.

convention, the policy of the government toward disaffected states, and the position the President should assume in his annual message to Congress. Secretary of the Treasury Howell Cobb of Georgia and Secretary of the Interior Jacob Thompson of Mississippi upheld the right of secession and opposed any Federal interference. Secretary of War John B. Floyd of Virginia disapproved of secession but objected also to coercion. Secretary of State Lewis Cass of Michigan and Attorney General Jeremiah S. Black of Pennsylvania dissented vigorously and demanded the immediate sending of reinforcements to Charleston Harbor. Both Cass and Black, along with Secretary of the Navy Isaac Toucey of Connecticut and Postmaster General Joseph Holt of Kentucky, denied the right of any state to secede.[19]

As the tension mounted, it became manifestly impossible to hold this cabinet together. Black and Cass continued their pressure upon the President and nearly persuaded him to send additional troops to Fort Moultrie. But the southern members threatened to resign if this step were taken, and Floyd prevailed upon Buchanan to agree to a temporary delay. The Secretary of War assured Trescott that he would cut off his right hand before signing an order for reinforcements.[20] The friction between Cobb and Black soon grew to a point where the latter insisted that it was imperative for one of them to leave the cabinet. He finally suggested that they see the President; the one Buchanan endorsed should remain and the other should resign.[21]

Although the issue was never presented to Buchanan in this fashion, he decided between the factions no less clearly as he carefully composed his annual message. When that document was completed Buchanan had made his choice. Once decided, he adhered to his position consistently for the remainder of his term.

3

Northerners waited suspiciously for the message Buchanan would send to Congress on December 3. Few of them doubted

[19] Auchampaugh, *Buchanan and His Cabinet*, 131.
[20] Crawford, *Genesis of the Civil War*, 25–35; William N. Brigance, *Jeremiah Sullivan Black* (Philadelphia, 1934), 82–83.
[21] Brigance, *Black*, 90. For a clear expression of Black's views on the crisis see Black to George W. Woodward, November 24, 1860, copy in Black Papers.

that its sentiments would border upon treason. Editors reminded
the President of his duty to the country but despaired of him; he
was no man for the emergency, no Jackson.[22] It would be good
for loyal men to have the facts. "If we have got a President who
is too weak to withstand the menaces of the disunionists about
him, . . . the people of the Union should know it." [23] It was
time for Buchanan to speak out so that all could judge his position.[24]

Unfortunately for the President, most Yankees had judged
before he spoke. Unfortunately, too, his message was full of tight
constitutional reasoning that could not bear a swift reading without being liable to misinterpretation. Before transmitting the document to Congress, he consulted his cabinet and various outside acquaintances. On points of constitutional law he relied
mainly upon his able Attorney General, Jeremiah S. Black, and
incorporated many of Black's opinions in his message. When this
became generally known, as it soon did, the Attorney General
often got credit, or blame, for the President's attitude.[25]

In his message Buchanan blamed the crisis on the constant interference of the northern people with the institution of slavery.
This meddling, he said, had produced a feeling of insecurity in
the South. Still, he insisted that the elevation of any man to the
presidency did not "of itself afford just cause for dissolving the
Union." The election had been held in accordance with strict
constitutional forms, and the Federal government was not yet
guilty of any violation of southern rights. "Reason, justice, a
regard for the Constitution, all require that we shall wait for some
overt and dangerous act on the part of the President elect, before
resorting to such a remedy." Buchanan went on to deny the legal
right of secession. The nation was no mere voluntary association
of states. Secession was a revolution, no less. "It may or may not
be a justifiable revolution, but still it is revolution."

[22] Detroit *Free Press*, November 14, 1860; *Daily Boston Traveller*, November
12, 1860; Boston *Herald*, November 26; December 3, 1860.

[23] Boston *Daily Journal*, November 15, 1860.

[24] *Morning Courier and New-York Enquirer* ("Washington Correspondence"), December 3, 1860.

[25] Brigance, *Black*, 84–89; Crawford, *Genesis of the Civil War*, 23–25; Philadelphia *Press*, December 10, 1860; New York *World*, December 11, 1860; George
W. Woodward to Black, December 10, 1860, Black Papers.

What, then, he asked, was the duty of the chief executive when confronted by such a movement? According to his oath it was to execute the laws, "and from this obligation he cannot be absolved by any human power." He would be compelled to collect the revenues and hold Federal property. He had instructed officers in the southern forts to remain "strictly on the defensive." If they were attacked, "the responsibility for consequences would rightfully rest upon the heads of the assailants." He himself, as President, lacked authority to alter the relationship between the national government and the disaffected states. That was a matter for Congress alone to decide.

Having said all this, Buchanan believed, as did Black, that a serious problem of executive responsibility would appear if events, such as the resignation of judges and other Federal officers, should make law enforcement impossible. The President could not assume powers he did not possess; he had no right to send a hostile army into a state to wage war upon its people. This would become another problem which only Congress could settle. Its members would have to consider whether they should delegate additional authority to the President for such an emergency.

Congressmen would also have to decide whether they had power to compel a state to remain in the Union by force of arms. On strict legal grounds Buchanan doubted that the legislative branch had the constitutional right to coerce or wage war upon states. They could not, for example, be forced to send representatives to Congress. War, he feared, would destroy the Union forever; conciliation was the nation's last hope. Closing on this theme, he outlined his compromise proposals and appealed for mutual sacrifices for the sake of the beloved Union.[26]

Buchanan's plea for peaceful adjustment, his stand against secession, and his assertion that the laws must be enforced brought from the North scattered expressions of approval.[27] But these were exceptions to the general run of comments. Indignant Republicans

[26] Moore (ed.), *Works of Buchanan*, XI, 7–43; James D. Richardson (comp.), *A Compilation of the Messages and Papers of the Presidents, 1789–1897* (Washington, 1897), V, 623–59.
[27] New York *World*, December 5, 1860; Springfield (Mass.) *Daily Republican*, December 5, 1860; Boston *Post*, December 6, 1860; Providence *Daily Post*, December 7, 1860; Curtis, *Buchanan*, II, 353–54.

lashed out angrily at the President, distorted his message, and held him up to ridicule. "I think the President has conclusively proved two things," sneered Seward, "1st, That no state has the right to secede unless it wishes to; and 2d, That it is the President's duty to enforce the laws, unless somebody opposes him." [28] The message was the "cowardly twaddle" of a "degenerate and degraded Democrat," an "incendiary document" designed to encourage the South in its most unreasonable demands.[29] Buchanan had "evoked but the shifts and evasions of a second-rate attorney," wrote James Russell Lowell. "He has always seemed to consider the Presidency as a retaining-fee paid him by the slavery-propagandists, and his Message to the present Congress looks like the last juiceless squeeze of the orange which the South is tossing contemptuously away." [30]

Buchanan's assailants were angered more by his interpretation of the causes of the crisis and his appeal for compromise than by any weakness in his attitude toward disunion. Friends of the administration charged that the Republicans were disappointed because the President had not declared war upon the South, thus shouldering a responsibility which they sought to evade.[31] In fact, Buchanan was guilty of nothing more than indulging in the common constitutional quibbles of the time. He had simply made the usual differentiation between "enforcing the laws" and "waging war upon a state." If he denied the right of Federal coercion, so did most of his critics. If he failed to see the sophistry of simultaneously pledging the continued maintenance of national authority in the South, so did they. Like them he accepted the subtle distinction between "defense" and "aggression." In the melee of partisan politics the President's clear acceptance of the nationalist

[28] New York *Evening Post* ("Washington Correspondence"), December 6, 1860; Seward, *Seward at Washington*, II, 480.

[29] New York *Times*, December 5, 1860; New York *Evening Post*, December 5, 1860; Springfield (Mass.) *Republican*, December 18, 1860.

[30] [James Russell Lowell], "The Question of the Hour," *Atlantic Monthly*, VII (January, 1861), 117–21. For equally bitter criticism from pro-Douglas Democratic papers see Detroit *Free Press*, December 18, 1860; Buffalo *Daily Courier*, December 6, 1860, quoted in Howard C. Perkins (ed.), *Northern Editorials on Secession* (New York, 1942), II, 138–40. Perkins' selection of editorials provides an excellent and well-organized cross section of northern press opinion on the crisis.

[31] Boston *Post*, December 7, 1860; Philadelphia *Morning Pennsylvanian*, December 21, 1860; Chas. Levi Woodbury to Buchanan, December 17, 1860, Moore (ed.), *Works of Buchanan*, XI, 67–68. Original in Buchanan Papers.

doctrine of a perpetual Union was all but ignored.[32] The average Yankee had concluded long before that there was no good in "Old Buck," the "doughface."

But if most Northerners were blind to the implications in Buchanan's message, southern secessionists were not. Before its submission to Congress, Cobb, Thompson, and other disunionists had protested vehemently against its affirmation of the integrity of the Union. In the Senate both Iverson and Wigfall attacked the President for rejecting the right of secession. Nor did they overlook his declaration in favor of the enforcement of the laws. They insisted that it was impossible to coerce individuals without coercing a state, and, significantly, they predicted that Buchanan's course would terminate in war.[33] A few days after the delivery of the message, Cobb expressed his displeasure with its tone by tendering his resignation from the cabinet.[34] He at least understood the President's verdict as between him and Black. Buchanan had, in fact, taken the first major step toward the alienation of the South.

4

The final break between Buchanan and his former southern allies grew out of the problem of Federal property in the seceding states. Though the President had declined to send reinforcements, this did not mean that he intended voluntarily to surrender the government's forts. Rather, he considered it his duty to hold on tenaciously wherever such a course was practicable. Conforming with the ideas embodied in his message, though still hoping to prevent bloodshed, he proposed to keep the military garrisons on the defensive and to have them simply resist any attack. This, he felt, would fulfill his constitutional obligation, demonstrate his conviction that secession was illegal, and yet leave a way open for compromise. It was a course which would in no way tie the hands of his successor.

[32] For defenses of Buchanan's message see [Buchanan], *Buchanan's Administration*, 111–33; Curtis, *Buchanan*, II, 318–29; Buchanan to Henry M. Phillips, December 5, 1860, Moore (ed.), *Works of Buchanan*, XI, 55.

[33] *Congressional Globe*, 10–14.

[34] Auchampaugh, *Buchanan and His Cabinet*, 67.

The situation in Charleston Harbor was the most pressing of Buchanan's immediate problems. Late in November, Major Robert Anderson, who commanded the small garrison of seventy men at Fort Moultrie, requested reinforcements because of the threatening attitude of the Charlestonians. The President could not agree to this, lest it impair the opportunity for conciliation. But on December 1 the War Department instructed Anderson to maintain his position to the best of his ability. Ten days later the Moultrie commander received oral instructions to refrain from aggressive action. "But you are to hold possession of the forts in this harbor, and if attacked you are to defend yourself to the last extremity." Then, on December 21, Buchanan ordered these instructions modified to permit the avoidance of a useless sacrifice of life if Anderson's garrisons should be assaulted by an overwhelming force.[35] Even so, the President had clearly endorsed the idea of trying to hold the Charleston forts.

Meanwhile, because of the critical situation, General Scott went to Washington from New York. In an interview with Buchanan on December 15 he urged that three hundred men be sent at once to Fort Moultrie. But the President again refused, explaining that he wished to avoid such a provocative step as long as Anderson did not seem to be in danger of immediate attack. That night, Scott sent Buchanan a note reminding him that President Jackson had not hesitated to send reinforcements to Moultrie during the nullification controversy of 1832. The northern press, getting the details of this interview, had additional evidence to show that Buchanan was ignoring the advice of his patriotic general in chief.[36]

On the day of the Scott interview, Secretary of State Cass tendered his resignation from the cabinet on the grounds that the President would not heed his repeated advice to send aid to Major Anderson. The defection of an old Jacksonian Democrat at that

[35] Crawford, *Genesis of the Civil War*, 60–61, 75; *War of the Rebellion: A Compilation of the Official Records of the Union and Confederate Armies* (Washington, 1880–1901), Ser. 1, I, 74–76, 78–79, 82–83, 89–90, 103. Hereafter cited as *Official Records*.

[36] Curtis, *Buchanan*, II, 364–65; Scott to Buchanan, December 15, 1860, Buchanan Papers; New York *Evening Post*, December 17, 1860.

particular moment was a source of extreme embarrassment to the administration. Cass became a great hero for a season; his Washington house was crowded with admirers. And the loyal press found a new reason for censuring the "traitor" Buchanan.[37]

But there were other facts involved in Cass's resignation which place him in a less heroic light. Buchanan and Cass, old political rivals, had never been on cordial terms. Buchanan reluctantly took Cass into his cabinet, for reasons of political expediency. Still, Cass, as Secretary of State, endorsed the President's message and even concurred in denying the right of coercion. And now, in submitting his resignation, he doubtless did not overlook the probable effect upon the prestige of his chief. There followed an anticlimax. After reconsidering his action for two days, Cass actually asked permission to withdraw his resignation. Buchanan stubbornly refused to permit it.[38] So the northern people believed the man they considered one of the few patriots in the administration left it to avoid tarnishing his reputation with treason.

At that time Buchanan was still being harassed by continued pressure from the secessionists to abandon the pro-Union doctrines of his message. On December 8 the congressional delegation from South Carolina called upon the President to assure him that sending reinforcements to Charleston Harbor would be the surest way to provoke an attack. They believed the forts would not be disturbed until after the ordinance of secession had been passed and commissioners had been sent to Washington to seek a peaceful settlement. At Buchanan's request they reduced this opinion to writing and handed it to him on December 10. He at once objected to a significant reservation—"that no reinforcements shall be sent into those forts, and their relative military status remain as at present." This, he said, "might be construed into an agreement on my part which I never would make." The delegation replied that it was not their intention to force him into such a position. Evidently Buchanan then led them to believe that he did not

---

[37] Horatio King to Holt, December 14, 1860, Holt Papers; New York *Daily Tribune*, December 15, 1860; New York *Leader*, December 15, 1860; New York *Evening Post*, December 17, 1860; *Morning Courier and New-York Enquirer*, December 17, 1860; Andrew C. McLaughlin, *Lewis Cass* (Boston, 1891), 334–41.

[38] Moore (ed.), *Works of Buchanan*, XI, 57–65; Curtis, *Buchanan*, II, 396–400.

propose at that time to send reinforcements or change the military status of the forts.[39]

A few weeks later the South Carolinians and the President's northern critics interpreted these negotiations as evidence that he had agreed to a formal truce involving a mutual pledge to preserve the *status quo*. Assuming there was actually such a truce, Northerners were to accuse Buchanan of disloyalty, and Southerners were to accuse him of double-dealing. Buchanan himself always insisted that there had been no truce and that he had in no way committed himself.

The trouble was that two constructions were easily deducible from the interview and correspondence. There seems to be little reason to doubt that the South Carolinians really *thought* the President had made them a pledge. To be sure, he did tell them that he had no immediate plans to change the status of the forts; but he also specifically refused to make that a binding promise for the future. Buchanan was probably right in maintaining that no formal truce had been made.[40] Nevertheless, these negotiations doubtless provided the reassurance that Buchanan needed to confirm his decision not to send reinforcements for the present. In other words, he proceeded as if there *were* a truce, even though technically none existed. Altogether it was a confused situation.

But the President never allowed the secessionists to have the slightest doubt as to what his reaction would have been had they demanded the surrender of any of the forts in Charleston Harbor. On December 17, Governor Francis W. Pickens of South Carolina suddenly asked permission to place a small force of state troops in Fort Sumter. Pickens said that if this request were refused he would be unable to answer for the consequences. Buchanan promptly drafted a sharp response in which he denied that he had power to surrender Federal property. He concluded: "If South Carolina should attack any of these forts, she will then become the assailant in a war against the United States. It will not then become a question of coercing a State to remain in the Union, to which I am utterly opposed, as my message proves, but it will be a question

[39] Curtis, *Buchanan*, II, 377; Moore (ed.), *Works of Buchanan*, XI, 56–57; Crawford, *Genesis of the Civil War*, 37–43; *Official Records*, Ser. 1, I, 125–28.

[40] [Buchanan], *Buchanan's Administration*, 162–79; King, *Turning on the Light*, 154–86.

of voluntarily precipitating a conflict of arms on her part, without even consulting the only authorities [Congress] which have power to act upon the subject." [41]

When Trescott and the South Carolina congressmen learned the contents of Governor Pickens' letter, they realized that his demand would nullify the supposed agreement which they had recently made. They knew that Buchanan would have to reject it and thus produce a crisis before the state commissioners had time to try peaceful negotiations. At the last minute the South Carolinians prevailed upon Pickens to withdraw his letter, and it became unnecessary for the President to send his challenging reply.[42] He was probably gratified that the impasse had been removed and that the opportunity for conciliation had not been lost entirely.

For Buchanan still struggled feebly toward that objective. In desperation he sent Caleb Cushing as his special messenger to South Carolina. Cushing was to communicate with Governor Pickens "for the purpose of changing or modifying the contemplated action of the State." It was a futile gesture; the emissary arrived in time to witness the formal passage of the state's ordinance of secession.[43]

The heartsick President, turned at last to implore divine guidance, proclaimed January 4 a day of fasting and prayer. To his enemies this was a confession of complete inadequacy. "God helps those who help themselves," snapped the New York *World*. "There are no records of miracles on behalf of the sluggard. . . ." [44] Others found Buchanan "so depressed in mind as to be practically incompetent to perform the duties of his office. . . . He is the most pitiable object in the country. . . ." The whole purpose of his policy, they asserted, was simply to stave off the crisis until his term expired. Demands for his impeachment were mixed with the common cry of loyal men: "Oh for an hour of Jackson!" [45]

[41] Moore (ed.), *Works of Buchanan*, XI, 71–72; Curtis, *Buchanan*, II, 384–85; Nicolay and Hay, *Lincoln*, III, 2–9.
[42] Crawford, *Genesis of the Civil War*, 81–86.
[43] Moore (ed.), *Works of Buchanan*, XI, 68.
[44] New York *World*, December 18, 1860.
[45] Boston *Evening Transcript*, December 28, 1860; Boston *Daily Advertiser*, December 17, 1860; Springfield (Mass.) *Daily Republican*, December 17, 1860; J. Leavitt to Sumner, December 17, 1860, Sumner Papers.

These were the daily greetings sent to Buchanan from the North. And they came at the very time that Southerners were becoming increasingly frigid toward him. The President was a lonely man in those December days. Some said that he wept a little.

V

Disunion Becomes a Reality

WHILE Buchanan was evolving his policy toward the disaffected states, the second session of the Thirty-sixth Congress assembled on December 3 in a tense atmosphere. "In truth it was a wretched time," Charles Francis Adams, Jr., afterward recalled. "Terribly anxious, we watched the daily papers with feverish interest, snatching at every straw." [1]

Seldom has there been a legislative body from which so much was expected and by which so little was achieved. It was not that the members suffered from a dearth of talent, for its personnel compared favorably with previous Congresses. There were able politicos—as many as could reasonably be expected. It was not the incompetence of its members that caused the failure of this Congress. To succeed, it would have had to remedy the errors of a whole generation and rectify the deficiencies of all its predecessors. What overwhelmed Congress was the size of the problem, the lateness of the hour.

Because it was their platform and projected policies that had provoked the wrath of Southerners, the focus of attention was generally upon Republican lawmakers, even though they constituted a minority in both House and Senate. How would they respond to the secession threat? Would they permit peaceful separation? Would they sponsor legislation to strengthen the hand of the executive department? Would they accept the compromise proposals expected to be advanced by northern Democrats and southern conservatives? Everyone was interested in what Seward would have to say, for he was still the pre-eminent Republican. When people learned that he was to enter Lincoln's cabinet as

[1] Adams, *Autobiography*, 71.

Secretary of State, they assumed they needed only to watch him to forecast the attitude of the new administration.

The resulting publicity which the Republicans received, the close scrutiny given to the most casual utterance of each member, promised to become a source of great embarrassment to the party. All this attention worried those who like Seward were unprepared for immediate action because of their continued belief in the ultimate triumph of southern unionism.[2] Publicity threatened to magnify the irresponsible statements of those with lingering doubts about the seriousness of the secession movement. Above all, publicity promised to illuminate the party's internal divisions. This conglomeration of Free-Soilers, old Whigs and former Democrats, radicals and conservatives, conciliators and "stiff-backed" Republicans, was still sadly lacking in organic unity. There was the ever present possibility that the organization would disintegrate at the first effort to formulate a positive policy.

These were the perils that faced Republicans as they gathered in Washington for the opening of Congress. And it was these perils which made most of them decide spontaneously that silence, delay, and inaction would best serve their needs for the present. "At all events," concluded conservative Senator James Dixon of Connecticut, "the longer action is postponed, the less will be the danger that an irretrievable and fatal step will be taken." [3] The radical Chase gave the same advice to Senator Henry Wilson of Massachusetts. He believed that Republicans were helpless until Lincoln's inauguration, "and all attempts, on their part, to do anything, under existing circumstances will, I fear, prove unfortunate." So it would be best to say little, avoid "intemperate denunciations," and concentrate upon necessary legislation such as the admission of Kansas, the new tariff, and the homestead bill.[4] Sumner's friends, too, urged him to hold his tongue and leave the debate to Southerners and northern Democrats.[5] A newspaper

[2] See Chapter II.

[3] James Dixon to Black, November 14, 1860, Black Papers.

[4] Chase to Henry Wilson, December 13, 1860, in *Diary and Correspondence of Salmon P. Chase* in American Historical Association, *Annual Report*, 1902, II (Washington, 1903), 293–95.

[5] E. R. Hoar to Sumner, December 11, 1860; George Livermore to *id.*, December 12, 1860; Edward L. Pierce to *id.*, December 15, 1860, Sumner Papers;

reporter found the Republicans viewing the crisis "with entire calm and self-possession"; they seemed to be determined upon a policy of "masterly inactivity." [6]

On December 3 this course received the formal sanction of the party caucus. Republicans were to shun all exciting discussions, push forward the public business, and await future developments.[7] Having nothing to apologize for or repent, like Lincoln in Springfield they would sit quietly by while their opponents held the floor. The subsequent decision in each house to create a special committee to consider the President's message and the various proposals for adjustment neatly fitted the strategy of the Republicans. As a device to remove the issue from general discussion most of them gave it their support.[8]

During the month of December, Republicans generally abided by the caucus decision, even when their critics abused them unmercifully for their silence. Seward, pleasant to all, said nothing in the Senate until January. Sumner gave a remarkable and uncharacteristic exhibition of self-discipline. Most of their fellow partisans likewise ignored the barbed taunts or confined their indignation to private letters. There were exceptions, however, for the party still lacked the discipline that comes with age alone. On the one side a few succumbed to outside pressures and, to the dismay of the radicals, began to speak in conciliatory tones or even to offer moderate concessions.[9] By mid-December these evidences of "timidity" caused some to fear that party ranks were breaking. "All the mean material we've got is coming out now," wailed Henry Adams to his brother.[10]

But the menace from the "backsliders" was small compared with that from the minority of "irrepressibles" who soon broke the party pledge with angry replies to the southern fire-eaters. In the Senate on the first day Republicans listened sullenly as Thomas

Laura A. White, "Charles Sumner and the Crisis of 1860–61," in Avery Craven (ed.), *Essays in Honor of William E. Dodd* (Chicago, 1935), 151–52.

[6] New York *Evening Post*, December 3, 1860.

[7] Charles Francis Adams to R. H. Dana, Jr., December 3, 1860, Dana Papers; James Dixon to Welles, December 8, 1860, Welles Papers; New York *Herald* ("Washington Correspondence"), December 5, 1860.

[8] *Congressional Globe*, 6–7, 117.   [9] See Chapter VII.

[10] Henry Adams to Charles Francis Adams, Jr., December 13, 1860, in Ford (ed.), *Letters of Henry Adams*, 64.

L. Clingman of North Carolina defended disunion and launched a violent attack upon the North. On that occasion they were content to leave the rebuttal to a conservative old Henry Clay Whig, John J. Crittenden of Kentucky.[11] The incitement became more intense, however, as Clingman was followed by Iverson, and the latter by the iconoclastic Wigfall. In an incendiary speech the sharp-tongued Texan sneered that if conflict came "the next treaty which was signed would be in Faneuil Hall, in the town of Boston, and in the state of Massachusetts."[12]

As early as December 5 the radical Senator John P. Hale of New Hampshire was on his feet with a speech loaded with sarcasm and defiance. He began with acid remarks about the alleged inconsistencies in Buchanan's message and demanded that the issue be faced squarely. Either the crisis would result in the absolute submission of the North—"or it looks to open war." Was war to be the alternative to surrender? "Let it come in any form or in any shape." Was the decision at the ballot box to be disregarded? "Then, sir, this is not a Union of equals; it is a Union of a dictatorial oligarchy on the one side, and a herd of slaves and cowards on the other." Either the incoming administration would do its duty, or Hale would oppose it.[13]

On December 17, "Bluff Ben" Wade (who was accused of aspiring to become a northern Cromwell) was "boiling over" before packed galleries with a two-hour speech which moderate colleagues had been unable to dissuade him from delivering.[14] He vowed that the day of compromise had passed. "This long, chronic controversy that has existed between us must be met, and met upon the principles of the Constitution and laws, and met now." Were it not for the dangerous precedent, Wade would have been glad to be rid of the "miserable" state of South Carolina. But the laws had to be enforced; the only way to destroy the Union was for disaffected states to "hew out their independence by violence and war." The Constitution had to be maintained unless the government was defeated by superior force.[15]

[11] *Congressional Globe*, 3–5.   [12] *Ibid.*, 72–76.   [13] *Ibid.*, 9–10.
[14] New York *Herald* ("Washington Correspondence"), December 15, 18, 1860.
[15] *Congressional Globe*, 99–104.

Congratulatory letters, filled with violent denunciations of the South and expressions of a readiness to fight for the Union, poured in upon Wade from many northern states. "Every true Republican," one correspondent assured him, "carries his head higher now that we *know* our sentiments are spoken in Congress. . . ." [16] Commentators heralded this speech as evidence that Wade's party, especially its western and rural members, was stiffening up. This "whiff of the old Jackson doctrine" sent "a thrill of satisfaction through the national heart." [17]

Hale and Wade were only two of a number of Republicans who were now ready to meet the crisis head on.[18] Even before the secession of South Carolina, Trumbull and Senator Preston King of New York had publicly pronounced for the enforcement of the laws.[19] On the day of Wade's speech Senator Daniel Clark of New Hampshire precipitated a heated debate by pointedly proposing an investigation of the military situation in Charleston Harbor.[20] In private, Senator James R. Doolittle of Wisconsin favored sending 800 men to Moultrie. And Representative James M. Ashley of Ohio wanted to raise and arm 50,000 volunteers to guard Lincoln's inauguration, hold the capital, and defend the forts.[21]

Private caucuses of members from various northern states were declaring themselves in favor of strong action. The delegations from New Hampshire, Pennsylvania, and Illinois, after vigorous speeches, resolved individually that the Union must be preserved, the laws enforced, and public property protected.[22] The New

[16] See especially letters to Wade from J. D. Cox, December 21, 1860; C. Delano, December 21, 1860; B. F. Hoffman, December 21, 1860; Daniel Hamilton, December 22, 1860; and C. Grant, December 23, 1860, Wade Papers.

[17] New York *Evening Post*, December 18, 20, 1860; New York *World*, December 19, 1860; Springfield (Mass.) *Daily Republican*, December 19, 1860.

[18] New York *Herald* ("Washington Correspondence"), December 19, 1860.

[19] *Congressional Globe*, 154–56; Preston King to Dr. S. N. Sherman, December 17, 1860, quoted in New York *Evening Post*, December 29, 1860; King to Welles, December 15, 1860, Welles Papers.

[20] *Congressional Globe*, 96, 154–56, 159.

[21] James R. Doolittle to his wife, December 2, 1860, Doolittle Papers, Historical Society of Wisconsin; J. M. Ashley to Chase, December 18, 1860, Chase Papers.

[22] New York *Herald* ("Washington Correspondence"), December 18, 1860; Arthur C. Cole, *The Era of the Civil War, 1848–1870* (Springfield, Ill., 1919), 255.

York delegation met at Willard's Hotel on December 19 and passed a resolution demanding "a prompt and energetic enforcement of all the laws of the General Government . . . and . . . the preservation of the Union." [23] A few days later the rooms of Francis Preston Blair were the scene of another large Republican confabulation. Among those present were Trumbull, Doolittle, Governor-elect John A. Andrew and Representative Anson Burlingame of Massachusetts, and Representative Mason W. Tappan of New Hampshire. They agreed unanimously "that the integrity of the Union should be preserved, though it cost millions of lives." [24]

On December 20 the disunion question suddenly became something more than the academic abstraction it had been for so many years. That was the day when Washington received the news that the South Carolina convention had unanimously passed an ordinance of secession. Immediately the South Carolina congressmen notified Speaker William Pennington that their people had "resumed the powers heretofore delegated by them to the Federal Government of the United States," and had thereby dissolved their connection with the House of Representatives.[25] Disunion had become a reality!

Or had it? Not if the views of most northern politicians were to be accepted. Indeed South Carolina's action simply completed the breakdown of the original Republican caucus agreement and spurred the coercionists on to stronger statements in the days that followed. Now they could "swell their cheeks, talk of treason, force laws, hanging," [26] while the press agreed that the ordinance was a "farce." [27] The state was in the Union as much as before, though the New York *Courier and Enquirer* decided that its people were "no longer our brethren, but a band of Rebels

---

[23] New York *Evening Post* ("Washington Correspondence"), December 18, 21, 1860; New York *Herald* ("Washington Correspondence"), December 20, 1860; New York *Daily Tribune*, December 28, 1860.

[24] New York *Times*, December 25, 1860; Boston *Daily Courier*, December 27, 28, 1860; Springfield (Mass.) *Daily Republican*, December 27, 1860.

[25] *Congressional Globe*, 190.

[26] New York *Herald* ("Washington Correspondence"), December 23, 1860.

[27] New York *Evening Post*, December 21, 1860; New York *World*, December 21, 1860; Boston *Daily Advertiser*, December 22, 1860.

and Traitors." [28] The Springfield *Illinois State Journal*, to whom many looked for hints of what Lincoln's attitude might be, asserted that South Carolina could not get out of the Union except by fighting. The revenues would have to be collected, and resistance would lead to conflict. "If she violates the laws, then comes the tug of war. The President of the United States, in such an emergency, has a plain duty to perform. . . . The laws . . . must be executed. . . . Disunion by armed force, is treason, and treason must and will be put down at all hazards." [29]

Then ensued a critical month when a succession of irritating incidents drove the sponsors of compromise to the edge of despair. The chance of continued peace seemed to become increasingly remote. The New York *Times* confessed gloomily that South Carolina was so firm in her course that there was no chance of her turning back. Everywhere people were saying: "Civil war is imminent—peace is impossible. . . . There is no longer any more hope of peace than of compromise. . . ." Especially violent were northwestern congressmen, with their "flaming tirades against disunion, coupled with direct threats of coercion." [30]

The will to peace was evaporating; a popular leader might easily have precipitated matters and sounded the call to arms. And so, temporarily, the eyes of the country shifted from the Republicans in Congress to the troubled man in the White House. What would the terms of his recent message imply in the face of the challenge from South Carolina?

2

The pressure of events gave Buchanan little time for contemplation. Without delay South Carolina sought to implement its independence by severing all remaining ties with the Union. The state convention appointed Robert W. Barnwell, James H. Adams, and James L. Orr as commissioners to treat with the Federal gov-

[28] *Morning Courier and New-York Enquirer*, December 22, 1860.
[29] Springfield *Daily Illinois State Journal*, December 20, 1860, quoted in Perkins (ed.), *Northern Editorials on Secession*, I, 121–22.
[30] New York *Times*, December 21, 1860.

ernment about the transfer of forts and other Federal property lying within the new "Republic," about the apportionment of the public debt, and about other matters of interest to the two countries.[31]

While the unhappy President awaited the coming of these diplomats, there were restless stirrings throughout the North. As South Carolinians prepared to leave the Union many indignant Yankees began to itch for "a chance to flog those hot headed fools." Politicians received assurances that "the rapid spread of treasonable sentiments at the South" was producing "a counter-current in public sentiment." [32] While General John E. Wool proposed "a judicious application of the army and navy," Buchanan's Assistant Postmaster General resumed his campaign to purge the administration of disunionists. "For God's sake," he wrote Black, "let us see the Government placed squarely and unequivocally on the side of the Union." [33] With the passage of the secession ordinance, the appointment of commissioners, and the circulation of wild rumors of rebel attacks and assassinations, northern anger mounted rapidly. The loyal press called upon the states to mobilize and upon Federal authorities to blockade Charleston.[34] Individual patriots demanded the suppression of treason in letters to their congressmen and in the columns of their newspapers.[35]

Reports that Buchanan would yield to the South Carolina commissioners elicited still more bitter attacks upon him. Even a conservative Bell paper like the Boston *Courier* insisted that public property must be defended and urged the sending of reinforce-

31 *Official Records*, Ser. 1, I, 109–10.

32 N. G. Olds to Sherman, December 19, 1860; H. B. Carrington to *id.*, December 20, 1860, Sherman Papers; George Opdyke to Trumbull, December 17, 1860; W. H. Hanna to *id.*, December 19, 1860, Trumbull Papers; S. Allibone to Edward McPherson, December 15, 1860, McPherson Papers, Library of Congress.

33 New York *World*, December 14, 1860; Horatio King to Black, December 14, 1860, Black Papers.

34 New York *World*, December 25, 1860; Philadelphia *Press*, December 22, 24, 1860; Columbus *Daily Ohio State Journal*, quoted in Columbus *Daily Ohio Statesman*, December 26, 1860; Indianapolis *Daily Journal*, December 22, 1860.

35 New York *World* (letter from "Madison"), December 26, 1860; J. G. Bigelow to Sherman, December 25, 1860; W. C. Scott to *id.*, December 26, 1860, Sherman Papers; E. B. Ward to Wade, December 21, 1860; J. Thomas to *id.*, December 22, 1860; D. Cadwell to *id.*, December 25, 1860, Wade Papers.

ments to Anderson.[36] Others warned him that he had no legal right to receive the commissioners and that it was his responsibility to be ready to resist an attack from South Carolina.[37] His enemies prayed that an "outraged and betrayed people" would be avenged for the "treason and imbecility [which] preside in the Whitehouse," that "some Brutus . . . would arise and remove him from the scene of his earthly labors." [38]

The Palmetto State commissioners reached Washington on December 26. But before they approached the President, sensational news of activities in Charleston Harbor increased immeasurably the sectional tension. The very night of their arrival Major Anderson secretly spiked his guns at Fort Moultrie and moved his men and most of his supplies to the stronger and more easily defended position at Fort Sumter. Having proposed this step to the War Department several days earlier, Anderson cited his instructions of December 11 as authority for his action. The menacing attitude of the Charlestonians, the imminent danger of attack, convinced him that the shift of positions was the best way to avoid bloodshed. Now with a four months' supply of provisions, even though some items such as soap, candles, and coal were short, he was in a position where the Federal government could send him additional troops "at its leisure." [39]

Anderson's action seemed like a bold challenge to southern treason. It brought fame overnight to "the gallant Major." Northerners, desperately in need of a hero, overwhelmed Anderson with promises of reinforcements, lavish praise for his loyalty, and thanks for this refreshing contrast with the "cowardice" of the administration. "The Lord bless your noble soul!" wrote one delirious admirer. "Oh, my dear sir, the whole country will triumphantly sustain you." [40] The anti-Republican Boston *Courier* confessed that it received the news from Charleston "with a

[36] Boston *Daily Courier*, December 24, 1860.
[37] New York *Evening Post*, December 26, 1860; New York *World*, December 24, 1860.
[38] Doolittle to his son, December 22, 1860, Doolittle Papers; A. F. Randall, Jr., to E. B. Washburne, December 22, 1860, E. B. Washburne Papers; Simeon Rush to Wade, December 24, 1860, Wade Papers; Boston *Daily Advertiser*, December 22, 1860. [39] *Official Records*, Ser. 1, I, 2–4, 105–106, 120.
[40] Edmund Morris to Major Robert Anderson, December 28, 1860, Anderson Papers, Library of Congress.

prouder beating of the heart. We could not but feel once more that we had a country. . . ." [41] From New York, the stronghold of the "dry goods party," John A. Dix expressed a doubt that any military man could have avoided the step that Anderson had taken. "His conduct is approved here by all parties, even by the warmest advocates of Southern rights." [42]

On the morning of December 27, Buchanan faced three indignant Southerners—Trescott, Jefferson Davis, and Robert M. T. Hunter—who had come to protest and demand that he order Anderson back to Moultrie. The President wailed bitterly about the calamities befalling him and swore that he had not authorized Anderson's move and did not approve it. But, after wavering momentarily, he refused to comply with his visitors' demand until he had consulted his cabinet and given Anderson time for an explanation. Nor would he permit them to telegraph Governor Pickens that the *status quo* would be restored if the Sumter garrison were not attacked. Other southern politicians who sought to influence Buchanan had no greater success than these three. [43]

The next day the President had his only interview with the South Carolina commissioners. They contended that there was a truce which their state had faithfully observed but which the Federal government had violated when Anderson took up a new position in Charleston Harbor. Buchanan again asked for time before he decided whether the garrison was to be recalled from Sumter. The commissioners pressed him, demanded an immediate order, and insisted that his personal honor was involved. The President stubbornly refused to be intimidated, and the interview ended with the issue still unsettled. [44] The South Carolinians then sent Buchanan a note in which they repeated the charge of plighted faith, argued that the occupation of Sumter had changed the whole situation, and refused to negotiate further until they had satisfaction upon this matter. They asserted, moreover, that the

[41] Boston *Daily Courier*, December 28, 1860.

[42] Dix to King, December 29, 1860, quoted in King, *Turning on the Light*, 36–37. See also A. Hamilton to Caleb Cushing, December 30, 1860, Cushing Papers, Library of Congress.

[43] Crawford, *Genesis of the Civil War*, 142–45.

[44] *Ibid.*, 148–49; Curtis, *Buchanan*, II, 370–82; [Buchanan], *Buchanan's Administration*, 180–85.

Federal forces in Charleston Harbor were a "standing menace" to peace and must be evacuated forthwith.[45]

As the harried President labored over a reply to this letter, additional news from Charleston increased the complexity of his problem and substantially lessened the chance for a peaceful settlement. Immediately after Anderson's removal to Sumter, South Carolina retaliated by occupying Fort Moultrie and Castle Pinckney and by seizing the customhouse, post office, and arsenal in Charleston. Simultaneously all Federal officers in South Carolina resigned, so as to signalize the end of national authority in their state. The Federal garrison in Fort Sumter remained as the last vestige of the old relationship.

Meanwhile, the mere fact that Buchanan was conferring with Southerners caused most Yankees to assume the worst about him. Even Democrats denounced what they supposed was his spineless abandonment of Major Anderson to the rebels.[46] Republicans believed him guilty of treason, an eligible candidate for the gallows, and clamored for his impeachment. "People here are becoming frantic," reported Horace White of the Chicago *Tribune*. "If Old Buck should show his corpus in these parts he would be hung so quick that Satan would not know where to look for his traitorous soul." [47] Even so conservative a man as Edward Everett talked of superseding the President and making General Scott a military dictator for the duration of the crisis.[48] One of Buchanan's political friends confessed privately that he seemed to be "execrated now by four-fifths of the people of all parties." [49]

[45] *Official Records,* Ser. 1, I, 109–10; Moore (ed.), *Works of Buchanan,* XI, 76–77.

[46] Albany *Atlas and Argus,* December 29, 1860, quoted in New York *Evening Post,* January 2, 1861.

[47] Horace White to E. B. Washburne, December 30, 1860, E. B. Washburne Papers. See also George G. Fogg to Welles, December 30, 1860, Welles Papers; Thomas Earl to Wade, December 28, 1860, Wade Papers; New York *Evening Post,* December 29, 1860; New York *Daily Tribune,* December 31, 1860; New York *World,* December 31, 1860; Bangor *Daily Whig and Courier,* January 1, 1861; Philadelphia *North American and United States Gazette,* December 31, 1860; Cincinnati *Daily Gazette,* January 1, 1861; Chicago *Daily Tribune,* December 27, 1860; Madison *Wisconsin Daily State Journal,* December 28, 1860.

[48] Edward Everett to Mrs. Charles Eams, December 31, 1860, Everett Papers, Massachusetts Historical Society. See also Cincinnati *Daily Commercial,* January 2, 1861; Philadelphia *Press* (Washington dispatch), December 29, 1860.

[49] Sidney Webster to Cushing, December 28, 1860, Cushing Papers.

The South Carolina *émeute* was fusing northern political factions into a solid mass for national defense and creating a war spirit that threatened to get out of control. John Sherman's mail from his constituents was typical of what every northern congressman was receiving at the time. Sherman was urged to send an appeal from Washington that would "rally the freemen of the North" and was assured that thousands would respond to the call to fight. "There is now but one party—one earnest and angry sentiment, ready to break forth at any moment and wipe out the traitors. . . ." [50] A Democrat informed Holt that South Carolina's acts had "succeeded in uniting Bell Men, Douglas Men and Breckinridge Men with the Lincoln Men at the North in one unbroken phalanx. . . ." [51] The conservative business community was equally agitated, and New York merchants gave ample signs of displeasure with Buchanan's seeming weakness. [52] In Boston, Amos A. Lawrence, wealthy merchant and champion of compromise, warned Senator Crittenden that the first blow struck by the South would "arouse and unite the whole Northern people." "The destruction of . . . [Anderson's] little force *would bring out the warlike feeling in a day.* . . ." [53] Even Seward momentarily lost his equanimity. He filled his letters to Lincoln and Weed with excited rumors of southern plots. He was sure there would be an "explosion" if Buchanan yielded. [54]

The tone of the Republican press was like the blare of bugles calling men to the colors. "Our advice . . . to every Northern man is, Arm yourself at once," cried one Republican editor. [55] Others chimed in. The rebels were guilty of overt acts; they had defied Federal authority. "Since they have invited open war with the General Government, let them have it to their hearts' con-

[50] See especially letters to Sherman from Thomas Earl, December 28, 1860; Dr. Reidling, December 28, 1860; Jacob Brinkerhoff, January 1, 1861; H. C. Johnson, January 1, 1861; Officers of the Young Men's Republican Union, January 1, 1861, Sherman Papers.

[51] Howard Crosby to Holt, December 31, 1860, Holt Papers.

[52] W. H. Cobb to Cameron, December 28, 1860, Cameron Papers; Foner, *Business & Slavery,* 239-43.

[53] Amos A. Lawrence to Crittenden, December 29, 1860, Crittenden Papers.

[54] Barnes (ed.), *Memoir of Thurlow Weed,* 315; Seward, *Seward at Washington,* II, 486-89.

[55] *Daily Pittsburgh Gazette,* December 27, 1860, quoted in New York *Daily Tribune,* December 29, 1860.

tent." [56] There was no time to wait for a "perjured Executive" to move; the initiative for saving the Union must come from the loyal states. The people themselves must "draw the sword . . . to quell Rebellion [and] punish Traitors." [57] Even Democratic editors felt the growing war spirit. The editor of the New York *Herald*, for one, abruptly turned from apologies to threats. "South Carolina has placed herself in open and armed hostility to the government of the United States. . . . This is war. The ice is broken. Revolution is no longer a threat, but a reality, and the time for action has come." [58] Hostilities seemed inevitable.

3

Buchanan, by one false step, could easily have set off the "explosion" Seward predicted. His northern sympathizers feared that because of his desire for peace he might do something to injure the Union cause and infuriate the North. So his friends urged him to stand firm. Senator William Bigler of Pennsylvania, Representatives John Cochrane and Daniel Sickles of New York, and other Democratic politicians visited the White House to notify him that he would lose their support if he failed to maintain the supremacy of the government or evacuated the Sumter garrison.[59]

Again Buchanan turned for advice to his cabinet, which he had remade since the beginning of the crisis. Cass and Cobb had retired. Black, formerly Attorney General, had become Secretary of State. Philip F. Thomas of Maryland was the new Secretary of the Treasury. And Edwin M. Stanton, an unconditional Unionist,

---

[56] Trenton *Daily State Gazette and Republican*, January 1, 1861; New York *World*, December 29, 31, 1860; New York *Evening Post*, December 29, 1860; Boston *Daily Journal*, January 1, 1861; Providence *Daily Journal*, December 29, 1860; Philadelphia *North American and United States Gazette*, December 29, 1860; Philadelphia *Public Ledger*, December 28, 1860.

[57] *Morning Courier and New-York Enquirer*, December 29, 1860; January 1, 1861.

[58] New York *Herald*, December 29, 1860; Philadelphia *Press*, December 27, 28, 31, 1860; Boston *Herald*, December 29, 1860; Boston *Post*, December 31, 1860; Hartford *Daily Times*, quoted in Boston *Post*, December 31, 1860; Albany *Atlas and Argus*, quoted in Boston *Post*, December 31, 1860.

[59] New York *Daily Tribune* (Washington dispatch), December 29, 1860; Boston *Daily Advertiser*, January 2, 1861; Chicago *Daily Tribune* (letter from "Chicago"), January 3, 1861; Morgan Dix (comp.), *Memoirs of John Adams Dix* (New York, 1883), I, 361.

had filled the vacant post of Attorney General upon the recommendation of Black.[60] But the reformed cabinet, still disunited, was soon quarreling over the Sumter issue. Once more the President had to choose between opposing points of view.

In the first stage of another cabinet rift Secretary of War Floyd appeared as the central figure. It was a wretched period in his public life, from which he emerged tainted with scandal, divested of his former pro-Union sympathies, and a prime object of northern hatred. Up to this point Floyd had been generally regarded as an opponent of secession, although he had not doubted the "right" of a state to take such action and had opposed all measures of Federal coercion. An apparent shift in his views began almost simultaneously with the discovery on December 22 of serious and complicated financial irregularities in the War Department. These involved the theft of $870,000 of Indian trust bonds from the Interior Department and their exchange by Floyd for the dubious bills of a government contractor. The Secretary did not personally profit from these transactions, but they showed extreme administrative laxness on his part. Buchanan promptly informed Floyd that he must have his resignation, to which the latter agreed.[61]

But Floyd, delaying his departure, was still in the cabinet when Anderson transferred his garrison to Fort Sumter. He then blatantly sided with the secessionists, assuring them that the move was unauthorized and telegraphing a sharp rebuke to Anderson.[62] On December 27 the War Secretary came uninvited to a meeting of the cabinet and heatedly denounced the Sumter commander for breaking the government's pledge to South Carolina. In the resulting fray Black, Holt, and Stanton denied his charges; Thompson and Thomas supported Floyd; Toucey and Buchanan were undecided. That night Floyd, in great agitation, read a paper to his colleagues which declared that the only way to avoid civil war was to withdraw the garrison from Sumter. Boldly he demanded immediate authority to issue such an order. After

[60] George C. Gorham, *Life and Public Services of Edwin M. Stanton* (Boston, 1899), I, 121–26.

[61] Rhodes, *History of the United States*, III, 236–41; [Buchanan], *Buchanan's Administration*, 185–88; Curtis, *Buchanan*, II, 406–10; Brigance, *Black*, 93; Auchampaugh, *Buchanan and His Cabinet*, 92–96.

[62] *Official Records*, Ser. 1, I, 2–4.

the Secretary had finished, both Black and Stanton angrily retorted that such a course would be treason. Two days later Floyd
used the failure of the President to meet his demands as an excuse
for a formal letter of resignation.[63] Amid a torrent of northern
abuse the discomfited former Secretary retired to his home in
Virginia.[64]

At length, on December 29, Buchanan completed a reply to the
South Carolina commissioners which he read to his cabinet. This
document—no copy of which has survived—evidently indicated
that the President was faltering. He did not yield upon the right
of secession, as Black later explained, but he "dallied" with the
secessionists on points where the Secretary of State believed he
should have been inflexible. So the next day Black told Toucey
that if that letter were used he would be compelled to resign.
Stanton certainly, and Holt probably, would have followed.
When Buchanan learned of the intention of his old friend, he
called Black in and pleaded for his continued support. But the
Secretary again said he could not defend the administration upon
such principles. Buchanan then handed over the letter for Black
to revise as he wished. Black hastened to the Attorney General's
office and dictated his suggestions to Stanton. After the paper was
completed both Stanton and Holt read and approved it.[65]

A comparison of Black's opinions of the previous November
with those submitted to Buchanan on December 30 reveals, not
a change in basic theories, but a distinct shift of emphasis. By the
end of December, Black's position had grown decidedly stronger.
He now stressed the powers rather than the limitations of the
government. He cautioned the President against making even an
indirect admission that South Carolina had a right to be represented in Washington by "diplomatic officers." He urged Bu-

[63] Crawford, *Genesis of the Civil War*, 146; [Buchanan], *Buchanan's Administration*, 185–88; Curtis, *Buchanan*, II, 408–10; Brigance, *Black*, 94–96; Auchampaugh, *Buchanan and His Cabinet*, 77; Black to Charles R. Buckalew, January
28, 1861, copy in Black Papers.
[64] See Chapter XII.
[65] Crawford, *Genesis of the Civil War*, 160; Curtis, *Buchanan*, II, 379–91;
Brigance, *Black*, 97–102; Chauncey F. Black (ed.), *Essays and Speeches of Jeremiah S. Black* (New York, 1885), 14–17; Auchampaugh, *Buchanan and His
Cabinet*, 161–65; Gorham, *Stanton*, I, 121–26; Frank A. Flower, *Edwin McMasters
Stanton* (Akron, 1905), 88–95. Stanton's biographers exaggerate his role in the
cabinet crisis.

chanan to deny emphatically that Federal forts could be surrendered and to drop even an "implied assent" to the idea that
a truce had existed. Above all Black insisted that the President
avoid abstractions concerning the right to coerce a state and
instead center his attention upon the power to defend Federal
property and resist attack. Black wrote:

> . . . The power to defend the public property—to resist an
> assailing force which unlawfully attempts to drive out the
> troops of the United States from one of their fortifications and
> to use the military and naval forces for the purpose of aiding
> the proper officers of the U. S. in the execution of the laws—
> this as far as it goes is *coercion* and may very well be called
> "coercing a State by force of arms to remain in the Union."
> The President has always asserted his right of coercion to that
> extent. He merely denies the right of Congress to make offen-
> sive war upon a State of the Union as such might be made upon
> a foreign government.[66]

Seldom did a contemporary confess more eloquently the fraudu-
lency of the distinction between "coercing a state" and "enforcing
the laws"!

On December 31, with Black's memorandum before him, Buchanan redrafted his reply to the commissioners. The new document was entirely satisfactory to the Unionists in the cabinet.
In it the President denied that any truce had been made. He did
admit that he had decided against sending reinforcements so long
as no attack seemed imminent. He admitted also that Anderson
had moved from Moultrie to Sumter upon his own responsibility.
(Indeed Buchanan confessed that his first impulse had been to
order the garrison back to its original location; but before he
could do this the news arrived that South Carolina forces had
captured Moultrie and Castle Pinckney.) Concerning a complete
withdrawal from Charleston Harbor, Buchanan now wrote:
"This I cannot do; this I will not do. Such an idea was never
thought of by me in any possible contingency." Instead, he intended to defend Fort Sumter as part of the Federal property.[67]

---

[66] Undated "Memorandum for the President on the Subject of the paper
drawn up by him in reply to the Commissioners of South Carolina," copy in
Black Papers.

[67] Moore (ed.), *Works of Buchanan*, XI, 76–84.

After four days of indecision Buchanan again had ranged himself on the side of the (northern) angels. As Toucey said, any other course "was impossible in the face of northern sentiment." [68]

Convinced that they were the victims of Executive duplicity, the South Carolina commissioners sent a stinging rejoinder to Buchanan's letter. They marshaled the evidence that a formal truce had existed and accused the President of violating "the pledged faith of the Government." The occupation of Sumter was a "hostile act," and the response of their state was an act of self-defense. After sharply upbraiding Buchanan for his conduct, they concluded that his course had "probably rendered civil war inevitable." This South Carolina was ready to accept if it were forced upon her. Finally, since they saw they could get no satisfaction from further negotiations, they announced their decision to return to Charleston at once.[69] The gulf between even a "doughface" President and these Carolinians was wide indeed!

Buchanan received the commissioners' second note in the midst of a cabinet meeting on January 2. Acting on the advice of the Union members, the President sent it back without an answer. He now agreed that reinforcements must be speeded to Fort Sumter. Now that the negotiations had been terminated and the vexed commissioners were hurrying home, he believed the direct menace to Anderson was sufficient to justify the step he had long refused to take.[70] At the end of another cabinet crisis the stalwart Unionists had emerged triumphant.

Rejoicing that the Palmetto commissioners had "gone home with fleas in their ears," the New York *World* expressed the "unexpected pleasure" of many Northerners who had found that the President was "not wholly insensible to the force of northern public opinion." [71] But Henry Wise of Virginia testified to the progress of southern alienation as he sneered at "Mr. Buchanan's new allies, the Black Republicans and coercion Democrats, his latter day friends." [72]

[68] Crawford, *Genesis of the Civil War*, 158–59.
[69] *Official Records*, Ser. 1, I, 120–25.
[70] [Buchanan], *Buchanan's Administration*, 183; Curtis, *Buchanan*, II, 392 n.; Moore (ed.), *Works of Buchanan*, XI, 100–101.
[71] New York *World*, January 4, 1861.
[72] Auchampaugh, *Buchanan and His Cabinet*, 177.

4

A fast side-wheel steamer laden with supplies and concealed reinforcements for Sumter departed from New York on January 5 as an earnest of the administration's new policy. Evidently, sniffed a Buchanan critic, "at the last gasp of his official life he has in some measure repented and is stiffening himself up to the performance of his duty." [73] The North waited tensely for the response of the secessionists, for it seemed likely that the *Star of the West* was sailing into civil war.

The President had authorized Scott as early as the morning of December 31 to prepare such an enterprise, using the sloop of war *Brooklyn*. But Scott later decided that the need for speed and secrecy required the use of a merchant vessel rather than a warship. Buchanan and Black reluctantly agreed to the change, and the unarmed *Star of the West* was chartered.

Shortly after the departure of the relief ship, the War Department received a report from Major Anderson that he was secure in his new position and had no immediate need of supplies or reinforcements. This seemed to justify a cancellation of the whole enterprise. But the recall order came too late to catch the ship, and the expedition was carried through.[74] It must have caused Buchanan much anguish to have sponsored this apparently unnecessary challenge when peace was still his earnest wish.

Now it was too late to turn back. On January 8 the President sent Congress a special message which transmitted his correspondence with the commissioners and explained the menacing situation which had prompted the dispatch of reinforcements. Again guided by Black, he emphasized the government's obligation to suppress rebellion. Neither he nor Congress, he said, had the right to make war upon a state. *"But the right and the duty to use military force defensively against those who resist federal officers in the execution of their legal functions, and against those who assail the property of the federal government, is clear and undeniable."*

---

[73] *Morning Courier and New-York Enquirer*, January 7, 1861.
[74] *Official Records*, Ser. 1, I, 112, 119, 128–32, 134, 136–37; Curtis, *Buchanan*, II, 445–48; [Buchanan], *Buchanan's Administration*, 188–92.

Accordingly, if South Carolina's seizure of government property resulted in civil war, the administration would not be responsible for commencing it. Finally, it was for Congress to decide what new legislation the emergency required; Congress alone was qualified "to declare war, or to authorize the employment of military force." [75]

By this time Buchanan's break with the southern wing of his party was complete, and the final reorganization of his administration soon followed. After Floyd's resignation, Holt was shifted to the War Department, whereupon, reported Dix, "for the first time we began to breathe freely." [76] King's promotion to the position of Postmaster General was another victory for the Unionists. Secretary of the Navy Toucey, responding partly to outside pressure,[77] loyally supported the President's stiffened policy. (In this same period Buchanan also severed his ties with the Washington *Constitution*, a secessionist paper, and withdrew its government patronage.[78]) Secretary of the Interior Thompson was the next to separate from the administration. He had strongly opposed reinforcing Major Anderson and had assured his southern friends that there would be no reinforcement while he was in the cabinet.[79] And so, after the sailing of the *Star of the West*, he resigned.[80]

Conservative financiers of New York played a major role in forcing the withdrawal of Secretary of the Treasury Thomas, who had favored the evacuation of Sumter. Late in December, when the government advertised for bids on a $5,000,000 loan at 12 per cent, the financiers withheld their support because of their disapproval of Buchanan's apparent indecision and their lack of confidence in Thomas. They informed the administration that money would not be forthcoming until a "sound" man whose loyalty they could trust was at the head of the Treasury Department. They let it be known that John A. Dix was such a man. Buchanan promptly summoned Dix to Washington, accepted Thomas'

[75] Moore (ed.), *Works of Buchanan*, XI, 94–99; Brigance, *Black*, 106.
[76] Dix to King, January 3, 1861, quoted in King, *Turning on the Light*, 39–40.
[77] L. F. S. Foster to Welles, January 2, 1861; Welles to Isaac Toucey, January 3, 1861, copy in Welles Papers.
[78] Moore (ed.), *Works of Buchanan*, XI, 75; Philadelphia *Press* (Washington dispatch), January 12, 1861.
[79] *Official Records*, Ser. 1, I, 252.
[80] Moore (ed.), *Works of Buchanan*, XI, 100–101, 102–103.

resignation, and appointed Dix in his place.[81] The appointment of Dix, "made as much to restore confidence in the financial world . . . as for any other reason," had its desired effect; the government now received the money it badly needed. On January 12 a group of merchants and financiers gathered at the New York Bank of Commerce and resolved that Dix, because of "his devotion to the Union, and his determination to maintain the laws," would "inspire throughout this community increased confidence in the administration of that Department and in the stability of the Government." [82]

The New York *Times* observed that Buchanan had emerged at last with a "united Union Administration." With the Southerners gone, no man remained "whose fidelity to the Constitution he had any reason to distrust." [83] But even the *Times* failed to grasp the full meaning and the deep irony of this development. The "dough-face" Buchanan, eager for peace and compromise, was ending his public career as the head of a northern, sectional administration! This old friend of slaveholding politicians was now being accused of hostile aggression against the South! National disaster could not be far off. "When Lincoln comes in," Jefferson Davis wrote gloomily, "he will have but to continue in the path of his predecessor to inaugurate a civil war. . . ." [84] And Davis was right.

[81] New York *Times*, December 29, 1860; *Morning Courier and New-York Enquirer*, January 1, 1861; Philadelphia *North American and United States Gazette*, January 15, 1861; Moore (ed.), *Works of Buchanan*, XI, 105; Dix (comp.), *Memoirs*, I, 362–64; King, *Turning on the Light*, 40–41; Foner, *Business & Slavery*, 243–47; Auchampaugh, *Buchanan and His Cabinet*, 67–69.

[82] New York *Herald*, January 12, 1861; New York *Evening Post*, January 14, 1861; *Morning Courier and New-York Enquirer*, January 14, 1861; New York *World*, January 16, 1861.

[83] New York *Times*, January 12, 1861.

[84] Jefferson Davis to Franklin Pierce, January 20, 1861, in "Some Papers of Franklin Pierce, 1852–1862," *American Historical Review*, X (1905), 366.

VI

The First Uprising

W E ARE all feeling better here, than we have done for weeks," exulted a Republican member of the Ohio legislature early in January. " 'Old Buck' . . . threatens to go out of office the most popular man at the North. The people . . . are so relieved at the indications that *we have a Gov^t* . . . that they feel disposed to . . . forgive Old Buck." [1] Buchanan enjoyed a fortnight of popularity such as he had never before experienced in his own section. Those who had been accusing him of treason now welcomed him into the ranks of loyal men. "Wonder of wonders," conceded an astonished Lincolnite, "he is supported by the republicans and is now to most intents and purposes as good as a republican." [2] But with all factions rising in defense of the Union "one party name . . . [would] soon be as good as another." [3]

Lincoln as President, it was confidently predicted, would pursue the same policy. Thus "the two Administrations, the present and the incoming, are, in the most material respect of all, brought into harmony." There was abundant evidence that Northerners would have backed Buchanan in punitive measures against secessionists, even to the extent of military action. "Whether war or peace follow in the footsteps of a vigorous policy are matters of secondary consequence." [4]

---

[1] R. C. Parsons to Sherman, January 8, 1861, Sherman Papers.

[2] Boston *Daily Advertiser*, January 10, 1861.

[3] Boston *Daily Journal*, January 4, 1861; Edward McPherson to Francis Lieber, January 2, 1861, Lieber Papers, Henry E. Huntington Library, photostat in possession of Professor Frank Freidel.

[4] New York *Evening Post*, January 3, 8, 11, 1861; New York *Times*, January 3, 1861; *Morning Courier and New-York Enquirer*, January 10, 1861; Boston *Daily Journal*, January 4, 9, 1861; Cincinnati *Daily Commercial*, January 12, 1861; Chicago *Daily Tribune*, January 7, 1861.

The administration's special friends in the free states were relieved. They assured Buchanan that his cabinet purge had improved his reputation and that his message to Congress had "thrilled the popular heart." If he would but "stand by the Union," the people would praise his name "as long as history shall last." Black was informed that the South had lost its northern friends through its "treachery to the President." "Were you to go one step farther and get back the forts and man them at Charleston I think the North would be willing to make Mr. Buchanan king." [5] The New York *Herald* now described the President as a man who rightly comprehended "his position, his responsibilities and the expectations of the American people." [6] The supporters of Douglas and Bell were equally generous in their expressions of gratification and encouragement.[7]

On January 8, the anniversary of General Jackson's victory at New Orleans, delegations of politicians of all parties visited Buchanan to voice their pleasure at his recent course.[8] Among them were men who in past years had belabored him as a "tool of the slave power," as an "imbecile," a "coward," and a "traitor." But his past errors seemed forgotten as men magnanimously clasped the hand of this convert to the doctrine of the "irrepressible conflict."

2

On the night of that anniversary so full of meaning to American patriots the *Star of the West* arrived off Charleston Harbor. The next morning as it approached Fort Sumter the South Carolina batteries on Morris Island opened fire. The secessionists elected not to disturb Sumter, but their guns soon drove the relief ship out of the harbor. Having failed to fulfill its mission but escaping

[5] Jos. C. Herr to Buchanan, January 5, 1861; E. Littell to *id.*, January 7, 1861; Charles L. Lamberton to *id.*, January 14, 1861, Buchanan Papers; Silas Reed to Holt, January 4, 1861; Wm. Macwherter to *id.*, January 13, 1861, Holt Papers; Richd. Schell to Black, January 7, 1861; Geo. W. Harris to *id.*, January 9, 1861, Black Papers.

[6] New York *Herald*, January 3, 1861.

[7] New York *Leader*, January 5, 12, 1861; Philadelphia *Press*, January 4, 8, 9, 10, 1861; Providence *Daily Post*, January 5, 1861; New York *Morning Express*, January 8, 10, 1861.

[8] New York *Daily Tribune* (Washington dispatch), January 9, 1861.

without casualties, the *Star of the West* returned to New York.[9]

Public attention had been riveted upon the voyage of that vessel, and the warning had already been sounded: If she is attacked, "we are at war with South Carolina." [10] Hence, as the report of her fate spread through the North it brought to a climax the growing popular wrath. The event, widely accepted as the beginning of civil conflict, provoked a flurry of martial activity. Newspapers everywhere, regardless of party, reported an unprecedented "state of excitement . . . produced by the news." "We are on the eve of war. The first gun has been fired. . . ." [11] A Buchanan Democrat admonished the President: *"The Star of the West must return to Charleston and land her troops at Fort Sumter,* or your administration will be disgraced through all coming time. . . . It is not your duty to count the cost. The salvation of our country is worth more than the lives of all the traitors it contains." [12]

The firing upon the *Star of the West* afforded the first opportunity for a practical application of the northern defensive concept. Union apologists took pains to demonstrate the Federal government's patience in the face of repeated provocation as well as the peaceful purpose of the relief expedition. The guilt of aggression rested solely upon South Carolinians. They had "assumed the terrible responsibility" and had "deliberately begun the war." "They have fired the first gun." They had "laid aside the pretense of 'peaceable secession' " and were "making open and treasonable war against the general government." The administration, on the other hand, had "exercised forbearance to the last." Now the full force of Federal power must be applied; "only a dreadful experience can bring the mass of people in the cotton states to realize the evils they are incurring." Since the conflict

[9] *Official Records,* Ser. 1, I, 9–10.

[10] New York *Evening Post,* January 9, 1861.

[11] New York *Herald,* January 11, 1861; New York *Daily Tribune,* January 12, 1861; *Morning Courier and New-York Enquirer,* January 11, 12, 15, 1861; New York *World,* January 10, 1861; Boston *Daily Courier,* January 12, 1861; Boston *Post,* January 12, 1861; Boston *Daily Journal,* January 11, 1861; Boston *Daily Advertiser,* January 12, 1861; Worcester (Mass.) *Daily Spy,* January 11, 1861; Philadelphia *Press,* January 10, 1861; Philadelphia *North American and United States Gazette,* January 11, 1861; Philadelphia *Daily Evening Bulletin,* January 10, 1861; Indianapolis *Daily Journal,* January 11, 1861.

[12] W. O. Bartlett to Buchanan, January 15, 1861, Buchanan Papers.

had already begun, Yankee rectitude was submitted to the judgment of Providence: "May God defend the right!" [13]

3

While Northerners still chafed at the rebels' humiliation of a Federal ship in Charleston Harbor they saw their government exposed to further indignities in other parts of the South. By February 1 conventions in Georgia and the five Gulf states had followed South Carolina in the passage of ordinances of secession. State troops took possession of additional national forts, arsenals, customhouses, post offices, United States revenue cutters, hospitals, and of the navy yard at Pensacola and the mint at New Orleans. Only Fort Sumter, Fort Pickens off Pensacola, and Forts Taylor and Jefferson off the southern coast of Florida had garrisons of sufficient size to discourage immediate secessionist attempts at seizure. The nationalists, viewing such acts as unmitigated aggression, asked bitterly how long the "atrocities" of these "pirates" were to be tolerated. To them the alternatives seemed to be a "base submission" to continued depredations, or at once to send a force which could "restrain the licentious excesses of the madmen." [14]

That "submission" was not the northern choice soon became clear enough. Again the loyal press was in the vanguard of a zealous movement for reprisals. With scarcely an exception Republican newspapers exploded with fresh cries "for 'coercion,' 'fight,' 'drums,' 'gunpowder,' 'bombs,' 'shells,' &c." [15] "FORBEARANCE HAS CEASED TO BE A VIRTUE" was the much-overworked title for editorials dealing with southern "brigandage." "The flippant talk against coercion is worn threadbare. Likewise the pathetic sniveling about shedding fraternal blood. . . . If traitors attempt to destroy the Government, and the Government turn and overwhelm them, can the Government be held responsible for the

[13] New York *World*, January 11, 12, 1861; Springfield (Mass.) *Daily Republican*, January 12, 1861; Providence *Daily Journal*, January 11, 1861.

[14] New York *Daily Tribune*, January 17, 1861; Philadelphia *North American and United States Gazette*, January 12, 1861.

[15] New York *Morning Express*, January 12, 1861.

civil war involved, and the pouring out of blood?" [16] From Maine to Iowa editors clamored for a prompt reorganization and mobilization of the state militias to punish the secessionists.[17] Editors like Greeley who had toyed with the idea of peaceful secession now spoke as violently as the rest.[18] Democratic journalists also kept time with the music of the Union; weathercock James Gordon Bennett urged Congress to empower the President to call out 60,000 militiamen.[19]

Individual Yankees poured their militancy into literally thousands of letters to their congressmen which all but unanimously expressed their desire to reassert Federal authority in the South. Horace White wrote Trumbull, "Every man I meet (Republican or Democrat) is perfectly frantic in view of the treason which is being consummated. . . ." Cameron heard that in Pennsylvania there was substantially "one great consolidated party in favor of a fight and especially in favor of blotting out the city of Charleston." An Illinois constituent apprised Representative Washburne of a willingness "to meet those poor, miserable Sneering . . . low degraded pusilanimous [sic] . . . rebel Imps . . . upon any ground at any time with any kind of arms or weapons." [20]

Throughout the month of January, Major Anderson continued to receive benedictions for his "glorious deed in that nest of devils," and assurances that the North was solidly behind him.[21] Countless names appeared upon a flood of petitions and memorials to Con-

[16] Columbus *Daily Ohio State Journal*, January 15, 1861, quoted in Perkins (ed.), *Northern Editorials on Secession*, I, 214-16.

[17] Bangor *Daily Whig and Courier*, January 1, 1861; Boston *Daily Journal*, January 2, 1861; Providence *Daily Journal*, January 2, 1861; Philadelphia *North American and United States Gazette*, January 4, 1861; Cincinnati *Daily Commercial*, January 11, 1861; Chicago *Daily Tribune*, January 3, 4, 1861; Madison *Wisconsin Daily State Journal*, January 4, 1861; Milwaukee *Daily Sentinel*, January 21, 1861.

[18] New York *Daily Tribune*, January 4, 11, 1861; Springfield (Mass.) *Daily Republican*, January 9, 25, 1861; Indianapolis *Daily Journal*, January 17, 1861.

[19] New York *Herald*, January 3, 1861; New York *Leader*, January 5, 12, 1861; Philadelphia *Press*, January 7, 1861; Providence *Daily Post*, January 7, 1861.

[20] Horace White to Trumbull, December 30, 1860, Trumbull Papers; A. H. Reeder to Cameron, January 11, 1861, Cameron Papers; Jonas Wilson to E. B. Washburne, January 8, 1861, E. B. Washburne Papers. During the month of January the papers of Sumner, Chase, Trumbull, Sherman, Cameron, and Washburne were filled with letters demanding the use of force against the South.

[21] See especially John Bonner to Anderson, January 8, 1861; James E. Morse to *id.*, January 15, 1861; J. D. Reeves to *id.*, January 15, 1861, Anderson Papers.

gress which admonished that body to provide for the enforcement of the laws.[22] Northern newspapers frequently commented upon the pervasiveness of this ardent spirit. They found in the talk of the people a sound "like the heavy booming of cannon and the sharp, decisive crack of musketry," a sound which betokened "a determination to defend the country against all conspirators." [23]

Even men who themselves preferred conciliation were able to recognize the fact of northern ire. Amos A. Lawrence confessed to Senator Crittenden, "If the Gov[t] sh[d] call for enlistments of State Militia the applicants would be more numerous than could be received, & there would be as many Democrats & Union men, as Repub[ns]." [24] Bell-Everett men in New England vented their indignation in the columns of the Boston *Courier*.[25] Buchanan Democrats agreed, "The rash unreasonable & treasonable proceedings at the South is rapidly destroying all sympathy & rendering the entire population an unit in the free states." These Democrats made it perfectly obvious that in almost every case their purpose, like Buchanan's, was adjustment *within* the Union, but that they would never tolerate national disintegration.[26]

During the first feverish weeks of the new year there was hardly a Yankee community that was not the scene of excited meetings, patriotic speeches, and stern resolutions. At Trenton a large gathering of New Jersey's conservative citizens, Republican and Democratic, pledged their "earnest and undivided support to the general Government in its efforts to put down treason, execute the laws, and maintain the Constitution." [27] A huge nonpartisan mass meeting in Philadelphia applauded resolutions branding secessionists as "public enemies" and promising aid to the

[22] New York *World* ("Washington Correspondence"), January 7, 1861; *House* and *Senate Miscellaneous Documents*, 36 Cong., 2 Sess.

[23] Springfield (Mass.) *Daily Republican*, January 3, 1861; New York *Evening Post*, January 14, 1861; Boston *Daily Courier*, January 18, 1861; Chicago *Daily Tribune*, January 9, 1861.

[24] Amos A. Lawrence to Crittenden, January 12, 1861, Crittenden Papers. See also N. P. Tallmadge to *id.*, January 7, 1861, *ibid.*

[25] Boston *Daily Courier* (letter from "H"), January 7, 1861.

[26] N. G. Upham to Buchanan, January 1, 1861; Richard D. Davis to *id.*, January 5, 1861; Wm. S. Hodge to *id.*, January 8, 1861, Buchanan Papers; Wm. Jessup to Black, January 7, 1861, Black Papers; Sidney Webster to Cushing, January 5, 1861, Cushing Papers.

[27] Trenton *Daily State Gazette and Republican*, January 16, 1861.

President.[28] In Chicago, where a Democrat presided over a bipartisan audience, the people resolved that efforts to break up the Union were the "basest treason." *"The laws should be enforced at whatever cost, and by the whole power of the Nation."* [29] In Massachusetts, Governor Andrew encouraged such demonstrations; he explained that the people needed "to get accustomed to the smell of gunpowder." [30]

Buchanan's day of fasting and prayer, coming amid this tumult, was hardly the occasion its author intended. In Madison, Wisconsin, people observed the day "in a somewhat different manner from that advised by the President." Over the state capitol floated the flag "without a star obscured," and at noon a salute of thirty-three guns honored the Sumter garrison.[31] In Boston the Reverend Jacob Manning, addressing a crowd in Old South Church, deplored the signs that "the hanging of traitors" had "gone out of fashion." He was no "man of blood," he said, but great principles were at stake. "It is a duty to lay down our lives for them." [32]

Volunteers to man the guns would not have been lacking if Buchanan had called for troops. Northern governors were receiving numerous tenders of militia companies; vigorous recruiting drives were being launched; new regiments were being formed.[33] Militiamen were "putting on their war paint to fight for the Union"; they were drilling; their arms and accouterments were being "burnished up." [34] In many localities the young men's Re-

[28] Philadelphia *Press*, January 7, 1861.

[29] Chicago *Daily Tribune*, January 7, 1861; E. C. Larned to Trumbull, January 7, 1861, Trumbull Papers.

[30] Henry G. Pearson, *Life of John A. Andrew* (Boston, 1904), I, 143. For other reports of these patriotic activities see New York *Herald*, January 4, 9, 1861; New York *Daily Tribune*, January 4, 7, 9, 1861; New York *Evening Post*, January 8, 9, 1861; New York *World*, January 9, 1861.

[31] Madison *Wisconsin Daily State Journal*, January 4, 1861.

[32] Providence *Daily Journal*, January 5, 1861; Boston *Daily Advertiser*, January 5, 1861.

[33] See, for example, the many tenders of troops to Governor Oliver P. Morton during January, in Morton Papers, Indiana State Library. See also Indianapolis *Daily Journal*, January 8, 9, 1861; New York *World*, January 10, 18, 1861; New York *Herald*, January 19, 1861; New York *Daily Tribune*, January 18, 1861; Boston *Evening Transcript*, January 18, 1861; Boston *Daily Journal*, January 25, 26, 30; February 1, 4, 1861; Providence *Daily Journal*, January 18, 1861.

[34] New York *World*, January 18, 1861; *Morning Courier and New-York Enquirer*, January 17, 1861; Springfield (Mass.) *Daily Republican*, January 22, 26; February 11, 1861.

publican organizations, the Wide-Awakes who had recently campaigned for Lincoln, were being converted into new militia units.[35] In Ohio a Bell-Everett partisan offered to "raise a Regiment of good old Clay Whigs." [36] In Pennsylvania the enrollment of recruits went on briskly while "the question of republican or democrat" was "sunk." [37] By the end of January nearly a half-million men of all parties had placed themselves at the disposal of the government to protect public property and preserve the Union.[38] From Yankee cities, villages, and farms a citizen army was to be had for the asking.

4

This mass uprising received abundant encouragement and direction from northern governors and legislatures. The state governments, close to the grass roots, reflected popular sentiment far better than the national Congress. Except in Rhode Island and New Jersey the legislatures were controlled by Republicans; the only Democratic governors, William F. Packer of Pennsylvania and Abram A. Hammond of Indiana, retired at the start of the new year. Among the incumbent and newly inaugurated state executives were conservatives such as Charles S. Olden of New Jersey ("Opposition party") and William Sprague of Rhode Island ("Fusion party"), moderates such as Edwin D. Morgan of New York and Andrew G. Curtin of Pennsylvania, and radicals such as John A. Andrew of Massachusetts and Austin Blair of Michigan. But, conservative or radical, the northern governors underwrote the popular demand for the defense of the government.

Early in January most of them aired their views in inaugural addresses or messages to the legislatures. Governor Olden was the most conciliatory of the group, but even he vowed that secession was anarchy and that the people of New Jersey were ready to support the Union.[39] Morgan and Curtin, while relatively cau-

---

[35] New York *Herald*, January 7, 1861.
[36] Alfred Minnse to Sherman, January 26, 1861, Sherman Papers.
[37] New York *Herald* ("Washington Correspondence"), December 29, 1860.
[38] *Ibid.*, February 11, 1861; Philadelphia *Press*, February 12, 1861.
[39] Trenton *Daily State Gazette and Republican*, January 11, 1861.

tious, both affirmed that the citizens of their states desired to see the Union preserved at every hazard.[40] Governor Israel Washburn, Jr., in a more representative message, pledged the full cooperation of Maine in any enterprise to assert Federal authority in the South. "The divisions of party will disappear among us, . . . and all will be known as Patriots and Defenders of the Union." [41] In Massachusetts, Governor Andrew spurned the slightest gesture toward compromise and reported that his state would supply men and money to aid the national cause. Pointing proudly to his Commonwealth's Revolutionary War record, he vowed his people would fight again if necessary.[42] Governor William Dennison of Ohio insisted that Ohioans had no terms to offer traitors except the enforcement of the laws.[43] "It took seven years to establish our independence," asserted Governor Richard Yates of Illinois. "For seven years yet to come, at least, we will struggle to maintain a perfect Union, a Government of one people in one nation, under one Constitution." [44] Governors Blair of Michigan and Alexander Randall of Wisconsin were even more belligerent.[45] But Governor Oliver P. Morton of Indiana was the most warlike of them all. At a flag-raising ceremony in Indianapolis on January 22 he rallied Hoosiers to the colors with an impassioned oration:

> . . . We live at a time when treason is running riot throughout the land. . . . It is a time when the hearts of all men should beat in unison, and every patriot join hands with his neighbor and swear eternal devotion to Liberty, the Constitution and the Union.
>
> In view of the solemn crisis in which we stand, all minor, personal and party considerations should be banished from every heart. . . . For myself . . . I will only know the man who vows fidelity to the Union and the Constitution, under all circumstances and at all hazards; . . . who, when he stands in

[40] New York *Herald*, January 3, 1861; Philadelphia *Press*, January 16, 1861.
[41] Bangor *Daily Whig and Courier*, January 5, 1861.
[42] Springfield (Mass.) *Daily Republican*, January 7, 1861.
[43] Columbus *Daily Ohio Statesman*, January 7, 1861.
[44] Chicago *Daily Tribune*, January 15, 1861.
[45] Detroit *Free Press*, January 4, 1861; Madison *Wisconsin Daily State Journal*, January 10, 1861.

the base presence of treason, forgets the contests and squabbles of the past in the face of the common danger; who then recognizes but two parties—the party of the Union, and the base faction of its foes.[46]

State legislators, coming fresh from agitated constituencies, presently added their voices to the angry hum in the North.[47] They gave defiant speeches, offered coercive resolutions, discussed measures to enlarge and revitalize the state militias, and offered men and money to the President. Only in Rhode Island and in New Jersey did the more conservative members have the upper hand, and even in New Jersey the legislature affirmed the principle that it was the duty of all citizens "to stand by and sustain the Union." [48]

The legislature of New York, assembling on January 2, proceeded along lines that set a pattern for many others. "The American eagle has been screaming in both houses," wrote a reporter after listening to the speakers for several days.[49] The delegate who attracted the most attention was Democratic Senator F. B. Spinola of Brooklyn. He proposed that the Governor volunteer the services of state troops to be used as the President might "deem best to preserve the Union and enforce the constitution and laws of the country." [50] After the firing on the *Star of the West* Spinola announced his readiness to shoulder a musket. On January 11 the New York Senate and House, by votes of 28 to 1 and 117 to 2, resolved that the secessionists had "virtually declared war," tendered to the President whatever aid in men and money might be required to "enforce the laws," and announced that "in defense of the Union" the legislators were ready to devote their fortunes,

[46] Indianapolis *Daily Journal,* January 23, 1861. For the role of the northern governors during the secession crisis see William B. Hesseltine, *Lincoln and the War Governors* (New York, 1948), 115–30.
[47] Only the legislatures of New Hampshire, Vermont, Connecticut, and Iowa were not in session during the crisis.
[48] Trenton *Daily State Gazette and Republican,* January 24, 1861; Charles M. Knapp, *New Jersey Politics during the Period of the Civil War and Reconstruction* (Geneva, N.Y., 1924), 46–50.
[49] New York *Herald* ("Albany Correspondence"), December 30, 1860; January 3, 8, 9, 1861; Sidney D. Brummer, *Political History of the State of New York during the Period of the Civil War* (New York, 1911), 106–10.
[50] New York *Herald,* January 3, 1861; New York *Evening Post* ("Albany Correspondence"), January 7, 1861.

their lives, and their "sacred honor." [51] After several more days of spread-eagle oratory the Senate passed a bill appropriating $500,000 to equip the militia, but the House deferred action.[52] The New York resolutions were sent to the other northern legislatures and were duplicated in Wisconsin, Michigan, and other states.[53] The Massachusetts legislature went even farther and early in February passed a new law empowering the Governor to enlarge the militia.[54]

Meanwhile some of the vigorous northern governors busied themselves with military preparations. In Vermont, Erastus Fairbanks ordered militia companies to recruit to capacity and to be ready to answer a Federal call. He instructed the state congressional delegation to assure the President that he was ready to mobilize and expand the militia, if necessary, without waiting for legislative action.[55] In Connecticut, William A. Buckingham urged militia officers to fill their ranks by enlistments, to inspect arms and accouterments, and to perfect their companies in discipline and drill.[56] In Indiana, Morton applied at once for all guns due his state under the Federal militia law, began a search of the counties for arms previously distributed to state troops, and called in all muskets not held by effectively organized militia companies. Morton also traveled to Washington to try to get additional arms.[57]

In Massachusetts, Andrew, hearing reports of rebel plots against the national capital,[58] sent confidential messengers to relay these

[51] New York *Evening Post* ("Albany Correspondence"), January 11, 1861; New York *Herald* ("Albany Correspondence"), January 11, 12, 13, 1861.

[52] New York *Evening Post* ("Albany Correspondence"), February 8, 1861.

[53] Madison *Wisconsin Daily State Journal*, January 14, 16, 17, 1861; Detroit *Free Press*, January 15, 16, 20, 1861.

[54] Boston *Daily Advertiser*, January 30; February 8, 1861; Springfield (Mass.) *Daily Republican*, January 21; February 4, 9, 1861.

[55] Erastus Fairbanks to Andrew, January 7, 19, 1861, Andrew Papers; Springfield (Mass.) *Daily Republican*, February 1, 1861; New York *World* ("Montpelier Correspondence"), February 22, 1861.

[56] New York *Herald*, January 26, 1861.

[57] *Official Records*, Ser. 1, I, 54; William D. Foulke, *Life of Oliver P. Morton* (Indianapolis, 1899), I, 104; Morton Papers for January and February, 1861.

[58] Charles Francis Adams to Andrew, January 4, 1861, Andrew Papers; Henry Wilson to Adj. Gen. William Schouler, February 1, 1861, Schouler Papers, Massachusetts Historical Society; Pearson, *Andrew*, I, 134–37, 159–63; Benjamin F. Butler, *Autobiography and Personal Reminiscences of Major-General Benjamin F. Butler: Butler's Book* (Boston, 1892), 161–66.

frightful rumors to the other New England governors. On January 12 he wrote General Scott to ask how "to meet any demand for patriotic citizen soldiers to assist . . . in maintaining the laws. . . ." If they were needed Massachusetts would "respond with . . . alacrity." [59] Andrew next issued a general order to the state militia: All men unfit for active service were to be eliminated and replaced by volunteers ready for "any public exigency." The Governor exerted all his influence to get the militia law amended in the legislature, and that achievement was largely his personal triumph. [60]

Late in January, Andrew got another batch of alarmist reports. Virginia was about to secede; her troops would attempt to seize Washington! The Governor gave this information to his legislators in a dramatic secret session, and they quickly placed at his disposal a $100,000 emergency fund to assist in the defense of the Union. He sent instructions to all militiamen to prepare for speedy mobilization. He prepared detailed plans for sending troops to Washington by boat. Though the necessary appropriation had failed to pass the lower house, he contracted for military overcoats, knapsacks, blankets, and cartridges. [61] Then he waited eagerly for the call to arms, as did Morton and some of the other governors.

But the call was not forthcoming. Not till after two months of agonizing drift.

5

"One short year ago the country was at peace," wistfully recalled the New York *Herald* early in February. "Within a month we have seen the bristling of bayonets, the heavy tread of artillery, and the incipient efforts of military leaders preparing the way for a chaos of ruins. . . ." [62] Truly during those frantic January days

[59] *Official Records*, Ser. 1, I, 36–37.

[60] Boston *Daily Advertiser*, January 17, 18, 19, 20, 1861; Pearson, *Andrew*, I, 147–48.

[61] Pearson, *Andrew*, I, 159–62; J. M. Forbes to Andrew, February 2, 6, 7, 1861, Andrew Papers; Boston *Daily Advertiser*, February 4, 1861; Boston *Daily Journal*, February 7, 1861; Springfield (Mass.) *Daily Republican*, February 7, 8; March 30, 1861.

[62] New York *Herald*, February 9, 1861.

Northerners were ready and eager for the President to send warships to Charleston Harbor and summon volunteers to the colors. If Buchanan had done so, he would undoubtedly have retired at the end of his term amid the encomiums of Yankees.

He chose instead to let the "opportunity" pass, to ignore the cry for retaliation, and to rest content with the continued possession of the few southern forts that remained in Federal hands. These, he felt, would suffice as symbols at least of the persistence of national supremacy—of the Union's perpetuity which he never forswore. By not pressing for the immediate repossession of seized government property Buchanan could cling to the withering hope for peace and ultimate reconciliation. But his decision merely produced a period of stalemate and uncertainty which lasted until almost a month after Lincoln's inauguration.

His decision also abruptly terminated Buchanan's brief period of popularity among Northerners. When it became evident that he would neither dispatch another relief expedition to Sumter nor attempt the recovery of other forts, his old enemies resumed their vilification. Once again they complained that "the silence and utter inactivity of the Government" created "general disgust and indignation." Though the flag of the Republic was "trailing in the dust, disgraced," the insult was "solemnly pocketed" by Buchanan "the coward and villain." [63] Some patriots were ready once more to ignore the administration and avenge the national honor on their own initiative. They urged the President to weigh the probability that there would be less bloodshed if traitors were punished through regular government processes than if the people were driven, "by their impatience of official imbecility, to take the remedy into their own hands." Patriots hinted at the possibility "of one of those things done by Napoleon III, a *coup d'état* on the part of the American people." [64]

Matters would have to wait, it then appeared, for the inauguration of Lincoln, and that was still a month away. In the interim

[63] New York *Times*, January 16, 1861; *Morning Courier and New-York Enquirer*, January 19, 1861; New York *World*, January 15, 16, 1861; Chicago *Daily Tribune*, January 17, 1861.

[64] New York *Evening Post* (letter from "Ready"), January 15, 1861; New York *World*, January 16, 1861; New York *Daily Tribune* (letter from Gabriel Harrison), January 17, 1861.

the relative absence of further irritating incidents, the assembling of the Peace Conference in Washington, and the rejection of secession in Virginia and Tennessee all helped to create a temporary calm. "Little or nothing can be done until after the fourth of March," a Connecticut Republican observed. "Though it is necessary to prepare . . . for the suppression of rebellion, it would nevertheless be improper at the present time to make any show or unnecessary display. . . ." The existing calm, however, was only "the stillness that precedes the tempest." [65]

This first upheaval of the northern people, which diminished toward the end of January, left irritants and disturbing lessons for the future. War had been avoided simply because secessionists left Fort Sumter undisturbed and because Buchanan did not again attempt reinforcement. The focus of public attention upon it, rather than its intrinsic strategic importance, made the Sumter question a "point of honor" and a potential source of hostilities. Either a northern move to strengthen the garrison or a southern attack upon it would inevitably break the peace. Here neither side could afford to "lose face." Here, as the New York *Herald* admitted, an assault would arouse the North "as one man" and compel it "to suffer all the horrors of a fratricidal conflict." [66]

And so Major Anderson's mail in February continued to emphasize Yankee determination to keep him where he was. A correspondent from Vermont assured him that New Englanders still wanted him sustained and were ready to fight whenever he needed their support. A friend in Albany vowed that a secessionist attack would bring swift retribution: "Woe! to the South if 'Sumter' is taken. . . ." If Sumter were attacked, Northerners would not wait for "sneaking & cowardly" Federal officials to dispatch aid. But "with 'Sumter' for our battle cry [we] will succor you in spite of the Government—in spite of the South—yes! even through rivers of blood." [67] The Sumter issue remained alive and dangerous.

Equally dangerous was the facility with which Northerners

[65] [?] to Trumbull, January 21, 1861, Trumbull Papers.
[66] New York *Herald*, January 17, 1861.
[67] See especially A. Y. Morey to Anderson, February 6, 1861; Chas. Townsend to *id.*, February 11, 1861, Anderson Papers.

had applied their concepts of "rebel aggression" and "Federal defense" to the train of events accompanying the secession movement. Indeed those terms had been used so broadly as to cover every effort of Southerners to give reality to their alleged independence—the nullification of Federal laws, the seizure of government property, and the appropriation of its revenues. In view of the experiences of January it was an absolute certainty that no conflict could begin without Yankees' assigning the role of "aggressor" to the South. And that in turn promised to consolidate them for the "defense" of the Union.

Had Sumter been surrendered, shrewdly observed the New York *Courier and Enquirer*, Lincoln's first duty would have been to retake it, and that might have forced the Federal government to initiate a war. "Not so now. If there should be Civil War, South Carolina must become the assailant. . . ." [68] After the *Star of the West* affair the coldly realistic Henry Adams was "utterly delighted with the course of things down there." "It puts them so in the wrong that they never will recover from it." Much could be gained, he thought, from "a little bit of a fight," especially if the North were worsted. "If Major Anderson and his whole command were all murdered in cold blood, it would be an excellent thing for the country, much as I should regret it on the part of those individuals." [69] Another optimist consoled himself by saying, "This apparent misfortune will operate to render more universal at the North the sentiment that the South is wrong & palpably the aggressor." [70] A friend of Sumner's believed, however, that Republicans had "lost an opportunity which they ought to have improved—an opportunity of consolidating and sustaining the party, and of placing themselves clearly and unmistakably in the right." [71] The advocates of a forceful "defense" were to find other opportunities to "improve" in due course.

A few of the more perspicacious saw one other important lesson in the events of January. They saw that the northern people were

[68] *Morning Courier and New-York Enquirer*, December 29, 1860.
[69] Henry Adams to Charles Francis Adams, Jr., January 11, 17, 1861, in Ford (ed.), *Letters of Henry Adams*, 78–79, 82.
[70] A. B. Eaton to Trumbull, January 18, 1861, Trumbull Papers. See also J. Watson Webb to Lincoln, January 12, 1861, Lincoln Papers.
[71] Paul P. Andrews to Sumner, February 6, 1861, Sumner Papers.

eager for strong leadership and willing to respond to a positive policy. Buchanan's experience had demonstrated this. The President was condemned for indecision in December; he was sustained and cheered when he showed signs of boldness in early January; he was execrated again when he appeared to resume his former inertia. The New York *Times* penetrated the meaning of this phenomenon in a most discerning editorial. What the country craved above all, the *Times* explained, was "courage and firmness at headquarters." ". . . It is not disunion,—nor the prospect of war that alarms our people:—it is the utter lack of stability, of courage, and of patriotic purpose in the men who are placed at the head of affairs. It is the failure of the Government, and not the hostility of its enemies, that discourages and alarms the American people. . . . If this apprehension could be removed, the whole country would be relieved and would rouse itself with vigor and courageous wisdom to meet the emergencies which are gathering around it." [72]

This was the lesson to be derived from the Yankee response to the January crisis. Northerners craved a leader willing to act with energy and decision. Their Unionism made them deeply sensitive to southern defiance of Federal authority—to "aggression," as they understood the meaning of that term. And they had come to believe that to lose Fort Sumter was to lose the whole game, to surrender the nation itself. In Springfield, Illinois, the President-elect, closely studying the course of events, took the whole lesson to heart.

[72] New York *Times*, January 1, 1861. See also New York *Evening Post*, December 28, 1861; Boston *Daily Advertiser*, January 1, 1861.

VII
Deadlock

DESPITE the adjectives Buchanan's enemies attached to his name, his course after the attack upon the *Star of the West* still yielded nothing in principle to the displeased secessionists. "I . . . never swerved to the right or to the left from the policy enunciated in my last message," he later wrote in defense of his record. "Intensely anxious that no collision should occur at Charleston which might precipitate the country into civil war, I was yet ever ready and willing to send reinforcements to Major Anderson had he requested them." Even though he wanted desperately to prevent hostilities, he scrupulously avoided any commitment which might impede a relief project if the necessity arose.[1] Secretary Holt instructed the Sumter commander to continue "strictly on the defensive." If, however, additional men or supplies should be needed, he advised Anderson, "you will communicate the fact to this Department, and a prompt and vigorous effort will be made to forward them." [2]

Anderson never again made such a request. Quite the contrary. His daily reports conveyed the impression that he felt secure and were so phrased as actually to discourage attempts to relieve him. Some Northerners began to doubt his loyalty. In particular they criticized him for his failure to return the rebel fire during the shelling of the *Star of the West*. After that, the New York Assembly tabled a resolution to present him with a sword, and the *Evening Post* recommended a pause in the rush to bestow honors upon him. He was, after all, one of the Southerners himself, "and it would not be extraordinary if his failing was too great sympathy with their cause." [3]

[1] Buchanan to Holt, March 16, 1861, Holt Papers.
[2] *Official Records*, Ser. 1, I, 136–37, 140.
[3] New York *Evening Post*, January 15, 16, 1861; New York *Herald* ("Washington Correspondence"), January 14, 1861.

But the Kentucky Major's "failing" was not partiality toward secessionists; it was the dread he shared with Buchanan of initiating civil conflict. That fear had been the real cause for his decision to move to the less exposed position at Fort Sumter; that fear drove him to abandon his earlier supplications for reinforcements. That same motive restrained him at the last moment from turning his guns upon the secessionists while they were driving the relief vessel out of the harbor. Searching frantically for some escape, he gave Governor Pickens of South Carolina an opportunity to disavow the act. In a note to the Governor, Anderson expressed the hope that the attack was without his sanction. Otherwise, "I must regard it as an act of war."

Pickens, in accepting full responsibility for the assault, reminded Anderson that South Carolina was no longer in the Union, a fact that did not "admit of discussion." In Pickens' view the occupation of Sumter was "the first act of positive hostility," and the subsequent effort at reinforcement was "coercion of this State by the armed force of the Government." The people of South Carolina were entitled "to repel such an attempt" and defend their shores. The Governor denied aggressive intentions. He hoped "to conduct the affairs of the State [so] that no act, however necessary for its defense, should lead to an useless waste of life." Hence, if any new attempt were made to bring relief to Sumter, the ships would receive adequate warning before being bombarded.[4] This response, which to Governor Pickens seemed the essence of restraint, came to Anderson like the sound of doom.

Anderson had not recovered from this rebuff when, on January 11, Pickens presented him with a new demand for the surrender of Fort Sumter. Anderson promptly refused but hopefully offered "to refer the matter to Washington." "It would afford me the sincerest pleasure to depute one of my officers to accompany any messenger you may deem proper to be the bearer of your demand." Pickens consented to this proposal, and on January 13, Colonel Isaac W. Hayne, Attorney General of South Carolina, and Lieutenant J. Norman Hall arrived in Washington to present the issue to the President. During the ensuing negotiations a temporary truce existed at Charleston, a truce that was neither

[4] *Official Records*, Ser. 1, I, 134–36.

initiated nor approved by Buchanan, but was the exclusive responsibility of Major Anderson and Governor Pickens.[5]

Colonel Hayne had a preliminary talk with the President on
January 14. He promised to deliver a letter from Governor Pickens
the following day. Before Hayne could do this, however, a group
of ten southern senators intervened to urge that he withhold the
Governor's communication while they sought to execute an
armistice at Sumter to last until the fourth of March. When the
emissary accepted their request, Senator Clement C. Clay, Jr., of
Alabama visited Buchanan to suggest such an agreement.[6] But
the President refused to negotiate orally, and Clay agreed to submit the appeal for an armistice in writing.

Buchanan's formal reply was written by Secretary Holt and
dated January 22. Holt stressed the President's desire to preserve
the peace and avoid bloodshed. For that reason the government
had assumed a defensive position and would make no demonstration against the people of South Carolina unless they committed a
hostile act. But it was impossible to pledge that reinforcements
would not be sent to Sumter: "The President has no authority to
enter into any such agreement or understanding." All that could
be said was that, since Anderson had made no request, it was not
presently deemed necessary to send aid. "Should his safety, however, require re-inforcements, every effort will be made to supply
them."

Colonel Hayne immediately denounced this response as utterly
unsatisfactory; nevertheless he sent it to Governor Pickens with a
request for further instructions. The Governor also rejected it
and ordered his agent to deliver forthwith the original demand
for the surrender of Sumter. This Hayne did on January 31, accompanying the demand with a long letter which argued that the
continued Federal possession of the fort was an act of aggression
against the state.

It fell to Holt once more to construct an answer. On February
6 he informed the Colonel that Buchanan was unable to see how
"the presence of a small garrison" could "compromise the dignity

[5] [Buchanan], *Buchanan's Administration*, 192–205; Curtis, *Buchanan*, II, 448–
52.
[6] Moore (ed.), *Works of Buchanan*, XI, 109–11. Buchanan's memorandum of
this interview, dated January 16, 1861, is in Buchanan Papers.

or honor of South Carolina, or become a source of irritation to her people. . . ." The garrison was not there for any unfriendly purpose; the people of South Carolina could "never receive aught but shelter from its guns, unless, in the absence of all provocation, they should assault it, and seek its destruction." If, despite "all the multiplied proofs . . . of the President's anxiety for peace," state authorities should attack Fort Sumter "and peril the lives of the handful of brave and loyal men shut up within its walls, and thus plunge our common country into the horrors of civil war, then upon them, and those they represent, must rest the responsibility." But the President had no more constitutional power to cede or surrender the fort than he had to sell the Capitol to Maryland.[7]

This answer roused Colonel Hayne to excited anger. After sending what Buchanan regarded as an "outrageous & insulting" rejoinder, he departed for Charleston at once.

After Hayne's abrupt leave-taking former President John Tyler of Virginia interceded with Buchanan in another effort to secure an armistice at Sumter. But the President refused to discuss it and said flatly, "I could not agree to bind myself not to reinforce the garrison in case I deemed it necessary." [8]

This impasse, of course, terminated the truce which had been concluded by Major Anderson, and neither he nor the administration ever renewed it. The first impulse of Governor Pickens was to proceed at once to reduce the fort by force, but ultimately he acceded to more cautious counsels and handed the problem over to the newly established Confederate government at Montgomery. President Jefferson Davis decided to await the inauguration of Lincoln, to whom commissioners would be sent to negotiate a surrender.

Meanwhile local troops continued to erect batteries and fortifications which put Sumter at their mercy and increased immeasurably the difficulty of reinforcement. It then appeared that ultimately exhaustion of the garrison's supplies would deliver the fort safely into Confederate hands. State authorities now even agreed to grant the Federal troops the use of the mails and the

[7] Moore (ed.), *Works of Buchanan*, XI, 126–41; Curtis, *Buchanan*, II, 452–60.
[8] Curtis, *Buchanan*, II, 460; Moore (ed.), *Works of Buchanan*, XI, 141–43.

right to purchase fresh meats and vegetables in the Charleston market.[9] Such was the *modus vivendi* in the harbor at the close of Buchanan's term.

2

The stalemate at Fort Sumter was characteristic of the general status of the secession crisis during the final weeks of Buchanan's administration. To the end the President remained unswervingly true to the Union. "It was his policy," Secretary Holt later testified, "to preserve the peace if possible and hand over the Government intact to his successor." And the members of his cabinet, although differing occasionally as to how that could best be done, were in essential agreement upon the wisdom of his objective.[10] Lincoln would thus find no obstruction to his inauguration in Washington, and he would be unencumbered by either the action or the commitments of his predecessor. So, at least, Buchanan reasoned.

But many patriots were unimpressed by what the President had achieved and complained bitterly about the numerous things he had failed to do. He had issued no call for volunteers to enforce the laws and defend the Union; had made no attempt to recover Federal property which fell into Confederate hands; had never sent warships to southern ports to force the continued collection of government revenues. The mere refusal to surrender Sumter or recognize secession was not enough; these other shortcomings destined him to appear weak and vacillating to northern nationalists.

To Buchanan, however, there always seemed to be abundant extenuating circumstances which justified his course. Nearing retirement, he might well have longed, perhaps unconsciously, to escape the crisis and leave its solution to his successor. Yet he was not devoid of loftier motives: a sincere desire to avoid hostilities, to have the issue finally settled by compromise. In February, Buchanan looked hopefully to the Peace Conference, whose chance for success he would not impair by menacing movements.

Moreover, the President could defend his static policy in terms

[9] *Official Records*, Ser. 1, I, 151, 153, 160, 254–57; Charles W. Ramsdell, "Lincoln and Fort Sumter," *Journal of Southern History*, III (1937), 263.
[10] Auchampaugh, *Buchanan and His Cabinet*, 81.

of practical and legal limitations of power. Never were there available sufficient Federal troops for the repossession of government property. He denied that he could legally call out the militia without a prior request from United States marshals in the rebellious states. (These officers, of course, had resigned and the courts had ceased to function.) He felt he lacked authority under existing laws to muster volunteers into the national service. Finally, he was not entitled by any statute to use warships to collect the revenues or to close the southern ports.

Buchanan later noted in his defense that Congress did nothing to strengthen his hands. "It failed to furnish the President or his successor with a military force to repel any attack which might be made by the cotton States." It neither empowered him to call for volunteers nor appropriated money for the defense of the Union. It made no provision for the enforcement of the revenue laws. Congress, if anyone, must bear responsibility for the deadlock.[11] (There was, to be sure, the alternative of proceeding without legal authority—as did Lincoln—but that was not a course Buchanan was given to pursue.)

Still, within the limits fixed by law and by the desire for compromise, the administration continued to defend the nation's integrity. Holt promised to redeem a request from Major Anderson for reinforcements, even though Anderson's later dispatches had "relieved the Government of the apprehensions previously entertained" for his safety.[12] Black and Stanton wanted to forward relief without waiting for the Major's requisition. The South Carolinians, these advisers said, "are improving every moment, and increasing their ability to prevent re-enforcement every hour, while every day that rises sees us with a power diminished to send the requisite relief." After consulting New York pilots they were convinced that a warship could defy the hostile batteries and deposit troops and supplies at Sumter. Suppose rebel guns should fire? "Is it necessary that this intolerable outrage should be submitted to? Would it not be an act of pure self-defense on the part of Major Anderson to silence Fort Moultrie?" So it appeared to Stanton and Black! [13]

[11] [Buchanan], *Buchanan's Administration*, 134, 153–61.
[12] *Official Records*, Ser. 1, I, 140.   [13] *Ibid.*, 140–42; Brigance, *Black*, 105–106.

Buchanan did not subscribe to the views of his bold Secretaries, but he did agree that tentative plans for succoring the garrison should be perfected in case the need arose. On January 30 the President ordered Holt and Scott to devise a plan.[14] These men, together with Secretary Toucey and Captain J. H. Ward of the Navy, finally agreed upon one that seemed to promise success. Ward, in command of a squadron of four small Treasury Department steamers, was to slip into Charleston Harbor at night and anchor under the guns of Sumter. In February, Ward waited eagerly for the expected order. It did not come, because of Anderson's failure to apply for aid.[15] Buchanan, however, could cite this project as further evidence of his solicitude for the Union cause.

The President also took what precautions he could, without inciting a collision, to secure Fort Pickens, commanding Pensacola Bay. In January, after secessionists occupied the Pensacola Navy Yard, Lieutenant A. J. Slemmer and seventy-odd Federal troops withdrew to Pickens and prevented its seizure by the Florida militia. But this small garrison needed reinforcements and supplies. On January 24 the warship *Brooklyn* started toward Fort Pickens with provisions, military stores, and a company of artillery. Four other naval vessels followed.

On January 28, Senators John Slidell of Louisiana, Robert M. T. Hunter of Virginia, and William Bigler of Pennsylvania handed the President a telegram from Senator Stephen R. Mallory of Florida. This dispatch tendered a pledge, endorsed by Mallory, that Pickens would not be assaulted if reinforcements were not landed. Buchanan, more anxious than ever to prevent conflict now that the Peace Conference was about to assemble, sought the advice of his cabinet. Every member, plus General Scott (though he later denied it), favored accepting the proposal and establishing what would actually constitute a military truce. Holt and Toucey then sent a joint order to Lieutenant Slemmer and the various naval officers instructing them to keep the artillery company on board the *Brooklyn*—"unless said fort shall be attacked, or preparations shall be made for its attack." Provisions were to

14 Moore (ed.), *Works of Buchanan*, XI, 123–24.
15 *Ibid.*, 363–64; *Official Records*, Ser. 1, I, 177, 179, 180–81; Crawford, *Genesis of the Civil War*, 248–51.

be transferred to the garrison; the troops and naval vessels were to remain near by. "You will exercise the utmost vigilance, and be prepared at a moment's warning to land the company at Fort Pickens. . . ." [16]

Thus the Federal government was reserving the right to land supplies and to keep on hand adequate reinforcements and naval protection. But since the secessionists made no hostile movement, the government forces did not increase the size of the garrison. This "quasi armistice" still prevailed at Fort Pickens at the time of Lincoln's inauguration.

Meanwhile rumors recurred in Washington that secessionists were conspiring to seize the city. On January 22, Black, too ill to attend a cabinet meeting, sent Buchanan a note warning him that the ultimate aim of the disunionists must be the possession of the national capital. Nothing less than this could give their project the real attributes of success. He advised the President not to heed the promises of those who had already betrayed him, but to bring in troops and prepare the city's defenses. Holt, Stanton, and Dix endorsed this recommendation. Early in February a force of 650 men was stationed in Washington. "Had I refused to adopt this precautionary measure," Buchanan later reported to Congress, "and evil consequences, which many good men at that time apprehended, had followed, I should never have forgiven myself." [17]

In the handling of other governmental problems also the President and his Secretaries clearly demonstrated their impeccable Unionism. When, on January 24, John D. Ashmore, resigned Representative from South Carolina, inquired whether he might continue to frank public documents, the Postmaster General assented with pleasure. King explained, "The theory of the administration is that the relations of South Carolina to the general Government have been in nothing changed by her recent act of secession; and this being so, you are of course entitled to the franking privilege. . . ." [18]

One of Holt's first steps as Secretary of War was to remove

[16] Curtis, *Buchanan*, II, 461–66; Auchampaugh, *Buchanan and His Cabinet*, 86–88.
[17] Black to Buchanan, January 22, 1861, copy in Black Papers; Brigance, *Black*, 110–11; Moore (ed.), *Works of Buchanan*, XI, 152–54.
[18] King, *Turning on the Light*, 48–49.

Major P. G. T. Beauregard of Louisiana as Superintendent of West Point because of his suspected secession sympathies. When Senator Slidell, Beauregard's brother-in-law, protested to Buchanan, the President assured him that he had full confidence in Holt. His acts "are my own acts, for which I am responsible." [19]

Secretary of State Black shortly before his retirement began the long struggle to prevent the Confederacy from winning support abroad. In a circular to all American ministers in foreign capitals, dated February 28, he instructed them to use all proper means to prevent recognition. "This government," he added, "has not relinquished its constitutional jurisdiction within the territory of those States, and does not desire to do so." Hence it expected foreign countries to refrain from any step which might encourage the seceders. Should their independence be recognized, "it would tend to disturb the friendly relations, diplomatic and commercial, now existing between those powers and the United States." [20]

Black, the ablest and most trusted of Buchanan's advisers, never hesitated to give expression to his patriotic impulses. To a friend he wrote that there might be justice in allowing the "Black Republicans to . . . have a civil war of their own making" and "reap the wirlwind [sic] which must grow out of the storm they sowed." But he believed that the issue was now "beyond party considerations." It was simply a question of whether the nation was to submit to its own destruction or defend itself. Black had no desire to coerce South Carolina so long as she refrained from coercing the government. "But she kicks, cuffs, abuses, spits upon us—commits all kinds of outrages against our rights—and then cries out that she is coerced if we propose to hide our diminished heads under a shelter which may protect us a little better for the future." [21] These views Black frequently expressed in cabinet meetings.

To Secretary of the Treasury Dix fell the vexatious problem of the revenues in the seceded states. Though the customs officers continued to collect duties at the ports of entry, they acted under the authority of state governments and held the money subject

[19] *Ibid.*, 55–58; Moore (ed.), *Works of Buchanan*, XI, 122.
[20] Copy of circular to foreign ministers, dated February 28, 1861, Black Papers.
[21] Black to A. V. Parsons, January 17, 1861, copy in *ibid.*

to their wishes. Dix, helpless to prevent this, could only denounce the collectors.[22]

He also tried, without much success, to prevent Federal revenue cutters from falling into secessionist hands. In January he sent W. Hemphill Jones, a Treasury clerk, to the various Gulf ports to aid in the rescue of vessels belonging to his department. Subsequently Dix received a telegram from Jones in New Orleans reporting that the commander of the revenue cutter *McClelland* refused to obey his orders. The Secretary replied with instructions that the next-ranking officer place the unfaithful commander under arrest and treat him as a mutineer if he resisted. "If anyone attempts to haul down the American flag," he added dramatically, "shoot him on the spot."

This bold order drew wide acclaim from the northern people, and Secretary Dix took a prominent position in the galaxy of heroes of the secession crisis. But an anticlimax followed when the second in command on the *McClelland* also proved to be a disunionist and the ship was nevertheless surrendered to Louisiana. Dix regularly dismissed these disloyal officers from the Treasury service, but this saved neither the vessels nor the government's revenues.[23]

Although he was an ally of New York merchants and a friend of compromise, Dix never counseled the administration to pursue anything but a vigorous policy. "The Southern Secessionists," he affirmed, "are acting as badly as the Northern abolitionists. We ought to sustain the Constitution and the government against both." To Major Anderson he wrote: "I approve heartily of all you have done. I need not say—maintain your ground to the last —because I know you will do it at all hazards." [24] Having the confidence of Wall Street, he was able to borrow money and maintain the credit of the government. When Dix retired in March, Governor Morgan of New York praised him for having "brought order out of chaos," and for giving "capitalists and . . . others confidence and assurances that treason and traitors had

[22] Dix (comp.), *Memoirs*, I, 366–67.

[23] *Ibid.*, 370–73, 375–76; New York *Evening Post*, February 4, 6, 1861.

[24] Dix to Geo. W. Clinton, February 16, 1861, copy in Chase Papers; *id.* to Anderson, January 21, 1861, Anderson Papers.

done their worst, and that henceforth law and order were to bear sway in the councils of the Federal Government." [25]

Attorney General Stanton, in his own peculiar way, was another forceful Secretary who consistently seconded the suggestions of his mentor, Black. While in Buchanan's cabinet, he first demonstrated his penchant for intrigue by becoming a source of information for leading Republicans in Congress. He kept them posted on administration plans and was the author of many of the wild reports of impending secessionist attacks upon Washington. In the basement of Seward's office, and in secret midnight conferences with Sumner, Stanton perfected the art of conspiracy and began his gradual conversion to Republicanism. [26]

March 4 came at last, and Buchanan was freed from his disagreeable responsibilities. As the new Chief Executive took office, the old bachelor and his charming niece, Harriet Lane, retired to Wheatland, his Pennsylvania home. There, between frequent illnesses, he spent his declining years assembling the materials for a defense of his record during the secession crisis. This became almost an obsession, as is shown by the many pathetic letters, reviewing the past, which he wrote to his former Secretaries. (How it pained him to see one after another of these men—Holt, Dix, King, and Stanton—make their peace with the Republicans and take favors from their hands! Only Black and Toucey stood aloof.) In 1866, two years before his death, the former President completed and anonymously published a small volume of vindication. Though omitting a few things, his book was essentially accurate and presented a solid case in his behalf. But contemporary Yankees were not convinced, and they contemptuously relegated "Old Buck," the last "doughface," to oblivion.

[25] Edwin D. Morgan to Dix, March 9, 1861, quoted in Dix (comp.), *Memoirs*, I, 387; New York *Herald* (Financial column), February 26, 1861; Barnes (ed.), *Memoir of Thurlow Weed*, 319.
[26] Weed to Lincoln, January 10, 1861, Lincoln Papers; Sumner to Andrew, January 28, 1861, Andrew Papers; Boston *Evening Transcript*, January 8, 1861; Seward, *Seward at Washington*, II, 492; Nicolay and Hay, *Lincoln*, III, 139–40.

3

While the executive department labored over the crisis, the Thirty-sixth Congress continued to present a study in futility. The loud cacophony of its proceedings added to the confusion and uncertainty of the secession winter. "Seven weeks of its session have passed," complained a reporter late in January, "and still it meets, and makes long speeches which nobody reads, and adjourns, without doing anything for the country." [27] When Congress dissolved in March, its limited accomplishments had not altered the essential validity of this earlier review.

The reasons for congressional impotence—for the failure to give legislative expression to the northern demand that the Union be preserved—were evident enough. In the first place, even after the withdrawal of members from the seceded states, Republicans never secured a clear majority in the upper chamber. Senators from the slave states remaining in the Union, aided by a few northern friends such as Joseph Lane of Oregon, William M. Gwin of California, and Jesse D. Bright and Graham N. Fitch of Indiana, still retained considerable power. In the House southern resignations did not give Republicans control until late in January, after the first period of excitement had passed. By that time the lawmakers were showing increased interest in the position of the upper South, especially Virginia and Tennessee. Approaching elections in those two states would determine whether or not they favored immediate secession, and the majority in Congress was not inclined to aid the disunionists by provocative measures. Seward helped to block drastic legislation, for it would have destroyed his hope for peaceful reconstruction.

By February many Republicans had concluded that it would be best to stall for time until after Lincoln had taken office. Previously a few might have hoped to force a showdown while Buchanan was still President; this hope was offset, however, by the fear that an early conflict would prevent the orderly inauguration of Lincoln in Washington. The first objective of Republi-

[27] Cincinnati *Daily Commercial* ("Sigma" from Washington), January 21, 1861.

cans had become the safe installation of their new administration. Meanwhile the President-elect added to the indecision of Republican legislators by keeping them in the dark about what new laws, if any, he desired. "As it is," explained John Sherman, "we are powerless here because we dont know *what Lincoln wants.* . . . He communicates nothing even to his friends here & so we drift along. . . ." [28] Some party leaders finally decided that they would have to wait for a special session after the inauguration to make good any deficiencies in the existing laws. Others consoled themselves with the belief that the executive already had sufficient emergency powers.

Finally, President Buchanan, while disputing the adequacy of his authority and blaming Congress for failing to increase it, actually shared some of the responsibility for the unwillingness of Congress to act. He dutifully informed the lawmakers of the legal restraints which tied his hands, but he never really encouraged them to remove the restraints. Indeed he exerted what little influence he had in the opposite direction. For example, in his special message of January 28, transmitting Virginia's call for the Peace Conference, he admonished Congress "to abstain from passing any law calculated to produce a collision pending the proceedings contemplated by the action of the General Assembly of Virginia." [29] In the same spirit Holt discouraged Representative Benjamin Stanton, chairman of the House Military Affairs Committee, from sponsoring a measure authorizing the calling of volunteers. Holt did not apprehend the necessity for such a call, and the President "would not desire to have such a bill . . . submitted to Congress." [30]

Though congressmen did little they said much. By March there was hardly a Senator or Representative who had not formally registered his opinions. Only a few failed to emphasize that disunion was intolerable, that Federal authority must be maintained in the remotest corner of the country. Some couched these sentiments in cautious and conciliatory words; others, in reckless and defiant diatribes. Not merely a scattering of radicals such as Hale and Wade, but a majority of the Republicans and numerous

[28] Sherman to Frank Blair, February 9, 1861, Blair Papers, Library of Congress.
[29] Moore (ed.), *Works of Buchanan*, XI, 116–18.
[30] *Official Records*, Ser. 1, I, 55.

Democrats challenged the secessionists in sharp, incisive language. Typical of the polemics was the address of Democratic Representative Isaac N. Morris of Illinois on January 16:

> It is time, sir, that we should arouse [ourselves]. . . . All considerations of party should be lost with us, when our country is in danger. . . . Our national property, our citizens, public officers, and rights must be protected in all the States, and our men-of-war must be stationed off the southern ports to collect the revenue; and, if necessary, blockade them. . . . The enemy is battering at the very gates of the Capitol, and meditate a seizure of our national records, and the appropriation of its Army and Navy. Shall we wait until our flag is no longer respected, or shall we strike for the Constitution and the Union now? [31]

Republican Representative Stanton of Ohio in his speech on March 2 exemplified the calmer discretion of the moderates. Indeed the tone of his remarks was strikingly similar to that of Lincoln's inaugural address two days later. The new President, he said, could neither recognize secession nor ignore the duties imposed upon him by his oath of office. Still, Lincoln was a "prudent and sensible man" and would not attempt to execute laws which could be temporarily dispensed with. If, for example, Southerners preferred to do without Federal courts and their legal processes, he assumed there would be "no effort to force it upon them." But the collection of import duties was a different matter. Secessionists could not deprive the Federal government of the revenues which were "indispensable to its very existence." They must not attempt that. "Then we must have war; and upon their heads be the responsibility for all the horrors and calamities that may result from it." [32]

The near solidarity of free-state legislators on the issue of national supremacy was tested and proved during an encounter in the House on January 8. On that day Democratic Representative Garnett B. Adrian of New Jersey introduced a resolution endorsing Major Anderson's removal to Fort Sumter, approving Buchanan's decision to maintain him there, and pledging Congress to "support the President in all constitutional measures to enforce

[31] *Congressional Globe*, Appendix, 55.   [32] *Ibid.*, Appendix, 301.

the laws and preserve the Union." In the ensuing "Babel of voices" angry Southerners alternated attempts to table the subject with repeated motions to adjourn. But the northern majority, suspending the rules, finally passed the resolution by a vote of 124 to 56. No Republican, and only four northern Democrats, dissented.[33] This, at least, was common ground for Yankee congressmen!

On several other occasions verbal battles between free-state and slave-state members almost culminated in physical violence. A New York *Times* reporter described one such altercation which occurred when Representative William Barksdale of Mississippi heatedly announced his readiness for an immediate settlement with the North: ". . . Several Republicans and Northern Democrats responded spiritedly, 'Lets have it then!' Mr. McClernand, of Illinois [a Democrat], shook his finger at Barksdale and Hindman [of Arkansas], vocifering loudly, 'Come on! Come on! now we are ready to meet you, and settle it quickly.' Great confusion prevailed, which finally subsided through the efforts of Mr. Hill, of Georgia, Mr. Sherman, of Ohio, and others." [34]

Another animated debate was set off in the Senate on January 9 by Buchanan's special message of the previous day. When Jefferson Davis defended the conduct of South Carolina's commissioners, Preston King of New York compared them to Aaron Burr and Benedict Arnold. During the imbroglio Wigfall of Texas contributed a characteristically violent speech, after which he sarcastically expressed the hope that his remarks would "produce peace and harmony and good feeling on both sides of the Chamber." [35] Again, as Representative Miles Taylor of Louisiana announced his resignation in an address defending secession, Daniel E. Sickles, a New York Democrat, challenged his right to express such doctrines on the floor of the House. Sickles wanted to know whether it was "competent for a member, sworn to support the Constitution of the United States, to . . . avow, advocate, and justify treason to the United States, and to defend the stealing

[33] The four dissenters among the northern Democrats were John C. Burch of California, Thomas B. Florence of Pennsylvania, Charles L. Scott of Pennsylvania, and Clement L. Vallandigham of Ohio. *Ibid.*, 280–82; Chicago *Daily Tribune* ("Chicago" from Washington), January 11, 1861.
[34] New York *Times* (Washington dispatch), January 1, 1861.
[35] *Congressional Globe*, 284–89.

of United States forts, United States arsenals, United States hospitals, and United States ships." Other shouting congressmen joined in a general melee before Taylor was permitted to finish.[36]

These unseemly arguments, insignificant in themselves, revealed the depth of sectional animosity, the widening gap between politicians of the North and of the South, the great difference in the basic principles by which they rationalized their respective positions.

4

Despite the truculent debates and uncomplimentary epithets, Congress passed few laws that had a direct bearing upon the secession crisis. Congressmen approved no measure to heighten Executive authority; only with difficulty could they enact even routine appropriation bills. Although the Federal treasury was nearly empty, southern members objected to a bill authorizing a $25,000,000 loan to meet current expenses. Representative Thomas C. Hindman of Arkansas tried, unsuccessfully, to add an amendment prohibiting the expenditure of the money for troops or ships to make war upon the secessionists. Most of the slave-state representatives voted against the loan when Congress finally approved it.[37]

Southerners again objected when, to supply the government with needed funds, an amendment to the Morrill Tariff Bill was proposed. This provided that the Secretary of the Treasury could issue $20,000,000 worth of Treasury notes in small denominations if Federal bonds could not be sold at par. These notes, paying 6 per cent interest, might be offered to little investors whenever the great banks failed to furnish the desired financial support. "We ask you to put these bonds out in small sums," said Senator Daniel Clark of New Hampshire, "so that small holders of money can take them; and we will put our arms and our small means around this Government, and we will hold it so fast that no traitor shall overthrow it." The dissenting votes of southern congressmen were not sufficient to prevent the adoption of the amendment.[38]

[36] *Ibid.*, 754.   [37] *Ibid.*, 712–15; New York *Herald*, February 7, 1861.
[38] *Congressional Globe*, 1015–20.

The appropriation of money for the Navy Department was accompanied by another round of menacing speeches. In the House, Roger A. Pryor, the volatile Virginian, vowed that he would not vote a penny to the navy at a time when it was "to be employed for the inhuman purpose of subjugating sovereign States." Muscoe R. H. Garnett, another Virginian, demanded an amendment proscribing the use of this appropriation to coerce the southern states. After spirited replies by various Republicans and northern Democrats the bill passed.[39]

That, however, was merely the start of the battle over naval appropriations. When the question came up in the Senate, on February 11, Republicans proposed an additional grant of money for the construction of seven new steam sloops of war, of light draft, heavy armament, and great speed. Many Northerners endorsed this amendment on the ground that a strong navy would be needed if the South persisted in its secession project. "It must not be forgotten," remarked the New York *Times*, "that the 'coercion' by which the Federal Government will seek to preserve the integrity of the Union and the supremacy of the Constitution, must be coercion by sea. It must be mainly a matter of blockades." [40]

But southern senators also could see the relevance of the amendment to the crisis. They fought against it vigorously. James M. Mason and Hunter of Virginia, James S. Green and Trusten Polk of Missouri, all charged that these new ships were designed to support a blockade of southern ports, and they swore that they would vote no money for such a purpose. William P. Fessenden of Maine retorted by suggesting that they either support the government or resign. He denied that these vessels would ever be used to attack the South. "But it may be that . . . war will come; it may be that these difficulties are to grow vastly greater than they are now. When that time comes, I trust we shall be ready to meet all our responsibilities like men." King of New York favored naval expansion because "treason" was "abroad in the land." He wanted peace. "But I would amply provide means for the defense of the country by war, if necessary." The struggle went on in the Senate for two days before the amendment won approval by a vote of 27 to 17. Except for Johnson of Tennessee, Southerners voted

[39] *Ibid.*, 345–46.   [40] New York *Times*, January 26; February 8, 1861.

solidly against it; the Republicans, aided by four northern Democrats, put it through.[41]

The House concurred in this amendment on February 20, after two more days of sectional recriminations. Garnett complained that it was a "direct proposition to raise a naval force to carry on war upon one portion of the Union." Edward J. Morris of Pennsylvania countered with the accusation that the opposition plotted to strip the government of all means of defense so that it would "surrender at will to all who attack it." "I see very clearly," said Curtis of Iowa, "that every measure, from this time forward, is to be opposed in this Hall as a force measure and a war measure. Why, sir, we are trying to keep the peace; and for the purpose of keeping the peace, we want an Army and we want a Navy." The final vote on the amendment was 112 to 38, the Southerners and a small minority of northern Democrats dissenting.[42]

The army appropriation bill had to travel the same rough road before it was adopted by either chamber. In the House its introduction on February 20 led to two days of mutual incivilities. John Sherman opened the discussion by confessing that he favored the bill with the expectation that the Army would be used "in protecting the acknowledged property of the United States, in recovering that which has been unlawfully taken, and in maintaining the Union." Although the regular military establishment was small, at least it formed "a nucleus capable of any reinforcement demanded by the exigencies of the times." Albert G. Jenkins of Virginia replied crisply that the measure, as construed by Sherman, was "nothing more or less than a force bill." It meant war upon the seceded states; he appealed to every southern member to vote against it. Even the legal precepts which Sherman defended were, in themselves, enough to dissolve the Union:

> . . . If we are to understand that, at any time hereafter, under any circumstances . . . no portion of the States of this Confederacy . . . shall be allowed quietly to act upon the great principle of self-government and confederate together, but that the strong arm of the Army and Navy will be used by the

[41] Northern Democratic support for the amendment came from Bigler, Douglas, John R. Thomson, and Milton S. Latham. *Congressional Globe*, 844–46, 850–53, 865–69, 870.

[42] *Ibid.*, 1039–40, 1067–76.

old Government to bring them into subjection—I say even if the slavery question were dead to-day, the fact that the dominant section stand upon a proposition of that sort, . . . is enough to make any southern man desire to get out of the Confederacy as soon as possible.

Henry C. Burnett of Kentucky then offered the usual amendment: No part of the army appropriation is to be applied to "any attempt to subject any State which has or may hereafter secede from the United States." He introduced this amendment to test whether the North was concealing under such terms as "enforcing the laws" a desire to commit aggressions against the South. Indignant Republicans were quick to take umbrage. "There is no war contemplated by the Government," said Stanton of Ohio, "except a defensive war, for the protection of its executive officers, and of the men engaged in the discharge of executive and ministerial duties." And thus the members from the two sections entered again into a fruitless discussion of what constituted aggression and defense, what distinguished coercion from the enforcement of the laws. After they tired of the subject, Burnett's amendment was defeated and the army was granted its appropriation.[43] No provision was made, however, for any increase in its size, which some northern legislators had favored.

But these men had already launched a movement to supplement the power of the Regular Army by permitting the enlistment of volunteers and by amending the militia laws. As early as January 16, John A. Gurley, a rabid Representative from Ohio, advocated a "force act" to allow the President to accept volunteers to sustain the government. If it were passed, he cried exuberantly, the West would furnish 500,000 men. Ohio alone had nearly 300,000 ready to "defend our glorious flag" as long as they had "a loaf of bread to eat or a gun to fire." [44] Two weeks later the House committee to which was referred the President's special message reported a bill "further to provide for calling forth the militia of the United States in certain cases." The accompanying report discussed the present danger and the duty of the executive to protect the public property. The majority of the committee believed there was sufficient authority under existing laws, but this

[43] *Ibid.*, 453, 461-63, 477. [44] *Ibid.*, 418.

bill would remove any doubts on the matter. Despite southern opposition, it was read a second time, ordered printed, and re-committed to the committee.[45] There it still remained at the end of the session.

In February another "force act," sponsored by Stanton of the House Committee on Military Affairs, received the endorsement of the Republican caucus and held the attention of the lower chamber.[46] The bill specifically provided that the militia acts of 1795 and 1807 were "hereby extended to the case of insurrec-tions against the authority of the United States." Further, it en-abled the President to accept the services of volunteers and pre-scribed how they were to be organized. This legislation was needed, explained Stanton, because of the narrow construction given the earlier laws by the administration. Buchanan believed that the act of 1795 only sanctioned the use of the militia to aid the officer of the court—the United States marshal—to execute its processes and disperse hostile combinations; that the laws did not apply to the suppression of a general rebellion. Stanton's bill would make the old laws apply specifically to this latter case.

The prolonged fight over this measure began on February 18 when Thomas S. Bocock of Virginia moved that it be rejected. His motion was promptly defeated by a vote of 68 to 110, the minority consisting of Southerners and seventeen northern Demo-crats. (At least one of the Democrats—Morris of Illinois—ex-plained that he voted for rejection only because he believed the law of 1795 provided enough authority to overcome the secession-ists.) In the ensuing controversy the rival factions inevitably re-verted to a discussion of the meaning of aggression, each pro-claiming its love for peace and reviewing the hostile acts of the other. Some Southerners resisted by dilatory motions and threat-ened to debate it indefinitely. Others, like Hindman and Pryor, thought it might be well to let the bill pass so that the people of the South could see what was coming. To Hindman it was "one of the best disunion propositions made in this Congress." While

[45] *Ibid.*, 645-46; Appendix, 304-305.
[46] Cincinnati *Daily Commercial* ("Sigma" from Washington), February 18, 1861.

he expected to vote against it, he was quite willing "to give gentlemen a chance to try steel if they prefer it." [47]

A week later, on February 26, Stanton's "force bill" was taken
up again, even though Southerners tried desperately to prevent
it. Thus began another day of rancorous debate. Pryor and William E. Simms of Kentucky called the measure "a bill of murder,"
an instrument "to carry slaughter and the sword into the bosom
of the Republic." It was nothing of the sort, countered Curtis of
Iowa: "The object of this bill is to send our eagles to protect our
citizens, and shield them against revolution, . . . and against all
the ills of anarchy, civil war, and oppression." At length Thomas
Corwin of Ohio moved to postpone further discussion—a motion
which, in effect, would prevent passage because of the limited
time for business which remained. But the postponement was
agreed to by a vote of 100 to 74. Among the majority were the
Southerners, most northern Democrats, and a few conservative
Republicans such as Corwin, William Kellogg of Illinois, and
David Kilgore of Indiana. The minority was largely Republican—
indeed, Republicans were overwhelmingly opposed to postponement.[48] The "force bill" was debated in the House on several later occasions, but it never came to a vote in either chamber.

The same fate awaited the various proposals advanced for the
collection of customs in southern ports. On January 9, Representative Stanton urged a simple repeal of the laws making them ports
of entry. Thus foreign commerce would be excluded and the
government would be relieved of the necessity of trying to enforce its revenue laws.[49] A few days later Representatives James
B. McKean of New York and Thaddeus Stevens of Pennsylvania
introduced bills for that purpose.[50] On January 30, John Cochrane,
Democratic Representative from New York City, reported a
similar bill from the select committee to which was referred Buchanan's special message. Cochrane was close to New York's mer-

[47] *Congressional Globe*, 1001–1002, 1031–33.
[48] *Ibid.*, 1199–1202, 1225–32; New York *Herald* ("Washington Correspondence"), February 27, 1861.
[49] B. Stanton to Holt, January 9, 1861, Holt Papers.
[50] *Congressional Globe*, 363, 510.

cantile interests and spoke vigorously in defense of the measure, although he naturally professed at the same time his intrinsic opposition to coercion! [51]

But the revenue bill to win the approval of the Republican caucus was the one advanced by Representative John A. Bingham of Ohio.[52] Rather than closing the southern ports, it authorized the collection of the customs from the decks of warships. Should this be resisted, the President could use the army, navy, and militia to protect Federal revenue officers. This bill provoked violent debates in the House off and on until the end of the session. On March 2, Bingham made one last attempt to pass the measure by suspending the rules. But the motion to suspend was lost.[53]

Another issue was the status of Federal postal facilities in the seceded states. Disunionists had cautiously refrained from interfering with the post-office system, and southern postmasters continued to settle their accounts with the government in Washington. But many outraged Yankees demanded that secessionists be deprived of this service, especially since it placed a burden upon loyal taxpayers.[54] Accordingly, on January 22, Schuyler Colfax, chairman of the House Committee on Post Offices and Post Roads, reported a bill authorizing the Postmaster General to suspend the mail wherever its contents could not be preserved inviolate because of an insurrection or resistance to the laws of the United States.[55]

The debate which followed was one of unmatched confusion. Republicans supported the bill as a measure of justice—the "merest, meekest self-defense." Northern Democrats, like Sickles, ridiculed Southerners who claimed these states were independent and yet expected the Union to provide them with such benefits. Some slave-state representatives pointed to the injustice and inconsistency of seeking to enforce oppressive laws while suspending beneficial ones; they would only approve the suspension of *all*

[51] *Ibid.*, Appendix, 307–308; New York *Evening Post*, January 31, 1861.
[52] New York *World* ("Washington Correspondence"), February 16, 1861; New York *Herald*, February 17, 1861.
[53] *Congressional Globe*, 1422–23.
[54] Rhodes, *History of the United States*, III, 142; New York *Evening Post*, January 21, 1861.
[55] *Congressional Globe*, 498, 509–10.

Federal laws in those states. Hindman, on the other hand, again advocated it as "a disunion measure." When the bill finally passed the House on February 6 (by a vote of 131 to 28), most of the opposition was southern.[56] The bill never became a law, however, because the Senate added an amendment in which the House failed to concur.[57] This, then, was one more bill that died with Congress in March.

There were two other measures relating to the crisis that Congress considered in January. Representative Stanton introduced a bill to eliminate secessionists from the militia of the District of Columbia by requiring each member to take an oath of allegiance. After another animated debate, it passed the House by a vote of 119 to 42, only eight northern Democrats opposing.[58] But the Senate took no action. Another bill, sponsored by Representative Morris of Illinois, provided penalties for any person found guilty of giving aid to the people of a state which had declared itself out of the Union.[59] It received only brief consideration and passed neither chamber.

However deficient Congress proved to be in these matters, the House at least showed great diligence in investigatory work. Most of this business was handled by the committee which received Buchanan's special message. The committeemen probed into the rumors of treason in the District of Columbia but uncovered no evidence of a conspiracy to seize the place. They investigated the matter of the southern forts and submitted a report strongly coercionary in tone. They reviewed the charges that Floyd had treasonably transferred arms to the secessionists but found no grounds to substantiate the charges. Finally they inspected Toucey's administration of the Navy Department and brought forth a sensational "exposure." On flimsy evidence this partisan committee charged that the whole Atlantic seaboard had been left defenseless and that the navy had been deliberately scattered in distant seas. In particular the committee condemned Toucey for accepting the resignations of various naval officers

[56] *Ibid.*, 755–58, 775–77; New York *World*, February 7, 1861; New York *Evening Post*, February 8, 1861.
[57] *Congressional Globe*, 1044–46, 1078–82, 1160–64.
[58] *Ibid.*, 605–606.   [59] *Ibid.*, 498.

who had joined the enemies of the Union.[60] So the House, as one of its last acts, passed a resolution, by a party vote of 95 to 62, that in accepting these resignations Toucey had "committed a grave error," for which he deserved the censure of the House.[61]

In the end, when the furious congressional debates closed on March 3, the power of the government to proceed against secessionists was almost precisely the same as it had been in December. Congress had provided for the following: a meager loan of $25,000,000 in bonds or $20,000,000 in Treasury notes, small normal appropriations for the army and the navy, the construction of seven new warships, and the reprobation of the Secretary of the Navy. The rest of the emergency laws lay strangled in committee pigeonholes or dead on the crowded calendars of House and Senate. They were, in fact, the casualties of the deadlock which still prevailed at the time of Lincoln's inauguration.

[60] *Ibid.*, 295–96, 572, 913–17, 1095–96, 1256–57; *Reports of Committees of the House of Representatives*, 36 Cong., 2 Sess., Nos. 79, 85, 87, 91. Hereinafter cited as *House Reports*.

[61] *Congressional Globe*, 1422–24.

VIII

Compromise Debacle

A T L E N G T H Congress disappointed not only those Northerners who desired an enforcement of Federal laws in the
seceded states but also those who hoped earnestly for a sectional
adjustment that would make force unnecessary. On the last night
of the session Senator John J. Crittenden of Kentucky, worthy
heir to Henry Clay's title of Great Compromiser, poured forth
his vexation in an extended farewell speech: "We are about to
adjourn. We have done nothing. Even the Senate of the United
States, beholding this great ruin about them, . . . have been able
to do nothing; we have done absolutely nothing." [1] Though
Crittenden seemed unwilling to credit his senses, before the legislators adjourned that night they had in fact done something: they
had delivered the *coup de grâce* to the cause of conciliation.

But the battle for compromise was not lost until after a long
and persistent struggle by its champions. [2] The most ardent of
them came from among those who keenly felt the economic impact of the secession movement and suffered most directly from
the business panic which continued throughout the crisis period.
It was a particularly wretched time for eastern merchants, who
generally agreed that the commercial slump was as severe as the
one following the panic of 1857. The shipowners, dry-goods
dealers, and cotton exporters of New York, Boston, and Phila-

[1] *Congressional Globe*, 1375–80.
[2] Cf. Frederic Bancroft, "The Final Efforts at Compromise, 1860–61," *Political Science Quarterly*, VI (1891), 401–23; Foner, *Business & Slavery*, 248–74;
Gilbert G. Glover, *Immediate Pre-Civil War Compromise Efforts* (Nashville,
1934), *passim;* Dumond, *Secession Movement, passim;* Clinton E. Knox, "The
Possibilities of Compromise in the Senate Committee of Thirteen and the Responsibility for Failure," *Journal of Negro History*, XVII (1932), 437–65; Potter,
Lincoln and His Party in the Secession Crisis, passim; Mary Scrugham, *The
Peaceable Americans of 1860–1861* (New York, 1921), *passim.*

delphia felt a sharp decline in their rich southern trade; and many feared the loss of their southern investments variously estimated at from $150,000,000 to $300,000,000. The heavy dependence upon slave-state markets of a great cluster of northern mercantile interests was clearly demonstrated by the thousands of bankrupt-cies which occurred during the secession winter. Capitalists saw millions in paper values wiped out in the downward trend of stocks and bonds; the accompanying decline in New York real estate drove investors "well nigh out of their senses." August Belmont, wealthy banking associate of the Rothschilds, estimated a 30 per cent depreciation in the worth of his property. Every-where financiers tightened their credits, and before the end of November, Philadelphia banks had suspended specie payments. The merchant princes of Pine Street and Wall Street trembled as they saw New York toppling from her commercial and financial pinnacle; they visualized the disunion movement reducing her to the condition of a decaying fishing village! [3]

Eastern industrialists felt the same terrible shock as their south-ern markets began to evaporate. There was a bitter wail from a Bridgewater, Massachusetts, cotton-gin manufacturer who feared that his whole capital investment would be liquidated. There were pathetic groans from New Haven carriage makers whose entire business was connected with the South. The same cry of agony was echoed by Philadelphia boot manufacturers and New Eng-land cotton-factory owners. Between January, 1860, and Janu-ary, 1861, the average price of a share of stock in forty-four cotton and woolen mills declined from $518.34 to $304.22. [4]

In addition, the curtailment of production meant widespread unemployment and suffering among the operatives in the factory towns. "Boston streets to-day are full of discharged workmen,"

[3] Business failures and the commercial and stock-market panics can be traced in the files of the New York *Herald*. See also Philadelphia *Public Ledger*, De-cember 7, 1860; Boston *Daily Journal*, January 9, 1861; Arthur C. Cole, *The Ir-repressible Conflict, 1850–1865* (New York, 1934), 279; Emerson D. Fite, *Social and Industrial Conditions in the North during the Civil War* (New York, 1910), 105–10; Foner, *Business & Slavery*, 1–14, 208–23; Frank H. Taylor, *Philadelphia in the Civil War* (Philadelphia, 1913), 9–12.

[4] J. E. Carver to Andrew, January 7, 1861, Andrew Papers; D. J. Wilcoxson to Sherman, January 7, 1861, Sherman Papers; Boston *Daily Journal*, January 31, 1861; Taylor, *Philadelphia in the Civil War*, 9–11.

reported the Boston *Courier.* "Our laboring population have a dreary winter before them, unless the business pressure is taken off. . . ." By December nearly 20,000 were without employment in Philadelphia. The *Herald* painted a shocking picture of the misery among the families of discharged workers in the New York hat trade.[5]

Western merchants, bankers, and river-boat operators experienced the blight of commercial panic almost as acutely. As late as 1860 the West was still profiting from a flourishing river trade with the South, but the disunion movement brought general stagnation to this business also. "Wheat cannot be sold at present, and we have therefore no quotations," ran the market report of one western paper, which repeated this dismal account for pork, hogs, wool, and flour.[6] Scores of banks in that section had heavy investments in southern state bonds and were forced to close their doors as these securities depreciated.[7] The people of southern Ohio, Indiana, and Illinois, especially those in the Ohio River communities, were hit hardest of all. From the Kentucky border of Indiana came the complaint, "All looks gloomy . . . in this part of the country where the people depend on the South for a market for their produce. It is feared that river traders will suffer great loss. . . ." [8] Throughout the North, then, the bleakness of the secession crisis was increased by a creeping economic paralysis.

With so many suffering serious financial losses, it was not surprising that there soon appeared abundant signs of a political reaction. The conservative trend was encouraged by the northern friends of Douglas, Breckinridge, and Bell, but it gained some support from the right wing of the Republican party—among those who had voted for Lincoln for reasons other than opposition to slavery expansion. In Syracuse and Boston this general drift

[5] Boston *Daily Courier,* December 3, 1860; New York *Herald,* December 23, 1860; Philadelphia *Morning Pennsylvanian,* December 11, 1860; Philadelphia *Press,* December 18, 1860.

[6] Detroit *Free Press,* December 2, 1860; Chicago *Daily Tribune,* January 1, 1861.

[7] Fite, *Social and Industrial Conditions,* 110–12.

[8] Elizabeth S. Craft to Henry Clay Craft, December 22, 1860, Daniel D. Pratt Papers, Indiana State Library; New Albany (Ind.) *Weekly Ledger,* November 7, 21, 1860; February 6, 1861; Columbus *Crisis,* January 31, 1861.

found expression in mob attacks, participated in by "gentlemen
of property and standing," upon abolitionist meetings.[9] In Philadelphia the Republican mayor prevented a riot on December 13
by forcing the radical George William Curtis to cancel his lecture
engagement. Instead, on that day there was a huge meeting in
Independence Square, directed by the business interests, which
adopted conciliatory resolutions and forwarded them to South
Carolina.[10] Other evidence appeared in conservative gains in New
England's local elections in December; [11] in the processions and
demonstrations of New York City's unemployed, or in workers'
mass meetings, there and elsewhere, which called for concessions
to the South; [12] and in the hundreds of procompromise Union
meetings held in every city of the North, gatherings which almost
invariably had the support of a few moderate Republicans. These
Union rallies were most numerous in the large cities of the East
and in the border areas of the West where the people favored
conciliation overwhelmingly.[13] There the specter of financial ruin
made other issues shrink into insignificance.

Because of their commanding political and economic positions
the compromise drive was always spearheaded by eastern merchants and manufacturers. A contemporary found the conservative leaders generally "men who are well to do worldly speaking,
. . . usually found in warm parlors, . . . remarkable for good
feeding, . . . sleek and comfortable. I notice also that they pay
great attention to the prices of stock." [14] Among them were afflu-
ent Republicans—bankers, shippers, commission and hardware
merchants such as William A. Booth, A. A. Low, Peletiah Perit,
and William E. Dodge—who joined with their Democratic and
Whig business associates to save their country—and themselves.

[9] New York *Evening Post*, December 4, 1860; January 30, 1861; Boston *Daily
Advertiser*, December 4, 1860; Boston *Liberator*, December 7, 1860.

[10] Taylor, *Philadelphia in the Civil War*, 11–12; Stanton L. Davis, *Pennsylvania Politics, 1860–1863* (Cleveland, 1935), 144.

[11] New York *Herald*, December 14, 1860.

[12] *Ibid.*, December 12, 13, 1860; January 10, 16, 1861; Philadelphia *Press*, January 28, 1861; Indianapolis *Indiana Daily State Sentinel*, February 16, 20, 1861.

[13] Edward C. Smith, *The Borderland in the Civil War* (New York, 1927),
135–36.

[14] Trenton *Daily State Gazette and Republican* (letter from "Hunterdon"),
January 28, 1861.

This was a matter which transcended politics, and capitalists were in essential agreement regardless of party preferences.[15]

The work began on December 15, when practically every prominent New York capitalist met on Pine Street in the city's commercial heart. Here they framed an appeal to the South, urging it to avoid hasty action, and adopted a series of compromise resolutions. Richard Lathers, president of the Great Western Marine Insurance Company, immediately departed for the slave states to deliver personally this message from their northern friends.[16] In the following weeks there were numerous private consultations of businessmen, which culminated in a meeting at the rooms of the Chamber of Commerce on January 18. There they approved a memorial to Congress pleading for compromise and appointed a committee to circulate it for signatures. After more than 30,000 names had been attached, a delegation of merchants carried it to Washington for Seward to present to the Senate. During January various other groups of New York capitalists approached congressmen to coax or threaten them into yielding to the South.[17]

Merchants elsewhere applied themselves diligently to the same task. Committees from Boston and Philadelphia also poured into the capital, while others put intense pressure upon state politicians. In December, Boston's men of substance signed an address to the people of Massachusetts recommending the repeal of their personal-liberty law; in February they delivered to Senator Crittenden a compromise petition with 22,000 signatures.[18] With equal determination northern railroad men exerted their considerable influence in this direction. Thus, on January 24, a convention of railroad executives in Washington resolved in favor of

[15] New York *Morning Express*, January 21, 1861; Foner, *Business & Slavery*, 232–38.

[16] New York *Herald*, December 15, 16, 1860; New York *Evening Post*, December 17, 1860; Dix (comp.), *Memoirs*, I, 347–60; Foner, *Business & Slavery*, 227–32. Lathers' compromise efforts can be traced through his papers in the Library of Congress.

[17] New York *Evening Post*, January 19, 1861; *Morning Courier and New-York Enquirer*, January 30, 1861; Foner, *Business & Slavery*, 248–58.

[18] Boston *Daily Courier*, December 18, 1860; New York *Evening Post* ("Washington Correspondence"), January 28; February 8, 1861; *Congressional Globe*, 862–63; Davis, *Pennsylvania Politics*, 143–44.

compromise, while individually they improved their opportunity to intercede with the legislators.[19]

In the mail of northern politicians were numerous letters from the merchants describing the disaster before them and begging for concessions to appease their southern customers.[20] It was a bold Republican indeed who could stand up to the richest land-owner or dry-goods merchant in New York, to a powerful rail-road president from Albany, or to a wealthy textile manufacturer from Boston, and not cower before the ammunition he could draw from his long purse. As the moneyed ones swarmed through the lobbies of the Capitol many politicians must often have thought that they truly did speak the voice of the North—at least the only voice that counted in a practical sense. Certainly the capital-ists were not backward in asserting that their immediate interests were the ones most worthy of the attention of Congress. Re-peatedly they noted how many hundreds of millions they had at stake, how trivial by comparison was the sacrifice of a few party principles.

Inevitably, then, much of the time of Congress was consumed by the discussion of compromise proposals. Most border-state legislators and northern Democrats strove eagerly for their en-actment, and the ranks of the Republicans began to waver before the onslaught. "Politically there is a terrible panic," nervously wrote Henry Adams from Washington. "As yet there has been no open defection, but the pressure is immense and you need not swear too much if something gives at last." [21] (Not long thereafter even his scrupulous father began to "give" before the pressure.) A radical Republican wrote Chase of his "solicitude . . . about

[19] J. W. Foster to George B. McClellan, January 31, 1861, McClellan Papers, Library of Congress; New York *World*, January 25, 1861; New York *Evening Post* ("Albany Correspondence"), January 25, 1861.

[20] See especially the many letters from merchants in the Crittenden Papers. See also the letter to Lincoln signed by New York's leading capitalists, including J. A. Hamilton, J. J. Astor, Jr., Shepherd Knapp, M. H. Grinnell, Hamilton Fish, R. M. Blatchford, George D. Morgan, and P. Townsend, dated January 29, 1861, Lincoln Papers; Geo. M. Davis to Trumbull, January 28, 1861, Trum-bull Papers; Barnes (ed.), *Memoir of Thurlow Weed*, 310, 319-20; August Bel-mont, *Letters, Speeches, and Addresses of August Belmont* (privately printed, 1890), 30-47.

[21] Henry Adams to Charles Francis Adams, Jr., December 9, 1860, Ford (ed.), *Letters of Henry Adams*, 62. See also Potter, *Lincoln and His Party in the Seces-sion Crisis*, 112-33.

the state of things here, both in regard to measures and men. . . . I have been here only two days; but long enough to be alarmed." [22] Most sensational was the "backing down" of Thurlow Weed, who began to advocate concessions, especially the restoration of the Missouri Compromise line, in his Albany *Evening Journal*. "Poor Weed," mocked a critic. "His glory has departed —his metal is broken—his pride is humbled—his self reliance is gone. . . ." And the "knowing ones" had no trouble in finding the cause. "They easily traced the wonder to Wall Street. They found in the condition of the stock market a perfect means of explanation." [23]

The hopes of the compromisers were strengthened when the Senate and House voted to create Committees of Thirteen and Thirty-three respectively. To them would be submitted the various plans of adjustment, from which they could draw ideas for their own specific recommendations. These committees received propositions from northern Democrats such as Douglas and Bigler; from border-state men such as Crittenden, Emerson Etheridge, and Andrew Johnson; and even from a few Republicans such as John Sherman, Charles Francis Adams, David Kilgore, William M. Dunn, and William Kellogg. Although the Senate committee soon broke up in disagreement, Thomas Corwin, chairman of the House Committee of Thirty-three, ultimately reported a scheme of conciliation approved by the majority. It was debated in a desultory fashion for more than a month.[24]

But interest had long since focused upon Crittenden as the chief of the compromisers; and his plan, presented to the Senate on December 18, won by far the greatest attention in and out of Congress. Even after its defeat in the Committee of Thirteen, to a very large extent the serious compromise movement was directed to the adoption of his proposal as the most comprehensive settlement and the one most likely to satisfy the South. In brief, Crittenden advocated the passage of six constitutional amendments: (1)

[22] Henry B. Stanton to Chase, January 7, 1861, Chase Papers. See also George G. Fogg to Lincoln, December 19, 1860, Lincoln Papers.
[23] New York *Herald*, December 6, 1860.
[24] *Journal of the Select Commitee of Thirteen*, in *Reports of Committees of the Senate*, 36 Cong., 2 Sess., No. 288; *Journal of the Select Committee of Thirty-Three*, in *House Reports*, 36 Cong., 2 Sess., No. 31.

In all territory, now held "or hereafter acquired," slavery was to be prohibited north of the line 36° 30', and recognized and protected south of it. (2) Congress was to have no power to abolish slavery in places under its jurisdiction when it existed in the surrounding state. (3) The same restriction was to be applied to the District of Columbia. (4) Congress was to be denied authority to interfere with the interstate slave trade. (5) Slaveholders prevented from recovering a fugitive by violence were to be compensated by the Federal government. (6) No future amendment to the Constitution was to affect these five preceding articles, nor to give Congress the right to abolish slavery in the states. In addition Crittenden introduced resolutions declaring the fugitive-slave law constitutional and personal-liberty laws null and void.[25] It was this scheme that legislators discussed most frequently, that northern merchants endorsed most often, and that Union meetings advocated most persistently in their petitions to Congress.

Second only to Crittenden's efforts toward a peaceful settlement was the work of the Peace Conference which assembled in Washington on February 4. That enterprise was sponsored by the legislature of Virginia, and ultimately twenty-one states sent delegates. After wrangling for more than three weeks, on February 27 they reported a compromise which resembled the one advanced by Crittenden. The chief difference was its application of the Missouri line only to present territory and its prevention of future acquisitions without the approval of a majority from each section.[26] Again the merchants were hopeful and applied their influence to get it adopted by Congress.[27] In the last days of the session the labors of the compromisers were directed toward its passage. Thus from start to finish there was scarcely a day that the legislators did not spend part of their time considering one or another of the measures of conciliation.

Outside Congress the state legislatures also received numerous proposals for reconciliation and gave them extended consideration.

[25] *Congressional Globe*, 112–14.
[26] Lucius E. Chittenden, *A Report of the Debates and Proceedings . . . of the Conference Convention . . . Held at Washington, D.C. in February, A.D. 1861* (New York, 1864).
[27] Foner, *Business & Slavery*, 266–73.

In New Jersey the Democratic majority carried through an endorsement of the Crittenden compromise.[28] Rhode Island repealed
her personal-liberty law, and Maine deleted the allegedly unconstitutional clauses in hers.[29] Indiana's general assembly resolved
in favor of calling a national convention, though not until after
Congress had adjourned.[30] And in the states, as in Congress, there
were always some Republicans who joined with their political
opponents in these movements for appeasement. Indeed, recalled
one radical Republican, "To the very last the old medicine of
compromise and conciliation seemed to be the sovereign hope of
the people of the free states. . . ." [31]

And he was right, for the evidence was strong that the majority
of Northerners favored some kind of an adjustment during the
secession crisis. Democrats and Bell men desired it overwhelmingly, and a minority of Republicans were ready for "reasonable
and honorable" concessions. That the masses wanted the laws enforced did not mean that most of them were unwilling simultaneously to seek a peaceful settlement. Their basic aim was to preserve the Union, and conciliation might be applied if it could
achieve that end. After all, "the old medicine of compromise" had
been holding the Union together from its birth.

Because of this tradition and the conservative reaction during the
secession winter it seems astonishing, at first glance, to find that
the compromise movement ended in a complete fiasco. Despite the
long debates no northern legislature except that of New Jersey
voted to sponsor either the Crittenden amendments, the Peace
Conference settlement, or any other general adjustment. In its
last hours Congress approved a new constitutional amendment,
to be binding for all time, prohibiting that body from interfering
with slavery in the states. But every other compromise had been
defeated; the efforts of Crittenden, Douglas, Bigler, Corwin, and
the other conservative leaders bore no fruit at all. The tremendous
pressure of the propertied interests was of no avail; the pleas of the
border states were snubbed. In the end the northern people were

[28] Trenton *Daily State Gazette and Republican*, January 24, 25, 26, 1861.
[29] Providence *Daily Post*, January 26, 1861.
[30] Indianapolis *Indiana Daily State Sentinel*, March 12, 1861.
[31] George W. Julian, *Political Recollections, 1840 to 1872* (Chicago, 1884), 186.

left with the alternatives of accepting disunion or trying force, unless they preferred to trust to the escapist formula of "masterly inactivity" which Seward still pursued.

Hence an account of the northern reaction to the disunion movement would be incomplete without a qualitative evaluation of the factors which defeated compromise. To begin with, was the alternative of appeasement ever truly open to the North to accept or reject? Was the will of the people actually frustrated by their own stubborn politicians? Did the majority really desire a comprehensive settlement that would satisfy the South, or did they deceive themselves again with ambiguous phrases which implied one thing but meant another? Could the sectional conflict have been resolved without a drastic change in the economic philosophy and social institutions of one of the two sections? Did either section show any evidence of a desire to submit to such institutional remodeling? These are questions which drive to the core of the problem—to the core of the crisis itself.

2

In December, despite the accumulating signs of political reaction, Joshua R. Giddings, the old antislavery radical, was not discouraged. Although some of the Republicans were wavering, he believed that in the end "the Southern States will do more for us than we can do for ourselves." [32] Obviously, northern conservatives would be unable to engineer a compromise if the men who had political control in the Deep South were not willing to entertain propositions in that direction. It was not enough that the majority in the border states, who were merely the brokers between the factions, favored conciliation. They were not the ones who had to be appeased; rather, it was the cotton states which were actually in the process of dissolving the Union. If the Deep South had no interest in compromise, then the whole movement was doomed from the start and that alternative was never actually open.

This being the case, it was of the utmost significance that Gid-

[32] Joshua R. Giddings to George W. Julian, December 14, 1861, Giddings-Julian Papers, Library of Congress.

dings' prediction proved to be true. There is no escaping the fact that the dominant political faction in the cotton states was trying neither to bluff nor bully the North into a surrender, that the election of Lincoln had converted this group to a program of immediate secession. The southern-rights men, who controlled the governments of all these states [33] and most of their congressional seats, went ahead without pause to achieve that objective. Every convention in the Deep South contained a majority which voted for disunion without showing the slightest interest in a compromise of any sort. Not one of these bodies offered to remain in the Union if a satisfactory settlement could be reached.

When Congress met, only a negligible minority among the twelve senators (those from South Carolina had already resigned) and thirty-two representatives from the cotton states showed any desire to discuss compromise. Rather, they spent their time arguing that adjustment was impossible, defending the right of secession, and citing the menaces to the South that Lincoln's election entailed. When the House approved the creation of the Committee of Thirty-three, sixteen of the twenty-two members present from those states refused to vote. Otho R. Singleton of Mississippi explained that he was not there "for the purpose of making any compromise, or to patch up existing difficulties." George S. Hawkins of Florida gave notice that he opposed "all and every compromise. The day of compromise has passed." William Porcher Miles of South Carolina said: "We consider our State as already withdrawn from the Confederacy in everything except form." James L. Pugh of Alabama added curtly: "I pay no attention to any action taken in this body." [34] After being appointed to represent their states on this committee, Hawkins and William W. Boyce of South Carolina declined to serve; Reuben Davis of Mississippi accepted simply to see that nothing was done to arrest the secession movement.[35] Thus the House had scarcely convened when the representatives from the Deep South had taken a stand against an adjustment.

[33] Governor Sam Houston of Texas was an exception. Houston refused to cooperate with the secessionists and forced them to resort to extralegal tactics to achieve their objective.

[34] *Journal of the House of Representatives*, 36 Cong., 2 Sess., 38, 50–51, 59, 77, 90, 146, 222; *Congressional Globe*, 6–7.

[35] *Congressional Globe*, 22–33, 59–62.

Their counterparts in the Senate also proscribed compromise—and simultaneously notified their states that all hopes for concessions were futile. Not until after two weeks of bickering did the Senate agree to create the Committee of Thirteen. During the debate, various southern-rights senators made known how certain they were that the Union would be dissolved. In nearly every case their aim was not to promote an adjustment but to achieve the strategic advantage of throwing the responsibility for its failure upon the North. When the Senate committee was created on December 20, Jefferson Davis asked to be released from his appointment because of the position held by himself and his state. The next day, however, Davis reconsidered and agreed to serve.[36]

The cotton-state congressmen had already made another major contribution to the cause of immediate secession. On December 13, before the House committee had well begun its work, before the Senate committee had even been appointed, thirty of these legislators sent an incendiary address to their constituents: "The argument is exhausted. All hope of relief in the Union . . . is extinguished. . . . We are satisfied the honor, safety and independence of the Southern people require the organization of a Southern Confederacy. . . ." Obviously these men were not seeking accommodations within the Union; they were simply rationalizing a program upon which they had already determined![37]

The conduct of the southern-rights men did not change during the few remaining weeks they spent in Washington. Toombs and Davis represented the Deep South in the Senate Committee of Thirteen. Both voted against the Crittenden amendments because, they said, the Republican members had also opposed them; both helped to defeat the more moderate propositions offered by Seward. Their impelling motive was not so much to save the Union as to pin upon Republicans the blame for its destruction.[38] Davis may also have feared to mislead southern moderates with false

[36] *Ibid.*, 19, 24–35, 117, 158.

[37] Alda Gregory, "The Southern Congressional Delegation and Compromise, 1860–1861" (unpublished M.A. thesis, University of Maryland, 1944), 30–36; Potter, *Lincoln and His Party in the Secession Crisis*, 200–18.

[38] *Journal of the Committee of Thirteen, passim;* Gregory, "Southern Congressional Delegation and Compromise," 46–55.

hopes. But it is significant that he was one of the senators who signed the prosecession address of December 13. On January 7, Toombs announced to the Senate that disunion was an "accomplished fact." [39]

In the House on that same day Etheridge of Tennessee asked for the suspension of the rules to call up his compromise proposal. His motion was defeated, most of the cotton-state representatives again refusing to vote.[40] At the same time Crittenden, having failed in the Committee of Thirteen, sought to bring his amendments before the full body of the Senate. On January 11 a motion to make them the order of business was rejected; six Southerners joined with the Republicans in the negative.[41] Five days later the Republicans were able to pass, by a vote of 25 to 23, an anticompromise resolution as a substitute for Crittenden's plan because six Southerners refused to vote.[42] They could have killed the substitute and forced the Kentuckian's measure to be discussed, but they deliberately scuttled the opportunity. Thereafter, as their respective states seceded, congressmen from the Deep South one by one announced their resignations in long farewell speeches.

By February the cotton-state legislators were no longer in the chambers of Congress to receive whatever concessions might be offered; at home they cast no backward glance. None of their states sent delegates to the Peace Conference in Washington—nor did its deliberations check in any way the progress of secession. Indeed the very day it assembled, the seceders met at Montgomery to begin the work of constructing a government for the Confederate States of America. Before the Peace Conference had adjourned, President Jefferson Davis and the Confederate Congress had served notice that the Deep South was out of the Union, unconditionally and for all time.

These southern-rights men need not and cannot be held responsible for the failure of Congress to adopt a compromise. Though they contributed to that result, they lacked the votes to prevent compromise without the support of Republicans. The important point, however, is that after the election of Lincoln most of them

[39] *Congressional Globe*, 267.   [40] *Ibid.*, 275, 279–80.   [41] *Ibid.*, 326–27.
[42] *Ibid.*, 409. Those who refused to vote were Judah P. Benjamin, John Hemphill, Alfred Iverson, Robert W. Johnson of Arkansas, John Slidell, and Louis T. Wigfall. All the other senators from the cotton states were absent.

had shown a persistent unwillingness even to *consider* concessions as an alternative to disunion. In their eyes the rights and interests of the South could no longer be guarded in the Union. No new compromise could alter northern hostility to slavery, to further southern expansion, to the fugitive-slave law. With the inauguration of Lincoln the executive department would be controlled by those opposed to southern interests, and more than ever the patronage and favors of the Federal government would be at the disposal of the South's foes. The future promised nothing but increasingly galling economic exploitation by the dominant section and the rapid reduction of the South to political impotence. To the ruling faction in the cotton states it was a choice between separation and ruin.[43]

In summary, the secession movement was undertaken by its sponsors in good faith. Those who favored prompt and unqualified disunion were in the saddle in the Deep South, and the votes for delegates to the state conventions indicated that they spoke for a majority of their constituents. By its own acts the southern party in the sectional dispute had taken a stand against conciliation.

3

John Sherman's most vivid recollection of the House of Representatives during the secession winter was that it "was almost constantly occupied in considering and rejecting the many schemes 'to save the country.' . . ."[44] More accurately it was a *portion* of the House—specifically, his party friends—who battled unremittingly for that objective. Despite the fears of "stiff-backed" Republicans and the publicity given to their less steadfast brethren, only a small minority were willing, when the votes were actually tallied, to make any significant concessions or surrender any of the planks in their Chicago platform. The majority clung tenaciously to their creed, rejected every scheme of adjustment, and threatened their fainthearted associates with the penalties of party discipline. "Now and then one of their number wavers," observed a cor-

---

[43] These were the general arguments used by the cotton-state congressmen to defend secession.

[44] John Sherman, *Recollections of Forty Years in the House, Senate and Cabinet* (New York, 1895), I, 215.

respondent, "but he is shot down in an instant by his comrades." [45]

Not the handful of "backsliders" but those who yielded nothing were the typical Republicans in Congress. The "stiff-backed" members expressed the real sentiments of the party. Washburne of Illinois was "satisfied with the present constitution," and Stevens of Pennsylvania sneered at the Committee of Thirty-three as the "committee of incubation." [46] Roscoe Conkling of New York insisted that Southerners must "return to their allegiance, haul down their palmettos and pelicans, [and] doff their cockades" before he would listen to pleas for concessions. [47] Owen Lovejoy of Illinois, even though identified with the extreme antislavery radicals, was not out of step with his more moderate colleagues on this issue. For too many years, thought Lovejoy, the South needed only to threaten, and there rose "a Judas to betray, a Peter to deny, and a hired soldier to drive the nails" which fastened freedom, "bleeding and quivering, to the accursed wood of compromise." [48] When Thurlow Weed visited Washington in early January he soon discovered that he was almost "alone" in favoring a course of appeasement. Senator Fessenden of Maine believed that a few Republicans would bear watching but that most of them were "generally right and firm." Even in December, when the "weak-kneed" Republicans seemed most dangerous, Senator James W. Grimes of Iowa discounted the talk of compromise and predicted confidently, "There is not the slightest probability that anything will be done." [49]

And nothing *was* done. The first in the series of anticompromise victories was won by the five Republicans (Seward, Wade, Jacob Collamer, Grimes, and Doolittle) on the Senate Committee of Thirteen. Under its rule that a majority of both Republicans and anti-Republicans must approve any settlement, they defeated Crittenden's proposal and everybody else's by their unanimous nega-

[45] Boston *Post* ("Washington Correspondence"), January 1, 1861; Wade to his wife, February 14, 1861, Wade Papers.

[46] *Congressional Globe*, 231. See also Doolittle to Lincoln, January 10, 1861, Lincoln Papers.

[47] *Congressional Globe*, 649–52.   [48] *Ibid.*, 84–87.

[49] Charles Sumner, *The Works of Charles Sumner* (Boston, 1874–1883), V, 452; Francis Fessenden, *Life and Public Services of William Pitt Fessenden* (Boston, 1907), I, 119–21; William Salter, *Life of James W. Grimes* (New York, 1876), 132.

tive votes.[50] On December 31, Chairman Powell of Kentucky reported that the committee had concluded its work and had been "unable to agree upon any general plan of adjustment." [51] Two weeks later twenty-five Senate Republicans passed the resolutions opposing concessions, introduced by Clark of New Hampshire, as a substitute for the Crittenden amendments; not one member of the party voted against them. Although the conservatives mustered a majority on January 18 to reconsider the Clark substitute,[52] in the following weeks Republicans repeatedly blocked further discussion or a vote on Crittenden's proposals.

The role of the sixteen Republicans on the House Committee of Thirty-three was essentially the same. Despite conciliatory gestures by some, such as Kellogg and Dunn, they voted unanimously against (and thus defeated) a border-state proposition to reestablish the Missouri Compromise line.[53] Late in December the Republican members sponsored and helped pass two recommendations, one for a new constitutional amendment protecting slavery in the states (an idea suggested by Seward in the Committee of Thirteen), and one for the admission of New Mexico, presumably as a slave state. The favorable Republican votes on these two measures were 11 to 3 and 9 to 6 respectively.[54] Even though the committeemen from the cotton states spurned these as entirely inadequate, this was as far as any voting majority of Republicans in Congress ever went toward an accommodation. In fact they never went that far again. Thus when the House committee later passed on a specific bill to admit New Mexico the Republicans reversed themselves and voted 6 to 9 against it. Charles Francis Adams, who had originally agreed to sponsor the proposal, now opposed it on the ground that the Deep South would not acquiesce peacefully in the legal election of a President. Finally, when the committee's work was finished, fifteen of the Republicans and most of the slave-state members refused to recommend that the House accept their propositions; instead they simply agreed to report their action to

[50] *Journal of the Committee of Thirteen, passim;* New York *Times,* December 24, 1860; Rhodes, *History of the United States,* III, 151–55.
[51] *Congressional Globe,* 211.   [52] *Ibid.,* 409, 443.
[53] *Journal of the Committee of Thirty-Three,* 9–10.
[54] *Ibid.,* 19–21; Potter, *Lincoln and His Party in the Secession Crisis,* 290–94.

that body.[55] Beginning on January 21 the House debated this report intermittently until the end of February.

It was in the last week of the session that Republicans, after protracted stalling, slaughtered every meaningful compromise that had been presented. As late as February 26 most Republicans in the lower chamber were still voting to postpone consideration of the report of the Committee of Thirty-three, and John Hickman of Pennsylvania and Washburne of Illinois led a filibuster to prevent a vote that night.[56] But the next day they went to work in earnest. First, the House killed the proposal of John C. Burch of California to call a constitutional convention. This was largely the work of Republicans, though the balloting was confused, some Republicans favoring the idea as a means to sidetrack other compromises and some Democrats and border-state representatives opposing it from a desire to obtain something more specific.[57] Next, the House finally took up the Crittenden plan and rejected it by a vote of 80 to 113. Not one Republican favored it.[58] The House then refused, on the first ballot, to approve even the proposed constitutional amendment to guarantee slavery in the states. Later, on February 28, the congressmen agreed to reconsider and passed the resolution by a vote of 133 to 65, but most of the Republicans were still against it.[59]

This amendment proved to be the sole achievement of the conciliators. On March 1 the House voted 115 to 71 to table the bill to admit New Mexico as a state. Only a few Republicans favored it; and some Southerners and northern Democrats, still hoping to win something more substantial, cast their ballots with the majority.[60] The last chance of the compromisers was to bring the report of the Peace Conference before the House. But that would require a suspension of the rules, which the Republicans were determined to prevent. "We have saved the Union so often," sarcastically remarked Thad Stevens, "that I am afraid we shall save it to death." A motion to suspend the rules was then defeated, most of the Re-

[55] *Journal of the Committee of Thirty-Three*, 33–39; Potter, *Lincoln and His Party in the Secession Crisis*, 296–99.
[56] *Congressional Globe*, 1232–43.
[57] *Ibid.*, 1258–59.
[58] *Ibid.*, 1260–61.
[59] *Ibid.*, 1263–65, 1283–85.
[60] *Ibid.*, 1326–27.

publicans balloting in the negative.[61] The compromise movement died in the House.

In the Senate the filibustering and delaying tactics of the "stiff-backed" Republicans held up the decisions on measures of adjustment until the last meeting on Sunday night, March 3. Even then the voting did not begin until almost midnight, the earlier hours having been occupied in further protracted speechmaking. The first vote was taken on the motion of Senator Pugh of Ohio to substitute the Crittenden propositions for the constitutional amendment already passed by the House. Pugh's motion was defeated by a vote of 14 to 25, with every Republican in opposition. (Even Crittenden voted against his own plan in his eagerness to pass the House amendment through the Senate!) Johnson of Arkansas then introduced the report of the Peace Conference as another substitute. This the senators rejected almost unanimously. Then they passed the amendment to protect slavery in the states by a bare two-thirds vote of 24 to 12, every opposing vote being Republican.

The last act in the Senate drama had in it a bit of cruel irony. In the early morning hours of March 4 the Republicans finally agreed to have a direct vote on the Crittenden amendments. But at that point Crittenden himself moved to substitute the Peace Conference proposals for his own because he thought they afforded the best opportunity for agreement among the states. Indeed he believed they offered an even better settlement of the territorial question than the one he had suggested. But most of the slave-state senators disagreed; they united with the Republicans to defeat the substitute by a vote of 7 to 28. After that the Senate rejected the Crittenden propositions, 19 to 20. None of the *yeas* and all the *nays* were Republican votes.[62] Then the exhausted senators wound up their routine business and adjourned.

The alarm of the anticompromise Republicans about their wavering colleagues had been ill-founded. Some of them spoke the language of conciliation but only a few of them voted that way. Not only did Republican senators and representatives stand unanimously against the Crittenden amendments, but they were

[61] *Ibid.*, 1331–33.   [62] *Ibid.*, 1386–1405.

overwhelmingly opposed to every other plan of adjustment that
came before either chamber. They voted, by 62 to 44 and 12 to 8,
against the constitutional amendment that finally won the approval of Congress. They opposed this measure to protect slavery
in the states even though it in no way violated their party platform. To the Republicans, then, belonged the responsibility for the
fact that no compromise was ever offered to the South.

4

In estimating the unyielding position assumed by Republicans
in Congress two questions remain to be answered: (1) Did they reflect fairly the general attitudes of those who had voted them into
office? (2) How did they rationalize their hostility to compromise? The first question poses few difficult problems; the
second is riddled with complexities.

The most cursory examination of the Republican press, the
correspondence of the national leaders, and the sentiments of state
and local party politicians provides convincing evidence that the
great mass of Republicans were unalterably opposed to compromise. Those who faltered in the commercial and industrial
cities and in the border areas of the West were no more representative of popular Republican opinion than Kellogg and Corwin were
of their party colleagues in Congress. It would be a safe estimate
that not more than a few hundred thousand of the 1,866,000 voters
who supported Lincoln were willing to follow Thurlow Weed in
his proposed retreat. This fraction when combined with the million and a half anti-Lincoln votes in the free states was doubtless
large enough to form a northern majority in favor of *some* concessions, but it was not sufficient to justify any assertion that Republican congressmen misrepresented the men who had elected
them. Senator Wilkinson of Minnesota understood the minds of
rank-and-file Republicans at least when he invited his colleagues to
look away "from the sidewalks of our cities": ". . . If Senators
would ascertain what the true sentiment of the country is, they
must go to the wool-growing regions of Vermont, to the wheat-
fields of New York, to the agricultural and mining districts of

Pennsylvania. Yes, sir; they must penetrate to the very heart of the eight million of people residing on their own acres in the great Northwest, and ask them this question: are you prepared to make a surrender of your convictions, of your principles, of your honor, at the bidding of organized rebels and traitors?" [63]

The letters Republican congressmen received from their constituents certainly would have given pause to any who might have contemplated abandoning party principles. In every instance the authors were overwhelmingly opposed to "backing down"; in some cases—as in the mail of E. B. Washburne, for example—there was scarcely a letter that indicated a willingness to make a single additional concession to the South. Slavery, insisted a typical correspondent, was to "have its pound of flesh according to the bond and nothing more." [64] Legislators were cautioned against assuming that the eastern cities sounded the voice of the North: "Artful politicians—rich merchants and speculators, whose god is money, will counsel peace, regardless of principle: see that you yield not to their solicitations." [65] Others contended, "The Chicago Platform is the written contract between the Republicans and every man that was elected by them, and we expect them to live up to it to the very letter." If there were another surrender the Republican party "would be *smashed into a thousand fragments!*" [66] "Mr. Sherman," pleaded an average Republican, "what ever you may do in Congress this winter, *for God sake* . . . dont . . . Compromise." [67]

Politicians who ignored these admonitions and favored conciliation exposed themselves to torrents of abuse from angry partisans. When Weed advocated the restoration of the Missouri line he was attacked by Republicans throughout the North; from upstate New York came an almost universal protest that his *Evening Journal* was no guide to opinion there. "Do not judge New York State by Mr. Weed. He no longer speaks for her when he suggests

[63] *Ibid.*, 896.   [64] C. M. Bowers to Sumner, December 8, 1861, Sumner Papers.
[65] J. P. Fessenden to William P. Fessenden, January 10, 1861, Fessenden Papers; W. A. Baldwin to E. B. Washburne, January 4, 1861, E. B. Washburne Papers.
[66] J. H. Smith to Trumbull, January 7, 1861; J. H. Jordan to *id.*, February 26, 1861, Trumbull Papers.
[67] A. M. Sattig to Sherman, December 13, 1860, Sherman Papers. See also Fessenden, *Fessenden,* I, 117; White, *Trumbull,* 117-19.

a Compromise. . . ." [68] After Representative Kellogg delivered a compromise speech on February 8, he was repudiated by a convention of his own constituents and read out of the party by the Chicago *Tribune;* others invited him to resign and go home.[69] Corwin of Ohio suffered the same penalty; the general opinion was, "If ever Corwin was a Republican, the sooner he is classed against us the better. . . ." [70] When Senator Cameron of Pennsylvania indicated his readiness to make concessions to slavery he received considerable praise from Philadelphia but precious little from other parts of his state. Russell Errett, one of the editors of the Pittsburgh *Gazette,* wrote Cameron a letter which must have given a fright to that ambitious politician:

> I find upon my return home, that the public mind is so inflamed against Compromise and so bitter against all efforts at concession, that my colleagues thought it most prudent to enter their dissent, in to-day's paper, to the views you expressed on Monday. This was deemed essential to maintain the position of the paper here, and means nothing unkind to you. Those who are familiar only with the public sentiment at Harrisburg, Phila., N.Y. and Washington can have no idea of the fierceness of the sentiment here in opposition to anything that looks like Compromise. It amounts almost to a fury.[71]

Even Seward, Adams, and Sherman, who offered the most modest propositions (none of which could be justly called an abandonment of party principle), were rewarded with condemnation by most of their political associates. When Sherman proposed to settle the territorial question by the formation of new states he was scolded by the Republicans in his district. They criticized him for suggesting anything "that even squinted toward

[68] Ebenezer Griffin to Sumner, December 3, 1860; George E. Baker to Sumner, December 3, 1860, Sumner Papers; New York *Daily Tribune* ("Rochester Correspondence"), December 6, 1860; Brummer, *New York during the Period of the Civil War,* 99–101.

[69] Chicago *Daily Tribune,* February 4, 13, 23, 1861; New York *Herald* ("Washington Correspondence"), February 9, 1861; F. A. Dallam to Trumbull, February 6, 1861, Trumbull Papers.

[70] Geo. T. Brown to Trumbull, December 18, 1860, Trumbull Papers; O. B. Chapman to Sherman, December 19, 1860, Sherman Papers.

[71] Russell Errett to Cameron, January 23, 1861, Cameron Papers. See also John Blodgett to *id.,* February 1, 1861; Saml. Snyder to *id.,* February 18, 1861, *ibid.*

a surrender" and warned that he would lose the sympathy of "masses of live working Republicans." [72] That Adams should have sponsored the admission of New Mexico as a state was an unpleasant shock to his friends in Massachusetts, and they were quick to express their displeasure.[73] Seward, because of his moderation rather than for any actual compromise that he publicly endorsed, lost favor with great numbers of his former admirers. Some bitterly and indiscriminately lumped "old grandmother Seward" with "the host of creeping things, called compromisers. . . ." The Chicago *Tribune* catechized him tartly in an editorial under the heading "HOW THE MIGHTY HAVE FALLEN!" A western Democratic paper agreed, "Mr. Seward . . . is not the idol to-day in this section that he was before the election." [74]

Reports from all parts of the North were almost unanimous that local Republicans were generally standing firm. In December, Carl Schurz traveled through Pennsylvania, New York, and New England and noted, "outside of the large commercial cities I have not found one single Republican who did not scorn the idea of receding from a single principle laid down in the Chicago platform." [75] The essential truth of this was evident not only in the mail of individual congressmen but in the resolutions of Republican mass meetings in every northern state, in a flood of petitions to Congress, and in the thousands of letters in the columns of party newspapers. Even Republican meetings in Newark and Trenton in conservative New Jersey re-endorsed the party platform and resolved against any compromise.[76] The Republican Central Club of New York City on two separate occasions affirmed that it was the duty of the government "to hold fast to the constitution as it is." [77] A prominent Democrat believed that the number of Lincoln

[72] See especially letters to Sherman by Jas. D. Whitney, February 2, 1861; Silas H. Mead, February 5, 1861; R. P. Spaulding, February 7, 1861; Thos. J. Butman, February 13, 1861; B. P. Baker, February 15, 1861, Sherman Papers.

[73] Edward L. Pierce to Sumner, December 31, 1860, Sumner Papers; George G. Fogg to Lincoln, January 1, 1861, Lincoln Papers.

[74] Atlantic (N.J.) *Messenger*, quoted in New York *Daily Tribune*, February 16, 1861; Chicago *Daily Tribune*, February 4, 1861; *Daily Chicago Post*, January 31, 1861.

[75] Bancroft (ed.), *Speeches, Correspondence, and Political Papers of Carl Schurz*, I, 168–70.

[76] New York *Evening Post*, January 12, 1861; Trenton *Daily State Gazette and Republican*, February 7, 1861.

[77] New York *Evening Post*, December 28, 1860; February 6, 1861.

men who would sign the compromise memorial sponsored by the New York merchants, "though respectable in character and position," were "a small minority in the republican organization." [78]

That being the case in the eastern bailiwicks of the conservatives, there was little cause to doubt the faith of party members in the Republican strongholds of the Northwest. Listening to the anticompromise chorus in that section, the *Wisconsin State Journal* had reason to gloat: "The North-west, thank God, has stood erect and firm." [79] Even in Chicago, with its great commercial interests, the number of Republicans who wavered was small. "Chicago has not yet descended to the dead level of New York," exulted the Chicago *Tribune*. "Cotton has not usurped the functions of Conscience; Pork has not conquered Patriotism; Lard has not dethroned Loyalty; nor have Cut Meats amended the Constitution. The city is sound." [80] The strong German-Republican element in the Northwest was a special bulwark against retreat; that group was uniformly opposed to compromise. [81]

With this strength behind them, local Republican politicians stood almost solidly upon the party platform. This was generally true even in the areas where the conservatives were most powerful. Thus the Republican Central Committee of New York City urged Congress "in no manner, come what may, to further compromise with the slave power." [82] The Rhode Island Republican State Central Committee opposed further concessions or even the repeal of the state's personal-liberty law. [83] On December 20 a secret caucus of New Jersey party leaders resolved, with only three dissenting votes, against yielding any of the principles of the Chicago platform. The proceedings and resolutions of this meeting, signed by Thomas H. Dudley, chairman of the State Central Committee, were printed in circular form and sent to every Republican member of Congress. [84]

[78] Sidney Webster to Cushing, December 31, 1860, Cushing Papers. See also George Opdyke to Chase, December 26, 1860, Chase Papers.
[79] Madison *Wisconsin Daily State Journal*, December 22, 1860.
[80] Chicago *Daily Tribune*, February 15, 1861.
[81] See, for example, Theodore Canisius to Trumbull, February 8, 1861, Trumbull Papers.
[82] New York *Evening Post*, February 1, 1861.
[83] Providence *Daily Journal*, January 22, 1861.
[84] Copy in E. B. Washburne Papers. See also Thomas H. Dudley to Sherman, December 22, 1860, Sherman Papers.

The Republican-controlled state governments also resisted resolutely the appeals of the compromisers. Of the Republican governors only Olden of New Jersey ever gave a formal endorsement
to an adjustment. Most of the rest were even hostile to the appointment of delegates to the Peace Conference. Rhode Island repealed
her personal-liberty law over the opposition of the Republican minority; the New Jersey legislature endorsed the Crittenden amendments without the support of a single Republican in either chamber. In the other states every compromise proposal was thrust
aside. The New York legislature contained a few Republicans who
favored the admission of the territories as states; but the majority
caucus voted 67 to 5 against the discussion of any concessions. One
member remarked acridly that some thought that Weed "had only
to wave his wand over the Assembly and a majority of the knees
would bow, but if the wand was waved to encompass the passage
of these [compromise] resolutions it would be found to have lost
its magic power." [85] In the lower house of the Pennsylvania legislature, on January 12 the Republican majority resolved "That we
affirm the doctrines of the Chicago platform as expressing the
sentiment of a large majority of the people of Pennsylvania. . . .
We do not believe that anything in our political condition demands concessions on our part." [86] Republicans in the Wisconsin
legislative assembly made short work of an opportunistic Democrat's resolution praising the moderation of Seward; they rejected
it by passing a substitute lauding Major Anderson! [87] Clearly, if
northern senators had any mandate from the bodies that had
elected them it was to stand firm.

And, finally, throughout the secession winter the Republican
press stood guard over the political morals of the North. The position of Weed's Albany *Evening Journal* received cautious and
almost apologetic support from the New York *Times*, the *Courier
and Enquirer*, and a scattering of papers elsewhere. But these were
exceptions; by and large, Republican editors, guided by the
Tribune twins of New York and Chicago, added their voices to
the cry against conciliation. "These journals," complained the

[85] New York *Herald* ("Albany Correspondence"), January 9, 23, 31, 1861;
Brummer, *New York during the Period of the Civil War*, 106–10.
[86] Philadelphia *Press*, January 14, 1861.
[87] Madison *Wisconsin Daily State Journal*, January 21, 1861.

Bell-Everett New York *Express*, "but little lower their flag of insolence. . . ." Instead they "crack whips over their Representatives in Congress, to stiffen them in stubbornness, or frighten them" away from concessions.[88] An editorial in the *Illinois State Journal* on December 19, entitled "STAND FIRM—BE TRUE," came close to typifying the position of the Republican press: ". . . We have done nothing wrong. We have nothing to apologize for, nothing to take back, as a party.—We have fought a hard battle; we have come out of it victorious; and shall we now call back the routed, flying enemy, and basely surrender all that we have gained? Never. . . . Let there be no wavering, no faltering here —no treacherous counsel, no base surrender of principles. Let there be justice, moderation, prudence, but unflinching firmness." [89]

It was not surprising, then, that the Republicans in Congress rejected compromise. They did it in the belief that the men who had placed them in office would tolerate nothing else, that if they yielded "they would be swept from the face of the earth at home." Seward dared do nothing more than "make fine promises," the New York *Herald* correctly explained, because there was "a power behind him, in the Republican camp, stronger than his own." [90]

5

After the election of 1860, Republican leaders had an experience that was almost unique in the annals of American politics. Ordinarily, victorious parties have been taunted by their rivals for their subsequent betrayal of promises made in platforms and campaign oratory. During the secession winter, however, Republican politicians chose to stand by the commitments they had made at the Chicago convention: to check the further spread of slavery, to admit Kansas as a free state, to increase the tariff, to pass a home-

[88] New York *Morning Express*, January 1, 1861; New York *Herald*, January 3, 1861; Boston *Post*, January 4, 1861. For a broad sampling of Republican-press opinion see New York *Daily Tribune*, February 25, 26, 28; March 2, 1861.

[89] Springfield *Daily Illinois State Journal*, quoted in Columbus *Daily Ohio Statesman*, December 24, 1860.

[90] New York *Herald*, December 17, 1860; March 3, 1861.

stead act, and to subsidize internal improvements. And their reward was an equal measure of abuse from contemporary opponents and more recent critics for their "obstinate adherence to a mere party platform," their refusal "to sink the partisan into the patriot." But if they had pursued another course and repudiated their previous pledges, presumably they would have been accused of the insincerity and opportunism of time-serving politicians. History had entrapped the Republicans in a moral dilemma!

Why were the adherents of Lincoln so fastidious at this particular time about their political integrity? That is a question which permits no simple explanation. Perhaps a few of the Republicans actually made opposition to compromise a matter of high principle, sincerely believed in the essential wisdom and justice of their party's program, and had no feelings of guilt or responsibility for the secession crisis. The mental rigidity of these "doctrinaires" may have been incomprehensible or offensive to practical politicians whose minds were more flexible, but the "doctrinaires" were nevertheless a group to be reckoned with among the Republicans of 1860.

In those early years the Republican party was not yet completely fettered by machines whose only rule was expediency. Originally it had absorbed in its complex body much of the political wing of a great crusade, namely, the antislavery radicals who had fused the remnants of the Liberty and Free-Soil parties with the new organization. Their hostility to slavery and the southern way of life was a partial expression of the broader nineteenth-century middle-class liberalism which they espoused. They put their faith in individual freedom, in the right of each man to the fruits of his enterprise. They placed their hope in the "music of the loom," in the material progress and abundance they foresaw in a nation of shopkeepers, mechanics, and free farmers. Actually they had simply adapted to the realities of the northern milieu the economic creed of Adam Smith and the English Manchester School. To its propagation they brought an intense degree of moral fervor. In a very real sense it was this group which gave the Republicans their *raison d'être*, their driving force, and their only common principle, namely, opposition to slavery expansion. Without these men it is doubtful that the party could have survived.

The radicals had endured too much, bolted the major parties and supported forlorn hopes too often, stood outside the gates of power too long, to permit any doubt of their devotion to principle. For such representatives of the antislavery crusade as Charles Sumner, Joshua R. Giddings, Owen Lovejoy, and George W. Julian to have yielded anything to the Slave Power after the victory had finally been won was unthinkable. They *believed* in the doctrine of the "irrepressible conflict" and denied that it could be removed by any feasible compromise; they insisted that their platform, so far from being sectional, actually contained the only true formula for national well-being. Republicans stood by their principles, explained one, simply "because *they know their principles to be essential to the welfare and even to the very existence of the Union.*" [91] James Russell Lowell encompassed the thoughts of this group precisely:

> . . . It is quite time that it should be understood that freedom is also an institution deserving some attention in a Model Republic, that a decline in stocks is more tolerable and more transient than one in public spirit, and that material prosperity was never known to abide long in a country that had lost its political morality. The fault of the Free States in the eyes of the South is not one that can be atoned for by any yielding of special points here and there. Their offence is that they are free, and that their habits and prepossessions are those of Freedom. Their crime is the census of 1860. Their increase in numbers, wealth, and power is a standing aggression. It would not be enough to please the Southern States that we should stop asking them to abolish slavery,—what they demand of us is nothing less than that we should abolish the spirit of the age. . . . It is time that the South should learn . . . that the difficulty of the Slavery question is slavery itself,—nothing more, nothing less. It is time that the North should learn that it has nothing left to compromise but the rest of its self-respect.[92]

Still, granting the depth and sincerity of their convictions, was it not possible that these "doctrinaires" in refusing to yield on the issue of slavery expansion were contending for a mere abstraction? Certainly a plausible case could be made to show that none of the

[91] Bangor *Daily Whig and Courier*, February 16, 1861.
[92] [Lowell], "The Question of the Hour," *loc. cit.*, 120–21.

existing territories was suitable to slavery and the plantation system, that the radicals therefore were endangering the Union over a meaningless point of honor.[93] Representative Daniel E. Somes of Maine, while hardly answering the question, made the most obvious reply by turning the point against the South: "You say it is a mere abstraction for which we are contending, because slavery cannot possibly go there. And yet you regard this abstraction of so much importance to you that you say you are willing to dissolve the Union . . . to secure it. If it is an abstraction with us, of course it must be an abstraction with you." [94] But the fact of the matter was that, rightly or wrongly, many in both sections believed that the issue had substance to it. There was still the vivid memory of the recent struggle in Kansas, the reality of a comprehensive slave code in the Territory of New Mexico; and there was the very live problem of whether slavery was to enter the future territories that Manifest Destiny seemed to promise to the expanding Americans.[95] Finally, in a broader sense this "point of honor," this "abstraction," was but a symbol of the many basic issues which divided the sections; for slavery expansion, after all, was only one facet of the "irrepressible conflict." And symbols are exceedingly important in a struggle between rival ideologies and rival social patterns.

In addition to the radical moralizing on the penalties of deserting eternal principles, Republicans offered a more specific rationale for their refusal to back down. They asserted, for example, that their opponents did not ask for a compromise (which involves a mutual give-and-take) but only for a one-sided yielding on the part of the North. Yet the North also had grievances to be considered if there were to be a general adjustment of sectional relationships. For one thing, Northerners demanded protection from proslavery mobs when traveling in the South and the repeal of state laws which imprisoned Negro seamen when their ships

[93] New York *Journal of Commerce*, December 14, 1860; Detroit *Free Press*, January 13, 1861. The fact that Republican congressmen voted to organize the territories of Colorado, Dakota, and Nevada without any reference to slavery indicated that they had no fear that the "peculiar institution" would spread into those areas.

[94] *Congressional Globe*, 968.   [95] See Chapter IX.

stopped at southern ports.[96] In addition they insisted that revisions would have to be made in the fugitive-slave law before northern personal-liberty laws were repealed: jury trials and other safeguards would have to be provided to prevent the return of free Negroes.[97] Above all, a *sine qua non* of any settlement must be southern recognition of the perpetuity of the Union, a disavowal of the right of secession. As one Republican phrased it: "Let us hereafter know beyond a doubt that we have a government. What will compromise amount to if a state can secede at will [?]" [98]

But Southerners showed no desire to grant any of these; not even the politicians of the upper South would deny the legality of secession. What was required of the North, in fact, was not a compromise but a complete surrender. "Allow the South to govern this country, and you would reach the real difficulty," protested an indignant Yankee; no other terms would satisfy her.[99] Secessionists, opined a correspondent of Trumbull, ". . . will be satisfied with nothing less than the repeal of our Revenue Laws, of our Navigation Laws, of our Fishing Bounties,—in fact of all legislation that is not demanded by the wants of the peculiar interests of the South. They complain of the political and commercial supremacy of the North, and will be content with nothing less than a reduction of their more prosperous neighbor to their own level." [100] The end result of further concessions must be the utter humiliation and subordination of every northern interest. If the North temporized, explained Wade, Southerners would

[96] J. H. Alderman to Trumbull, December 13, 1860; Rev. John Van Cleve to *id.*, December 13, 1860, Trumbull Papers; E. Spoford to Crittenden, January 16, 1861, Crittenden Papers; message of Governor Austin Blair to the Michigan legislature, quoted in Detroit *Free Press*, January 4, 1861.

[97] Charles Ingersoll to Andrew, January 9, 1861, Andrew Papers; New York *Daily Tribune*, November 23, 1860.

[98] Stewart Pearce to Andrew Johnson, December 24, 1860; Wm. G. Leader to *id.*, January 31, 1861, Johnson Papers, Library of Congress; H. F. Page to Sherman, December 31, 1860; J. Sturges to *id.*, January 28, 1861, Sherman Papers; *Morning Courier and New-York Enquirer*, February 15, 1861; Springfield (Mass.) *Daily Republican*, January 21, 1861.

[99] Speech of Representative Emory B. Pottle of New York, *Congressional Globe*, 570. See also speech of Representative C. C. Washburn of Wisconsin, *ibid.*, 513; New York *World*, February 21, 1861; Worcester (Mass.) *Daily Spy*, December 19, 1860.

[100] C. B. Custiss to Trumbull, December 10, 1860, Trumbull Papers.

"consider it a victory and become ten times more insolent than ever." In the opinion of another Republican, any yielding would virtually assure the South that "Whenever you are beaten at the ballot-box you have only to steal the public property and declare war against the Government, and we will make concessions. . . ." [101] Representative Orris S. Ferry of Connecticut drew a startling picture of the future:

> . . . Suppose we yield; sacrifice the moral convictions of the North, and the revolted States return to their allegiance: the tariff bill . . . is taken from the table of the Senate and passed; forthwith the hosts of sedition are rallied, secession again raises its hideous front, and amid the clangor of arms sounding from the Gulf, the industrial interests of the nation are immolated upon the altars of treason. . . . After peace has been restored by the new surrender, the homestead bill is reached upon the Calendar of the Senate, guns roar from Fort Moultrie, bayonets bristle at Pensacola, batteries are planted on the banks of the Mississippi, and amid shouts of "compromise" the Government yields once more, and the free emigrant of every section is sacrificed to the plantation.[102]

Equally frightening to the nationalists was the dangerous example of surrendering to rebels in arms, of placing a premium upon rebellion which could easily lead to national suicide. With this as a precedent a pattern might be established which would be followed thereafter by the defeated party in every national election. Any bargaining with Southerners would be a practical recognition of the right of secession, and that would make a mockery of the authority of the Federal government. In essence the Union would be lost as surely as if the independence of the South were conceded at once. "I am afraid to compromise," confessed a Republican, "for fear of demoralizing the government." In short, compromise, so far from being a remedy for disunion, would only aggravate the evil. "Instead of healing the disease, concession will make that disease constitutional, chronic, and fatal." [103] A "patch-

[101] Wade to Schouler, January 7, 1861, Schouler Papers; speech of Representative Daniel E. Somes of Maine, *Congressional Globe*, 969.
[102] *Ibid.*, 554.
[103] Philadelphia *North American and United States Gazette* (letter from "Independent"), January 29, 1861; New York *Independent*, January 3, 1861.

ing up" would only "postpone the evil day"; it would bequeath to the future an issue that would still one day have to be faced.[104] Republicans also bolstered their case by citing the past conduct and present attitude of the South. In the past the Southerners had allegedly violated every compromise that had been made. "We can make no compromise that will be more binding or conclusive than that which secured the admission of Missouri," asserted the New York *Tribune*, "yet that Compromise, which was effected by an almost unanimous vote of the South, was repudiated by a like vote within the next quarter of a century." "No more compromises with the covenant-breakers!" insisted another. "Not another concession from freedom to the treacherous south." Sumner argued bitterly, "*They are all essentially false, with treason in their hearts, if not on their tongues.*"[105]

Finally, it was easiest of all to present the evidence that secessionists had no desire to receive concessions from the North. This was a constantly recurring theme in Republican speeches and newspapers; it seemed convincing because of such incidents as the manifesto of the thirty southern congressmen to their constituents and such statements as those of fire-eaters like Wigfall. After the Deep South had refused to attend the Peace Conference, Thad Stevens could declaim with an air of finality: "Thus ends negotiation; thus ends concession; thus ends compromise, by the solemn declaration of the seceding party that they will not listen to concession or compromise."[106] Ironically but inevitably, the refusal of one side to entertain an adjustment, and of the other to offer it, provided reciprocal advantages for the policy of the dominant political group in each section.

6

One other factor helped to shape the course of the compromise battle: party politics. In the last analysis the issue was settled in Congress by a group of professional politicians who, according to

[104] F. D. Parish to Sherman, January 19, 1861, Sherman Papers.
[105] New York *Daily Tribune*, November 27, 1860; Indianapolis *Indiana American*, December 5, 1860; Sumner to Andrew, January 28, 1861, in Sumner, *Works*, V, 462.
[106] *Congressional Globe*, 621.

the normal standards of their trade, attached much significance to considerations of personal and party gain. To deny that many northern congressmen adjusted their views about conciliation to the requirements of political expediency would be to overlook one of the functional concepts of the American party system. Through the minds of these politicians, believed the New York *World*, always ran the question, "How shall the republican party be annihilated, or preserved [?] . . . On all sides there seems to exist this selfishness of party. . . ." [107]

Indeed this opportunism was not the responsibility of any one faction, for the Democrats were just as solicitous of party interests as were the Republicans. Unquestionably the Democrats felt most keenly the political consequences of compromise failure and secession, for with the South out of the Union their power was substantially weakened. Moreover, in a narrower sense, the Democrats strove for the advantage of portraying themselves as the would-be saviors of the Union and their opponents as a standing menace to its survival. In effect they invited the Republican party to abandon its platform, "repent of its iniquities, reform its policy," and confess that it had "thus far proceeded upon false pretenses of morality and philanthropy. . . ." [108] More precisely, Republicans were urged to disband. What Douglas men really hoped for, complained a Lincoln paper, was that the Republican party would "destroy itself" so that the Democratic party might be "reconstructed on its ruins." [109]

During the secession crisis, Democrats lost no opportunity to foster disunity in the ranks of their rivals or to mock them when they showed any signs of weakening. Thus Douglas chided the Republicans in Congress for allegedly adopting his platform when they voted to organize the territories of Colorado, Nevada, and Dakota without forcing a restriction upon slavery. To Senator Henry Wilson this furnished proof of the hypocrisy of Douglas' professed nonpartisanship and evidence that his primary aim was to rebuild "the broken ranks of the Democracy." [110] The New

[107] New York *World*, December 26, 1860.
[108] Boston *Post*, December 21, 1860.
[109] Springfield (Mass.) *Daily Republican*, February 4, 1861. There are many letters in the Douglas Papers which indicate that Democratic politicians were trying to make political capital out of the secession crisis.
[110] *Congressional Globe*, 1088–94.

York *Times* when it opposed the immediate passage of the Wilmot Proviso was rewarded with tart sarcasm from the Democratic Boston *Post:* "Verily the work goes bravely on! . . . Mischief has done its work! The storm is raised! Still here is more backing down. It is good to see repentance." [111] As a result the *Times* complained bitterly that conciliatory Republicans were "taunted with tardy cowardice and with a disposition to abandon their party. . . . The hypocritical insincerity of these [Democratic] appeals for compromise . . . is becoming too glaring to deceive any portion of the community much longer." [112]

But while Democrats coveted the political profit from splitting their opponents and promoting appeasement, Republicans looked upon compromise as the shortest route to political suicide. It would necessarily have required a repudiation of their platform, especially their one common principle of opposition to slavery expansion; it would have been a virtual admission that southern complaints were valid, that the Republican victory at the polls justified southern secession; and it would have involved a disastrous public humiliation. A terrible fear of these consequences ran through the speeches and writings of numerous Republican leaders. Over and over they droned that a Republican who favored compromise would simply furnish "proof that he is *scared,*" that he would achieve "the annihilation of the party," that he would promote "the re-establishment in power of the Democratic party," or that he virtually confessed that "Republicanism is a 'dead dog.' " Representative Cadwallader C. Washburn of Wisconsin was even convinced that the bill to admit New Mexico was a conspiracy to weaken the Republicans by adding two more proslavery senators to the upper chamber. To another Republican the whole compromise movement was simply a "plott [sic] by the slave holders & democrats to regain control of the Federal Government." Weed, during his visit to Washington in January, found his party friends obsessed with this dread. [113]

Panicky Republicans had before them a lesson from the Whigs, who, many believed, had been wrecked by compromise a decade

[111] Boston *Post,* November 15, 1860.
[112] New York *Times,* December 6, 1860.
[113] *Congressional Globe,* 514; F. D. Parish to Sherman, February 2, 1861, Sherman Papers; Barnes (ed.), *Memoir of Thurlow Weed,* 312–13.

before. "Beware of Compromise," ran a typical admonishment. "It killed Clay and Webster. It killed the old Whig party, and if you are not careful it will slaughter the present generation of politicians." [114] The inevitable result would have been fragmentation because antislavery Republicans would not tolerate concessions; they would have quit the organization first. Radicals warned that those who had been "educated by the Kansas tyrannies" meant "to stand firmly by this [antislavery] principle, cutting loose from any party that deserts it." Giddings' newspaper promised that if the Republican party yielded, "we will repudiate it with a full heart, and counsel all our friends to do the same. We have degraded ourselves enough." [115] Thus it was all too evident that reunion through compromise was impossible without the death of the Republican party, and there were few of its members who chose to make that sacrifice.

Yet it would be wrong to assume that most Republicans *consciously* placed party considerations above peaceful reunion. Even those not properly classified among the "doctrinaires" generally would have denied that their chief concern was the salvation of their party and would have insisted that their solicitude was for the well-being of the whole nation. Representative Somes of Maine gave an exceptionally clear illustration of the way concepts of party advantage and public weal were often fused in the politician's mind. "In a new country like ours," he told his colleagues, "where everything is yet undeveloped, . . . the bold and courageous are bound to succeed, while the timid will complainingly follow after them." Hence he commended to Republicans a course of boldness and rectitude, for "I would save this young champion of freedom and true democracy—the Republican party —from internal dissension and dissolution." [116]

There was still another factor which mitigated the seeming crassness of Republicans weighing the effects of compromise on the scale of party gain. Their attitude posed the general problem

[114] Henry F. Page to Sherman, December 17, 1860, Sherman Papers. See also speech of Representative James M. Ashley of Ohio, *Congressional Globe*, Appendix, 62.
[115] New York *Daily Tribune* (letter from "Citizen"), November 29, 1860; Jefferson (Ohio), *Ashtabula Sentinel*, February 13, 1861.
[116] *Congressional Globe*, 969.

of political responsibility. Whatever others may have desired, Republican voters overwhelmingly opposed concessions. Consequently, to say that compromise would have destroyed the Republican party is simply to say that the congressmen who supported it would have been repudiated by the party rank and file.

More than that, it was quite evident that the dissolution of the Republican organization would merely have paved the way for the formation of a new northern antislavery party which would have resumed the fight against the Slave Power. The elimination of the Republican party would neither have produced political harmony nor have removed the fundamental causes of sectional conflict. The radical Free-Soil Republicans made it incontrovertibly clear that they would build another party before yielding any of their principles. Many of Sumner's friends hinted that it might be necessary "to fight the battle all over again," or that "by a new 'bolt' . . . the fight with the Slave Power must be begun anew." "I helped to make the Republican party," vowed William H. Herndon, Lincoln's abolitionist law partner, "and if it forsakes its distinctive ideas, I can help to tear it down, and help to erect a new party that shall never cower to any slave driver." [117] Representative John F. Potter of Wisconsin believed that there were enough of the faithful left "to form a nucleus for a genuine republican party, should the conservative influence in the present one destroy or demoralize us." [118] And Owen Lovejoy laughed at the talk of reorganizing the Republican party with the radicals excluded: "I wish you a merry time of it my masters. A very interesting play, Hamlet with Hamlet left out!" [119]

And this tentative discussion of a new sectional party only provided further proof that there were certain basic sectional issues which could not be compromised away. The champions of appeasement were always breaking their lances on the tough realities of the "irrepressible conflict." They could neither silence the northern antislavery radicals nor prevent them from prosecuting

[117] D. W. Alvord to Sumner, December 12, 1860; Wm. H. Herndon to id., December 10, 1860, Sumner Papers.
[118] J. F. Potter to Jerome R. Brigham, December 18, 1860, Brigham Papers, Historical Society of Wisconsin. See also W. Taliott to E. B. Washburne, December 14, 1860; H. Whitney to id., December 17, 1860, E. B. Washburne Papers.
[119] *Congressional Globe*, Appendix, 85–86.

their fight through political action. Much less could they devise constitutional amendments which would obliterate the chronic antagonisms between agrarian and industrial economies. At best the work of the northern compromisers was superficial; at worst it was fraudulent.

IX

The Fraud of the Conciliators

AT THE March meeting of the New York Chamber of Commerce there was one item on the agenda that hardly anyone noticed except the merchants. They were considering a proposal to repeal the Federal law giving American shippers a monopoly of the coasting trade and to open this lucrative business to the British on a reciprocal basis. Except to these commercial men the final disposition of the matter seemed to be of small importance during the dramatic weeks of the secession crisis. And yet nothing illustrated more clearly the real essence of sectionalism and the tendency of northern compromisers either innocently to deceive themselves or deliberately to deceive others.

Conservative New York merchants had spent three months passing resolutions, circulating petitions, and visiting Washington to advance the cause of appeasing the secessionists. Repeatedly they had professed their friendship for the South and their eagerness to defend her rights in the Union. Now they had an opportunity to give tangible proof of their sincerity, not by the sacrifice of some remote territory to slavery but at the cost of risking their own profits for the sake of sectional harmony. For many years Southerners had protested against the monopoly enjoyed by northern shipowners in the coasting trade and had charged that it was one of the artificial devices by which the slave states were subjected to Yankee exploitation. The repeal of that law would have reduced the freight charges levied upon the planters by exposing northern traders to foreign competition. It would have removed one source of southern complaint.

Nevertheless a special committee of the Chamber of Commerce reported against sharing with Britain "our great and rapidly increasing coasting trade." Rather, the committee believed, "our interests demand we should cherish this trade, and establish our own system, irrespective of this or other nations." Ultimately the whole subject was indefinitely postponed.[1] Evidently some of the merchants could not understand the relevance of their action to the crisis and harbored the smug belief that the only remedy required was to disperse the abolitionists. Others seemed to think that the business of conciliation could be carried too far!

This decision of the New York merchants was no isolated phenomenon. Throughout the secession winter, the northern compromisers generally showed great enthusiasm for concessions on matters that seemed to have no direct bearing upon their particular interests, but they displayed an unfeeling obduracy toward concessions on subjects that touched them closely. In Congress nearly every type of sectional legislation came up for debate; and Northerners, whether radical or conservative, Republican or Democratic, refused to surrender any law which brought special benefits to their constituents. Southerners could cry out against discrimination and northern tyranny, but Yankee congressmen were unmoved.

As a result, when Congress adjourned, the navigation laws which benefited eastern merchants were still on the statute books. So was the grant of a Federal bounty to New England fishermen. Even though an Alabama congressman bitterly called the fishing bounty a device by which Northerners were "permitted to fleece" his constituents, a southern proposal that it be repealed was defeated.[2] When slave-state congressmen opposed additional appropriations for the United States coast survey which aided merchants by removing or charting hazards to shipping, eastern Democrats joined with Republicans in smothering the opposition.[3] The vote to admit Kansas as a free state divided the legislators along essentially sectional rather than party lines.[4] Despite longstanding southern opposition the House passed another homestead bill (though the Senate failed to act), and on this measure northwestern Democrats voted solidly with the Republicans. The South was also defeated by this same alliance when her congress-

---

[1] New York Chamber of Commerce, *Fourth Annual Report* (New York, 1862), 5–8.

[2] *Congressional Globe*, 191, 1057–58.   [3] *Ibid.*, 297–300.

[4] *Ibid.*, 489, 603–604.

men proposed to pledge the revenues from the sale of public lands to the redemption of Treasury notes. Northerners rejected this because it might interfere with their homestead policy or with the disposal of these lands as subsidies to internal improvements. Southerners angrily charged that selfish Yankees had the dual motive of monopolizing the public domain and of eliminating the revenue from this source to ease the way for higher tariff schedules.[5] Most slave-state congressmen were equally indignant when the two houses considered a Pacific Railroad bill which offered a huge Federal grant to the enterprise. (This bill did not actually become law because the session ended before the House had concurred in various Senate amendments.) Southerners were particularly indignant because of a provision which required the exclusive use of American iron in the construction of the railroad. It was at this point, by the way, that Pennsylvania's Senator Cameron, one of the more conciliatory Republicans, reached the limits of his interest in appeasement.[6]

Finally, while the country had the general subject of economic sectionalism under review it was altogether appropriate that the problem of the tariff should have had a thorough airing. Southern agrarians had long since made known their intense hostility to protective duties which they considered a burdensome tax upon their enterprise for the benefit of northern manufacturers. It was this issue which had driven South Carolina to the edge of rebellion thirty years before, and ever since 1846 southern influence had kept tariff schedules at low levels. Inevitably any attempt to increase them at this time would aggravate relations between the sections. New York merchants and western Democrats, both of whom also opposed protection as importers and consumers, were understandably eager to give the South no further irritation on this matter.[7]

But a tariff increase had been one of the major planks in the Republicans' Chicago platform. Its appeal had won them many

[5] Ibid., 15-16, 42-45, 65-71.   [6] Ibid., 169, 171, 544, 638-39, 880-82.

[7] New York Chamber of Commerce, Fourth Annual Report, 2-4; New York Evening Post, January 25, 30; February 1, 4, 1861; New York Herald, January 31, 1861; Cincinnati Daily Commercial, February 18, 1861; Indianapolis Indiana Daily State Sentinel, March 4, 19, 1861; New Albany (Ind.) Weekly Ledger, February 13, 1861.

votes in the East, especially in New Jersey and Pennsylvania. Accordingly they were determined to redeem their pledge without delay; indeed they were warned repeatedly that failure to act would ruin them in Pennsylvania. Governor Curtin assured Sumner that such a result would "annihilate" the Republicans. "We promised the people of Penna that the Republican party w[ou]ld be faithful to the principle of protection and you know the result." [8] Cameron's correspondence made it evident that conservative Pennsylvanians were determined to have a higher tariff regardless of consequences, that this was not an issue which they regarded as properly open to compromise. In the Pennsylvania legislature Republicans and Democrats unanimously passed a resolution demanding a "sound tariff bill" which would "afford protection to the labor and industry of the country." [9] With some the tariff seemed to come before everything else, as it did with one conservative who hoped that Southerners would leave their seats in Congress just long enough to permit the enactment of a new revenue law.[10] Henry C. Carey of Philadelphia, the doctrinaire protectionist who was ready to concede almost anything else to the South, comforted his sympathizers with a unique diagnosis of the secession crisis which absolved them from any responsibility. In begging northern congressmen to raise the tariff, he argued that free trade was actually "the cause of the discord with which we are troubled." Only protection could form a sound foundation for a prosperous and harmonious Union.[11]

In any event Republicans lost no time in bringing the tariff question before Congress. A bill sponsored by Representative Justin S. Morrill of Vermont, which provided substantial protection for Pennsylvania iron and other northern manufactures, had passed the House at the previous session. Cameron pressed for its consideration in the Senate as early as the second day of the new

[8] Andrew G. Curtin to Sumner, February 19, 1861, Sumner Papers. See also A. K. McClure to Fessenden, February 19, 1861, Fessenden Papers; id. to McPherson, February 19, 1861, McPherson Papers; Thos. P. Stotesburg to Wade, February 18, 1861, Wade Papers.

[9] Philadelphia Press, January 25, 1861.

[10] Philadelphia North American and United States Gazette, November 13, 1860.

[11] Henry C. Carey to Sherman, February 20, 1861, Sherman Papers. See also Carey's speech in Philadelphia, December 1, 1860, in Philadelphia North American and United States Gazette, December 3, 1860.

session. Ultimately the task of guiding the Morrill bill to passage was assumed by Senator Simmons of Rhode Island, who was appointed chairman of a special tariff committee. Significantly, however, few senators championed the bill more ardently than Bigler of Pennsylvania, who took sufficient time from his labors for compromise to advance this vital interest of his state. Crittenden was repeatedly exasperated when eastern Democrats such as Bigler and Thomson of New Jersey voted with the Republicans to postpone discussion of his compromise and to take up the tariff. Southerners and western Democrats protested in vain; when Douglas begged for the defeat of the Morrill bill to pacify the South, it was Bigler who rose to refute him.[12]

Senator Hunter of Virginia, defending the rights of farmers and consumers, led the opposition to the new tariff. His attack was centered upon the high duties on iron and on cotton bagging and gunny cloth, indispensable items to every cotton planter. To Virginia and the rest of the South this bill would be ruinous.

> . . . But, sir [he concluded], I do not press that view of the subject. I know that here we are too weak to resist or to defend ourselves; those who sympathize with our wrongs are too weak to help us; those who are strong enough to help us do not sympathize with our wrongs, or whatever we may suffer under it. No, sir; this bill will pass. And let it pass into the statute-book; let it pass into history, that we may know how it is that the South has been dealt with when New England and Pennsylvania had the power to deal with her interests.[13]

A week later an amended version of the Morrill Tariff passed the Senate by a vote of 25 to 14, the opposition coming exclusively from Southerners and western Democrats.[14] The House ultimately concurred in the amendments of the upper chamber, but not until it had given another illustration of the depths of sectional antagonisms and the inconsistency of northern compromisers. Representative Sickles of New York City reflected the views of the merchants when he protested that this bill would further alienate the South from the Union, for "our southern friends perceive that . . . you intend . . . to tax them on the

[12] *Congressional Globe*, 46, 518–21, 1051–53.   [13] *Ibid.*, 898–905.
[14] *Ibid.*, 1065.

necessaries of life in order to enrich the manufacturing classes of the North. . . ." Again the refutation came from a conservative Pennsylvania Democrat, Jacob K. McKenty, who blamed the southern low-tariff policy for the defeat of his party in the last election. After McKenty had finished, Roger Pryor of Virginia delivered a blistering tirade against the "dogmatic school of [Henry C.] Carey." ". . . The importunate protectionists of Pennsylvania [he cried], . . . after higgling successively with every party for a stipend from the Treasury, at last caught the Republicans in a moment of exigent need, and from their lust for place, extorted the promise of a bounty to iron. This bill is the issue of a carnal coalition between the Abolitionists of New England and the protectionists of Pennsylvania." McKenty's reply to Pryor was more bitter than that of any Republican, and he concluded with a significant confession: "I am here to represent the interests of Pennsylvania." [15] The passage of the Morrill Tariff was a blow to border-state Unionists, but it brought joy to Pennsylvanians, both compromising Democrats and "stiff-backed" Republicans. Buchanan must have redeemed himself a little in his home state when, like a loyal son, he signed the new revenue law.

Thus not one iota of what Southerners considered "discriminatory legislation" was relinquished, and a higher tariff was added to their list of grievances. The program of compromise urged by the northern business community fell far short of a real attempt to grapple with the fundamental economic aspects of sectional conflict. The position of the Bell-Everett Boston *Courier* was quite representative of this group. That paper wanted to be generous in granting new guarantees to slavery in the territories and states, but it specifically rejected every proposal to alter the basic economic relationship between North and South. Concession here, it felt, was unthinkable. "The opinions held by many at the South," it concluded unctuously, "on the subject of the fishing bounties, the tariff and the navigation-laws, are special and sectional, not American." [16]

A few of the northern conciliators were surprisingly honest in admitting the emptiness of the concessions they offered the South. One, for example, thought it was harmless "to yield a little on

[15] *Ibid.*, 1151-52, 1190-91.   [16] Boston *Daily Courier*, November 24, 1860.

matters which will in no way affect our prosperity." [17] Similarly the Democratic Chicago *Post* felt that it was precisely because the North was now "master of the Union, dictator of the nation, ruler of this great American empire" that she could "afford to be profuse in her bounties to the comparatively weak and powerless South." [18] The trouble was that southern secessionists understood this game only too well; they had no desire to compromise the shell while the North held securely to the kernel. In short, they were unwilling to beg for small favors from the "master of the Union" so long as a chance remained to escape northern mastery entirely.

2

The tariff and other manifestations of the South's disadvantageous economic position, although fundamental aspects of the sectional conflict, were too cold and complex to dominate the minds of average Americans. Instead, attention was centered upon slavery, the most explosive issue dividing the nation and the focal point among many sectional irritants. That most Northerners were willing to make further concessions to the South's peculiar institution seemed, then, to be an auspicious sign. But the compromisers always needed to remember that they required the support of a fraction of the Republicans. Whenever they tried to grant more than conservative Republicans would yield, they were reduced to a minority.

It was important, therefore, to find out just how much the moderate followers of Lincoln were willing to concede. From their record in Congress, their private correspondence, and their newspaper organs it appeared that these "weak-kneed" Republicans approved the repeal of northern personal-liberty laws, compensation to Southerners for fugitive slaves which could not be recovered, and a constitutional amendment guaranteeing slavery in the states. There were probably enough of them to constitute a northern majority in favor of the admission of New Mexico or the organization of all the territories into states. Possibly most

17 J. W. Foster to McClellan, January 31, 1861, McClellan Papers.
18 *Daily Chicago Post*, January 30, 1861.

Northerners would have agreed to the re-establishment of the Missouri Compromise line in existing territories. But this last proposition certainly would have reached the limit beyond which practically no moderate Republican would have gone. Hence it was as much as any majority of Northerners could have been persuaded to accept.

And so the chance for a slavery compromise collapsed when Southerners indicated that none of these concessions was enough, indeed that all of them together were still not enough. The politicians from the Deep South treated every proposition approved by conservative Republicans with the utmost contempt, and even many of those from the upper South expressed their dissatisfaction. Some of the latter, for example, voted with the Republican majority in the House to table the bill to admit New Mexico.[19] Senators such as Mason and Hunter of Virginia, Green of Missouri, and Johnson of Arkansas asserted that neither the amendment to protect slavery in the states nor the recommendations of the Peace Conference would succeed in preserving the Union.[20] Thus every plan of adjustment that could command a majority in the North was denounced by most Southerners as inadequate. How ironic, then, that "stiff-backed" Republicans should have attacked their conciliatory colleagues so violently for favoring concessions that came nowhere near appeasing the South! In reality moderates such as Seward, Cameron, Sherman, Kellogg, and Adams were no closer to a satisfactory understanding with the southern-rights men than were radicals such as Sumner, Wade, and Chandler.

The only slavery compromise that had an outside chance of satisfying Southerners was Crittenden's. It was his plan that congressmen from the upper South demanded when they denounced the others; unquestionably it would have been acceptable to most of the people in the slave states that had not seceded. It was at least conceivable that its passage would have started a reaction against secession leaders in the Deep South and thus prepared the way for eventual reunion. In fact the Crittenden compromise was the minimum prerequisite for the possible (but by no means certain) success of Seward's formula of voluntary reconstruction.

[19] *Congressional Globe*, 1326–27.   [20] *Ibid.*, 1305–18, 1331–33, 1386–1405.

And yet Seward voted against it, as did every Republican in Congress. Not a Republican governor, nor a Republican state legislature, nor any other prominent Republican politician ever endorsed Crittenden's amendments. Scarcely a handful among the party rank and file approved of them. Not even all northern Democrats and Bell men would concede so much. Letters from some of Crittenden's northern friends endorsed the principle of compromise but protested that he was going too far, and several Democrats in Congress expressed the same view.[21] Similarly the pro-Douglas Boston *Herald* rejected the Crittenden propositions as an "outrageous attempt to force slavery on a free people. It is more infamous than the late Breckinridge platform, and deserves to be hooted out of sight." [22] Thus with Republicans almost unanimously opposed, with at least a few of their opponents sharing their antipathy, it was evident that a majority of the northern people spurned the one adjustment of the slavery issue that might have cut the ground from under secession leaders.

A single clause in the first section of Crittenden's plan caused most of the controversy. There it was provided that slavery was to be recognized and protected south of the 36°–30' line not only in existing territories but also in those "*hereafter acquired.*" To proslavery leaders that was the nub of the whole matter; it was that provision alone which promised some ultimate advantage to the South, and Crittenden's compromise was the only one to include it. Most Southerners agreed that there was little chance for slavery to enter any of the remaining territories, that probably even New Mexico would ultimately be lost to them. But this was the age of the Spread Eagle and Manifest Destiny when Americans generally took for granted the eventual annexation of such areas as Cuba, Mexico, and Central America. And it was precisely in these anticipated acquisitions that the question of slavery expansion would become something more than an abstraction. It was there that the South might find new opportunities for growth and, equally im-

[21] See, for example, speech of Representative Isaac N. Morris of Illinois, *ibid.*, Appendix, 56.

[22] Boston *Herald*, February 8, 9, 12, 1861. See also Providence *Daily Post*, November 27, 1860; W. S. Holman to Hamilton, January 11, 1861, Hamilton Papers, Indiana State Library.

portant, the chance to re-establish a sectional balance in the national Congress. Southern imperialists looked in that direction for their salvation.[23]

Crittenden never seemed to appreciate how vital the "hereafter" clause actually was. In fact it had originally been added to his compromise upon the suggestion of Senator Lazarus W. Powell of Kentucky. Crittenden accepted the amendment, but he did not regard it as especially important and several times offered to drop it.[24] But Southerners repeatedly asserted that without this provision for further expansion his compromise would be as worthless as the rest.[25] Senator Green of Missouri had the same desire in mind when he demanded the protection of slavery in the new territory of Colorado "simply to establish a rule of justice." [26] Representative James Wilson of Indiana was near the truth when he contended that Congress was exclusively "deliberating as to the future condition of territory not one inch of which we now own." [27] To Washburn of Wisconsin southern motives were obvious: ". . . The territorial question, so far as it relates to the territory we now have, is a question of no consequence whatever to the people of the South. . . . The [Crittenden] proposition is to adopt a constitutional amendment that shall recognize and guarantee slavery in territory hereafter to be acquired. . . . Southern gentlemen will in a moment yield up everything else that they clamor about, if we will only consent to that. . . . Gentlemen who suppose that they can take this territorial question out of Congress by admitting New Mexico, entirely misjudge what the territorial question is." [28]

But precisely because Northerners also believed in Manifest Destiny, most of them would not accept a compromise which surrendered in advance a rich empire to the South. A Massachusetts delegate to the Peace Conference warned that Southerners already had their eyes upon Mexico, that they desired to "annex her and all her neighbors," which to the North "would be lost

[23] See, for example, Charleston *Mercury*, February 28, 1860, quoted in Dumond, *Southern Editorials on Secession*, 40–48; Crenshaw, *Slave States in the Presidential Election of 1860*, 126, 195, 243–44, 288, 289–90.

[24] *Congressional Globe*, 403–404, 863, 865.

[25] See, for example, remarks of Toombs and Mason, *ibid.*, 270, 404.

[26] *Ibid.*, 639–45.   [27] *Ibid.*, Appendix, 132.   [28] *Ibid.*, 514.

forever." [29] Senator Wade pointed to the "fair fields of Mexico" whose people feared southern aggression and might therefore "invite us to take a protectorate over them." [30] The Crittenden plan would convert the United States into "a great slave-breeding and slave-extending empire"; it would "make Slavery the rule and Freedom the exception." Equally alarming, it would result "in the acquisition and admission of new slave States" to restore "the equilibrium of the sections." [31] In short, the "hereafter" clause might threaten the North's political supremacy and exclude her from the regions into which national expansion was most likely to proceed. This was the crucial point to nearly every northern critic.

Finally, Crittenden's opponents saw in his compromise an invitation to southern filibustering on a grand scale. Remembering the recent enterprises against Cuba and Nicaragua, they had no desire to stimulate their repetition by posting rewards "right in the bosom of the Constitution itself!" Most Yankees would never agree "thus to guarantee to slavery all the territory which can be stolen or bought or conquered on our southern border." [32] As Representative Roscoe Conkling saw it, the Crittenden plan ". . . would amount to a perpetual covenant of war against every people, tribe, and State owning a foot of land between here and Terra del Fuego. It would make the Government the armed missionary of slavery. Eternal quarrels would be picked across the frontier lines, the Government must protect its citizens and demand indemnity for hostilities; and thus, for purposes of land-stealing and slave-planting, we should be launched upon a shoreless and starless sea of war and filibustering." [33] Accordingly, many argued that this compromise would not produce a final peaceful settlement of the crisis; rather it would be an eternal source of

[29] George S. Boutwell, *Reminiscences of Sixty Years in Public Affairs* (New York, 1902), I, 280.

[30] *Congressional Globe,* 99–104.

[31] John Jay to Sumner, February 4, 1861, Sumner Papers; *Morning Courier and New-York Enquirer* ("Washington Correspondence"), January 10, 1861; Grimes to Governor Samuel J. Kirkwood, January 28, 1861, quoted in Salter, *Grimes,* 133–34.

[32] *Morning Courier and New-York Enquirer* ("Washington Correspondence"), January 10, 1861; Bangor *Daily Whig and Courier,* February 9, 1861; August Belmont to Douglas, December 31, 1860, Douglas Papers.

[33] *Congressional Globe,* 651.

trouble, as each section would vie with the other for new fields of political and economic conquest.

Thus the "hereafter" clause was at once the greatest hope for southern reconciliation and the point at which northern compromisers lost command of their own people. Once again great numbers of Yankees were innocently or deliberately guilty of a deception. On the surface they seemed willing to concede much to slavery, but none of their concessions actually promised to release the South from its minority position. Only the Crittenden compromise held out the hope of restoring the political balance between the sections. And the northern majority by rejecting it stood firm on the only territorial question that really mattered: the status of territories "hereafter acquired."

3

For a few brief hours on January 12 a spirit of cautious optimism permeated Washington. An expectant crowd packed the gallery of the Senate, and those unable to get seats milled about the Capitol corridors and grounds. On the Senate floor, attendance was exceptionally full and the members uncommonly attentive. This was the day when the "premier" of the incoming administration was to break his silence and address his colleagues on the national crisis. This was the day when many believed, or hoped, that Senator Seward would somehow save the Union. The *Star of the West* had just returned from Charleston Harbor, the cotton states were busy with their secession conventions, and angry Northerners were clamoring for the enforcement of the laws. But sectional leaders paused long enough to learn what remedy had been devised by this masterful New Yorker, upon whom, it appeared, hinged the last chance for peace.

But soon after Seward had finished his speech the feeling of hope gave way to the disappointing realization that the situation was essentially as it had been before. For all his silken words and calm reassurances the Union had not been saved or permanent peace established. Scarcely any but Seward's friends among the moderate Republicans were altogether pleased with his performance; the reactions of others varied only in the quality and degree of their displeasure. The result could hardly have been otherwise, for his speech was designed to advance his own formula of delay and voluntary reconstruction. Accordingly, it was conciliatory without actually conceding anything. Its essence was embraced in a single concluding sentence: "Soon enough, I trust, for safety, it will be seen that sedition and violence are only local and temporary, and that loyalty and affection to the Union are the natural sentiments of the whole country." [34] To radicals this was weak, to northern and border-state compromisers it was evasive, and to secessionists it was sheer treachery.

Radical Republicans were furious because Seward expressed a readiness to accept the repeal of personal-liberty laws, the adoption of an amendment to protect slavery in the states, and the granting of statehood to the remaining territories. Northern Democrats and border-state Unionists, however, considered these shallow gestures as little better than no concessions at all. Nor was their faith in Seward strengthened because he had also suggested a constitutional convention to meet several years hence when present passions had cooled. They generally agreed that "he might as well not have spoken," for he proposed "nothing—literally nothing." Many were simply perplexed by his vagaries: "Mr. Seward is of the Talleyrand school—and he needs an interpreter." [35]

Southerners discovered the sinister quality of his speech in the coercion threat which lurked amid its pleasantries. Seward had vowed that he never would accept "unopposed separation," that no state had power to absolve its people from their allegiance to the Union, and that Congress had the duty "to supply the President with all the means necessary to maintain the Union. . . ." A few weeks later secessionists saw another ominous sign when Seward presented the compromise petition of the New York merchants to the Senate. Without endorsing their petition, he paid flattering tribute to their patriotism and advised them to exhibit it "by speaking for the Union, by voting for the Union, and if it should be demanded, by lending and even giving money for the

[34] *Ibid.*, 341–44.
[35] Detroit *Free Press*, January 15, 1861; Philadelphia *Morning Pennsylvanian*, January 14, 1861; New York *Herald*, January 13, 1861; Columbus *Daily Ohio Statesman*, January 16, 1861.

Union, and fighting in the last resort for the Union. . . ." Senator Mason made a heated reply in which he attempted to expose Seward as a coercionist. When he had finished, Seward confessed with unusual candor: If at last "this Union is to stand or fall by the force of arms, I have advised my people to do, as I shall be ready to do myself: stand in the breach, and stand with it or perish with it." After that, Mason concluded with an air of resignation that war was inevitable; for Seward, after all, would not admit the *fact* of disunion.[36]

That was precisely the trouble: Seward neither recognized the right of secession nor yielded anything that was really fundamental. His northern friends praised his speech not as a settlement of sectional issues but as shrewd politics, a brilliant tactical maneuver against southern leaders. Or they defended it because it might encourage southern Unionists without departing from the principles of the Chicago platform.[37] As they saw it, "his propositions . . . seem at first sight to yield more than they prove to give up upon examination of them." They were "intended to gain time." [38] Some of Seward's defenders even interpreted the speech as a coercion document, a solemn promise that the laws would be enforced and the Union preserved. "If I were a disunionist," confessed one admirer, "I should say there was cats claws in all that soft fur." [39]

Thus Seward gave evidence that much of the appeasement talk of moderate Republicans was nothing but an ingenious ruse. The real purpose behind the conciliatory gestures of many of them was not to save the Union by compromise but to gain some strategic advantage over the secessionists. Seward's motive was to undermine them by encouraging a resurgence of Unionism in the South. His voting record in Congress showed his real position; he assured his wife (who was strongly opposed to concessions and evidently worried about her husband) that she need have no fear of his proposing a compromise.[40]

[36] *Congressional Globe*, 657–59.
[37] Boston *Daily Advertiser*, January 14, 15, 16, 1861.
[38] Charles E. Norton to Sumner, January 18, 1861, Sumner Papers; Bancroft, *Seward*, II, 16–17.
[39] Nath Vose to E. B. Washburne, January 27, 1861, E. B. Washburne Papers; *Morning Courier and New-York Enquirer*, January 14, 15, 16, 1861.
[40] Seward, *Seward at Washington*, II, 478–79.

To Seward, Weed, Adams, and numerous others a second objective of moderation was to bid for the support of the border slave states. It was a device to split the South, to isolate the secessionists, and to gain an ally for the North. Adams had this idea in mind when he sponsored the bill to admit New Mexico.[41] Repeatedly these conservatives offered to satisfy every "reasonable" demand of the border states and simultaneously agreed with the New York *Courier and Enquirer* when it said: "For the *Rebels* in the 'Cotton States,' we have no terms to offer either of conciliation or compromise." [42] Senator Edward D. Baker of Oregon desired an adjustment with the upper South because he thought it would be simple to suppress an insurrection in the cotton regions but far more difficult to coerce fifteen united slave states.[43] Weed's editorial policy in the Albany *Evening Journal* also grew partly out of his desire to narrow the boundaries of rebellion rather than from any hope of pleasing disunionists.[44]

Another result conservative Republicans sought to achieve was the consolidation of northern public opinion. They were convinced that their section could not be wholly united for the defense of the Union unless its record was clear and secessionists were forced to assume the responsibility for repelling friendly overtures. "Let us set ourselves right in the judgment of the world," wrote Weed, or there would be "a divided North and a united South." [45] This was the reason why many Republicans saw the wisdom of appointing delegates to the Peace Conference. Its work would not "amount to a row of pins, . . . [but] traitors . . . would use the refusal to send [delegates] against us with unsuspecting people. . . ." [46] A correspondent of Trumbull argued that some proposition had to be made to the South, because ". . . It would put the North right upon the record. It would place them in a position in which they could confidently appeal

[41] Adams, "Secession Winter," *loc. cit.*, 668–69, 674–77; *Morning Courier and New-York Enquirer*, February 2, 1861.

[42] *Ibid.*, January 23, 1861; Indianapolis *Daily Journal*, December 5, 7, 8, 1860.

[43] *Congressional Globe*, 1383–86.

[44] Barnes (ed.), *Memoir of Thurlow Weed*, 315–17; Brummer, *New York during the Period of the Civil War*, 106 n.

[45] Weed to Preston King, December 10, 1860, quoted in Barnes (ed.), *Memoir of Thurlow Weed*, 309.

[46] Th. Jayne to Trumbull, February 1, 1861, Trumbull Papers; Boston *Daily Advertiser*, January 30, 1861.

for moral support to the opinion of all candid men, to the sentiment of the civilized world, and to the enlightened judgment of
posterity. It would put at rest the charges of Northern aggression
and fix the responsibility of our calamities where they belong. It
would deprive the South of the countenance of their allies at the
North. . . ." [47]

The urgency of such a policy was made evident by the demands
of northern anti-Republicans that their section's hands be clean
if force were to be used against the South. Numerous Democratic
newspapers promised that thousands of their party associates
would agree to fight for the Union when "they are fully assured
that every guarantee which the South can in justice demand, or
the North in honor concede, has been proffered and rejected." [48]
A convention of Ohio Democrats warned: Not until "the people
of the North shall have fulfilled their duties to the Constitution
and the South . . . will it be proper for them to take into consideration the question of the right and propriety of coercion." [49]
The plea of Massachusetts conservatives for the repeal of the state
personal-liberty law contained the same admonition: "When we
have done altogether right ourselves, we can firmly demand all
that is due from others, and calmly abide whatever consequences
may ensue from insisting upon that demand." [50] Moderate Republicans had these men in mind when they showed sympathy for
conciliation. In a real sense their aim was to appease their northern
critics more than their southern foes.

Still another ill-concealed purpose behind the reassuring talk of
this Republican minority was to procrastinate, to hold off any
decisive action until after the inauguration of Lincoln. Senator
Dixon of Connecticut doubted that there was "the slightest pos-

[47] C. B. Custiss to Trumbull, December 10, 1860, Trumbull Papers. See also
Thomas Ewing, Jr., to Hugh Ewing, January 17, 1861, Thomas Ewing Papers,
Library of Congress; D. J. Hooker to Cameron, February 1, 1861, Cameron
Papers; New York *Times,* December 10, 1860.
[48] Philadelphia *Press,* January 12, 1861; *Daily Chicago Post,* January 30, 1861;
Boston *Herald,* November 26, 1860; Providence *Daily Post,* February 8, 14, 1861;
Montpelier *Vermont Patriot and State Gazette,* January 12, 1861. For similar
sentiments in a Bell paper see New York *Morning Express,* January 10, 12, 18, 21,
1861.
[49] Columbus *Daily Ohio Statesman,* January 24, 1861.
[50] "To the Citizens of Massachusetts," copy in Benjamin R. Curtis Papers, Library of Congress.

sibility of any compromise *of any kind*," but he firmly believed that "we ought to *gain time* by conciliatory measures & sentiments." [51] Adams "advocated the appointment of committees and the summoning of conferences,—the presentation and discussion of schemes,—anything, in fact, which would consume time and preserve the peace, until the interregnum should end." [52] Many moderates attended the Peace Conference with the same motive and echoed Chase's slogan of "Inauguration first—adjustment afterwards." [53] There they found the proposition to call a national convention at some future date the most useful dilatory device, and they sponsored it as an alternative to any specific settlement.

But none exceeded the deception practiced by those conservative Republicans who offered concessions which they knew had no substance to them and which would still leave the North in control of the territories and general national policy. The New York *Times*, for example, saw no need for Congress to prohibit slavery in the existing territories now that an antislavery administration was about to dominate the executive department. So long as the government made no open attempt to propagate slavery "every foot of the public domain will be converted into Free States by the free choice of those who are destined to settle on it." [54] John Sherman had no fears about organizing all the territories into states, because he was convinced that such a measure "would admit 8 *free* States and hence settle in favor of freedom. . . ." [55] As both Seward and Weed viewed it, the Slave Power was crushed by the election of Lincoln. "I implore you to remember that the battle for Freedom has been fought and won," Seward told a delegation of citizens from Illinois. "Henceforth

[51] James Dixon to Welles, December 22, 1860; January 2, 1861, Welles Papers. See also James C. Conkling to E. B. Washburne, December 29, 1860, E. B. Washburne Papers; W. Jayne to Trumbull, January 21, 1861, Trumbull Papers.
[52] Charles Francis Adams, Jr., *Charles Francis Adams* (Boston, 1900), 129–33; Adams, *Autobiography*, 73–75.
[53] Cincinnati *Daily Commercial*, February 2, 1861; John Jay to Sumner, February 7, 1861, Sumner Papers; Charles B. Going, *David Wilmot, Freesoiler* (New York, 1924), 562–70; Kenneth M. Stampp (ed.), "Letters from the Washington Peace Conference of 1861," *Journal of Southern History*, IX (1943), 395–403.
[54] New York *Times*, November 12; December 4, 1860.
[55] Sherman's notation at the bottom of a letter from J. C. Thompson, December 18, 1860, Sherman Papers.

forget that Freedom ever was in danger, and exert your best influence now to save the Union." [56] Seward had no more intention
of surrendering any essential portion of that victory than the most
ardent radical Republican. It was simply that to him moderation
and conciliation were the attributes of successful political generalship in the hour of triumph.

When at last the game was finished, all these devious motives
caused the sincere compromisers to feel a deep bitterness toward
the moderate Republicans. On the eve of Lincoln's inauguration
the New York *Herald* raged that their course had been "a fraud
and a cheat . . . a deliberate double game . . . to consolidate
the sentiment of the North." They had held out "delusive hopes
and expectations . . . to the border States, in order to gain
time. . . ." Seward was "a monstrous political charlatan," and
Weed's peace talk was but "a sham—a fraudulent trick, to aid his
master in bamboozling the border States. . . ." [57] Inevitably the
tortuous course of the moderates angered not only the radicals
and secessionists but also those who looked upon concession as a
solution to the crisis per se and not a mere device to gain something
else.

4

The cause of conciliation was undermined by the opposition of
secessionists and "stiff-backed" Republicans, by its dependence
upon moderate Republicans, most of whom deliberately betrayed
it, and by the reluctance or inability of contemporary Americans
to grapple with the deeper aspects of sectionalism. These factors
alone were enough to render powerless the compromise leaders,
but they met still another obstacle that scattered their forces at a
critical time. It seemed that even the logical and inevitable se-
quence of events during the disunion movement conspired to give
strength to the foes of appeasement.

During the crisis of 1850 the behavior of disaffected Southerners had not obstructed those who sought compromise. Then
the secessionists had committed no overt acts; their movement

[56] New York *Daily Tribune*, March 7, 1861; Barnes (ed.), *Memoir of Thurlow
Weed*, 303–304.
[57] New York *Herald*, March 2, 3, 1861.

eventually resolved itself into a southern convention at Nashville which formulated a specific list of demands. In 1860, however, the crisis took a different turn and developed with greater speed. There was no period of delay during which Congress and the nation could give their undivided attention to the problem of peaceful adjustment. In the Deep South, state conventions were called at once, ordinances of secession were passed, and more important, the necessary steps were taken to give reality to southern independence. All this occurred during the decisive months of December and January, and the result was that most Northerners were bursting with indignation at the very time that calm deliberation was needed if there were to be any hope of an amicable settlement. Every day brought some new seizure of national property or defiance of Federal laws, each of which provided the opponents of compromise with another opportunity for a diversion. To secessionists these acts were unavoidable unless they renounced their constitutional philosophy and accepted the shadow of independence without its substance. But they thereby deprived compromise leaders of the ability to hold the undivided attention and loyalty of their followers until it was too late.

Radical Republicans were not unaware of how the course of events was demoralizing their opponents. Carl Schurz, for example, predicted that "the force of circumstances" would "whip our weak brethren into line" and suggested ways to shift the discussion from compromise to other subjects. (His most arresting proposal was to start impeachment proceedings against Buchanan in order to "monopolize the attention of Congress and of the people" and "to drown the cry for a compromise." [58]) Horace Greeley seized upon each instance of southern "aggression" and waved it like a red flag in the faces of "sober, patriotic, conservative citizens, who do not regard Government as a farce." [59] To one critic the great interest of Republicans in military preparations looked "like hiding behind the glitter of war, to escape detection in refusing an amicable adjustment." [60]

Similarly the moderate Republicans were almost too eager to

[58] Schurz to J. F. Potter, December 24, 1860, in Bancroft (ed.), *Speeches, Correspondence, and Political Papers of Carl Schurz*, I, 172–75.

[59] New York *Daily Tribune*, January 4, 7, 1861.

[60] Columbus *Crisis*, January 31, 1861; Boston *Daily Courier*, January 29, 1861.

use the deeds of secessionists as an excuse for abandoning measures of appeasement. With a transparent feeling of relief the New York *Times* predicted that the loss of southern forts would "put an end to all attempts at conciliation,—to all thoughts of compromise, until they are again in possession of the Government of the United States." [61] Amos A. Lawrence, as did many others who had opposed Lincoln, believed that the "violence of the nullifiers" was the most important of the factors which "retard the reactionary movement." [62] The Democrats were no less offended than Republicans by secessionist attacks upon government property and resistance to Federal authority. Early in January they found little time to battle Republicans on the issue of compromise while they participated in the growing movement for the enforcement of the laws.

By February the first period of excitement had passed, and for a time there were relatively few incidents in the South to add to northern bitterness. Now the compromisers re-formed their lines and sought to revive their appeal. But by this time their position was hopeless. Congress was near adjournment, Lincoln was en route to Washington, and the inauguration of a new administration was not far away. Time was running out. A few weeks later as Lincoln stood before the Capitol reading the lines of his matchless inaugural address, the real friends of compromise suddenly realized that theirs was a lost cause. The new President was making it evident that he proposed to save the Union in some other way.

[61] New York *Times,* December 21, 1860; January 3, 1861. See also *Morning Courier and New-York Enquirer,* January 8, 1861; Boston *Daily Advertiser,* December 28, 1860; Indianapolis *Daily Journal,* January 17, 1861.

[62] Amos A. Lawrence to Crittenden, January 12, 1861, Crittenden Papers. See also Charles A. Davis to *id.,* January 7, 1861, *ibid.*

X

Mr. Lincoln Views the Crisis

I T W A S in February of 1861 that the American people first began really to know Abraham Lincoln. Most of them doubtless
remembered his recent debates with Douglas and his subsequent
national speaking tour which carried him as far as New England,
but he had nevertheless remained a secondary political figure
until his presidential nomination. Now, with a keen curiosity
thousands came to see and hear him in a score of cities and towns
during his slow and indirect journey to Washington; the rest read
his speeches and full descriptions of his appearance and behavior
in their newspapers. Despite the criticism of political opponents,
Lincoln seemed for the most part to please average Northerners,
perhaps because he acted and talked so much *like* an average
Northerner. In him they found the embodiment of the Yankee
middle-class spirit, the exponent of most of their cherished convictions. Mr. and Mrs. Lincoln, concluded a newspaperman who
saw them in Columbus, were perfect "representatives of the bour-
goise [*sic*], or citizen class of people. . . . If the idea represented
by these people can only be allowed to prevail in this government,
all will be well." [1]

It took a deep faith in the talents of the "citizen class of people"
to nourish even the hope that Lincoln might be able to cope with
the national crisis. The new President could not rely upon his national prestige, for he had little of that. He was, after all, merely
the "favorite son" of Illinois who had proved to be the most "available" candidate to the political traders at Chicago, the man behind
whom various groups had united to head off Seward. Nor could he

---

[1] Jefferson (Ohio) *Ashtabula Sentinel* (letter from editor William C. How-
ells), February 20, 1861. For a detailed and careful account of Lincoln's career
during the secession crisis see William E. Baringer, *A House Dividing: Lincoln
as President Elect* (Springfield, Ill., 1945).

capitalize upon the experience gathered from long participation in national politics, for that too was lacking. It was lacking, however, through no fault of his own; since early manhood this ambitious Springfield lawyer had been striving for public office. But his meager successes—four terms in the Illinois legislature and one undistinguished term in the House of Representatives—had scarcely compensated for the many disappointments and frustrations. His record had been little more than that of a local party hack until he suddenly tasted success and found himself elected to the highest office in the land. To all appearances he was utterly unprepared for his new responsibilities.

His strength could come from nowhere but within himself: from his native shrewdness, his instinctive feeling for trends in public opinion, above all, from his capacity for growth. The secession movement tested the sufficiency of these qualities and gave him his first real training in statecraft. By March of 1861 his mind had broken through the confines of Springfield and encompassed the whole country.

As he stepped gingerly upon the national stage Lincoln's inexperience was revealed at times by spells of irresolution or lack of self-confidence, at other times by impulsiveness or flippancy. Feeling his way through the crisis months he made mistakes, he was guilty of inconsistencies, and occasionally he showed startling gaps in his knowledge. These shortcomings would have been still more evident had he not determined at the time of his nomination to abstain from making public statements. Throughout the campaign, although Douglas went on an extended speaking tour, Lincoln remained quietly in Springfield. His letters to political associates were "private and confidential" and never for publication.

After the election, Lincoln continued his policy of silence. As the crisis deepened, the Democratic press attacked him violently for refusing to state his position and for failing to allay the excitement with a "generous Union speech." [2] To the pleas of letter writers and personal interviewers he simply replied that he was still only a private citizen and that it would be time enough for him to announce a program after March 4. His views on public ques-

[2] New York *Herald*, December 8, 1860.

tions, he explained, were to be found in his earlier speeches, where they could be read by all. He had not changed his ground since then and had no intention of changing. Simply to repeat himself to those who refused to listen would do no good, and it "would be wanting in self-respect, and would have an appearance of sychophancy and timidity which would excite the contempt of good men and encourage bad ones to clamor the more loudly." [3]

Those who went to the trouble of referring to Lincoln's record found him committed upon most of the issues which had been debated in recent years. They found him professing an intense nationalism and a thorough admiration for Henry Clay and his "American System": a friend of the tariff, sound banking, and a broad program of Federal aid to internal improvements. As a Westerner he advocated the homestead bill and a transcontinental railroad. He professed a deep belief in democracy, a confidence in the wisdom of the people and their capacity to govern themselves. Yet even in his age Lincoln was no social radical; for his was a belief in a democracy of property holders, in the virtues of the "citizen class of people." It was the "bourgeois" spirit of the American laboring man that he approved.

The President-elect's past attitude toward slavery made it evident that he was no "doctrinaire." To be sure, he was no apologist for Negro servitude; and he had wholeheartedly endorsed the Republican demand that it be confined to its present limits. Once, in his "House Divided" speech, he had even subscribed to the essence of the "irrepressible conflict" theory. But that was not typical; his debates with Douglas and later public statements were characterized by their conservatism. Not only did he confess the right of Southerners to hold their human property, but he admitted an obligation to respect the fugitive-slave law and denied any belief in racial equality. His position was, in fact, the lowest common denominator of the Republican antislavery creed. It was that of the majority of moderate, respectable, and "sound" Yankees.

A perusal of this record might well have reassured Northerners, but it was hardly calculated to calm the agitation in the South.

[3] *Ibid.* ("Springfield Correspondence"), November 11, 18, 1860; Nicolay and Hay (eds.), *Works of Lincoln*, VI, 68–69, 70–71, 74–75, 79–82.

Lincoln's ideas were essentially those that had been embodied in the Chicago platform, and it was the victory of that platform which had precipitated the secession movement. Anti-Republicans realized that a mere reiteration of such doctrines would not solve the problem; their demand for a statement from him was prompted by a desire to force him into a retreat. The President-elect, however, thoroughly understood their purpose and refused to fall into their trap.

But Lincoln's previous speeches provided few clues to his thoughts on the main issue before the American people after his election. What they wanted to know was how he proposed to deal with the secession movement. That was why his continued silence was so exasperating, why everyone was speculating or predicting what his course would be and seizing upon every rumor and newspaper report from Springfield. Even some of his close associates, like Herndon and Judge David Davis, confessed that they knew nothing of his plans.[4] Mr. Lincoln, remarked a newspaper correspondent, "keeps all people, his friends included, in the dark." He was "naturally sly as a fox and cunning as a weasel. Sharpened by legal practice and Western life . . . he humbugs all and is humbugged by none. . . . Mr. Lincoln promises nothing, but only listens." [5] With so many of his contemporaries utterly confused by his reticence it is not strange that a debate has waxed ever since over what it was that Lincoln intended to do.

2

Lincoln's reaction to the secession movement during the weeks before he left Springfield was revealed only in fragments, in fleeting glimpses through the screen which generally concealed his thoughts. Several times he exposed himself a little by sending advice in private letters to Republican leaders, or by suddenly blurting out some significant observation while conversing with friends. On rare occasions a newspaper reporter would elicit an incisive comment from him. Henry Villard, the shrewd and observant correspondent of the New York *Herald*, had relatively free access

[4] Angle (ed.), *Herndon's Lincoln*, 387, 408.
[5] New York *Herald*, February 27, 1861.

to him, and his daily letters were often more reliable than most of the "authoritative reports" from Springfield. But even Villard confessed that as a rule Lincoln "evaded answers to specific interrogatories, and confined himself to generalizations." [6] Finally, many contemporaries searched the columns of the *Illinois State Journal* for signs of what the President-elect was thinking. Because of the known intimacy between him and its editors there was a widespread assumption that they knew and expressed his views.[7] Although the *Journal* denied that Lincoln ever "dictated a line," the evidence is strong that he did have a hand in writing several of its most important editorials. And it did proclaim, with apparent justification, "When we assert anything positively respecting him or his intentions we know whereof we affirm." [8]

These scattered sources, then, provided what clues there were to the manner in which Lincoln evolved a policy for the crisis. Despite the gaps, they were sufficient to define a pattern in broad outline at least. They established the fact, for example, that not one of his responses was unique, and that he was unable to devise an original solution. Rather Lincoln shared or merely reflected the views of most Northerners, for he was being guided by and not controlling public opinion. Always he was careful to keep abreast of popular currents by listening to reports from his many visitors and by watching the trends in the northern press.[9]

Thus it was quite natural that, in November, Lincoln should have been optimistic and have doubted the seriousness of the southern movement. To him the commercial panic was entirely artificial, and he had no sympathy for the " 'respectable scoundrels' who got it up." His solution was simple: "Let them go to work and repair the mischief of their own making, and then perhaps they will be less greedy to do the like again." [10] Confident that the

[6] Henry Villard, *Memoirs of Henry Villard* (Boston, 1904), I, 140–47. Villard's Springfield letters are reprinted in Harold G. and Oswald Garrison Villard (eds.), *Lincoln on the Eve of '61* (New York, 1941).

[7] New York *Herald* ("Springfield Correspondence"), December 24, 27, 1860; Springfield (Mass.) *Daily Republican*, December 22, 1860; Cincinnati *Daily Commercial*, January 31, 1861; Baringer, *House Dividing*, 15, 19, 55–57, 215.

[8] Springfield *Daily Illinois State Journal*, quoted in Chicago *Daily Tribune*, February 16, 1861.

[9] New York *Herald* ("Springfield Correspondence"), December 4, 1860; Nicolay and Hay, *Lincoln*, III, 246–47.

[10] Nicolay and Hay (eds.), *Works of Lincoln*, VI, 68–69.

Unionists would soon regain control in the South, he faced events "with a philosophic calmness." When Lincoln met Vice-President–elect Hannibal Hamlin at Chicago late in November, Villard reported that they agreed that a "programme of 'masterly inactivity'" would be "strictly carried out." [11] Initially, at least, Lincoln seemed to have faith in Seward's formula for dealing with secession.

The events of late December, however, jolted Lincoln, like most other Northerners, into a growing realization of the gravity of the crisis. Although he maintained an outward serenity, he soon confessed privately that the future troubled him more than he felt it wise to show.[12] Perhaps the hoped-for reaction in the South would not occur and "masterly inactivity" would not be enough to save the Union; possibly a more drastic remedy would have to be applied. Lincoln never repudiated peaceful and voluntary reconstruction as a satisfactory and desirable solution, but it was quite evident that he calculated the increasing likelihood that his administration would be driven to pursue some other course. And failing to discover a new alternative, he was obliged to choose among the three that had come under general discussion.

Of these, Lincoln rejected two with scarcely any hesitation. The first, the recognition of southern independence, he never considered a practical remedy. He was too much of a nationalist and believed too thoroughly in the indestructibility of the Union to pay it even the lip service that some did.[13] Nothing stood out more distinctly in the record of the President-elect than his conviction that peaceful disunion was utterly impossible. After the southern states had adopted ordinances of secession, he asserted flatly that they were a nullity and that the nation remained an organic whole.[14] As a practical man he saw that the severing of the Union would cause a profound shock to the national economy and a serious loss of prestige to the party and leaders responsible for it.

[11] New York *Herald* ("Springfield Correspondence"), December 15, 1860.
[12] Nathaniel W. Stephenson, *Lincoln: An Account of His Personal Life* . . . (Indianapolis, 1922), 128.
[13] *Ibid.*, 142–43, 145.
[14] Lincoln expressed this opinion in his inaugural address. Nicolay and Hay (eds.), *Works of Lincoln*, VI, 169–85.

Whatever the consequences Southerners would have to continue their political affiliations with the North.

In a series of confidential letters to friends and critics Lincoln revealed that he was equally opposed to the second alternative: compromise. "I am not at liberty to shift my ground," he explained; "that is out of the question." On the territorial issue he was "inflexible," and he advised Republicans in Congress to "hold firm, as with a chain of steel." [15] Never did he indicate a desire to remove any of the sources of economic friction which had contributed so mightily to southern sectionalism. On other matters which involved no departure from the fundamentals of the Republican creed Lincoln was moderate enough. He referred to his past speeches for evidence that he would not interfere with slavery where it existed and that he would enforce the fugitive-slave law. He made no objection to the proposed amendment guaranteeing slavery in the states. As to personal-liberty laws, he would "be glad of their repeal." "Nor do I care much about [the admission of] New Mexico," he once wrote Seward, "if further extension were hedged against." [16] Thus he revealed his affiliation with Republican moderates who would respect the rights of the South. But he also showed that he would grant nothing more than what he considered due her under the Constitution, and that he did not include in this category the right to expand slavery. In short, Lincoln ruled out both compromise and peaceful disunion from the outset.

Why did the President-elect refuse to accept a compromise? His rationale was not always as precise as it might have been, but it generally resembled that advanced by other Republicans. He explained his opposition to Crittenden's or any other territorial adjustment on the familiar ground that it would encourage "filibustering for all South of us and making slave States of it." Within a year "we shall have to take Cuba as a condition upon which they will stay in the Union," and thus the nation would be "again on the highroad to a slave empire." [17] Several times Lincoln professed

[15] *Ibid.*, 70–71, 78–82, 93–94, 102–104; Tracy (ed.), *Uncollected Letters of Lincoln*, 171.

[16] Nicolay and Hay (eds.), *Works of Lincoln*, VI, 63–64, 66–67, 68–69, 70–71, 74–75, 79–82, 85–86, 87–89, 102–104, 119–21.

[17] *Ibid.*, 78–79, 82, 93–94, 102–104; Stephenson, *Lincoln*, 114–15; Emanuel Hertz, *Abraham Lincoln, A New Portrait* (New York, 1931), II, 795.

a belief that a new compromise would come no nearer solving the sectional conflict than previous ones, that more was to be gained by a decisive settlement of the questions of secession and slavery expansion. Besides, concessions won by the threat of disunion would mean "the destruction of the Government itself." "The tug has to come," he warned his political friends, "and better now than later." [18]

Other of Lincoln's statements suggested that either conscious or subconscious fear for the prestige of his administration and the danger of wrecking his party helped to mold his ideas upon compromise. On two occasions political supporters reported him as saying that before he would suffer the personal humiliation involved in proposals to "buy or beg a peaceful inauguration" he would "be hung by the neck till he was dead on the steps of the Capitol." [19] By backing down, he believed, Republicans would lose "everything we gain by the election"; it would be "the end of us." If the party were thus demoralized, "they have us under again: all our labor is lost, and sooner or later must be done over." [20] In a speech delivered in Kansas the previous year, Lincoln had shown that he understood the inevitable effect of compromise upon his party: "Simultaneously with such letting down the Republican organization would go to pieces, and half its elements would go in a different direction, leaving an easy victory to the common enemy." [21] Lincoln had no desire to contribute to such a result. Undoubtedly, in making this decision, he had utilized the politician's penchant for fusing in his own mind the interests of his party and those of the nation as a whole. He too may have been convinced that what was good for Republicans was good for everyone.

Of one thing Lincoln could be certain: that his hostility to compromise was not displeasing to the masses of Republicans, that any other course would have discredited him with his own supporters. His numerous callers, his wide correspondence, and the

[18] Nicolay and Hay (eds.), *Works of Lincoln*, VI, 77–78; Tracy (ed.), *Uncollected Letters of Lincoln*, 171; Hertz, *Lincoln*, II, 803.
[19] Th. Jayne to Trumbull, January 28, 1861, Trumbull Papers; New York *Daily Tribune*, February 8, 1861; Chicago *Daily Tribune*, February 12, 1861.
[20] Nicolay and Hay (eds.), *Works of Lincoln*, VI, 77–79, 82, 93–94; Hertz, *Lincoln*, II, 795; Tracy (ed.), *Uncollected Letters of Lincoln*, 171.
[21] Nicolay and Hay (eds.), *Works of Lincoln*, V, 274–75.

Republican press never let him forget what the party faithful thought of proposals to abandon the Chicago platform. Stout Republican organs, which Lincoln examined regularly, kept a constant pressure upon him; Greeley, Giddings, George G. Fogg of New Hampshire, and George W. Julian of Indiana were a few among the many leaders who visited Springfield to impart "any amount of backbone needed." [22] It was hardly surprising, therefore, that Lincoln once confessed a fear of losing "the confidence of our own friends." [23]

Only the third alternative remained, and this was the one which began to intrude upon Lincoln's mind in December. If events proved that state authorities in the South, supported by large bodies of disaffected citizens, seriously proposed to repudiate the basic powers of the Federal government, then it would be necessary to coerce obedience to the laws. Never did the President-elect, directly or indirectly, hint that the government could abstain from exercising such vital functions as collecting its revenues and holding its property. It was not that he regarded force as desirable in itself, or that he wished to provoke a war. Rather it was that he was profoundly impressed with the idea that there were points at which the government could not tolerate defiance without destroying itself, and that as President he would have an inescapable obligation to "enforce the laws." As a nationalist and a middle-class statesman he had a full appreciation of the worth of law and order and the value of the Union. These were public interests of prime importance, meriting defense and preservation by military power if they were menaced. Lincoln was no pacifist, and he gauged his course to conform with the generally accepted standards of "practical" statesmanship. In short, he *calculated* the possible necessity of coercion to maintain the Union. Whether or not the chance of a protracted civil war was part of his calculated risk there is no way of knowing. If it were, he was doubtless comforted by the belief that the responsibility would be upon those who resisted the performance of his simple duty as chief executive.

"The most distinctive element in Mr. Lincoln's moral composition," wrote Villard, "is his keen sense and comprehensive

[22] New York *Herald* ("Springfield Correspondence"), January 31; February 16, 1861.
[23] Nicolay and Hay (eds.), *Works of Lincoln*, VI, 94–95.

consciousness of duty. . . . That he will endeavor to fulfill the obligations . . . [of his oath of office] faithfully and fearlessly may be expected with the utmost certainty." [24] Just enough evidence survived to confirm the essential truth of Villard's assertion. As early as December 13 the President-elect stated privately his belief that the government had "the legal power, right, and duty of maintaining its own integrity," and that it was "the duty of the President to execute the laws and maintain the existing government." [25] A few days later he asked Representative Washburne to instruct General Scott "to be as well prepared as he can to either hold or retake the forts, as the case may require, at and after the inauguration." [26] Immediately after the secession of South Carolina, Lincoln assured friends that if the southern forts were occupied by disunionists, "my judgment is that they are to be retaken." [27] His response to the request of Governor-elect Curtin of Pennsylvania for advice regarding his inaugural address was equally pertinent: "I think of nothing proper for me to suggest except a word about this secession and disunion movement. On that subject, I think you would do well to express, without passion, threat, or appearance of boasting, but nevertheless, with firmness, the purpose of yourself, and your state to maintain the Union at all hazards. Also if you can, procure the Legislature to pass resolutions to that effect." [28]

In the early weeks of 1861 Lincoln gave no sign that these opinions had changed. The resolutions adopted by the Illinois legislature, demanding the preservation of the Union and pledging "the whole resources of the State . . . to the Federal authorities," were drawn by his own hand.[29] An editorial which appeared on January 22 in the *Illinois State Journal* and strongly called for the

[24] New York *Herald* ("Springfield Correspondence"), February 1, 1861.
[25] Nicolay and Hay, *Lincoln*, III, 249–51. See also Nicolay and Hay (eds.), *Works of Lincoln*, VI, 82.
[26] Nicolay and Hay (eds.), *Works of Lincoln*, VI, 84–85; Nicolay and Hay, *Lincoln*, III, 249–51.
[27] Nicolay and Hay (eds.), *Works of Lincoln*, VI, 86; Tracy (ed.), *Uncollected Letters of Lincoln*, 173; Ida M. Tarbell, *Life of Abraham Lincoln* (New York, 1900), I, 395–97; S. Noble to E. B. Washburne, December 17, 1860; [H.] Kreis[mann] to *id.*, December 27, 28, 1860, E. B. Washburne Papers.
[28] Paul M. Angle (ed.), *New Letters and Papers of Lincoln* (Boston, 1930), 260.
[29] Hertz, *Lincoln*, II, 809.

enforcement of the laws bore much evidence, as Villard noted, of being prepared "under the eyes of the President Elect," and it was accepted by many Republicans "as an authoritative exposition of Mr. Lincoln's views." [30] "I see the duty devolving upon me," he told an old friend, and added bitterly that he was "in the garden of Gethsemane now." [31] This duty, Orville H. Browning heard him explain, was "to maintain the Constitution and the Union," and in this purpose he was "entirely firm and decided." Browning recorded Lincoln's conclusion "that far less evil & bloodshed would result from an effort to maintain the Union and the Constitution, than from disruption and the formation of two confederacies[.]" [32]

In all this Lincoln did little more than echo popular sentiments among Northerners. If he betrayed a belief that all the power of the government must be used to preserve the Union and maintain its authority in the South, he merely accepted the responsibility which most Yankees felt would devolve upon him when he became chief executive. It was remarkable how universal throughout the North was the assumption that Lincoln would do whatever was necessary to hold or recapture Federal property and collect the revenues. Before the inauguration, his friends had promised that he would support a program of national vindication; any evidence of "weakness" or "timidity" would have utterly discredited him. Here was a potent force in shaping the thoughts of one as sensitive to the drift of public opinion as Lincoln.

3

On February 11, Lincoln began his northern tour which would carry him to Washington in time for the inauguration. Soon, he told his Springfield friends in a brief and sentimental farewell address, he would face a task "greater than that which rested upon Washington." [33] Doubtless it was more than the sorrow of leaving home that caused him to speak with such solemnity. His mind

[30] New York *Herald* ("Springfield Correspondence"), January 28, 1861.
[31] Tarbell, *Lincoln*, I, 405–407.
[32] Theodore C. Pease and James G. Randall (eds.), *The Diary of Orville Hickman Browning* (Springfield, Ill., 1927), I, 453–54.
[33] Nicolay and Hay (eds.), *Works of Lincoln*, VI, 110–11.

must have been burdened with the weight of events occurring in the South: the appropriation of Federal property and revenues, the threatening military preparations, especially the rapid organization of a Confederate government at Montgomery. Confronted by these developments, Lincoln retained little of his earlier confidence that voluntary reconstruction would solve the southern problem. It appeared far more likely that force—the only alternative he accepted—would have to be applied. And now he was no longer able to maintain his silence; the time had come for him to disclose his intentions.

When Lincoln began his journey he realized the need to speak circumspectly, not only to explain what he must do, but to say it in precisely the right way. To threaten the South bluntly with military coercion would have been foolhardy and tactless. That might easily have precipitated a disastrous crisis before the inauguration, whereas it was obviously desirable to delay decisive action until the new administration had been peacefully organized. Besides, such threats would have alienated many northern Democrats whose Unionism could otherwise add strength to the government.[34] Fortunately for Lincoln, he understood and evidently shared the prevailing northern belief that there was an immense difference between the hostile invasion or coercion of seceded states and a simple enforcement of the laws. He appreciated the vital importance of informing his listeners that it was the latter and not the former which he considered an inherent power of the government.

Lincoln also saw the need to utilize the northern concept of "defense," to emphasize that if war came the South must be the aggressor and assume the burden of striking the first blow. It had to be explained that the government would only defend its property and revenues, that it would patiently abstain from exercising less essential functions, and that Federal armies would not be marched into the South to overawe its citizens. This strategy of defense, a simple device whereby the initiative was thrown to the secessionists, became Lincoln's basic approach to his problem.

[34] For significant comments upon this problem see New York *Herald* ("Springfield Correspondence"), January 25, 1861; "The Diary of a Public Man: Unpublished Passages of the Secret History of the American Civil War," *North American Review*, CXXIX (1879), 139.

Again it required care to select the exact phrases which conveyed this purpose to the northern people. In short, he favored neither "coercion" nor "aggression" but only "enforcement of the laws" and "defense" of the Union.

Lincoln could hardly be credited with originality for advancing these ideas about the crisis. Large bodies of Yankees had spontaneously advocated both nonaggressive law enforcement and the strategy of defense.[35] The Republican press had already promised that Lincoln's efforts to preserve the Union would conform with these principles. The New York *Times* predicted that the new administration would not "declare war against the seceding States" nor would it "send armies to coerce them into availing themselves of the benefits of United States Courts [or] Federal Post Offices." Duties on imports, however, the President would have to collect, even if it required the use of "the entire naval force of the Union." "In this condition of affairs," the *Times* concluded, "the seceding States will find themselves in a dilemma— they must either admit their scheme of disunion to be a failure, or *must themselves declare war against the General Government*." The New York *Courier and Enquirer* outlined the same course and vowed that it would be impossible for "any reasonable man . . . to discover 'Coercion' in this proceeding." The new President would "quietly remain upon the *defensive*, ready to repel any assault which Rebels and Traitors may make upon the Union."[36] Thus if secessionists imposed upon Lincoln the necessity of using force, the Republican press had shown him how to cast coercion in the mold of "defense" and to shift the responsibility for consequences to his "dissatisfied fellow-countrymen."

During his trip to Washington the central theme of Lincoln's public utterances was the further development and clarification of the strategy of defense. Holding inflexibly to the view that his fundamental objective must be the preservation of the Union, he chose his words carefully and shrewdly to avoid any basis for charging him with aggression. Shrewd realist that he was, he recognized that hostilities might ensue, and he seemed preoccupied with an intense desire to leave the record clear, to make it evident

[35] See Chapter III.
[36] New York *Times*, December 21, 1860; *Morning Courier and New-York Enquirer*, February 1, 1861.

to his listeners that conflict could be initiated only by the South. Lincoln, however, was not consciously and deliberately plotting to deceive the northern people, for they had already deceived themselves. He merely avoided antagonizing them as he explained what he sincerely believed would be his duty as President.

Indianapolis was Lincoln's first stop. There he was greeted by the roar of thirty-four rounds of artillery, a great throng of Hoosiers, and an impressive delegation of state and city dignitaries. At the depot Governor Morton welcomed him with a short and pointed speech. He made a fervent appeal to Lincoln to accept his responsibility "to maintain the Union, promote national prosperity and restore peace to our distracted and unhappy country." (Significantly, even the warlike Morton could define his desired program as one calculated to "restore peace.") In an extemporaneous reply Lincoln modestly referred to himself as "an accidental instrument . . . of a great cause." He assured Morton that in his plea for the Union "you have my hearty sympathy, and, as far as may be within my power, will have . . . my hearty cooperation." Finally, he placed the issue squarely in the hands of the American people: "It is your business to rise up and preserve the Union and liberty for yourselves, and not for me. I appeal to you again to constantly bear in mind that not with politicians, not with Presidents, not with office-seekers, but with you, is the question: shall the Union and shall the liberties of this country be preserved to the latest generations." [37]

That night, from the balcony of the Bates House, Lincoln made a second brief address. But this one was no extemporaneous affair; rather it was his "keynote," his most important and forthright speech before the inaugural. [38]

> . . . The words "coercion" and "invasion" [he began] are much used in these days, and often with some temper and hot blood. Let us make sure, if we can, that we do not misunderstand the meaning of those who use them. . . . What, then, is "coercion"? What is "invasion"? Would the marching of an army into South Carolina without the consent of her people, and with hostile intent toward them, be "invasion"? I certainly

[37] Indianapolis *Daily Journal*, February 12, 1861; Nicolay and Hay (eds.), *Works of Lincoln*, VI, 111-12.

[38] John G. Nicolay, *The Outbreak of Rebellion* (New York, 1881), 48.

think it would; and it would be "coercion" also if the South Carolinians were forced to submit. But if the United States should merely hold and retake its own forts and other property, and collect the duties on foreign importations, or even withhold the mails from places where they were habitually violated, would any or all of these things be "invasion" or "coercion"? Do our professed lovers of the Union, but who spitefully resolve that they will resist coercion and invasion, understand that such things as these on the part of the United States would be coercion or invasion of a State? If so, their idea of means to preserve the object of their great affection would seem to be exceedingly thin and airy.

The President-elect brought forth a loud laugh from his audience when he finished by remarking with pointed humor, "I am not asserting anything; I am merely asking questions for you to consider." [39]

After many weeks of silence Lincoln had defined his position with such sudden clarity as almost to cause a national sensation. The conservative Washington *National Intelligencer* refused to believe that he had made such a speech and hopefully suggested that he might have been misquoted in that day of "sensation intelligence." [40] To Southerners like Representative Garnett of Virginia it was the equivalent of a "declaration of war." [41] The New York *Herald* interpreted the address as "the signal for massacre and bloodshed by the incoming administration." [42] But the "stiff-backed" Republicans were jubilant. "This little speech," exulted Joseph Medill of the Chicago *Tribune*, "has electrified the true Republicans and given the fishy ones 'fever and ague.' . . . They see fight in the old fellow's eye." [43] Most moderate Republicans also approved the address and made no effort to discount its sig-

[39] Indianapolis *Daily Journal*, February 12, 1861; Nicolay and Hay (eds.), *Works of Lincoln*, VI, 112–15.
[40] Washington *Daily National Intelligencer*, February 14, 1861.
[41] *Congressional Globe*, 893.
[42] New York *Herald*, February 13, 14, 1861; Philadelphia *Morning Pennsylvanian*, February 13, 19, 1861.
[43] Chicago *Daily Tribune* (letter from "Chicago"), February 16, 1861. See also *ibid.*, February 18, 1861; New York *Daily Tribune*, February 13, 1861; New York *Evening Post*, February 13, 15, 16, 18, 1861; G. W. Ashley to Schouler, February 17, 1861, Schouler Papers; Jas. H. Barrett to Wade, February 19, 1861, Wade Papers; James C. Conkling to Trumbull, February 12, 1861; L. B. Comins to *id.*, February 15, 1861, Trumbull Papers.

nificance. The New York *Times* saw that Lincoln maintained "the right and duty of the Government to enforce its laws, to hold its forts, and take such steps as may most effectually defeat all resistance to its authority." Nor did the *Times* doubt that he would "make this belief the basis of his action as President." [44]

Having proclaimed his determination to "enforce the laws," Lincoln thereafter stressed the point that secessionists would be the aggressors if this should result in war. At Cincinnati he reassured the South that its rights would be respected, and thus he denied that self-defense could be a rational cause for disunion.[45] That being the case, he insisted innocently at Columbus and Pittsburgh, there was "no crisis but an artificial one," there was "nothing that really hurts anybody," "nothing to justify the course they are pursuing." [46] Repeatedly he emphasized his determination to defend the Union.[47] He assured the legislature of New Jersey that no man lived who was "more devoted to peace" than he; yet it might be necessary "to put the foot down firmly." This renewed expression of firmness brought wild applause from the lawmakers of both parties, and another cheer went up when Lincoln concluded: "And if I do my duty and do right, you will sustain me, will you not?" [48]

But it was in the final series of speeches at Philadelphia and Harrisburg that Lincoln expounded most clearly his defensive concept. In these he expressed the distaste with which he contemplated "the possibility that a necessity may arise in this country for the use of the military arm," and he promised "that so far as I may have wisdom to direct, if so painful result shall in any wise be brought about, it shall be through no fault of mine." He could see in the "present aspect of affairs . . . no need of bloodshed and war. . . . I am not in favor of such a course; and I may say in advance that there will be no bloodshed unless it is forced upon the gov-

[44] New York *Times*, February 13, 1861. See also New York *World*, February 14, 1861; Boston *Daily Advertiser*, February 16, 1861; Providence *Daily Journal*, February 15, 1861; Trenton *Daily State Gazette and Republican*, February 19, 1861; Indianapolis *Daily Journal*, February 12, 1861.
[45] Nicolay and Hay (eds.), *Works of Lincoln*, VI, 119.
[46] *Ibid.*, 121–22, 124–29.   [47] *Ibid.*, 145–52.
[48] *Ibid.*, 152–54. For an eyewitness account of Lincoln's appearance before the New Jersey legislature see Richard B. Duane to Anderson, February 21, 1861, Anderson Papers.

ernment. The government will not use force, unless force is used against it." [49]

Up to this point Lincoln had been received everywhere by enthusiastic crowds, and the response to his speeches had generally been favorable. But the manner of his appearance in Washington on February 23 threatened to nullify the good impression he had made. Reports of a plot to assassinate him in Baltimore caused him to yield reluctantly to the advice of friends and make the rest of his trip to the capital in secret. The news of his arrival in this undignified fashion had a depressing effect upon public opinion. It exposed him to ridicule and to a charge of cowardice, and it weakened confidence in his strength of character. "We feel humiliated to the last degree by it," complained Governor Blair of Michigan, who expressed the general dismay of Republicans.[50] The psychological effect of this incident upon Lincoln cannot be measured precisely, but it cannot be overlooked as a possible influence upon him in subsequent weeks. He may have realized that he could not afford to provide critics with another opportunity to make invidious comparisons between him and the "weak" Buchanan.

During the nine remaining days before his inauguration, Lincoln was bombarded from all sides with advice about his cabinet, patronage, and crisis policy. But only one incident provoked a really significant statement from him. This occurred when the delegates to the Peace Conference paid him a complimentary visit. William E. Dodge, the New York capitalist, begged him to save the country from bankruptcy and left it with him to decide "whether grass shall grow in the streets of our commercial cities." Lincoln assured Dodge, "If it depends upon me, the grass will not grow anywhere except in the fields and meadows." The New York delegate asked whether that meant that the new President would yield to the "just demands" of the South. Lincoln's earnest reply was recorded by the secretary of the Peace Conference, who was present at the interview:

. . . If I shall ever come to the great office of President of the United States, I shall take an oath. I shall swear that I shall faith-

[49] Nicolay and Hay (eds.), *Works of Lincoln*, VI, 154–58, 160–65.
[50] Austin Blair to Zachariah Chandler, February 27, 1861, Chandler Papers, Library of Congress. See also "Diary of a Public Man," *loc. cit.*, 259–60.

fully execute the office of President of the United States, of all the United States, and that I will, to the best of my ability, preserve, protect, and defend the Constitution of the United States. This is a great and solemn duty. With the support of the people and the assistance of the Almighty I shall undertake to perform it. . . . The Constitution will not be preserved and defended until it is enforced and obeyed in every part of every one of the United States. It must be so respected, obeyed, enforced, and defended, let the grass grow where it may.[51]

It need not be left to speculation what Seward, the self-appointed "premier," thought of the remarks that Lincoln had made since his departure from Springfield. These speeches came as a great shock to Seward and others who had assumed that he was to dominate the new administration and that he had been expounding a prearranged program.[52] As Henry Adams recalled, it became painfully evident that "Mr. Seward had acted all winter on his own responsibility." [53] Charles Francis Adams told his sons that Seward was "depressed" and that "Lincoln's folly in not consulting with his official advisers" had made the Senator's position "lamentable." The President-elect, "with no apparent regard for the policy indicated" by Seward, was ruining everything! [54] Charles Francis Adams, Jr., seconded his father's opinion that the "premier's" power had been "impaired" by Lincoln's addresses, which "spread the impression that Seward's policy is not to be followed out." [55] There was deep resentment in the Adams household at Lincoln's presumption in speaking without Seward's approval.

A more modest man than Seward might have taken this as convincing evidence that Lincoln did not intend to be dominated by a "premier," that he expected to follow a course of his own

[51] Lucius E. Chittenden, *Recollections of President Lincoln and His Administration* (New York, 1891), 74–75; *id., Personal Reminiscences, 1840–1890* (New York, 1893), 391–93.

[52] Boston *Evening Transcript* (letter from "Conciliator"), February 23, 1861; New York *Journal of Commerce* ("Washington Correspondence"), quoted in Providence *Daily Post*, February 21, 1861.

[53] Adams, "Secession Winter," *loc. cit.,* 682–83. For evidence of Lincoln's resentment at Seward's efforts to dominate him see Baringer, *House Dividing,* 87, 88–89, 99–102, 109–11, 128–30, 137–38.

[54] Adams, *Autobiography,* 76–78.

[55] C. F. Adams, Jr., to Andrew, February 22, 1861, Andrew Papers.

choosing. But how could this powerful New Yorker believe that the self-effacing and untried Lincoln could do anything but submit to his will? Rather than yield, Seward redoubled his efforts to dominate the President-elect as soon as he reached Washington. He proceeded with complete confidence that his would be the controlling voice in the government, that he could make commitments which Lincoln would never dare disavow. It would take another month for Seward to realize that he had met his master.

4

On inauguration day the atmosphere of Washington was full of meaning to those who sought signs of what the future promised. Persistent rumors of secessionist plots to seize the capital and prevent Lincoln from being installed in office caused an unprecedented display of the military. Throughout the ceremonies General Scott remained at the War Department ready to quell any disturbance, sentinels stood watch on the roofs of prominent buildings, and four batteries of artillery were drawn up before the city hall. Everywhere the sound of drum and fife could be heard, "and the streets were thronged with the volunteer soldiery hastening to their respective rendezvous." [56] Here, wrote a critic, was a spectacle to "terrify the heart of every patriot." For the first time a President delivered his inaugural "surrounded and guarded not by the honest hearts of a happy people, but safely esconced [sic] out of the people's reach, within a military cordon bristling with bayonets." [57]

Yet most Yankees felt relieved that the fourth of March had come with the government still in possession of Washington and with the great principle of the Union not surrendered. Now, whatever "perils and toils" were still to come, at least the nation could feel that it had "once more a central government." [58] A "change of political dynasties" was about to take place "almost as radical as that which signalized the revolution of 1688 in Eng-

[56] New York *World*, March 4, 1861.
[57] Philadelphia *Morning Pennsylvanian*, March 4, 1861.
[58] New York *Evening Post*, March 4, 1861.

land." [59] And the change, many expected, would be celebrated by Lincoln's inaugural address.

It was late in January before the President-elect had begun to prepare this document, the reading of which the people awaited with mingled feelings of hope and anxiety. By then the secession movement was in an advanced stage, the first uprising of Northerners had occurred, and an awareness of the tremendous scope of the crisis had penetrated Lincoln's mind. By then he was conscious of the need for an alternative to voluntary reconstruction: He had already rejected compromise and peaceful secession, and he had privately expressed his belief that force might be required to save the Union. His task in composing the inaugural was to analyze this trying situation and to explain not only *what* had to be done but *how* it must be done. This he attempted to do with only four references before him: a copy of the Constitution, Jackson's proclamation on nullification, Clay's speech in the Senate in February, 1850, and Webster's reply to Hayne, which he admired as the "grandest specimen of American oratory." [60] Lincoln completed the address and had a draft printed before he left Springfield. During the following month he made some revisions in style and several deletions and insertions, but few of these were important. In its final form the document was faithful to the nationalist spirit of both its author and his sources.

Only a few men knew the contents of the address before its delivery. Lincoln read it to Carl Schurz as evidence "that I shall never betray my principles and my friends." [61] Unquestionably an editor of the *Illinois State Journal* saw the document, for he disclosed many of its ideas in an editorial which even used some of its exact wording.[62] Seward and Orville H. Browning also read it and recommended several changes which Lincoln agreed to make.

The inaugural was not altogether pleasing to Seward; there were portions of it that "impaired" his policy as seriously as Lincoln's remarks during the trip to Washington. The "premier" was especially opposed to one sentence which announced: "All the

[59] Boston *Daily Journal*, March 4, 1861.

[60] Angle (ed.), *Herndon's Lincoln*, 386.

[61] Schurz to his wife, February 10, 1861, in Bancroft (ed.), *Speeches, Correspondence, and Political Papers of Carl Schurz*, I, 179.

[62] Springfield *Daily Illinois State Journal*, February 13, 1861, quoted in Perkins (ed.), *Northern Editorials on Secession*, I, 228–30.

power at my disposal will be used to reclaim the public property and places which have fallen." By declaring this Lincoln would have simply reiterated what he had affirmed privately as early as December and again in his speech at Indianapolis. But Seward urged him to drop the sentence and composed a meaningless vagary to be substituted for it. Although Lincoln rejected the substitute, he finally heeded the advice of Browning and omitted the statement entirely. This deletion, however, did not necessarily imply either that Lincoln had changed his original plans or that Browning wanted him to change them. "The fallen places ought to be reclaimed," Browning advised. "But cannot that be accomplished as well or even better without announcing the purpose in your inaugural?" An attempt to send supplies or reinforcements to Fort Sumter, he shrewdly added, would "induce aggression by South Carolina," after which the government would "stand justified, before the entire country, in repelling that aggression, and retaking the forts." [63] Whether or not that was the argument that convinced Lincoln, the episode showed that he continued to feel an obligation to retake the lost property right down to his inauguration. And there is no evidence that he ever abandoned more than his intention to make a second public announcement of that obligation.

Seward was also dissatisfied with the way Lincoln originally planned to close the address. The President-elect again revealed how much importance he attached to his defensive concept by giving it one final statement in his proposed conclusion. He wanted to explain that while secessionists could "forbear the assault" upon the government, he could not "shrink from . . . [its] defense." Hence, "with you, and not with me, is the solemn question of 'Shall it be peace or a sword.'" To Seward this ending was entirely too abrupt, and he urged Lincoln to finish on a softer strain. So Lincoln agreed to substitute an appealing and sentimental concluding paragraph outlined by Seward, although the final wording was his own.[64]

[63] Nicolay and Hay, *Lincoln*, III, 333–34; Browning to Lincoln, February 17, 1861, Lincoln Papers. Seward's suggested revisions of the inaugural are also in the Lincoln Papers. Actually Seward wanted Lincoln to drop the whole paragraph in which he announced his purpose to "hold, occupy and possess" public property in the South.

[64] An excellent account of the revisions of the original inaugural address is in Tarbell, *Lincoln*, II, 6–11. See also Nicolay and Hay, *Lincoln*, III, 319–44.

But none of these alterations modified Lincoln's basic ideas. There was nothing in the address that was out of harmony with what he had written or said before. Rather it was a renewed expression of his nationalism, of his belief in the perpetuity of the Union, of his intention to maintain the most essential aspects of Federal authority in the South, of his willingness to respect the rights of Southerners, and of his unfolding strategy of defense. He merely quoted from an earlier speech when he denied any intention to interfere with slavery in the states. He made no original contribution to the classical nationalist argument when he attempted to prove that "the Union of these States is perpetual," that ordinances of secession were "legally void," and that resistance to the Federal government was "insurrectionary or revolutionary, according to circumstances."

I therefore consider [he continued] that, in view of the Constitution and the laws, the Union is unbroken; and to the extent of my ability I shall take care, as the Constitution expressly enjoins upon me, that the laws of the Union be faithfully executed in all the States. Doing this I deem it to be only a simple duty on my part; and I shall perform it so far as practicable, unless my rightful masters, the American people, shall withhold the requisite means, or in some other authoritative manner direct the contrary. I trust this will not be regarded as a menace, but only as the declared purpose of the Union that it will constitutionally defend and maintain itself.

In fulfilling his duty to enforce the laws, Lincoln could see no need for bloodshed or violence, and there would be none "unless it be forced upon the national authority." His power as chief executive would be used "to hold, occupy, and possess the property and places belonging to the government, and to collect the duties and imposts." But, he added, *"beyond what may be necessary for these objects"* [65] there would be "no invasion, no using of force." In other words, he would have to use whatever force was needed to hold Federal property and collect the revenues, but not for any purpose less vital. He would abstain from doing many things which he had a right to do, but which could be forgone temporarily without injury to the government. If, for ex-

[65] Author's italics.

ample, resident citizens could not hold Federal offices "in an interior locality," he would not appoint "obnoxious strangers" to
fill them and exercise their functions. Nor would he insist upon
providing mail deliveries to the South if such service were "re-
pelled."

Lincoln then appealed to Southerners to pause and consider well
what they were doing. It was their duty to submit to majority
rule; control by the minority was "wholly inadmissible" and
would lead to some form of "anarchy or despotism." If the people
desired to change the Constitution, that was within their power,
though he had no amendments to propose.[66] But, while he thus
refused to recommend a compromise, he pointed out that there
would be another election within four years when national issues
could be reconsidered. Meanwhile it was the President's responsibility "to administer the present government, as it came to his
hands, and to transmit it, unimpaired by him, to his successor."
And so the course of future events was beyond his control: "In
your hands, my dissatisfied fellow-countrymen, and not in mine,
is the momentous issue of civil war. The government will not
assail you. You can have no conflict without being yourselves the
aggressors. You have no oath registered in heaven to destroy the
government, while I shall have the most solemn one to 'preserve,
protect, and defend it.' " [67]

When Lincoln completed the delivery of his inaugural address
he had the disunionists hopelessly cornered. He had, as Samuel
Bowles of the Springfield *Republican* explained, placed "the secession conspirators manifestly in the wrong." He "hedges them in
so that they cannot take a single step without making treasonable
war upon the government, which will only defend itself." [68]
Southerners, who had their own ideas of what constituted "aggression" and "defense," were almost unanimous in asserting that
the inaugural was a declaration of war against the Confederacy.
All that Lincoln had said, they agreed, was that there would be
no war if the South accepted the enforcement of the laws; since

[66] Lincoln said, however, that he had no objection to the amendment passed
by Congress which would have guaranteed slavery in the states. That, he
thought, was already "implied constitutional law."
[67] Nicolay and Hay (eds.), *Works of Lincoln*, VI, 169–85.
[68] Springfield (Mass.) *Daily Republican*, March 6. 1861.

that was not possible, war was inevitable.[69] Prosouthern papers like the Philadelphia *Pennsylvanian* shared the opinions of secessionists: "The tiger's claws are not the less formidable because concealed under the velvety fur of Sewardism." [70]

But the majority of Northerners reacted favorably. Even the Democratic press was by no means entirely unsympathetic toward Lincoln's position.[71] A Democratic congressman confessed that he could "find no fault" with the address.[72] The conservative coalition which nominated William Sprague for governor of Rhode Island heartily approved of the inaugural and called upon every patriot "to rally around the Chief Magistrate . . . in his efforts to maintain the integrity of the government." [73]

Republicans fairly glowed with appreciation for the consummate skill with which Lincoln had at once hamstrung the South, satisfied the mass of northern people that he contemplated no aggression, and yet conveyed his determination to defend Federal authority. "No party can be formed against the administration on the issue presented by the inaugural," rejoiced one Republican editor.[74] Another noted: "The fiat of peace or war is in the hands of Mr. Davis rather than of Mr. Lincoln." [75] "The inaugural is the most masterly piece of generalship which human history has shown," exulted a friend of Chase's.[76] The *Wisconsin State Journal* declared in all sincerity: "It is truly a peace message. . . . But if it contains any affirmation more distinct than another, it is that in which the President declares his purpose to use every means at his command to maintain the Constitution and enforce the laws." [77] The Boston *Advertiser* penetrated its meaning with un-

[69] See, for example, remarks of Senators Wigfall, Mason, and Clingman, in *Congressional Globe*, 1436–46. See also *Official Records*, Ser. 1, I, 261, 263–64; Alexandria (Va.) *Sentinel*, quoted in Philadelphia *Press*, March 7, 1861; Wilmington (N.C.) *Journal*, quoted in Philadelphia *Press*, March 9, 1861; New York *Evening Post*, March 5, 8, 9, 1861.
[70] Philadelphia *Morning Pennsylvanian*, March 5, 1861.
[71] Philadelphia *Press*, March 8, 1861; *Daily Chicago Post*, March 6, 1861. For the comments of other Democratic newspapers see New York *World*, March 6, 1861.
[72] John Law to Trumbull, March 7, 1861, Trumbull Papers.
[73] Providence *Daily Journal*, March 7, 1861.
[74] Springfield (Mass.) *Daily Republican*, March 6, 1861.
[75] Boston *Daily Journal*, March 12, 1861.
[76] Elizur Wright to Chase, March 7, 1861, Chase Papers.
[77] Madison *Wisconsin Daily State Journal*, March 11, 1861.

common acumen. The President, it believed, had implied that he would be discreet and conciliatory, but that he recognized "the natural limits of that discretion."

> . . . The address itself [it concluded] contemplates the pos-- sibility of an interruption of the peace. We understand the President to disclaim the intention of doing many things which he thinks himself authorized to do, but which he can forbear doing without detriment to the claims of the government. . . . But there is obviously a limit to this forbearance, and a limit to the concessions which the government should make for the preservation of peace. . . . Such powers as are con- fided to him . . . the President will use, with a due regard to practical policy, but with no thought of forgoing the exercise of a right essential to the existence of the government, because resistance to it is threatened.[78]

That was it precisely: At no time did Lincoln deliberately seek to provoke a war with the South; if he could "enforce the laws" (or at least the most important ones) without a conflict, so much the better, for that would obviously mean the collapse of the Confederacy. And yet he understood that his rejection of com- promise, his determination to defend the Union, and his insistence that essential Federal functions be exercised in the South might very well lead to conflict. He accepted that risk, and for that reason he took such enormous pains to absolve himself from the charge of aggression. Lincoln's inaugural address explained his position brilliantly, and most Yankees were more than satisfied.

[78] Boston *Daily Advertiser*, March 8, 1861.

XI

Yankees Take Stock

BY THE time Lincoln took up his residence at the White House four frightful months of national crisis had elapsed. Four months was long enough for Northerners to have done considerable thinking, both serious and frivolous, about secession. By March they had developed some fixed notions of what the establishment of southern independence would entail, notions altogether so unpleasant as to make them look upon political separation as utterly unthinkable.

When compromise failed, as it had by the time of the inauguration, this attitude contained an ominous implication. It meant that the foundation of domestic peace was crumbling. Most of the conciliators had understood that the choice was not between compromise and disunion but between compromise and war. Conservative Union meetings had almost invariably tied their appeals for concessions to an unqualified demand for the defense of the nation's integrity. Democratic Representative William S. Holman of Indiana was quite typical when he hoped that his constituents would show "a willingness to concede & conciliate but still insist under all circumstances that the flag of the Union shall be sustained." [1] An old Whig's plea for compromise ended thus: "Struggling to the death against war, . . . if war is inevitable, we are hand and heart, life and limb, body and soul, with the North from that time forth forever more." [2] Clearly, as one newspaperman perceived, the failure of compromise eventually forced "conservative men . . . to take sides with one or the other party." [3]

[1] W. S. Holman to Hamilton, January 18, 1861, Hamilton Papers.
[2] Boston *Daily Courier* (letter from "Hannibal"), January 3, 1861.
[3] New York *Morning Express* ("Washington Correspondence"), January 14, 1861.

If frantic conservatives tried instead to find a refuge in Seward's program of "masterly inactivity," they were soon driven from that position. Although a southern Unionist reaction might have occurred at some distant date, the events of March placed time limits on the policy of delay. Conditions at Fort Sumter and complications growing out of the revenue question were bound to force some kind of action almost immediately. Equally important, there were accumulating signs of northern restlessness, of a growing feeling that movement of any kind was preferable to the existing paralysis.[4] And so the conservatives were quickly forced back to the point where they found it necessary to "take sides" for or against the Union.

Then, like other Yankees, they overwhelmingly chose the Union—even at the cost of war. Why this was the almost universal choice, why Northerners believed that the formation of a southern Confederacy would have been such a terrible disaster, is not easily explained. There were many reasons, and these were advanced by individuals in limitless combinations. Some emphasized the political consequences of disunion, others the economic; some were appalled by the immediate results, others by the ultimate; some eagerly welcomed a war for the Union as a national catharsis, others regretfully accepted it as a national tragedy; some saw through the "red gates of war" the way to a new era, others hoped merely to restore "the Union as it was." When at last the guns were unlimbered, Yankees could unite only upon the sentiment embraced in Jackson's famous toast: "Our Federal Union—it must be preserved!" *Why* it had to be preserved was a question they debated throughout the Civil War.

2

Just as politics had helped to determine the outcome of the compromise struggle it also played its part, openly or covertly, in shaping the final decision to fight for the Union. Sooner or later the Republicans were obliged to recognize that violence was the logical consequence of their rejection of appeasement. Some faced that fact realistically from the beginning; others tried to

[4] See Chapter XIII.

dodge it for a time with a course of "masterly inactivity," or to
disguise it with soothing words like "defense" or the "enforcement
of the laws." But one thing Republicans knew for certain: The
acceptance of peaceful secession would demolish their party as
surely as would the betrayal of its platform. They realized, as one
Democrat predicted, that southern independence would cause the
North to "look upon . . . [Republicans] as the destroyers of
the Union of our fathers." That would rouse "an agitation . . .
that would know no rest, day or night, until Black Republicanism
. . . should be effectually destroyed." [5] Accordingly, Republicans fully understood that the Union must be saved to make their
future secure.

Some of Lincoln's followers evidently believed that a war for
the Union promised other political benefits. It appeared to many,
in fact, as the *only* program that could hold their organization
together. For what other purpose could the diverse elements of
Republicanism co-operate? Lincoln's election had removed the
danger of slavery expansion, and thus, as the New York *Evening
Post* mourned, the party was deprived of its "one important bond
of union." [6] Chase wrote apprehensively that the most dangerous
disunion threat he perceived was "the disunion of the Republican
party." [7] No sooner was the election over than many Democrats
waited expectantly for the disintegration of their rivals. A Douglas supporter noted gleefully that during the campaign the Republican party had been forced to assume "as many shapes as
Proteus." "But," he concluded, "no matter what policy the Republican Administration of Lincoln shall adopt, one consequence
is sure to result within a very short time from the date of his inauguration, and that is the disruption of the 'Republican' faction.
It is morally impossible for any man . . . to so distribute his
patronage and shape the policy of his administration as to gratify
and keep together such a heterogeneous combination of discord-

[5] Philadelphia *Morning Pennsylvanian*, December 11, 1860. See also Boston
Daily Courier, January 5, 1861; Wm. Lawrence to Chase, March 26, 1861, Chase
Papers; remarks of Senator Preston King, in *Congressional Globe*, 853.

[6] New York *Evening Post*, November 7, 1860.

[7] Chase to Trumbull, November 12, 1860, Trumbull Papers. See also Alexander
K. McClure, *Abraham Lincoln and Men of War-Times* (Philadelphia, 1892),
60–63.

ant materials as that of which the 'Republican' party is composed." [8]

Soon, however, the Democrats began to perceive that these death notices were premature. For if the secession movement was a threat to the Republican organization, it was also an opportunity. James C. Stone, one of Sumner's Massachusetts friends, expressed with engaging frankness an idea that must have been in the minds of more than a few Republican leaders. He saw in the northern love for the Union a "glorious" chance for his party to win "the confidence and affections of the people." Yankees would "suffer and sacrifice" for their flag, and if need be would "fight and die for it; and the grand opportunity which the Republican party now has, is to unite together, and lead in one irresistible current, the love of liberty and the love of the Union." By doing this, Stone was convinced that Republicans would be "all-powerful" and secure a "permanent hold upon the government." [9] James S. Pike, the Washington correspondent of the New York *Tribune*, offered the same advice: "If the Republicans would secure their own overwhelming triumph, . . . they have only . . . to declare that their first and chief object is to protect and preserve the American Constitution, the American flag, and the American Government, against the world, against treason, and against traitors. . . . Let the Republican Administration but do this, and it will draw around it the enthusiastic support of all sides, and establish itself in the affections of a whole people so that it can never be shaken. Thus simple and clear is the path of the Republicans." [10]

Here was a solution to the Republican problem: A stand for the Union would certainly bind all the factions together. More, it would provide an appeal which, properly stated, few in the opposition would be able to resist. With that in mind, one Republican

[8] Columbus *Daily Ohio Statesman*, November 8, 1860. See also New York *Herald*, November 11, 1860; New York *Journal of Commerce*, November 9, 1860; Boston *Daily Courier*, November 7, 1860; Montpelier *Vermont Patriot and State Gazette*, November 17, 1860.

[9] James C. Stone to Sumner, December 17, 1860, Sumner Papers.

[10] New York *Daily Tribune* ("Washington Correspondence"), December 31, 1860. Democrats repeatedly charged that Republicans were seeking a war to save their party. See, for example, Philadelphia *Morning Pennsylvanian*, December 26, 27, 31, 1860.

urged his political friends to "drop the slavery question . . . & appeal to the national feeling of the North" so that Democrats would be "swayed to our side." [11] Justin Morrill reminded Democrats that Whigs had sustained Jackson in the nullification controversy, and he called upon them "in this crisis . . . [to] reciprocate that sort of patriotism." Men of all parties, he warned, would have to "unite with us in rescuing the Government from its present dangers." [12] Even before the war began, Republicans were drawing the line between those who would "uphold the Government in its integrity" and those who were "the instruments . . . of the traitors." A Northerner who was not ready "to do service under the old flag," they contended, was "a recruit under the rattlesnake banner." [13] Republicanism and loyalty were soon to become synonymous.

It is impossible to determine precisely how prominent the political motive was in the calculations of Republican leaders. Simply to prove that the Civil War saved their party from disintegration, as it may well have done, would not be to prove that Republicans deliberately started the war for that purpose. Yet the evidence is conclusive that politics was at least *one* factor, and often a surprisingly conscious one, which directed some of Lincoln's friends toward war.

3

So far as politics directly influenced the crisis thinking of northern Democrats, it encouraged them to seek compromise rather than war. But when the conflict was actually at hand most of them understood that political ruin was the likely penalty for all who exposed themselves to charges of disloyalty. In the early months of the war, opposition was limited to a few politicians such as Representative Clement L. Vallandigham of Ohio and Senator Jesse D. Bright of Indiana, and to a handful of newspapers such as Samuel Medary's Columbus *Crisis* and Benjamin Wood's New

[11] John Jay to Sumner, February 4, 1861, Sumner Papers.

[12] Justin S. Morrill to Hon. Stephen Thomas, December 23, 1860, Morrill Papers, Library of Congress; *Congressional Globe*, 1006.

[13] New York *Independent* (article by Horace Greeley), March 21, 1861; Chicago *Daily Tribune*, April 10, 1861.

York *Daily News*. The typical Douglas or Buchanan Democrat united with his opponents in support of Lincoln's military measures against rebellion.

The Confederate attack upon Fort Sumter was by no means the only reason for this result. Even before the war began, there were numerous signs that Democrats would rally to the government if secession should eventually lead to conflict. Their appeal for continued sectional peace always contained some intrinsic weaknesses. This was partly due to the fact that Democratic protests against force were never based upon inherent pacifist principles. Instead, these protests were a product of the northern Democrats' traditional alliance with the southern planters and their party's desperate need for the continued support of the South. The Democrats of the North would have been greatly weakened politically by the permanent alienation of their southern allies. Moreover, they shared the deep emotional and practical attachment to the Union which was common among all Northerners. When other means failed, there were only a few Democrats who still rejected military action against secessionists. Some, like Representatives Holman of Indiana and Sickles of New York, vowed early in the crisis that the southern states would never be held to the Union by force; but before long most of these had reversed themselves and endorsed the popular northern demand for the "enforcement of the laws." [14] In fact more Republicans than Democrats were temporarily guilty of vague and inconsistent talk of letting the South secede in peace. Many Democratic newspapers denounced Republicans who spoke of peaceful separation as "traitors to their country." [15]

In general, northern Democrats assumed the position that Jackson had taken during the nullification controversy: They combined a desire for conciliation with a willingness to apply force as a last resort. Douglas established the common pattern. In a campaign speech at Norfolk, Virginia, he gave Southerners advance warning that they would never be permitted to break up

[14] W. S. Holman to Hamilton, November 18, 1860, Hamilton Papers; Holman's remarks in the House on January 16, 1861, in *Congressional Globe*, 419; Sickles' remarks in the House on December 10, 1860, and January 17, 1861, *ibid.*, 40; Appendix, 87–91.

[15] See, for example, Columbus *Daily Ohio Statesman*, November 14, 1860.

the Union. In the Senate he pleaded for compromise, but on January 3 he defended the right of the government "to use all the power and force necessary" to maintain its authority in the southern states.[16] Other Democratic congressmen who vowed they would appeal to arms if necessary included Isaac N. Morris and John A. McClernand of Illinois, Samuel S. Cox and William Allen of Ohio, Jacob K. McKenty of Pennsylvania, and Garnett B. Adrian of New Jersey. Although McKenty represented one of the most conservative districts in Pennsylvania, he declared: "While we have stood by South Carolina at the ballot box we cannot sustain her act of treason against the General Government. . . . If the last page of our nation's history is to be a bloody one, let the responsibility rest with those who will make it so." [17] On January 8, Adrian proposed a resolution pledging support to the President "in all constitutional measures to enforce the laws and preserve the Union." It passed the House with only four northern Democrats opposing.[18] The majority of Buchanan's followers agreed with the Douglasites on this point. In December, for example, Benjamin F. Butler, the champion of Jefferson Davis at the Charleston convention, warned the Breckinridge National Committee that Northerners would fight for the Union and that he would fight with them.[19] Secessionists were mystified. Representative John H. Reagan of Texas complained that northern Democrats appeared to be "equally forgetful of our wrongs, . . . and equally anxious for this gunpowder enforcement of the laws." [20]

But Reagan's surprise merely indicated that Southerners had totally misunderstood the position of their Yankee friends. Demo-

[16] Philadelphia *Press*, October 1, 1860; *Congressional Globe*, Appendix, 39; George Fort Milton, *The Eve of Conflict: Stephen A. Douglas and the Needless War* (Boston, 1934), 520-21, 531-32. See also R. Hamilton to Douglas, December 4, 1860; L. B. Marshall to *id.*, December 13, 1860; Richard Stevens to *id.*, January 28, 1861, Douglas Papers.
[17] *Congressional Globe*, 48-57, 167-70, 281-82, 367-72, 372-77, 393-97.
[18] *Ibid.*, 280-82.
[19] New York *Times*, January 3, 1861; Butler, *Butler's Book*, 150-56, 161-66. See also J. G. Dickinson to Johnson, February 8, 1861, Johnson Papers; H. P. Laird to Black, January 16, 1861, Black Papers; M. W. Jacobus to Holt, November 27, 1860, Holt Papers; G. W. DeCamp to Buchanan, November 22, 1860; D. Salomon to *id.*, December 23, 1860; G. M. Wharton to *id.*, January 3, 1861, Buchanan Papers.
[20] *Congressional Globe*, 391.

crats explained that their defense of southern rights had been predicated upon the assumption that the remedy for alleged grievances would be sought *within* the Union. McClernand assured Southerners that so long as they were loyal to the government and sought redress through legal processes he would "still stand by them in the right." But if they abandoned the Union there would be a "revulsion of feeling" from them.[21] Few Democrats believed that Southerners had been injured sufficiently to warrant such extreme action, nor did they believe that immediate secession was justified by anticipated future wrongs. The friends of Buchanan felt this especially keenly, since they had been such consistent defenders of the South.[22]

Free-state Democrats also believed that their southern allies had a moral obligation to stand by them in defeat. To abandon them to the "Black" Republicans would indicate cowardice and ingratitude. Many felt the same indignation as John A. Dix when he protested to Howell Cobb: "We have fought your battles without regard to the political consequences to ourselves. It is neither chivalrous or brave to draw off because the common adversary has gained a momentary advantage, and leave us to continue the contest . . . without the support we have given to you." [23] When such appeals were ignored, countless Democrats were convinced that they had been betrayed, and some of them became bitterly hostile to the South.[24]

At times these disillusioned Democrats revealed a bitterness that was hardly exceeded by the most radical Republicans. Douglas Democrats could neither forgive nor forget southern "treachery" at the Charleston convention. They held that the slave states were themselves responsible for Lincoln's election, because it was they

[21] *Ibid.*, 39–40.

[22] G. M. Wharton to Buchanan, November 16, 1860; Charles A. Davis to *id.*, December 10, 1860; E. N. Paine to *id.*, December 13, 1860, Buchanan Papers.

[23] Dix (comp.), *Memoirs*, Appendix, 335–38. See also Belmont, *Letters, Speeches, and Addresses*, 23–29; Appeal of Philadelphia Democrats to the South, Philadelphia *Public Ledger*, November 13, 1860.

[24] S. F. B. Morse to Amos Kendall, February 15, 1861, letter-book copy in Morse Papers, Library of Congress; F. J. Parker to Johnson, December 20, 1860, Johnson Papers; Henry M. Phillips to Buchanan, December 12, 1860; Geo. Taylor to *id.*, December 17, 1860, Buchanan Papers; Sydney Stowe to Douglas, December 18, 1860; W. W. Wick to *id.*, January 18, 1861; C. B. Hartman to *id.*, February 5, 1861; Theo. Williams to *id.*, April 1, 1861, Douglas Papers.

who had disrupted the Democratic party. Now these "bolters" deserved the worst that they would receive from the Republicans. Indeed some Douglasites charged that southern traitors, who "styled themselves Democrats," had deliberately destroyed their party to ensure a Republican victory and provide an excuse for secession.[25] The Boston *Herald* believed that it was subservience to southern ingrates that had proved so disastrous, and it demanded that the party be "purged of its false doctrines and worse than false leaders." Now the South would climax its treason to the Democracy with treason to the country. Democrats, argued this paper, had but one course: "We must stand up in our boots, . . . haul out the old revolutionary muskets, pick the flints, fix bayonets, and if anybody runs against them, they may get hurt. *That's all.*" [26]

In April the northern followers of Douglas and Buchanan heeded that advice. Most of them were driven to "pick flints" and "fix bayonets" by their intense Unionism, some by resentment against southern political infidelity, and a few by the belief that there was no other choice once the decision was made. No one opposed war more earnestly than Caleb Cushing, the rich Massachusetts merchant and Buchanan politician. But he always knew where he would have to stand if the peace were broken. As early as November he had said: "If civil war comes, that war finds me a citizen of Massachusetts fatally committed by domicile to a cause, which . . . my legal duty would force me to support." [27]

4

One day in February, Zachariah Chandler of Michigan stood in the Senate chamber delivering another of his violent war speeches and pounding his desk with accustomed vigor. On this occasion the dwellers in eastern cities were the special targets of his wrath. After lauding the superior patriotism of Westerners,

[25] Remarks of Isaac N. Morris, William Allen, John A. McClernand, Garnett B. Adrian, and William S. Holman in *Congressional Globe*, 51–52, 167–70, 372, 393–94, 420–21; John Law to Martin Van Buren, January 7, 1861, Van Buren Papers, Library of Congress; Providence *Daily Post*, November 13, 1860.

[26] Boston *Herald*, December 25, 1860; January 12, 26; February 6, 8; March 25, 1861.

[27] Clipping, dated November 12, 1860, in Cushing Papers.

he sneered disdainfully: "Cities have always been ready to buy peace—never ready to furnish men to fight for their rights." Were all the eastern metropolises obliterated, the nation would be just as strong, and there would be "less disunion croaking." [28] A week later Powell of Kentucky read to the Senate a letter written by Chandler to Governor Blair of Michigan, which had fallen into the hands of a Democrat. In it Chandler had again denounced the East for its timidity: "Some of the manufacturing States think that a fight would be awful. Without a little blood-letting this Union will not, in my estimation, be worth a rush." [29] Chandler did not deny the authenticity of the letter, but reminded the Senate of Jefferson's opinion that the "tree of liberty" needed to be "refreshed from time to time with the blood of patriots and tyrants." [30]

Chandler was too radical to be classified as a representative Westerner. Nevertheless, his belligerent attitude toward secessionists was characteristic of a substantial group in his section. Most of the West's Republican congressmen, governors, and state legislators on some occasion matched the virulence of Chandler's tirades against southern treason. And many western Democrats also raised their voices to challenge the enemies of the Union. The prevalence of the fighting spirit in the West was striking enough to cause general comment in the eastern press. Editors in New England and the middle states observed that Westerners made the most warlike speeches in Congress. These editors predicted that the seven states of the Northwest, whose eight million citizens held the balance of power in the nation, would exert a decisive influence in the present crisis. Those commonwealths alone could muster an army of 400,000 to "roll down upon the South like an avalanche." Surely "an army of western pioneers . . . would be, by all odds the ugliest customer the southern rebels could deal with." [31] The conservative Boston *Courier* found less to admire

[28] *Congressional Globe*, 1015–20.

[29] *Ibid.*, 1246–47. See also Austin Blair to Chandler, February 27, 1861, Chandler Papers.

[30] *Congressional Globe*, 1370–72.

[31] New York *Herald*, December 24, 1860; January 3, 15, 1861; New York *Evening Post*, November 12, 1860; New York *World*, January 25, 1861; Philadelphia *Public Ledger*, December 29, 1860; Boston *Daily Journal*, January 18, 1861; Boston *Daily Advertiser*, January 2, 1861; Providence *Daily Journal*, De-

in the current set of war hawks: "The spirit evinced by these Western orators in their bombastic threats is not calculated to afford present or future peace to the Union. . . . It will be sad to those who have reared the territories into States, to find that they have reared a viper brood." [32]

If the West reacted most rabidly against disunion it was because of the fear that she would suffer a grievous injury. The typical Westerner believed that his political and economic destiny was wrapped up in the Union, that its dismemberment would make him a helpless victim of forces beyond his control. Besides, in the past he had depended upon the Federal government for protection and for various kinds of aid. It was not surprising, therefore, that strong emotions of nationalism and patriotism had grown within him. The end of the Union, he feared, would be the end of everything.

Among the evils Westerners anticipated from secession was being isolated in the interior of the continent and left to the mercy of surrounding foreign states. As Douglas explained to the Senate, "We can never consent to be shut up within the circle of a Chinese wall, erected and controlled by others without our permission. . . . Our rights, our interests, our safety, our existence as a free people, forbid it!" [33] Holman of Indiana reminded the House that his section had been taxed to erect defenses along the Atlantic coast, and it would not permit these safeguards against foreign invasion to be appropriated by individual states.[34] Governor-elect Morton of Indiana described vividly what disunion would mean to the West:

> If South Carolina may secede peaceably, so may New York, Massachusetts, Maryland and Louisiana, cutting off our commerce and destroying our right of way to the ocean. We would thus be shut up in the interior of a continent, surrounded by independent, perhaps hostile nations, through whose Territories we could obtain egress to the seaboard only upon such terms as might be agreed to by treaty. Emigrants from foreign

cember 13, 1860; Newburyport *Daily Herald*, quoted in Springfield (Mass.) *Daily Republican*, February 18, 1861.

[32] Boston *Daily Courier*, December 18, 1860.

[33] *Congressional Globe*, Appendix, 39–40.   [34] *Ibid.*, 420.

lands could only reach us by permission of our neighbors, and we could not reach any Atlantic port except by passports duly *vised*. In such a condition of affairs the seaboard States would possess immense advantages, which may be illustrated and understood by comparing the wealth, prosperity and power of the seaboard kingdoms with those shut up in the interior of Europe.[35]

More than anything else it was the thought of the Mississippi River again flowing through foreign territory that caused Westerners to burnish their muskets. They would not surrender the mouth of that great artery and thus jeopardize the existing right of free navigation. On this the West was all but unanimous, as even the peace-Democrat Vallandigham proclaimed in emphatic language. The unobstructed use of the Mississippi, he warned, "we demand, and will have at every cost; . . . and if we cannot secure a maritime boundary upon other terms, we will cleave our way to the sea-coast with the sword." [36] Secessionists understood the determination of the Northwest on that point and remembered how ready that section had been to fight for it in the past. A few Southerners wanted to use the river as a weapon to coerce the Northwest into co-operation with them; and, with this in mind, a few Westerners toyed with the idea of a Northwest Confederacy allied with the South.[37] But in both sections schemes of that kind were advanced by a small minority. Most Westerners preferred to maintain their rights on the Mississippi by preserving the Union. And secessionists generally promised that they would never disrupt river commerce.[38]

But such assurances from the South were simply not enough. These were mere "*paper* guarantees" which the West would enjoy by the sufferance of a hostile people. At any time navigation rights could be revoked or subjected to whatever taxes or tribute South-

[35] Indianapolis *Daily Journal*, November 27, 1860. See also Columbus *Daily Ohio Statesman*, December 14, 1860; Madison *Wisconsin Daily State Journal*, November 17, 26, 1860.

[36] *Congressional Globe*, 38.

[37] William C. Cochrane, "The Dream of a Northwestern Confederacy," Historical Society of Wisconsin, *Proceedings*, 1916, 213–53; Smith, *Borderland*, 99; Kenneth M. Stampp, "Kentucky's Influence Upon Indiana in the Crisis of 1861," *Indiana Magazine of History*, XXXIX (1943), 266–67.

[38] Robert R. Russel, *Economic Aspects of Southern Sectionalism, 1840–1861* (Urbana, Ill., 1924), 258–59, 261.

erners desired to levy.[39] In January, Westerners had what they considered a foretaste of southern independence when batteries were erected at Vicksburg and shipping was temporarily disturbed by the state of Mississippi. At once the whole Northwest was aflame. The Cincinnati *Commercial* described these acts as "piracy and murder," and Governor Yates of Illinois raged that the Mississippi River would become "a sepulchre of the slain" before such indignities were tolerated.[40] No other incident did more to nourish the western war spirit than this interference with river commerce. That memory was still bright the following April.

In March the Confederate government announced its own regulations governing the right to navigate the Mississippi. These did not deny the West free use of the river, but they did take precautions against violations of the Confederacy's revenue system. Westerners were alarmed by these regulations because they feared that the South might proceed next to levy duties, fees, and imposts. In fact they contended that free navigation had already been nullified by the establishment of "a complicated system of appraisement, inspection, surveying, [and] bonding." Hence the Chicago *Tribune* found it "impossible" to see how war was to be avoided.[41]

But did not Westerners attach an undue significance to their freedom to navigate the Mississippi? Were they not wedded to a tradition that was outdated in 1860? At first glance that might appear to be the case, because much of the produce destined for export to Europe now went east via the railroads. But this revolution in transportation only served to increase western devotion to the Union. It guaranteed the failure of proposals for a Northwest Confederacy tied to the South, for the West now realized the importance of its connections with the East.[42] Besides, there

[39] Chicago *Daily Tribune*, January 28; February 25, 1861; Cincinnati *Daily Gazette*, January 14, 1861; remarks of James R. Doolittle, John A. McClernand, Samuel S. Cox, and John A. Gurley in *Congressional Globe*, 200, 369-70, 375, 418.

[40] Cincinnati *Daily Commercial*, January 14, 28, 1861; Chicago *Daily Tribune*, January 14, 15, 1861; New Albany (Ind.) *Weekly Ledger*, January 30, 1861; Indianapolis *Daily Journal*, January 15, 1861; New York *Herald*, January 25, 1861; Smith, *Borderland*, 134-35.

[41] Chicago *Daily Tribune*, March 25, 1861; Milwaukee *Daily Sentinel*, March 4, 1861; New York *Evening Post*, March 28, 1861.

[42] Charles A. Davis to Crittenden, January 21, 1861, Crittenden Papers.

were large areas below the old National Road where railroads had not yet penetrated and where there was as much dependence upon the river as in the past. In actual fact, so far from declining, the river trade was larger than ever in 1860. But it was now chiefly an intravalley trade, with the South serving as a huge market for western goods.[43] The farmers of the Northwest were not inclined to let that market slip beyond national control. Nor would the merchants and shipowners in river towns like Cincinnati, New Albany, and Evansville endanger their business by recognizing southern independence. After compromise failed, the preservation of the Union was no less urgent to these western interests.

In 1860 many Westerners still cherished their traditional ties with the South. They felt a deep kinship with that section because of a common agrarianism and a mutual suspicion of the commercial and creditor East. To those who retained such sentiments the final decision to fight was extremely painful. But there were thousands of Westerners in whom southern sympathies had wholly disappeared. They had built up resentments toward the South which contributed significantly to their section's militancy. This attitude was partly a product of southern efforts to carry slavery into territories coveted by western farmers. It was also the result of prolonged southern opposition to the homestead bill and to Federal support of internal improvements. Senator James Harlan of Iowa cautioned secessionists not to seek any new political arrangement by which the Northwest would become subservient to the slave states. That would end his section's hope for a homestead bill, for "you have defeated this policy for the last ten years." The West desired a transcontinental railroad, but Harlan charged that southern votes had become "a more insurmountable barrier than the intervening mountains." Again, "The improvement of our rivers and harbors . . . you of the South oppose." In contrast, Harlan found Easterners willing to support these western demands:

[43] Remarks of Representative Carey A. Trimble of Ohio in *Congressional Globe*, Appendix, 169–74; Smith, *Borderland*, 24–25; Isaac Lippincott, *A History of Manufactures in the Ohio Valley to the Year 1860* (Chicago, 1914), 138, 144; E. Merton Coulter, "Effects of Secession upon the Commerce of the Mississippi Valley," *Mississippi Valley Historical Review*, III (1916), 275–300.

. . . They have already, by their capital and their science, overcome the only barriers between us and the great Atlantic. We are now within three days' journey of Boston, and of the Atlantic at any point; and we believe that . . . her capital . . . will enable us to connect ourselves with the Pacific States. Her great fleets of merchant ships, starting at the western terminus of our Pacific railroad, can connect us with the human hive that swarms on the other side of the Pacific, and thus reverse the world's travel, and send it, with a large proportion of the world's trade, by our doors, as it careers onward to the Atlantic cities and to the Old World.[44]

Before Sumter, then, the West had decided that its ties with *both* the South and the East were too vital to be surrendered. It refused to try its fortunes in a reconstructed Confederacy which excluded either of its neighbors. The West was determined to have "the Union as it was."

5

Throughout the secession crisis the northern businessman was a paradox. His radical critics deplored the seeming inability of men of his class to rise above temporary inconveniences or to endure pecuniary losses for the sake of great principles. Representative Daniel E. Somes of Maine sneered at the cowardice of both the merchants in the southern trade and the senile capitalists with fixed investments who had "retired to their easy chairs to doze out the balance of their days." Fearing any change or turmoil which might depress their stocks and bonds, these enervated fogies clung to everything that was "old, moldy, and stationary. The world whirls too fast for them; it makes them dizzy, and so they are anxious to stop it." [45] Somes explained the compromise movement in terms of this hostility to change; but what he failed to perceive was that this same motive also made the men of substance potential advocates of military force. For the propertied interests soon concluded that the destruction of the Union and the resulting decline of national prestige would be the most disastrous change of all. Not even civil war would injure them so grievously. At least a few

[44] *Congressional Globe*, Appendix, 47.
[45] *Ibid.*, 968. See also Chandler to Trumbull, November 17, 1860, Trumbull Papers; New York *Independent* (Commercial column), March 28, 1861.

contemporaries saw that the greatest opponents of Federal disintegration were those with "material interests in the country"
who were "willing and ready to protect and defend those interests." [46]

Actually there were some notable exceptions to the businessmen's general clamor for compromise, and some striking cases of
capitalists who assumed a belligerent attitude toward the secessionists. Not every eastern merchant was completely chained to
the southern trade, for many of them were becoming increasingly
aware of the economic potentialities of the West.[47] Besides, the
North was full of young, ambitious entrepreneurs who were less
fearful of risks than their cautious and better-established elders.
Finally, and more broadly, southern threats such as the black lists
of objectionable northern firms were a source of resentment on
the part of northern merchants. So were the contempt for trade
and the attitude of social superiority held by southern agrarians,
and with enough provocation these resentments could flare up
sufficiently to control the behavior of many men.

Zachariah Chandler, for example, was both a radical Republican
and a wealthy Detroit merchant. He had "over 100,000 $ in the
vortex of business, besides a large amount of stocks" which had
depreciated because of secession. But he still maintained that business ultimately would be better off "by settling this question . . .
now and *forever*." [48] E. B. Ward, a friend of Chandler's and a
powerful Michigan capitalist with interests in iron mines, was a
strong advocate of violent measures in behalf of the Union. Ward
offered to furnish the government with iron for cannon and rifles,
on credit or as a gift, if these weapons would be used to enforce
the laws.[49] John Murray Forbes, opulent Boston merchant and
investor in western railroads, demonstrated his preference for
force by assisting Governor Andrew in the preparation of the
state militia for action against the secessionists.[50] Other business-

---

[46] *Daily Chicago Post*, December 25, 1860.
[47] New York *Evening Post*, November 30, 1860; Chicago *Daily Tribune*,
January 21, 1861.
[48] Chandler to Trumbull, November 17, 1860, Trumbull Papers.
[49] Letter of E. B. Ward to Detroit *Daily Advertiser*, quoted in New York
World, January 23, 1861; E. B. Ward to Lincoln, January 4, 1861, Lincoln Papers.
[50] John Murray Forbes to Andrew, February 2, 6, 1861, Andrew Papers; Pearson, *Andrew*, I, 160–61.

men angrily attacked the South for creating a panic, for blocking a higher tariff, or for interfering with their business ventures. A Cincinnati commission merchant, who discovered himself on a New Orleans black list for supporting Lincoln, raged: "I am now, more than ever for the Chicago platform, the enforcement of the Laws, & the *Constitution as it is*." [51] Nor did war seem so terrible to the dozen Boston manufacturers who, in February, petitioned Governor Andrew for contracts to supply military equipment for the state troops.[52]

Jay Cooke, the Philadelphia banker, was a rising capitalist who had boldly backed the victorious Republican party and expected suitable compensation. Through his brother, Henry Cooke, the editor of the *Ohio State Journal*, Jay had given financial support to Salmon P. Chase, who became Lincoln's Secretary of the Treasury, and to John Sherman, who was elected to Chase's vacated seat in the Senate. Jay Cooke at once sought to profit from his contacts with the new administration through business with the Treasury Department. Nor was he slow to appreciate the opportunities that the war presented to his banking enterprise.[53] Inevitably Cooke's evaluation of the whole situation was different from that of an established capitalist or a New York dry-goods merchant.

But it was not exceptional individuals like Cooke, Ward, or Forbes who provided the real paradox of the propertied classes. This was found in the attitudes of the vast majority of businessmen who clamored so loudly for compromise and against war. The paradox was in their simultaneous protests against any sign of government weakness toward the secessionists, against the slightest tendency to yield the basic features of Federal authority in the South. In December, for instance, while the merchants were

[51] Benj. P. Baker to Sherman, January 2, 1861, Sherman Papers. See also G. F. Carpenter to *id.*, December 22, 1860; A. G. Bemon to *id.*, January 9, 1861; M. Coffin to *id.*, January 21, 1861, *ibid.*; Charles Winslow to Wade, December 31, 1860, Wade Papers; Cyrus Woodman to Andrew, February 16, 1861, Andrew Papers; John C. Dodge to Cyrus Woodman, November 19, 1860, Woodman Papers, Wisconsin Historical Society; George Livermore to Sumner, December 12, 1860, Sumner Papers; Worcester (Mass.) *Daily Spy* (letter from Francis J. Parker), December 17, 1860.

[52] These requests for contracts are in the papers of Adjutant General William Schouler between February 6 and 18, 1861.

[53] Henrietta M. Larson, *Jay Cooke, Private Banker* (Cambridge, 1936), 100–105; Ellis P. Oberholtzer, *Jay Cooke: Financier of the Civil War* (Philadelphia, 1907), I, 128–29, 131–33.

laboring mightily for concessions, they were also expressing mounting displeasure with Buchanan's alleged timidity. Stocks were depressed and business further upset because the President wavered and appeared on the verge of capitulating to the secessionists. At length a delegation of thirty New York merchants visited Buchanan to discuss the crisis. These men registered disgust with his lack of firmness and made it clear that they wanted the forts held and the revenues collected.[54]

Subsequent evidence that Buchanan had regained his nerve was received in business circles with great satisfaction, and the immediate result was renewed confidence in the future. The merchants showered praise upon Major Anderson for his move to Fort Sumter, and they insisted that the government sustain him there. On January 4 a meeting of Philadelphia businessmen urged Buchanan to send Anderson "such reinforcements as will convince him and the enemies of the Republic that the laws are to be enforced at all hazards." A day later the New York shipping merchants expressed their gratitude to Anderson for his "noble stand" and assured him that he was "heartily supported by the mercantile population of this city." [55] Before the *Star of the West* attempted to relieve Sumter a group of New York merchants tendered General Scott a proposal to send reinforcements through their private efforts.[56] Meanwhile these same men had played a decisive role in forcing the reorganization of Buchanan's cabinet and ensuring its control by Unionists.[57] A commercial commen-

[54] James D. Ogden to Crittenden, December 22, 1860; James B. Murray to *id.*, December 22, 1860; Daniel Lord to *id.*, December 22, 1860, Crittenden Papers; George Woodman to Cyrus Woodman, December 26, 1860, Woodman Papers; *Morning Courier and New-York Enquirer* (Commercial column), December 6, 1860; January 3, 1861; Boston *Daily Journal*, December 11, 1860; Foner, *Business & Slavery*, 240–41.

[55] Letters to Anderson from Chas. Thatcher, January 1, 1861; Leverett Saltonstall, January 3, 1861; C. G. Childs, January 5, 1861; John Hammond, January 7, 1861, Anderson Papers. See also letters to Crittenden from Daniel Lord, December 29, 1860; James D. Ogden, December 29, 1860; James B. Murray, January 5, 1861, Crittenden Papers; New York *Times* ("Monetary Affairs"), January 3, 1861; New York *World* (Commercial column), January 7, 1861; *Morning Courier and New-York Enquirer* (Commercial column), January 4, 12, 1861.

[56] James A. Hamilton to Maj. Gen. Sanford, December 28, 1860, copy in Anderson Papers; *id.* to Scott, December 29, 1860, Buchanan Papers; *Official Records*, Ser. 1, I, 119; New York *Morning Express*, January 8, 1861; Foner, *Business & Slavery*, 241–43.

[57] See Chapter V.

tator finally concluded: "It is anarchy that merchants fear, much more than bloodshed." [58]

During the stalemate that prevailed in February, businessmen still combined demands for compromise with appeals that Federal authority be maintained. They complained because Buchanan tolerated violations of the laws and made no effort to punish offenders.[59] New proposals for private relief to Sumter were sent to Secretary of War Holt.[60] After March 4 the New York merchants singled out retiring Secretary of the Treasury Dix for special commendation. They entertained him at a public reception and voiced their appreciation for his "decision, firmness and fidelity," through which "confidence was restored, the national credit preserved and the integrity of the laws vindicated." These grateful merchants referred to themselves as "members of a community deeply interested in the maintenance of all the authority of constitutional government." [61]

Thus by March it was evident that northern businessmen had carefully measured the consequences of disunion and the collapse of central authority and decided that they were intolerable. They had called for appeasement, but when that failed they were soon reconciled to the use of force. Many of them concluded that property had received about as much damage from the crisis as it could, that "no new phase which the [secession] movement may take can have any further effect." Stocks had reached their lowest average quotations in December when the government seemed weakest, and even the approach of war failed to depress them that much again. As one commercial writer saw it, business was already suffering "all it could from a state of actual war." [62] After four months of political panic, capitalists had discounted most of its economic effects and were prepared to see the issue through. All this had much to do with the general cry for action that arose

[58] New York *Herald* (Financial and Commercial column), December 28, 1860; January 3, 1861.

[59] *Ibid.* ("Washington Correspondence"), February 12, 1861; *Morning Courier and New-York Enquirer* (Commercial column), February 18, 1861.

[60] Letters to Holt from W. P. Thomasson, February 6, 1861; James N. Lawrence, February 12, 1861; John P. Crosby, February 12, 1861, Holt Papers.

[61] New York *Evening Post*, March 14, 1861.

[62] *Morning Courier and New-York Enquirer* (Commercial column), December 31, 1860; January 22, 1861; New York *Herald* (Financial and Commercial column), December 31, 1860; January 11, 12, 18, 19, 1861.

in business communities late in March. And when war finally came the northern men of property united behind Lincoln to save the Union and restore the prestige of the national government.

6

When Yankee capitalists at last endorsed the use of military force against secessionists, they accepted the final remedy for a solemn threat to their property and future profits. Inevitably the holders of government securities looked upon disunion as a menace to their investments. The value of national bonds declined dangerously with each evidence of government weakness, and many feared that Federal credit, at home and abroad, would soon be completely ruined. One conservative nervously declared: "So long as the right of secession is acknowledged, United States bonds must still be denounced as entirely unsafe property to hold. . . . One of the most substantial reasons for the formation of the present confederacy was the impossibility of raising money for the purpose of general defense and general government without a Union of a permanent character." To permit states to leave the Union at will, he warned, would mean that "United States stocks are really worth no more than old Continental money." [63] With this in mind, when another government loan was offered in January, an observer shrewdly predicted: "Every dollar N York takes binds her capitalists to the Union, and the North." [64]

Businessmen also believed that the reduction of the government to impotence would not only destroy its own credit but depress every form of private property. A basic tenet of the northern middle classes was that the value of property depended upon political stability. That condition was "the first necessity for business, . . . the life and soul of commerce," the pillar of capital,

[63] New York *Herald* (Financial and Commercial column), December 17, 1860; January 17, 1861. See also remarks of Rep. John A. Gurley of Ohio, in *Congressional Globe*, 418; Trenton *Daily State Gazette and Republican*, February 18, 1861; *Morning Courier and New-York Enquirer*, January 12; February 26; April 9, 1861; New York *Evening Post* ("Washington Correspondence"), February 14, 1861; Boston *Daily Advertiser*, February 14, 1861; Philadelphia *North American and United States Gazette* (letter from "Independent"), February 11, 1861; Washington *Daily National Intelligencer*, January 2, 1861.

[64] N. C. Nash to Sumner, January 15, 1861, Sumner Papers.

"whether it assumes the shape of land, labor, stocks or money." [65]
Once surrender the power of government and "down will go all
our stocks, . . . and every species of property will feel it." Then,
"No pursuit of life can be followed with the prospect of certain
rewards to honest industry. . . . [There] will never be a moment's certainty of that order and tranquility in which alone industry and commerce can thrive." Economic progress would
cease and business would languish.[66]

Another axiom of the middle classes was the sacredness and in-
violability of property rights. Accordingly they tended not only
to regard southern seizures of Federal forts and arsenals as a peril-
ous defiance of government authority but as a transgression upon
a vital social principle. In effect, secessionists had made an indirect
attack upon the possessions of every property holder. They had
virtually invited propertyless Northerners, the "revolutionary 'sans culottes,' " "the unwashed and unterrified," to precipitate the country into "rough and tumble anarchy." This "social
and moral deterioration" might easily infect the lower classes with
the radical idea "that a raid upon property can be justified by the
plea of necessity." Conservatives looked apprehensively at the
"immense foreign element" in northern cities and feared that revolution was "nearer our doors than we imagine." From these recent
immigrants could come the mobs to set aside all law and order
and, with "revolver and stiletto," sink the nation "into confusion
and riotous chaos." [67] The only alternative, it was repeatedly argued, was to enforce respect for the Federal government everywhere. The New York *World* explained:

> The conservative classes have the deepest stake in the pres-
> ervation of civil order. The supremacy of law, and the stability
> of which this supremacy is the foundation, are the theme of

[65] New York *Times*, April 12, 1861; New York *Evening Post*, January 3, 11,
1861; *Morning Courier and New-York Enquirer*, January 11, 1861; Chicago
Daily Tribune, April 6, 1861.

[66] Philadelphia *Public Ledger*, January 3, 1861; New York *Evening Post*,
January 31, 1861; Chicago *Daily Tribune*, January 14; February 15, 1861;
P. J. Joachimsen to Douglas, January 30, 1861, Douglas Papers.

[67] New York *World*, February 16, 1861; New York *Commercial Advertiser*,
April 11, 1861; New York *Morning Express*, January 11, 1861; *Morning Courier
and New-York Enquirer*, March 4, 1861; Bellows to "My dear friend" (Cyrus A.
Bartol), December 12, 1860, Bellows Papers; remarks of Representative Alexander H. Rice of Massachusetts, in *Congressional Globe*, Appendix, 275.

their constant eulogy, because there is no other solid support
for the rights of property, for the preservation of credit, the
safety of commerce, the tranquility and security of private
life. . . . It is for their advantage that all symptoms of in-
subordination to established law should be repressed with
wholesome vigor; for when an insurrectionary spirit once gets
the upper hand, there is no predicting how far it will spread,
nor where it will stop. . . . Our whole safety rests on the
strict and impartial enforcement of the laws.[68]

Secession, then, endangered the fabric of credit and the institution of property. Ultimately the business classes concluded that
it would impair the national economy in other ways as well. In
the early stages of the crisis many Northerners tried either to re-
assure themselves or restrain Southerners with the argument that
the Union was of greater value to the South than to the North.
But this feeble strategy was soon abandoned, and before long the
terror of disunion had doubtless produced an exaggerated picture
of its consequences. "It is often said," commented the New York
Times, "that the apprehension of danger is worse than the danger itself. It is not easy to say what evils would follow a dissolution of the Union,—but they could scarcely be more serious
than the general fear of that event has already caused to our business interests." [69]

One grim prospect before merchants and bankers was the repudiation of southern debts, perhaps even the confiscation of their
property holdings in that section. Despite numerous reassurances
that these obligations would be respected, the belief steadily grew
that secession was the work of "sundry persons whose debts to
the North are too grievous to be borne, and who look to repudiation as one of the effects of revolution." Proposals for debt
moratoriums or cancellations appeared in the southern press frequently enough to lend plausibility to this suspicion.[70] And so a

[68] New York *World*, December 31, 1860. See also New York *Times*, December
25, 1860; Philadelphia *North American and United States Gazette*, April 9, 1861;
remarks of Representative William A. Howard of Michigan, in *Congressional
Globe*, 1227.

[69] New York *Times*, December 7, 1860. See also Boston *Daily Journal*, November 16, 17, 19, 1860; remarks of Representative John B. Alley of Massachusetts,
in *Congressional Globe*, 584-85.

[70] Boston *Daily Journal*, November 16, 1860; New York *Times*, November
12; December 4, 1860; Clayton (Ala.) *Banner*, quoted in New York *Daily Trib-*

feeling crept "over the mercantile community, that . . . the *cheapest* course of all . . . will be to enforce the laws. . . . The money due the North may be long coming, . . . but [if secession were tolerated] it will never come." [71] John Bigelow knew one New York merchant who "had not a word to say in condemnation of the South till they stopped paying him. . . . Fortunately for his patriotism, they have refused to pay him and restored him to his country." [72]

Still other disturbing questions arose as the disunion movement proceeded: What would prevent secessionists from making depreciated paper money legal tender in the payment of private debts? What assurance was there that they would respect the constitutional mandate against violating the obligation of contract? "What becomes of the cases in law and equity, in Admiralty and maritime jurisdiction, now pending and undetermined in the United States Circuit and District Courts?" What chance would northern merchants have to obtain justice in southern state courts? What would happen to Federal land grants made to northern-owned railroads in various southern states? Finally, would not secessionists violate northern copyrights and patent rights? [73] The answer to this last question reputedly came from Judah P. Benjamin, the Confederate Attorney General. He informed a northern manufacturer that every Federal patent would have to be validated by the new southern government before it would be binding. If that were the case, might not Confederates seek to raise a revenue by levying heavy fees on patentees as the price for recognizing their patent rights? "What confusion and distress," wrote an observer, would "thus be created throughout our manufacturing regions!" [74]

At the same time, businessmen gradually became convinced that southern independence would be almost fatal to northern com-

une, December 28, 1860; Philadelphia *Press* (Washington dispatch), December 28, 1860; Philadelphia *North American and United States Gazette*, March 20, 1861; Boston *Daily Journal*, November 15, 1860; Cole, *Irrepressible Conflict*, 282–83; P. J. Joachimsen to Douglas, January 30, 1861, Douglas Papers.

[71] New York *World*, January 19, 1861.
[72] Bigelow Ms. Diary, quoted in Foner, *Business & Slavery*, 302.
[73] New York *Times*, January 3, 1861; Boston *Daily Courier*, December 25, 1860; Boston *Evening Transcript*, January 18, 1861.
[74] "Diary of a Public Man," *loc. cit.*, 139, 486.

merce. American maritime power in the Caribbean and Gulf of Mexico would vanish with the loss of such strategic positions as New Orleans, Mobile, Pensacola, and Key West. An independent Confederacy might seize Cuba, Mexico, and Central America, exclude the North from their trade, and convert the Caribbean into a "great inland lake . . . over which they . . . exercise complete control." The government would be deprived of naval bases to protect shippers from piracy and privateering. Even trade with the Pacific would be at the mercy of the South, for she would control the direct route through the Isthmus. Hence these Gulf positions were as essential to northern mercantile interests as Gibraltar was to Great Britain.[75] A newspaper correspondent explained precisely what the merchants had at stake:

> . . . Their commerce pours in an uninterrupted stream through the Gulf, and through every avenue of ingress and egress that leads to and from it. That commerce requires and will forever demand the security and protection of forts, and harbors, and military succor, whenever occasion necessitates it, somewhere within those waters. Key West, the Tortugas, and Pensacola belong more, a thousand times more, to the great maritime and commercial interests of the Free States. . . . Those posts are in themselves alone of sufficient importance to create and justify a war, even a long and bloody war, should their possession be contested.[76]

The northern monopoly in the coasting trade was a further casualty of the disunion movement. It was hardly surprising, but nonetheless disconcerting, when, in February, the Confederate Congress abrogated the United States navigation laws and opened their coastwise commerce to the ships of all nations.[77] An alarmed New York capitalist wrote Secretary Chase that foreign vessels would now enjoy a lucrative triangular trade, carrying European goods to New York, these and northern manufactures to the

---

[75] New York *Times*, January 19, 26; February 5, 7, 1861; New York *Daily Tribune*, January 25; March 16, 1861; Philadelphia *North American and United States Gazette*, January 25; March 13, 1861; *Daily Boston Traveller*, November 17, 1860; Worcester (Mass.) *Daily Spy*, January 19, 1861; *Official Records*, Ser. 1, I, 112; speech of George S. Boutwell, quoted in Boston *Daily Advertiser*, January 8, 1861; remarks of Representative John A. McClernand of Illinois, in *Congressional Globe*, 369.

[76] New York *Daily Tribune* (letter from J. S. Pike), January 11, 1861.

[77] Russel, *Economic Aspects of Southern Sectionalism*, 261.

South, and southern cotton back to Europe. Thus would emerge "a competing force, that under its arrangements would nearly impoverish our coasting trade." Vowing that he had "an interest and proprietorship in the Union of *all* these States," this New Yorker concluded that secession would have to be checkmated by "force of a most formidable character." [78] Since New York merchants had just rejected a proposal to repeal the coasting-trade monopoly,[79] they were not inclined to let disunionists deprive them of that valued prize.

Yankee manufacturers were equally apprehensive that selling their wares to an independent and hostile Confederacy would be extremely difficult and that much of this previously profitable market would be lost. Secessionists strengthened this opinion with their proposals to boycott or heavily tax the goods coming from the hated North.[80] Shipping to the South had already become a precarious business. Marine-insurance companies asked the government whether it would assume liability for disasters resulting from South Carolina's removal of lights and buoys from Charleston Harbor. They also inserted war clauses in their policies and considerably advanced their rates on risks from New York to southern ports.[81] Commerce with the South became still more difficult when the seceded states began issuing port clearances in their own names. Since no foreign country recognized their right to exercise that power, a vessel with such a clearance would be subject to seizure and detention in a European port.[82] The State Department was bombarded with demands from domestic merchants and foreign consuls that this situation be clarified. Black's replies were evasive, but he affirmed that the government would never "recognize clearances made by state officers or regard any payment of duties as an acquittance of an importer's

---

[78] Lorenzo Sherwood to Chase, March 14, 1861, Chase Papers. See also New York *Evening Post*, March 5, 1861; Boston *Daily Courier*, February 12, 1861; Springfield (Mass.) *Daily Republican*, March 30, 1861.

[79] See Chapter IX.

[80] New York *Herald*, March 26, 27, 1861; Dumond, *Secession Movement*, 142; Russel, *Economic Aspects of Southern Sectionalism*, 255.

[81] Alex. Fraser to E. B. Washburne, January 4, 1861, E. B. Washburne Papers; Boston *Daily Advertiser*, January 10, 1861.

[82] New York *Herald* (Financial and Commercial column), December 28, 1860; Philadelphia *North American and United States Gazette*, March 29, 1861.

obligation unless made to the proper federal officer." [83] This was a source of embarrassment to northern shippers which could only be removed by the re-establishment of national authority in the South.

A most irritating incident occurred in February, when the Governor of Georgia ordered the seizure of several New York ships at Savannah in retaliation for the detention in New York of arms destined for his state. The New York *Herald* called the Governor's act "the most grave and momentous event that has yet occurred, in the progress toward civil war." It created "naturally a very deep feeling of resentment in this city." [84] "Such a proceeding," raged the New York *World*, "is worthy of some half civilized Asiatic satrap, or some petty potentate of the Barbary states, . . . before the siege of Algiers." [85] Democratic Representative John Cochrane of New York immediately became interested in legislation to protect shippers from secessionist attacks upon their vessels. [86] This incident substantially increased the concern about the future of trade with the Confederacy.

Meanwhile many southern leaders had revived their longstanding interest in the establishment of direct commerce between their section and Europe. In March the Confederate Congress provided for a committee to promote this project, and President Davis sent William L. Yancey, Pierre A. Rost, and A. Dudley Mann to Europe to bid for recognition and commercial treaties. [87] Every southern port hoped to become a great metropolis in the new Confederacy. "In the Union," explained the Charleston *Mercury*, "our city has been tributary to New York; out of the Union, she will be the triumphant rival of her northern mistress." [88] Moses Kelly, chief clerk of the Department of Interior, heard numerous Southerners proclaim that secession was the

[83] J. A. Campbell to Black, January 23, 1861; Black to Campbell, January, 1861, Black Papers; New York *World*, February 5, 1861; Philadelphia *Press*, February 1, 1861; Boston *Daily Advertiser*, March 16, 1861.

[84] New York *Herald*, February 9, 10, 11, 24; March 17, 20, 1861; *Morning Courier and New-York Enquirer*, February 11, 1861; Philadelphia *Press*, February 11, 1861.

[85] New York *World*, February 11, 1861.

[86] New York *Herald*, February 10, 1861.

[87] *Ibid.*, March 16; April 1, 1861; Boston *Daily Advertiser*, March 8, 1861; Russel, *Economic Aspects of Southern Sectionalism*, 255-57.

[88] Charleston *Mercury*, quoted in New York *World*, December 12, 1861.

means "of accomplishing a long cherished plan . . . to make a
New York of *Charleston*. It is also said that this feeling is extending among those who are interested in Mobile, New Orleans and
other southern ports. . . ." [89] These direct-trade projects promised both to deprive northern merchants of their position as
middlemen and to eject northern manufacturers from the southern market in favor of European competitors. This prospect was
a major factor in driving businessmen, first, to efforts at compromise and, finally, to a desire to enforce the laws. The Philadelphia
Press asked rhetorically: "If South Carolina is permitted to establish a free port with impunity, and to invite to her harbor all the
ships of foreign nations, would not disaster in that event fall upon
all our great northern interests?" It accurately predicted "an
early reawakening of the Union sentiment in New York." [90]

By April few northern businessmen disputed the New York
Evening Post's argument that the Union was an economic necessity:

> We cannot afford to have established on this continent the
> intolerable restrictions to commercial intercourse, which are
> fast dying out among the nations of Europe. Our vast progress
> and unparalleled prosperity depend upon continental free
> trade, even more than upon our cheap and fertile lands. . . .
> We cannot permit the Gulf of Mexico to become a foreign
> sea to our shipping, now the greatest in the world. . . . We
> have come to a crisis where we have everything at stake. Lib-
> erty, morality, industry, commerce, progress, respect abroad
> and peace at home, all depend upon this, that the government
> shall assert its power, vindicate the outraged laws, and teach
> treason such a lesson that she will not soon raise her head again
> in the land.[91]

[89] Moses Kelly to Pierce, November 23, 1860, Pierce Papers. See also J. W.
Schaumburg to Chase, March 9, 1861, Chase Papers; Wm. W. Ellsworth to
Hon. James Dixon, in New York *Herald*, December 19, 1860; New York *Evening Post* (letter from South Carolina planter), November 30, 1860.
[90] Philadelphia *Press*, December 25, 27, 1860. See also A. G. Bemon to Sherman, January 28, 1861, Sherman Papers; New York *Herald*, December 15, 1860;
Boston *Herald*, November 12, 1860; Boston *Daily Courier*, November 20, 1860;
January 5, 1861.
[91] New York *Evening Post*, April 11, 1861.

7

A low tariff was to be the Confederacy's chief device for emancipating its planters and merchants from northern exploitation. And the tariff therefore became the challenge which, more than anything else, crystallized sentiment among Yankee businessmen in favor of applying force against the South.[92] Early in the crisis, a few merchants appreciated the complications that would result from the simultaneous operation of a northern system of protection and a southern system of free trade. This, they realized, would guarantee the establishment of direct commerce between the South and Europe. More, it would put a premium upon the smuggling of imported goods from the seceded states, where they escaped payment of the Union tariff, into the North. This difficulty was one of the major reasons why some observers believed all along that war was inevitable.[93]

By the time of Lincoln's inauguration the revenue question had become the most exasperating menace to northern business. In February the Confederate Congress had re-enacted the Federal tariff of 1857 and provided that its rates would be levied upon goods purchased in the North after March 1. This act brought a rush of orders from the South during the last days of February, and northern merchants enjoyed a brisk trade. But by March this flurry of commercial activity had ceased, and business again became stagnant.[94] Then the Yankee manufacturer suddenly found himself deprived of protection from his European competitors and forced to pay the same duties levied upon foreign goods in the southern market. The northern importer was at an even greater disadvantage. He saw that the southern tariff would "make goods imported into the Confederate States *via* the United States *pay double duty*," which was the equivalent of entirely forcing him out of this trade.[95]

[92] For a brilliant analysis of the effect of the tariff question upon the attitudes of New York merchants see Foner, *Business & Slavery*, 275–305.

[93] New York *Journal of Commerce* (letter from "T."), November 13, 1860; Philadelphia *North American and United States Gazette*, November 14, 1860; New York *Evening Post*, January 5, 1861; W. T. Sherman to John Sherman, February 1, 1861; E. W. Dunham to *id.*, February 8, 1861, Sherman Papers.

[94] New York *Evening Post*, March 1, 7, 1861; Foner, *Business & Slavery*, 277.

[95] *Morning Courier and New-York Enquirer* (Commercial column), February 25, 1861; New York *Herald*, March 16, 1861.

But soon an already deplorable commercial situation would become altogether hopeless. On April 1 the North and South would cease to have even the same schedule of duties, for that was the date when the new Morrill Tariff would go into effect. Thereafter the duties levied in northern ports would be almost double those levied in the ports of the Confederacy under the old tariff of 1857. Under those conditions every Yankee merchant was convinced that he faced bankruptcy. European goods would avoid northern entrepôts and flow directly to the South, whose cities would achieve a position of mercantile supremacy. "It is well known," reported a commercial paper, "that at least *one million dollars* in foreign orders, which have gone forward, have been *countermanded* and ordered from New York to Mobile and New Orleans." [96] The English and French press made it quite clear to American businessmen that foreign merchants and manufacturers intended to take full advantage of the low southern tariff.[97] Thus, wailed the Boston *Courier*, "the productions of the South, instead of benefiting its own kin in the North, and flowing back in innumerable channels, . . . would confer the same benefit upon merely self-interested strangers and foreigners. . . ." [98] The New York *Times* published a dismal editorial entitled "The Beginning of the End": ". . . The result of this policy cannot be doubtful. . . . We shall not only cease to see marble palaces rising along Broadway; but reduced from a national to a merely provincial Metropolis, our shipping will rot at the wharves and grass grow in our streets. No earthly influence, short of a reversal of the policy referred to, can save not only New York, but every Northern port from this frightful destiny." [99]

It was also feared that the Confederate revenue policy would become an irresistible lure to the border slave states and make it impossible to hold them in the Union. As the boundaries of the

[96] Boston *Commercial Bulletin*, quoted in Boston *Daily Journal*, April 1, 1861. See also Boston *Evening Transcript*, March 18, 1861; New York *Herald*, March 12, 14, 28, 1861.

[97] London *Times*, quoted in New York *Herald*, March 27, 1861; London *Examiner*, quoted in Boston *Daily Courier*, March 9, 1861; Paris *Le Pays*, quoted in Boston *Daily Courier*, March 8, 1861; Paris *Moniteur*, quoted in Boston *Post*, March 20, 1861.

[98] Boston *Daily Courier*, March 9, 1861.

[99] New York *Times*, March 29, 1861.

Confederacy thus expanded, the area of northern trade would be further contracted.[100] Then would follow the establishment of a long and expensive line of interior customhouses and all the resulting inconveniences of bonding goods and searching freight passing from one section to another. For instance, a Confederate Treasury circular instituted a set of complex regulations governing the importation of goods from the North over the railroads. Thereby the country would have on its own soil "a taste of the customs annoyances which . . . [were] so unbearable in Europe." [101]

But the most fearful aspect of the tariff conflict was the probability that the extended, unnatural frontier between the Union and Confederacy could not be effectively guarded, that smuggling from the South into the North would occur on an enormous scale. In that manner the Northwest would be able to purchase cheap European goods through the South and escape paying the high Morrill Tariff. Merchants read in their newspapers extracts from the London *Times* showing that European businessmen already perceived their chance to invade the northern market. After a violent denunciation of Yankee protectionists, the *Times* commented: "The smuggler will redress the errors of the statesman, as he has so often done before." [102] The New York *Evening Post* described the prospect before northern commercial interests:

> . . . Allow railroad iron to be entered at Savannah with the low duty of ten per cent, . . . and not an ounce more would be imported at New York; the railways would be supplied from the southern ports. Let cotton goods, let woolen fabrics, let the various manufactures of iron and steel be entered freely at Galveston, at the great port at the mouth of the Mississippi, at Mobile, at Savannah and at Charleston, and they would be immediately sent up the rivers and carried on the railways to the remotest parts of the Union. . . . The whole country would be given up to an immense system of smuggling, which,

[100] Foner, *Business & Slavery*, 283.

[101] New York *Evening Post*, March 26, 1861; Springfield (Mass.) *Daily Republican*, March 28, 1861; Philadelphia *Public Ledger*, March 16, 1861.

[102] London *Times*, quoted in New York *Herald*, March 17, 1861. See also *ibid.*, March 15, 16, 1861; New York *Commercial Advertiser*, March 28, 1861; Boston *Daily Advertiser*, March 14, 1861.

on near two thousand miles of coast, would meet with no obstacle. . . .[103]

Indeed, might not this free trade system soon persuade the agrarian West to join the southern Confederacy too? "And can New York," asked one merchant, "afford not only to lose its trade with the South, . . . but to hazard the loss of the trade of the eight millions of inhabitants of the Northwestern states?" [104]

Before long this danger had become a reality. A Cincinnati commercial house reported that goods were arriving at that city' from New Orleans tariff free. Since there were no customs officers at Cincinnati, there was nothing beyond a "moral obligation" to pay the duties. But "self protection would soon force any firm to pursue a different course if others get goods free." [105] Eastern businessmen were panic-stricken by a widely circulated news item from the St. Louis *Republican:*

> Every day our importers of foreign merchandise are receiving, by way of New Orleans, very considerable quantities of goods, duty free. . . . If this thing is to become permanent, there will be an entire revolution in the course of trade, and New York will suffer terribly. Our merchants have capital enough to justify them in making their purchases in Europe, and shipping to New Orleans; and in that city, because of the difference in the tariff, goods can be bought cheaper than in New York. With these advantages we shall be able to sell cheaper than any other city in the valley of the Mississippi.[106]

Yankee capitalists searched desperately for a remedy for this impossible condition. As a temporary expedient many Boston and New York importers formally protested the payment of customs rates prescribed by the Morrill Tariff. They argued that it was unconstitutional to charge those duties in northern ports so long

[103] New York *Evening Post*, March 12, 1861. See also *Daily Chicago Post*, March 16, 1861.

[104] New York *Journal of Commerce* (letter from "J.M.B."), February 25, 1861; Foner, *Business & Slavery*, 284.

[105] D. W. Fairchild to Chase, March 29, 1861, Chase Papers. See also New York *Evening Post*, March 21, 1861; Indianapolis *Indiana Daily State Sentinel*, March 25, 1861.

[106] St. Louis *Missouri Republican*, quoted in New York *Evening Post*, March 27, 1861.

as similar duties were not collected in southern ports.[107] But revenue officers ignored their complaints. Another alternative was to work for the repeal of the Morrill Tariff. Confirmed free traders seized this opportunity to discredit a piece of legislation they had always opposed. Papers like the New York *Evening Post* demanded a special session of Congress to save northern commerce by reducing duties to Confederate levels.[108] In the end their campaign failed, but not until it had aroused the powerful protectionist elements in New England and Pennsylvania. Then there were reports that some merchants planned to solve the problem by moving to the South, or by establishing branch houses in that section.[109] A few might have escaped the dilemma in that way, but the national commercial crisis would still remain for most northern merchants.

Meanwhile a handful of New York politicians and businessmen toyed with a more daring project: Their scheme was to establish New York as a Free City independent of all the states and released from any Federal control of its commercial intercourse. As early as January, Mayor Fernando Wood had hinted at this idea, and a few newspapers like the *Daily News* and *Journal of Commerce* had discussed it sympathetically.[110] After the tariff problem arose, wild rumors were afloat that a secret league, numbering 5,000 members, was plotting to seize the city and make it an independent republic.[111] New York could thus escape the burden of the Morrill Tariff and preserve its position in the southern trade. The trouble was that there were corresponding disadvantages which prevented the movement from ever assuming substantial proportions. Independence could not save the western trade for New

[107] *Ibid.*, April 3, 10, 12, 1861; Boston *Daily Advertiser*, April 6, 1861; Boston *Daily Journal*, April 8, 1861.

[108] New York *Evening Post*, March 20, 23, 25, 26, 28, 29; April 1, 1861; New York *Commercial Advertiser*, March 15, 26, 1861; New York *Leader*, March 9, 1861.

[109] New York *Herald*, March 16, 1861; New York *World*, March 23, 1861; Savannah *Republican*, quoted in New York *Evening Post*, March 29, 1861.

[110] New York *Herald*, December 8, 15, 21, 1860; January 8, 1861; New York *Evening Post*, January 7, 22, 1861; New York *Journal of Commerce*, December 15, 21, 1861; New York *Morning Express*, January 8, 1861; Foner, *Business & Slavery*, 285–96.

[111] John Jay to Chase, April 4, 1861, in Chase, *Diary and Correspondence*, 493; New York *Evening Post*, April 4, 5, 1861; New York *Herald*, April 3, 1861; *Morning Courier and New-York Enquirer*, April 6, 1861.

York; nor would it help commission merchants who did business with northern manufacturers. Actually the risks of this project were too great to appeal to any but the most extreme prosouthern merchants. The New Yorkers who sponsored it were as small a minority as the Westerners who favored the equally chimerical proposal for a Northwest Confederacy.[112]

After examining all the alternatives, the vast majority of merchants were driven to demand the defense of the Union and the enforcement of the revenue laws in the South. That seemed to be the only safe, permanent, and practical solution of the tariff muddle. By the end of March northern mercantile interests were clamoring loudly for government action, especially for a blockade of southern ports.[113] Their earlier misgivings about signs of government weakness had matured into a desire for a positive demonstration of government power. The Chicago *Tribune* jubilantly noted "a marked change of sentiment on the part of those connected with the great commercial interests of New York city." The southern threat to northern commerce was "more than the flunkeys of that city bargained for or expected," and now they were asking, "Have we a government?"[114] The New York *Herald* saw that Seward's program of "masterly inactivity" was utterly defeated: "Mr. Lincoln's administration will soon be compelled to do something to save itself, and the suffering people of the North . . . are anxiously waiting to know . . . what Mr. Lincoln intends to do."[115] Others recalled that a major objective of the framers of the Constitution was "the better protection of commerce" which had been embarrassed by the rival tariffs of the various states. "We are now going back to this ruinous system, . . . and no hand is stretched out to save us."[116] The New York *Commercial Advertiser* recorded the revolution in sentiment that had taken place among the merchants: "These grave hindrances to commerce . . . are working their natural effect upon the commercial mind, and the feeling deepens and widens that the work of disorganization now in progress *must be stopped* by one means or another. This utter inanition of the fed-

[112] Foner, *Business & Slavery*, 297.
[114] Chicago *Daily Tribune*, March 27, 1861.
[115] New York *Herald*, March 23, 28, 1861.
[116] New York *World*, April 5, 1861.

[113] *Ibid.*, 298–305.

eral government cannot much longer be tolerated. . . . Under the present condition of things no one knows where to find the protecting arm of his government. . . . How long is it possible for a government to live under such conditions?" [117]

The tariff crisis had an equally marked effect upon the attitudes of northern manufacturers. Low southern duties and the smuggling threat created a situation which nullified all they had gained by the Morrill act. Representative Morrill noted with alarm that free traders were trying to make his bill "the scape-goat of all difficulties." [118] Fearing both the movement to repeal the Morrill Tariff and the Confederate challenge to northern industry, protectionist organs such as the New York *Tribune*, Chicago *Tribune*, and Philadelphia *North American* begged for military action against the South.[119] A critic of Greeley heatedly asserted that the *Tribune* editor would have let the South go in peace "if the Montgomery Government had not made a fatal stab at the tariff system." [120] But Greeley congratulated the industrialists of Pennsylvania for coming "with alacrity and cheerful decision forward, contributing to the aid of the Government menaced by Southern rebels and Northern traitors." Here, he thought, was evidence "that with the passage of this [Morrill] tariff act confidence was born into the minds of the classes on whose aid and countenance so much depends in the present hour." [121]

In March, during the executive session of the Senate, Clingman of North Carolina mocked the northern protectionists for the prospective failure of the new tariff. He explained to them how goods would come into the North from southern ports so long as they acted upon the theory that the seceded states were still a part of the Union. Their only salvation, he argued, was to recognize

[117] New York *Commercial Advertiser*, March 25, 1861. See also New York *Times*, March 22, 27, 1861; *Morning Courier and New-York Enquirer*, April 2, 1861; New York *World*, March 25, 1861; New York *Evening Post* ("Washington Correspondence"), March 22, 1861.
[118] Morrill to Sherman, April 1, 1861, quoted in Sherman, *Recollections*, I, 233.
[119] New York *Daily Tribune*, March 11, 19, 28; April 12, 1861; Philadelphia *North American and United States Gazette* (letters from "Independent"), March 8, 16, 18, 1861; Philadelphia *Press*, April 1, 1861; Boston *Daily Advertiser*, March 25, 1861; Chicago *Daily Tribune*, April 3, 1861.
[120] Indianapolis *Indiana Daily State Sentinel*, April 15, 1861; Providence *Daily Post*, March 16, 1861.
[121] New York *Daily Tribune*, April 11, 1861.

the Confederate government and establish customhouses along the southern border. But Simmons of Rhode Island, who had guided the Morrill bill through the Senate, rose to offer a different solution. "I have no doubt we shall continue to collect the revenues as we have done," he remarked with considerable feeling. "I know part of this scheme has been to make Charleston the great commercial emporium of the South. I think the fate of Charleston will be written in other language than that if they continue long in this position." And then he called upon the government to "administer the laws for the benefit of the whole country, and see that they are faithfully executed. That is their duty." [122] Simmons spoke the mind of the business classes as it had evolved on the eve of war.

[122] *Congressional Globe*, 1472, 1476.

XII

The Components of a Crusade

SUCH mundane matters as politics, investments, markets, and trade were basic ingredients of the war spirit which finally overwhelmed the northern people. But those articulate Yankees who ultimately endorsed the appeal to arms generally rationalized such a course in terms that were at once broader and more elevated than these everyday affairs. Economic motives for enforcing the laws were translated, unconsciously perhaps, into such elusive or romantic concepts as "national interest" and "Manifest Destiny." The belief in the practical blessings of the Union was richly decorated with the jewels of patriotism, nationalism, equality, and self-government. Simultaneously the destroyers of the Union became the violators of all these accepted virtues. They became obstacles to national progress and prosperity, enemies of democracy and freedom, degraded defenders of an effete slave economy, and criminal advocates of treason and corruption.

The widespread northern contempt for southern society was not merely an impetuous reaction against secession; it was also the product of a generation of sectional conflict. But the compelling impulse to strike a blow at that society was largely an end result of the disunion crisis. By the time the war began, many Yankees had transformed their desire to enforce the laws into the spirit of a holy crusade. While the North would save the Union it would also carry its enlightenment into the citadels of slavery. In short, the South would be civilized!

2

"National interest" is a concept whose meaning is seldom defined and whose validity is doubtful. As the term is generally applied it presupposes a oneness of purpose and social aspirations among regions and classes that rarely exists. Not only can the interpretation of "national interest" be extremely narrow and shortsighted, but the policy makers who implement the principle are capable of the most cavalier disregard for the desires of politically ineffective groups.

During the secession crisis, the northern majority shared David Wilmot's belief that "every national and moral interest" required the preservation of the Union.[1] If Southerners thought otherwise it was because they were misinformed and failed to understand how much they profited from their affiliation with the northern states. By blocking the disunionists the government would be serving the best interests of the South as well as of the North. Secession was an issue that had to be settled from a "point of view that regards it in its great historic bearings." It was not the desires of any special group that mattered, but what was "demanded by the lasting interests of the thirty millions that now inhabit the country." Disunion would mean such "mutilation and weakness" as "the national instinct of self-preservation would in no case permit." What Southerners failed to understand was that "physical conditions" imposed certain basic policies upon nations, and that in their application, men were "but the passive instruments of Providence."[2]

Just as secessionists threatened to infringe upon the country's deep need for organic unity, they also threw themselves recklessly in the path of another providential force: Manifest Destiny. They sought to reverse the relentless trend of the last half century, to fragmentize the nation when its divine mission was endless growth and expansion. The blood and treasure of Manifest Destiny had won the lands from which had been carved such states as Florida, Louisiana, and Texas. Hence Florida belonged to the Union "and not to the few planters and squatters occupying it." Texas could not secede with northern gold in her treasury and northern sons buried in her soil.[3] Secession of the cotton states

[1] Going, *Wilmot*, 572–73.

[2] New York *Daily Tribune*, January 29, 1861; New York *World*, November 16, 1860; Boston *Daily Advertiser*, January 2, 1861; Princeton *Review*, quoted in Boston *Evening Transcript*, January 10, 1861; Detroit *Free Press*, May 11, 1861.

[3] Philadelphia *North American and United States Gazette*, December 14, 1860; January 18, 1861; *Morning Courier and New-York Enquirer*, January 19,

would not end the movement but would lead to endless future separations until nothing was left but a collection of diminutive republics. There seemed to be convincing evidence for this in the reports from California that people were discussing a Pacific Republic, in the talk of a Northwest Confederacy, in the project for a Republic of New York, and in the agitation for even an independent State of Maine.[4] While violating the old manifest destiny, some secessionists seemed to feel a new manifest destiny of their own. They exhibited a desire to annex territories which Northerners had long coveted for the Union. Would not the rivalries of two or more ambitious peoples lead to a bloody race for empire? In fact the time might not be far distant when the armies of North and South would match their destinies on battlefields in Mexico and Cuba.[5]

And so, according to the Yankee argument, only by preserving the Union could Americans fulfill the promise of their Manifest Destiny. Governor-elect Andrew assured a Boston audience that the Union would not only survive but that it would eventually be "bounded only by the everlasting ice and impenetrable heat on the north and the south, and on either side by the waves of the ocean." [6] This crisis, warned the New York *World*, was "the testing time of our destiny." This destiny was "to build up the new world with the institutions of Christian civilization—to spread over its vast domains the triumphs of industry, intelligence and virtue. . . . We cannot forego this design without defying the will of heaven, the conscience of the civilized world, and the undeniable purpose of the fathers." [7] Henry J. Raymond exuded

26, 1861; Springfield (Mass.) *Daily Republican*, November 15, 1860; remarks of Senator James R. Doolittle of Wisconsin, in *Congressional Globe*, 199.

[4] New York *World*, December 1, 1860; San Francisco *Mirror*, quoted *ibid.*, December 19, 1860; Portland (Me.) *Eastern Argus*, December 12, 1860; Boston *Daily Courier*, December 29, 1860; Philadelphia *Morning Pennsylvanian*, December 12, 1860; Philadelphia *North American and United States Gazette*, March 13, 1861.

[5] E. Geo. Squires to Sumner, February 10, 1861, Sumner Papers; New York *Times*, December 26, 1860; Chicago *Daily Tribune*, March 19, 1861; Adams, "Secession Winter," *loc. cit.*, 661.

[6] Springfield (Mass.) *Daily Republican*, November 9, 1860. See also S. G. Lane to McPherson, December 14, 1860, McPherson Papers.

[7] New York *World*, December 24, 1860. See also Philadelphia *Press*, December 22, 1860; [Lowell], "E Pluribus Unum," *loc. cit.*, 243; remarks of Representative James Humphrey of New York, in *Congressional Globe*, Appendix, 160.

the spirit of his bumptious contemporaries when he explained the sacrifices that disunion would entail:

> . . . We should be surrendering . . . all chance of future accessions from Mexico, Central America or the West India Islands. . . . Have you seen any indications which encourage the hope of so magnificent a self-sacrifice on the part of the people? What is there in our past history to lead you to consider us thus reckless of national growth and national grandeur? . . . Nine-tenths of our people in the Northern and Northwestern States would wage a war longer than the war of Independence before they will assent to any such surrender of their aspirations and their hopes. There is no nation in the world so ambitious of growth and of power,—so thoroughly pervaded with the spirit of conquest,—so filled with dreams of enlarged dominions, as ours.[8]

In another sense, this common belief in a great national mission was an expression of the nationalistic and patriotic impulses that swayed the northern masses. In his inaugural address Lincoln spoke feelingly of the "mystic chords of memory, stretching from every battlefield and patriot grave to every living heart and hearthstone all over this broad land. . . ." Such an appeal did much to "swell the chorus of the Union" at least among Yankees who could see all about them the tangible blessings of national unity. Because of their profound loyalty to their country and their intense pride in its achievements, they looked upon efforts to destroy it as a crime akin to parricide. The humiliation of their government by secessionists invoked within them a sense of personal shame.[9] Such identification of the individual with the national state meant that the enforcement of the laws was a means of personal self-fulfillment as well as an act of government vindication.

Throughout the secession crisis, northern nationalism was fed through every channel of human expression. Scarcely a public concert was given which did not include a rendition of "The Star

[8] Letter of Henry J. Raymond to William L. Yancey, in New York *Times*, December 13, 1860.

[9] For an able discussion of the evolution of American nationalism and the impact of secession upon it see Merle E. Curti, *The Roots of American Loyalty* (New York, 1946), 30–64, 92–121, 159–72.

Spangled Banner" or "Hail Columbia." Clergymen spiced their sermons with patriotic sentiments; newspapers abounded with ardent, though ill-contrived, patriotic poetry. American classics such as Webster's reply to Hayne, Jackson's Proclamation on Nullification, and extracts from the *Federalist Papers* appeared in pamphlet form for general distribution. Late in 1860 the last volume of James Parton's *Life of Andrew Jackson* reached the public to provide a worthy example of how a brave soldier-President had dealt with an earlier crisis.[10] Washington's Birthday was the occasion for patriotic celebrations in every northern city and for pointed recollections of the sacrifices of Revolutionary heroes. In January, Governor Andrew arranged a public ceremony to present the Massachusetts legislature with two Revolutionary War muskets bequeathed to the state by Theodore Parker. Andrew delivered a stirring address designed to "bring souls under conviction." Then, before presenting the muskets to the receiving committee, he raised one of them to his lips and kissed it. His audience was "exalted." It was a "melting time," the Governor wrote Sumner, "a good days work, happening at the right time." [11]

These appeals to patriotism touched a sensitive nerve in almost every Northerner. James Russell Lowell found comfort in the belief that the existing crisis would at least arouse the people to "a sense of national unity" and throw them "back on their national instincts." [12] Countless Yankees voiced the bitterness they felt at the evidences of national weakness and at the insults they had experienced as American citizens. What hurt them was that the United States was "to become a hissing and a by-word, of the nations of the earth. It is our degradation in the eyes of nations; it is the humility connected with the acknowledgment, that our government is a failure." [13] Mexican War veterans felt that their

[10] New York *Evening Post*, February 2, 1861; Rhodes, *History of the United States*, III, 140; Freidel, *Lieber*, 301–305. For a sample of the patriotic literature of the secession crisis see [Lowell], "E Pluribus Unum," *loc. cit.*
[11] Pearson, *Andrew*, I, 152–53.
[12] [Lowell], "E Pluribus Unum," *loc. cit.*, 235–36.
[13] Peleg Bunker to Sherman, January 12, 1861; Geo. B. Way to *id.*, January 19, 1861, Sherman Papers; Silas Reed to Trumbull, December 6, 1860; F. K. Bailey to *id.*, January 16, 1861, Trumbull Papers; T. A. Cheney to Chase, December 14, 1860, Chase Papers; C. K. Williams to E. B. Washburne, January 23, 1861, E. B. Washburne Papers; New York *Daily Tribune* (letter from "C.L.B."),

sacrifices gave them a special right to demand continued national unity. A man who had lost two sons in Mexico vowed that he would volunteer himself in a struggle for the Union.[14] The New York *Courier and Enquirer* achieved a skillful synthesis of the emotional and practical elements in Yankee patriotism:

> We love the Union, because at home and abroad, collectively and individually, it gives us character as a nation and as citizens of the Great Republic; because it gives us *nationality* as a People, renders us now the equal of the greatest European Power, and in another half century, will make us the greatest, richest, and most powerful people on the face of the earth. We love the Union, because already in commerce, wealth and resources of every kind, we are the equal of the greatest; and because, while it secures us peace, happiness and prosperity at home, like the Roman of old we have only to exclaim "I am an American Citizen" to insure us respect and security abroad.[15]

How, then, could a loyal Yankee feel anything but dismay at the prospect of his country's becoming as feeble as the Latin-American republics upon whom he had always looked with contempt? Even those petty states could "point scornful fingers at their once haughty but now humbled neighbor to the North." [16] By copying the "Mexican system of rebellion," by endorsing the principle of separatism, the secessionists were defying the spirit of the nineteenth century. This was an era of unification; nationalism was "the great political movement of this age." It was a force that stirred Germans, Italians, Hungarians, and Slavs, and it was a force that was certain to triumph. In such an age America could not tolerate "a Bomba at Charleston, a Pope at Washington, a Francis Joseph over New England, and an Empire in the West." Rather, in the "fierce outflaming of long smothered nationalities

March 5, 1861; H. D. Horton to Douglas, December, 1860; Richard Stevens to *id.*, January 28, 1861, Douglas Papers.

[14] Milton Jamison to Wade, December 24, 1860, Wade Papers; John Johnston to Crittenden, December 29, 1860, Crittenden Papers.

[15] *Morning Courier and New-York Enquirer*, December 1, 1860.

[16] New York *Daily Tribune*, January 17, 22, 1861; New York *Evening Post*, January 31, 1861; Philadelphia *Press*, January 29, 1861; Philadelphia *North American and United States Gazette*, February 9, 1861; Philadelphia *Public Ledger*, November 21, 1860.

in Europe . . . we may find . . . a fearful warning and a hopeful answer." [17]

Many Northerners were also convinced that the preservation of their nationality was the only means of ensuring American independence. Disunion would certainly destroy the Monroe Doctrine and open the Western Hemisphere once more to foreign intervention. Britain, France, and Spain would at once step in to re-establish or expand their imperial possessions, or to profit from the jealousies of rival American states. During the secession winter the northern press was filled with reports of foreign designs upon America. Early in April the Boston *Journal* published a sensational editorial entitled "The Gathering of the Vultures." It reported that Spain was already meddling in the affairs of the Dominican Republic, that France had been "stirred into activity by the prospects of our disintegration," and that Britain had dispatched a fleet to American waters. It was the secessionists, those "branded characters, lifting their hands against the government of their country," who were responsible "for the hovering of foreign fleets upon our coasts." These traitors were forcing patriots to choose "between the indefinite protraction of this degradation and its speedy removal." [18] Loyal men were left with no choice but to test the strength of American nationality, to discover "whether we have a *government* or a mere *league* of States." Either this would be achieved through existing political forms, or the North would rally behind some leader who, "like the Roman dictators," would see "that the Republic received no detriment." [19]

To Yankee patriots the preservation of America's political greatness was more than a duty they owed to themselves; it was a duty to mankind. Proud of their Republic, Northerners believed

[17] New York *Evening Post*, November 13, 1860; New York *World*, March 25, 1861; Washington *Daily National Intelligencer*, November 24, 1860; Boston *Post*, April 10, 1861; Simeon Nash to Chase, March 4, 1861, Chase Papers.

[18] Boston *Daily Journal*, April 3, 1861. See also Lucian Barbour to Trumbull, January 18, 1861, Trumbull Papers; New York *Times*, April 1, 1861; New York *Evening Post*, December 24, 1860; *Morning Courier and New-York Enquirer*, April 2, 1861; Philadelphia *Press*, April 1, 3, 4, 1861; Boston *Daily Courier*, April 8, 1861; remarks of Representative Daniel E. Sickles of New York, in *Congressional Globe*, 757.

[19] P. C. Smith to Sherman, December, 1860; Dexter A. Hawkins to *id.*, March 23, 1861, Sherman Papers; N. Ewing to Cameron, December 27, 1860, Cameron Papers.

that they were participating in a great experiment that would determine the future of democratic institutions throughout the world. The failure of the American experiment would be proof "that man cannot be ruled, save by force, and that freedom and civil liberty is too rare a gift to be enjoyed by our poor fallen nature." Were secession to triumph, European liberals would lose hope, and "the galling chains of tyranny" would everywhere fall more heavily "upon the down-trodden millions." Then, "Tyrants and all who govern by Divine right—all who, as Jefferson said, are born to ride, booted and spurred, upon the backs of the people, would rejoice in our downfall. The very Devils, in their place of torture, would triumph in such an outrage upon human nature." [20] With so much at stake, it was time for northern lovers of freedom to abandon their "mercenary spirit" and "sacrifice something for the sake of liberty and humanity." [21]

Many in the free states believed that the sectional conflict was itself a struggle between democracy and despotism. Liberal institutions had never taken root in the South with its slaves, degraded white masses, and aristocratic planters. Secessionists, it was charged, talked "openly of forming . . . a *monarchical* kingdom . . . an aristocratic oligarchy, out-torying in oppressive and illiberal measures even the British aristocracy." Southerners had repudiated the principles upon which their country was founded; their quarrel was not with the policy of the government but with the theory of democracy. Hence, proclaimed the New York *Tribune*, the climactic duel between two political philosophies had begun: "Despotism demands. Democracy refuses." [22]

[20] *Morning Courier and New-York Enquirer*, December 15, 1860; January 8; February 12, 23, 1861; New York *World*, December 12, 1860; New York *Daily Tribune*, February 11, 1861; New York *Commercial Advertiser*, March 15, 1861; New York *Independent*, January 17, 1861; Philadelphia *Press*, December 24, 1860; Boston *Evening Transcript*, March 28, 1861; Milwaukee *Daily Sentinel*, April 1, 1861; [Lowell], "E Pluribus Unum," *loc. cit.*, 242; Norman Campbell to E. B. Washburne, December 27, 1860; A. J. Betts to *id.*, December 31, 1860, E. B. Washburne Papers; Gideon Welles to Edgar [Welles], November 13, 1860, Welles Papers; Edwin Croswell to Crittenden, December 24, 1860, Crittenden Papers.
[21] Speech of Richard H. Dana, Jr., in Boston, February 11, 1861, quoted in Boston *Daily Advertiser*, February 12, 1861; Chicago *Daily Tribune*, February 12, 1861.
[22] New York *Daily Tribune*, November 27, 1860; April 9, 1861; [Lowell], "E Pluribus Unum," *loc. cit.*, 240; Philadelphia *Press* (letter from "Kappa"), December 14, 1860.

By preserving the Union, then, Yankee patriots would be pursuing the destiny that God had intended for them. They would ensure their continued political and cultural expansion into backward areas; they would contribute to the nationalism of their age; and they would advance the world-wide cause of freedom and democracy. And in the process, the spirit of the nineteenth century would at last be carried to the South itself.

3

Late in January, 1861, an antislavery editor wrote excitedly about the events that seemed to be carrying North and South toward war. With a fierce joy he concluded: "One great and glorious result at least must follow—*Slavery will surely die.*" [23] Thus he touched upon another thread that was being woven into the fabric of the northern crusade. It was the likelihood that civil war would destroy the South's "peculiar institution" that caused many veterans of the antislavery movement to demand the enforcement of the laws.

To be sure, the extreme Garrisonian abolitionists, the non-political sectarians of the antislavery cause, had long favored disunion as a means of freeing the North from the sin of slavery. They had always denounced the Constitution which recognized Negro servitude, as well as the Union which protected and preserved it. When secession came Wendell Phillips exulted: " 'The covenant with death' is annulled; 'the agreement with hell' is broken to pieces." [24] William Lloyd Garrison fervently hoped that "this pro-slavery Union" was "broken beyond the possibility of restoration." [25] On numerous occasions Henry Ward Beecher, Samuel G. Howe, John Greenleaf Whittier, James Freeman Clarke, Gerrit Smith, Charles Sumner, Joshua R. Giddings, and other abolitionists advocated the peaceful dissolution of "this blood-stained Union." That, they agreed, was infinitely more desirable than another cowardly compromise with the Slave Power.

[23] Centreville *Indiana True Republican*, January 31, 1861.
[24] Wendell Phillips, *Speeches, Lectures, and Letters* (Boston, 1884), 343-70.
[25] [Wendell P. Garrison and Francis J. Garrison], *William Lloyd Garrison, 1805-1879, The Story of His Life Told by His Children* (New York, 1885-1889), IV, 3-4; Boston *Liberator*, November 2, 30, 1860.

The compensations would be rich: a brilliant career for a Republic of free states and the speedy collapse of slavery in a weak southern confederacy.[26]

But the fact that this was the position of various outstanding abolitionists does not mean that the northern antislavery forces were unanimously or consistently disunionist. Such a generalization overlooks the fact that some abolitionists practiced the deception of Greeley and the New York *Tribune:* They qualified their support of disunion to the point where the formula lost its practical significance. James Freeman Clarke, for example, argued that the laws must first be enforced, after which the North might decide upon what terms the South could separate.[27] By February, Gerrit Smith had concluded that force ought to be used to prevent secession until the South had agreed to abolish slavery.[28] Even Wendell Phillips on one occasion refused to apply his disunion principle to Louisiana, because the West needed to control the mouth of the Mississippi. Louisiana, he said, could choose between remaining in the Union "as a State or a conquered province." [29] Strange doctrine from a Garrisonian!

Other antislavery leaders utterly disregarded consistency and alternated arguments for peaceful separation with demonstrations of warlike purposes. Charles Sumner advocated disunion—but only in private and largely as a kind of intellectual excursion into political theory. In practice he encouraged the movement to prepare the Massachusetts militia to defend Washington and enforce the laws.[30] On November 27, Henry Ward Beecher boldly proclaimed that he cared little whether the South seceded. Two days later he preached a Thanksgiving Day sermon which raised the banners for a war against the Slave Power: "The guns are loaded and the match prepared—the conflict is coming and you must take

[26] Paxton Hibben, *Henry Ward Beecher* (New York, 1927), 151; Edward L. Pierce, *Memoir and Letters of Charles Sumner* (Boston, 1878–1893), IV, 5–6; White, "Sumner and the Crisis," *loc. cit.,* 148–51, 171; Ralph V. Harlow, *Gerrit Smith* (New York, 1939), 428; James Freeman Clarke to Sumner, December 8, 1860, Sumner Papers; Th. Hielscher to George W. Julian, November 20, 1860, Julian Papers, Indiana State Library; New York *Evening Post*, February 7, 27, 1861; New York *Morning Express,* January 11, 1861.

[27] James Freeman Clarke to Sumner, December 8, 1860, Sumner Papers. See also New York *Independent,* April 11, 1861.

[28] Harlow, *Smith,* 428.   [29] Phillips, *Speeches,* 343–70.

[30] White, "Sumner and the Crisis," *loc. cit.,* esp. 155–57.

sides. . . . At last the North has been called upon to stand up and fight." [31] For a proponent of peaceful disunion Garrison's Boston *Liberator* grew surprisingly agitated about southern "treason." It charged that secessionists were determined to provoke a civil war and castigated the Democrats who allegedly opposed the punishment of "traitors." [32] Nor were the *Liberator*'s violent attacks upon the South calculated to instill pacifist sentiments in its readers: ". . . The brutal dastards and bloody-minded tyrants, who have so long ruled the country with impunity, are now furiously foaming at the mouth, gnawing their tongues for pain, indulging in the most horrible blasphemies, uttering the wildest threats, and avowing the most treasonable designs. . . . They are insane from their fears, their guilty forebodings, their lust of power and rule, their hatred of free institutions, their consciousness of merited judgments; so that they may be properly classed with the inmates of a lunatic asylum." [33]

More significant than such obvious contradictions, however, was the fact that many abolitionists opposed secession without qualification and bluntly demanded force to preserve the Union. This group had no faith in the Garrisonian approach. They did not agree that disunion would destroy slavery; rather they believed that it would strengthen and perpetuate it. One abolitionist of this persuasion admitted that secession would free Northerners from the responsibility for slavery, but he denied that it would advance the cause of the slave. The Negroes, he argued, would never win their freedom by their own efforts; without the North there could be no "development of a great emancipation plan." Hence: "I say the man cannot be truly anti-slavery who cares little if the South goes. . . . We mean both *Emancipation* and *Union*—the one for the sake of the other and both for the sake of the country." [34] Similarly, in February the Anti-Slavery Society of Worcester County, Massachusetts, rejected a disunion resolution. S. S. Foster, the chief speaker, asserted that by preserving the Union "and enforcing an anti-slavery construction of the constitution, slavery could ere long be wiped out." [35]

[31] New York *Journal of Commerce*, December 1, 1860.
[32] Boston *Liberator*, February 15, 1861.   [33] *Ibid.*, November 16, 1860.
[34] J. W. Bliss to Sumner, December 19, 1860; January 1, 1861, Sumner Papers.
[35] Worcester (Mass.) *Daily Spy*, February 11, 1861.

Those abolitionists who stood by the Union were certain that a civil war would hasten emancipation. Neal Dow, the Maine antislavery leader, predicted that once northern soldiers invaded the South to enforce the laws they would not return "until the question of slavery should be settled forever." [36] William H. Herndon, Lincoln's abolitionist law partner, begged the Republicans to strike at the South, to "let this inevitable struggle proceed . . . till slavery is *dead*." [37] Such men as these hopefully recalled the opinion of John Quincy Adams that a southern rebellion would confer upon the government the right to abolish Negro servitude as a war measure. A convention of the Church Anti-Slavery Society in New York resolved that, whatever the government's power over slavery in time of peace, the government had "in the present exigency, by the act of the southern states, and by the express provision of the constitution in case of rebellion or insurrection, the right to suppress rebellion and to abolish slavery, the cause of it." [38] The sectional impasse, then, was "the providential crisis of American slavery." And a significant element among the abolitionists welcomed this crisis in the belief that the hated institution was about to perish on the field of battle.[39]

More than that: by 1861 many antislavery leaders had concluded that force was the *only* means of reaching their goal. The strong religious element in this crusade mystically resigned itself to the will of an avenging God, for the shedding of blood would be His punishment for the terrible sin of slavery. Abolitionist clergymen such as the Reverend Henry W. Bellows of New York and the Reverend Jacob Manning of Boston deplored the need for bloodshed and yet defended the sacrifice of lives for great principles.[40] It was the "political parsons of New England," wrote

[36] Neal Dow to Andrew, January 19, 1861, Andrew Papers.

[37] W. H. Herndon to Sumner, December 10, 1860, Sumner Papers; *id.* to Trumbull, December 21, 1860, Trumbull Papers; David Donald, "Billy You're Too Rampant," *Abraham Lincoln Quarterly*, III (1945), 402–407.

[38] New York *Evening Post*, January 24, 1861. See also A. Brooke to Chase, April 8, 1861, Chase Papers; remarks of Representative James M. Ashley of Ohio, in *Congressional Globe*, Appendix, 61–70.

[39] New York *World*, January 1, 1861. See also Carl Wittke, *Against the Current: The Life of Karl Heinzen (1809–80)* (Chicago, 1945), 174–78.

[40] John Bigelow Ms. Diary, entry for January 27, 1861, New York Public Library; Boston *Daily Advertiser*, January 5, 1861; New York *Herald*, November 25, 1860.

an angry critic, who taught that "civil war and the resort to Sharpe's rifles were in accordance with the fundamental doctrines of Christianity." They put on the "sword of the Lord and Gideon" and instructed the people that God had "called them especially to the work of liberating the slaves." [41]

Thus it seems quite possible that during the secession crisis there were more abolitionists who desired a war against slavery than there were who sought absolution from the national curse by speeding the departure of the South. Although the antislavery movement was strongly tinged with pacifism, many of its leaders quickly made a moral distinction between the suppression of rebellion and the waging of international war.[42] Long before the attack upon Fort Sumter the militant spirit of John Brown had thoroughly permeated the ranks of abolitionism. By the end of April, even the orthodox Garrisonians were bidding the Yankee volunteers to remove the scourge of slavery from the land.

Potentially, a crusade against the Slave Power had an appeal for a larger segment of the northern public. It is true that thirty years of antislavery agitation had failed to convert the masses to abolitionism. But the deluge of propaganda had nevertheless made a decided impression upon the minds of many Yankees who were not active abolitionists. Few of them loved the Negro or believed in racial equality, but the majority opposed the further expansion of slavery and looked upon the institution as a national disgrace. Northerners almost unanimously believed in the superiority of their system of "free labor." Aside from slavery itself the years of sectional conflict and the labors of abolitionists had produced a deep hostility toward southern slaveholders. In popular parlance they were arrogant, immoral, undemocratic, and the foes of the ideals and aspirations of the northern middle classes. This does not imply that a large proportion of Northerners desired to *initiate* an antislavery war against the South. Rather, it meant that *if* force had to be used to preserve the Union, countless Yankees would quickly convert the struggle into an antislavery crusade.

That this would be the case was demonstrated by the radical wing of the Republican party during the secession crisis. Repre-

41 New York *Herald*, December 22, 23, 1860.
42 George C. Beckwith to Sumner, January 16, 1861, Sumner Papers; Edson L. Whitney, *The American Peace Society* (Washington, 1928), 111.

sentative Washburn of Wisconsin openly asserted, as did many of his Republican colleagues, that if civil war came, "we shall have the consolation of knowing that when the conflict is over, those who survive it will be . . . inhabitants of a FREE COUNTRY." Daniel E. Somes of Maine warned Southerners to abandon their "treasonable operations," or slavery would "go out in blood." The first blast of war, cried Sidney Egerton of Ohio, would be "the trumpet signal of emancipation." [43] Local Republicans freely expressed the same sentiment. An Illinois Republican wondered whether the North was being "forced into the fight for freedom," whether the present crisis would rid the country "of this curse much sooner than we expected." [44] And a Wisconsin Republican announced that he, for one, would be pleased with such a result: "It may be . . . that Providence . . . has ordained that Slavery shall die at its own hands.— It may be that the South are now determined at all hazards to push their institution 'upon the bucklers of the Almighty,' and thus seal its doom once and forever. If such is their will I for one would be the last to stay the hand of avenging justice, for the sake of preserving the institution of American Slavery." [45]

Thus when the conflict came, the most dynamic element in the Republican party at once demanded that the war be waged for a new Union purged of the barbarism of slavery. Representative Owen Lovejoy of Illinois, whose abolitionist brother had earlier been murdered by a proslavery mob, was a symbol of this spirit. Now, wrote a contemporary, "the long delayed, but long sought hour" had come when Lovejoy could "wreak a vengeance upon . . . 'the land of slavery.' " Now he would enforce the penalty upon secessionists, or "with fire and sword desolate their land." [46] At last the national sin would be atoned, the Declaration of Independence would cease to be a mockery, and America would truly become "the land of the free"!

[43] *Congressional Globe,* 516, 969; Appendix, 127–29.
[44] J. C. Allen to E. B. Washburne, February 7, 1861, E. B. Washburne Papers. See also Alfred E. Hale to *id.,* January 5, 1861; Nath Vose to *id.,* January 27, 1861, *ibid.;* D. D. Wolff to Sherman, December 24, 1860; S. T. Boyd to *id.,* January 25, 1861, Sherman Papers; Edward Wade to Benjamin F. Wade, January 22, 1861, Wade Papers; A. Harris to Chase, December 25, 1860, Chase Papers.
[45] Madison *Wisconsin Daily State Journal,* February 4, 1861.
[46] *Daily Chicago Post,* January 29, 1861.

4

Northerners believed that southern society was essentially degenerate. The want of national spirit, the rejection of political democracy, and the preference for slave labor were only a few of the many signs of social decadence. Secession itself was a "revolution against civilization," a southern attempt to take "revenge on the nineteenth century." [47] This, proclaimed Carl Schurz, was the "age of conscience ruled men," before which the "antisocial element" in the South must "break down." [48] Southerners needed to be taught the ways of the "progressive" North.

Such a worthy endeavor would have to begin with the elevation of the southern white masses who were kept subservient to an oppressive ruling class. In the North the common man had the benefits of free public education, a high rate of literacy, and a superior culture. In the South the people had few public schools and were left to wallow in ignorance. [49] Slaveholders feared mass education as much as they feared freedom of speech and press. "General intelligence," explained Charles Francis Adams, "might lead the poor white to . . . [perceive] an interest of his own antagonistic to the policy of King Cotton." [50] To the southern elite, slavery was the normal status of labor, as evinced by its use of such opprobrious terms as "greasy mechanics," "small-fisted farmers," and "mudsills." [51] Southern nostrils, asserted a Pennsylvania congressman, were "offended by too near a contact with the democratic masses"; southern masters wanted to make workingmen "soft, easy cushions" on which "sluggards" might "repose and fatten." [52]

[47] Philadelphia North American and United States Gazette, November 13, 1860; Bellows to Cyrus A. Bartol, November 7, 1860, Bellows Papers.

[48] Schafer (ed.), Intimate Letters of Carl Schurz, 239–41.

[49] Remarks of Representative John J. Perry of Maine, in Congressional Globe, 438–41; Philadelphia Daily Evening Bulletin, February 9, 1861; Milwaukee Daily Sentinel, April 15, 1861.

[50] [Charles Francis Adams], "The Reign of King Cotton," Atlantic Monthly, VII (1861), 451–65; remarks of Senator James Harlan of Iowa, in Congressional Globe, Appendix, 44.

[51] Chicago Daily Tribune, February 6, 1861; Philadelphia Press (letter from "Occasional"), December 21, 1860; Montgomery Blair to Gustavus V. Fox, January 31, 1861, in Robert M. Thompson and Richard Wainwright (eds.), Confidential Correspondence of Gustavus Vasa Fox (New York, 1918), I, 3–5.

[52] Remarks of Representative Edward J. Morris of Pennsylvania, in Congressional Globe, Appendix, 216.

By secession these autocrats hoped to tighten their grip upon the common people. Their next step would be to reopen the African slave trade (a design which many Northerners charged was the chief motive for disunion) and thus broaden the foundation of their "merciless despotism." [53] And so a fight for the Union would be a "struggle between the people on one side, and a privileged class on the other." [54]

In this southern land of darkness and decay, of arrogant aristocrats and brutish masses, life was as cheap as in all barbarous communities. Northerners learned from their newspapers that individual and mob violence were so common in the South as to be winked at by the courts. These unrestrained and passionate people, intolerant of criticism from within or without, made it unsafe for Yankees to travel among them or for natives to profess devotion to the Union. The South was gripped by a "Reign of Terror," dramatically proclaimed the northern press. The New York *Tribune*, for example, published two columns of murders, shooting affrays, and other "outrages" gleaned from "one hour's perusal of Southern papers." This account began with the headline:

LIFE IN THE LAND OF CHIVALRY.
HANGING, STABBING, SHOOTING, MURDERS BY THE DOZENS.[55]

The lynching of southern Unionists and the beating or tarring and feathering of Northerners appeared to be a common practice in the slave states. Loyal men were allegedly fleeing by the hundreds from the wrath of southern mobs. This "Terror," wrote Henry J. Raymond, stalked the South "like a hideous savage,— scornful of civilization, obeying only the impulse of its brutal nature." [56]

[53] New York *Times*, November 28; December 11, 1860; *Morning Courier and New-York Enquirer*, January 5, 8, 1861; Philadelphia *Press*, January 10, 1861; Worcester (Mass.) *Daily Spy*, November 28, 1860.

[54] Philadelphia *Daily Evening Bulletin*, February 9, 1861; remarks of Representative James M. Ashley of Ohio, in *Congressional Globe*, Appendix, 69; Walter S. Waldie to Johnson, February 3, 1861, Johnson Papers.

[55] New York *Daily Tribune*, April 2, 1861.

[56] Letter of Henry J. Raymond to William L. Yancey in New York *Times*, December 26, 1860. See also New York *Daily Tribune*, December 10, 1860; January 14; February 25, 1861; New York *Evening Post*, April 5, 1861; *Morning Courier and New-York Enquirer*, January 14, 23; April 8, 1861; Boston *Daily Journal*, November 15, 1860; January 2, 1861; Springfield (Mass.) *Daily Repub-*

Loyal Southerners, it was said, demanded the protection of the Federal government, whose duty it was to secure their lives and property from the maddened disunionists.[57] It was equally the government's duty to protect Yankees temporarily residing in the South. Never had the United States allowed foreign countries to treat its citizens as they were treated in the slave states. It was time to demonstrate that the rights of loyal Americans could not be violated with impunity.[58]

The prevailing ignorance, repression, and mob violence, many Northerners concluded, had enabled treason to flourish in the South. Secession was a manifestation of the real southern character. It was not simply a result of Lincoln's election. It had been planned for at least a generation: it was a plot "over which Calhoun's mind brooded for 30 years." [59] South Carolina had always been a center of disloyalty and treason; even during the Revolution the majority of her people had been Tories.[60] Confident of success and contemptuous of northern cowardice, secessionists were finally putting into effect the sinister aims they had long nourished. "Your flag has been insulted," Yankees heard Senator Wigfall of Texas sneer; "redress it if you dare. You have submitted to it for two months, and you will submit to it forever." [61] An old conspiracy had thus finally matured, and the South was arming to ensure its triumph.[62]

Northerners were especially shocked when Federal officers

---

lican, November 13, 20, 1860; April 3, 1861; Providence *Daily Journal,* December 7, 1860.

[57] *Morning Courier and New-York Enquirer,* April 4, 1861; Philadelphia *North American and United States Gazette,* April 6, 1861; Springfield (Mass.) *Daily Republican,* January 3, 1861; Chicago *Daily Tribune,* January 21, 1861; Milwaukee *Daily Sentinel,* April 11, 1861.

[58] Harley Wayne to E. B. Washburne, December 21, 1860, E. B. Washburne Papers; Daniel Hamilton to Wade, December 22, 1860; J. Thomas to *id.,* December 22, 1860; Jonathan Ward to *id.,* January 12, 1861, Wade Papers.

[59] F. P. Blair to Frank Blair, November 22, 1860, Blair Papers; New York *Daily Tribune,* November 16, 1860; Boston *Daily Journal,* March 28, 1861; Trenton *Daily State Gazette and Republican,* January 3, 1861.

[60] Letter of Henry J. Raymond to William L. Yancey, in New York *Times,* December 13, 1860.

[61] *Congressional Globe,* 1373; New York *Times,* April 11, 1861; New York *Herald,* December 13, 1860.

[62] New York *Evening Post,* January 7, 1861; Boston *Daily Advertiser,* December 12, 1860. The northern press was filled with accounts of southern military preparations, which justified appeals for countermeasures in the North.

from the South favored disunion. These men allegedly illustrated their depravity by using their high civil and military positions to promote treason. Howell Cobb, it was charged, had deliberately bankrupted the government before resigning as Secretary of the Treasury. Jacob Thompson had packed the Interior Department with traitors and plunderers. Secretary of War Floyd became the greatest villain of them all. The fact that he had been a Unionist until December was ignored as the northern legend developed that he had long aided the secession conspiracy. Among his supposed contributions to the cause were the weakening of Federal-occupied southern forts and the sending of arms to the South.[63] Actually, Floyd's record of loyalty was not clearly vulnerable until shortly before his resignation. On December 20 he had directed heavy ordnance to be sent from Pittsburgh to two uncompleted southern forts at Ship Island and Galveston. This order created a near riot at Pittsburgh, and violent protests poured in upon Washington. But the transfer of ordnance had not been made when Holt replaced Floyd and countermanded the order.[64]

Meanwhile the northern press described the "great plunderer" Floyd and the "faithless" Cobb as representative men of the secession movement. They and "wretches" like the "profligate adventurer" John Slidell and the "unprincipled" Judah P. Benjamin of Louisiana were "sharpers and thieves," the "spawn of hells and bagnios—men who come reeking from the haunts of vice." Like burglars "firing the house they . . . [had] robbed" they sought to cover up their crimes through disunion and civil war.[65] Yankees could render a service to the entire country by sweeping such men from their positions of power in the South.

[63] Boston *Daily Courier*, March 6, 1861; Philadelphia *North American and United States Gazette*, December 12, 1860; January 12, 1861; New York *Evening Post*, December 24, 26, 27, 28, 29, 1860; New York *Daily Tribune*, December 28, 1860; New York *Times*, December 29, 1860. For defenses of Floyd see Auchampaugh, *Buchanan and His Cabinet*, 89–99; Curtis, *Buchanan*, II, 411–17; Rhodes, *History of the United States*, III, 236–41. Floyd's policies can be traced in *Official Records*, Ser. 3, I, 1–22, 30–31, 36, 42–46, 51–52; Thos. F. Drayton to Wm. H. Gist, November 3, 6, 19, 23, 1860, copies in Stanton Papers.

[64] W. Robinson *et al.* to Black, December 25, 1860, Black Papers; *Official Records*, Ser. 3, I, 15, 30, 33–36; *Morning Courier and New-York Enquirer*, December 28, 1860.

[65] New York *Times*, December 29, 1860; New York *Evening Post*, February 8, 13, 1861; Providence *Daily Journal*, February 6, 1861; Springfield (Mass.) *Daily Republican*, February 4, 1861; Worcester (Mass.) *Daily Spy*, February 14, 1861; Chicago *Daily Tribune*, January 1, 1861.

Indeed Yankees would be forced to do it, because these traitors would never let them live in peace. Not satisfied with dividing the Union, secessionists already plotted to overthrow the government of the remaining loyal states. First, it was widely reported that they would seek to prevent the counting of the electoral vote.[66] Then, there were sensational and persistent rumors that they planned either to assassinate Lincoln or to resist his inauguration at Washington.[67] Finally, the North was kept in a state of perpetual agitation by the fear that Southerners would seize the capital city. These conspirators understood that "he who holds Paris rules France." The capture of Washington would win foreign recognition for the Confederacy and give it control of the army.[68] Hence the North had to choose between mobilization and complete destruction.

Late in the crisis, Yankees found another southern officer upon whom to pour their wrath. In February, Major General David E. Twiggs, commander of the Department of Texas, agreed to surrender all his army posts and other Federal property to the secessionists. President Buchanan immediately ordered Twiggs's dismissal from the army for "treachery to the flag." [69] Northern indignation again rose to great heights. Even the conservative Boston *Courier* asserted that Twiggs's conduct consigned him to "lasting infamy." Should secessionists honor him they would "furnish an argument in favor of the demoralizing influences of slavery." [70]

But loyal Northerners scarcely needed further evidence of the "demoralizing influence" of the whole southern way of life. The "lazy, idle gentry," the debased masses, the narrow bigotry, the mob violence, the political dishonesty, and the rampant treason all proved that there was something inherently wrong with south-

[66] Boston *Daily Advertiser* ("Washington Correspondence"), February 15, 1861.

[67] Mark Skinner to Trumbull, January 18, 1861, Trumbull Papers; H. Kreismann to E. B. Washburne, December 26, 1860; D. C. Mallory to *id.*, January 27, 1861, E. B. Washburne Papers.

[68] Philadelphia *Public Ledger*, January 28, 1861; Philadelphia *Press*, January 9, 1861; New York *Daily Tribune*, January 8, 15, 28, 1861.

[69] *Official Records*, Ser. 2, I, 1–60; William B. Hesseltine, *Civil War Prisons: A Study in War Psychology* (Columbus, 1930), 2–4; French E. Chadwick, *Causes of the Civil War* (New York, 1906), 275–77.

[70] Boston *Daily Courier*, March 2, 1861. See also Boston *Post*, February 28, 1861; New York *Evening Post*, February 26, 1861; Philadelphia *North American and United States Gazette*, February 26, 1861.

ern society. The basic trouble seemed obvious enough. What the South lacked was a sound and vigorous economy, a healthy spirit of enterprise, and a love for honest toil. Florid oratory had always been her rankest crop. She matched "every yard of printed cotton from the North with a yard of printed fustian, the product of her own domestic industry." Her rewards, however, were meager. And so Southerners resented "the wealth, the power, the intelligence, the . . . advanced civilization" of the North. It was the "infirmity of semi-barbarous men to hate what they cannot imitate." [71] It was this "infirmity" which motivated secession. Hence, until the disease was cured, the southern "problem" would remain unsolved.

Here was another opportunity for a northern crusade. Throughout the secession crisis there was much talk of the need to reform southern society, to rebuild it in the image of the North. King Cotton, many argued, should be dethroned and commerce, industry, and diversified agriculture given a chance to grow. Southerners should be made to appreciate the superiority of "free labor." One capitalist proposed that the government "buy up South Carolina, clear the people all out & stock it anew with good honest northern men willing & able to work with their own hands." [72] The New York *Tribune* believed that industrialization alone could achieve the redemption of the slave states:

> The South must learn to do her own manufacturing. She must make agriculture an incidental not the primary interest it is now. Her industry must be thoroughly diversified. She must build factories and furnaces, open her inexhaustible coal mines, make her own iron, convert it into locomotives, spin her own cotton, weave it into cloth, tan her own hides, make her own shoes and clothing, and condescend to manufacture even pails and hobby horses for herself. She must in fact adopt the thrift and industry of the North, bringing the consumer and producer together on her own soil. This course will stop the drain of capital which now exhausts her, and will enable

[71] *Morning Courier and New-York Enquirer*, April 12, 1861; Springfield (Mass.) *Daily Republican*, March 15, 1861; Chicago *Daily Tribune*, February 21, 1861; [Lowell], "E Pluribus Unum," *loc. cit.*, 237.

[72] George Woodman to Cyrus Woodman, December 4, 1860, Woodman Papers. See also [Adams], "The Reign of King Cotton," *loc. cit.*, 451–65.

her to pay her debts and make a respectable figure in the world.[73]

This economic reorientation, said its advocates, would benefit the rest of the country as well as the South. It would open immense new opportunities for the free laborers and capitalists of the "over-flowing North." The South's natural resources—her "undeveloped treasures"—would become "favorite fields for . . . [northern] energy and wealth." Southerners would be encouraged to produce coarse and bulky manufactured goods. This would increase their population and purchasing power and enable them to buy more of the "finer, lighter, [and] costlier productions" of the North. Then the South would naturally adopt "new views of public interest and public duty"—the whole section would be converted to the gospel of the high tariff. In short, the South would "pass under the control of free labor and become northern in sentiment and institutions." [74]

Such a crusade promised to usher in a new era of national harmony. The "irrepressible conflict" would vanish with the decline of slavery, the improvement of southern education and culture, and the development of a decent respect for labor and enterprise. In the New South, freed from the shackles of a dead past, there would grow for the first time a deep loyalty to the American Union.

5

Northern idealists did not overlook their obligation to posterity. They argued that their children and their children's children would suffer if southern treason went unpunished because of a distaste for bloodshed. Better use the bayonet now than leave an "unhappy legacy" to future generations. Suppressing secession with force would at least have the virtue of permanence.[75] "We

---

[73] New York *Daily Tribune*, March 5, 15, 1861. See also "A Genuine Republican" to Crittenden, December 21, 1860, Crittenden Papers; remarks of Representative Daniel E. Somes of Maine, in *Congressional Globe*, 969.

[74] New York *Daily Tribune*, February 7, 1861; New York *World*, November 26, 1860; Philadelphia *North American and United States Gazette*, October 19; November 22, 24, 1860; Springfield (Mass.) *Daily Republican*, February 27, 1861.

[75] James C. Stone to Sumner, December 17, 1860, Sumner Papers; Montgomery Blair to Andrew [January, 1861], Andrew Papers; James C. Smith to Chase,

are heartily tired," wrote a western editor, "of having this [dis-union] threat stare us in the face evermore. . . . We have never been better prepared for such a crisis than now. We most ardently desire that it may come." [76] The past thirty years of agitation had brought great material losses and much suffering. Now that the country was half through the struggle, "let us finish it like men, and be done with the controversy forever." [77] Nothing was to be gained by another truce.

The wisdom of forcing an immediate settlement became more evident when Yankees decided that two independent republics could not live side by side in peace. Most Republicans and Democrats shared the conviction that southern independence would ultimately lead to war. Typically the pro-Breckinridge Boston *Post* declared: "We have no faith, if the states separate, that there can be a peaceable issue of the vast interests, and the public property, at stake." [78] Secession would simply increase the sources of friction. The New York *Times* explained:

> . . . Questions of commerce, of the rights of navigation, of extradition,—cases of insult or maltreatment of citizens,—a thousand sources of hostility would be created by the very fact of separation,—and all the restraints which now prevent war, would be removed. . . . It would be impossible for two nations, so hostile to each other in the basis and groundwork of their society,—separated under circumstances of mutual distrust and dislike, lying side by side, with only an invisible boundary, touching each other upon a long frontier, and having a thousand sensitive points of dissension and discord, to avoid hostilities for any considerable length of time.[79]

Thus Northerners had persuaded themselves that acquiescence in disunion was in no sense a peace formula. Their only choice was

March 13, 1861, Chase Papers; J. Hamer to Trumbull, February 7, 1861; James J. Ferrel to *id.*, December 24, 1860, Trumbull Papers.

[76] Indianapolis *Indiana American*, November 21, 1860. See also New York *Daily Tribune*, January 4, 1861; Worcester (Mass.) *Daily Spy*, December 4, 1860; Anson S. Miller to Trumbull, January 14, 1861; G. Goodrich to *id.*, January 20, 1861, Trumbull Papers.

[77] Boston *Daily Advertiser* (letter from a Boston merchant), December 20, 1860; New York *Daily Tribune*, December 19, 20, 1860.

[78] Boston *Post*, December 15, 1860. See also New York *Herald*, November 19, 1860; Providence *Daily Post*, February 8, 1861; Philadelphia *Press*, December 5, 1860; January 18, 1861; Columbus *Crisis*, February 28, 1861; Columbus *Daily Ohio Statesman*, December 8, 1860.

[79] New York *Times*, March 21, 1861.

to fight against foreign enemies or enforce the laws against domestic insurgents.

A crusade against the South lost none of its lure when Yankees
speculated about the comparative strength of the two sections.
The South assuredly was no match for the North, for she lacked
the wealth, resources, and population to wage a successful war.
In such a contest the "cool, calculating energy and endurance of
the more phlegmatic Northerners" would overwhelm the "bluster and dash of the excitable and enervated Southron." Even the
little state of Connecticut could sell military supplies to the South
"and then send armed men enough down to take them back again,
without exhausting her resources." [80] Although conservative compromisers often predicted years of bloody strife, the average
Northerner believed that a civil war would be brief. Estimates of
its duration were repeatedly fixed at "sixty days," "three short
months," "one campaign . . . finished before haying time." The
crusaders expected that the "thunder of the first cannon . . .
[would] scarcely cease its reverberations" before the "inherent,
intrinsic weakness" of the South would bring her to her knees.[81]
So much could be gained with so little effort!

6

The impending Yankee crusade involved, like all such enterprises, a strange blending of human emotions. Into the blend went
the idealism of strong-minded men who would foster political
democracy, destroy slavery, and redeem the South. Into it also
went the conviction that the shedding of blood was justified for
these great objectives. Had not war always been one of the chief
instruments of progress? God, proclaimed one mystic, had frequently been "prodigal of human life & suffering in advancing the
cause of civilization." [82]

The blend contained one other essential emotion. Crusades, of
course, are launched against an evil, and they are joined by those

---

[80] New York *Evening Post*, November 2, 1860; Boston *Daily Journal*, December 24, 1860; New York *Independent*, January 3, 1861; remarks of Representative
John B. Alley of Massachusetts, in *Congressional Globe*, 585.

[81] E. Wright to Sumner, January 17, 1861, Sumner Papers; Chicago *Daily
Tribune*, April 9, 1861; Milwaukee *Daily Sentinel*, March 18, 1861.

[82] Homer Goodwin to Sherman, February 22, 1861; Saml. D. Cochrane to *id.*,
February 4, 1861, Sherman Papers.

who have learned to despise that evil. Or, more accurately, they have learned to despise the men with whom the evil is associated. Inevitably, then, the moral drive behind the antisouthern crusade was the usual combination of idealism and hatred. Even before the war began, the process of sectional alienation had given many Yankees an extreme dislike for Southerners. One Northerner described a not uncommon feeling that "some misterious [sic] and wicked influence had transformed them into a different race of people." Another declared: "If there is anything which I hate, I hate Englishmen and Southerners." [83] Such men as these felt no compunctions about shedding "brothers' blood." A Democratic orator proclaimed: ". . . This squeamish, sickly sentimentalism finds no sanction in the laws of humanity. . . . My friends, are you willing to own a traitor as a brother? . . . The man who lifts his hand against my country and my liberties—call him anything else you please, but O, insult me not by calling him my brother!" [84]

By April the ground had been prepared for what was to follow. Yankees had come to appreciate the practical reasons why disunion could not be tolerated. These practical matters had already been coated—or fused—with the idealism which invited a great crusade. Meanwhile sectional hatred had been intensified by the conduct of Southerners after Lincoln's election. All that was lacking was one last provocative incident. That came soon enough.

[83] Thomas R. Mott to Sherman, January 26, 1861, *ibid.;* M. L. Baxter to Morrill, January 20, 1861, Morrill Papers; Franklin Livingston to Hon. A. Burnam, March 6, 1861, Chandler Papers.

[84] Address of John Y. Smith before Wisconsin Assembly, March 14, 1861, in Madison *Wisconsin Daily State Journal,* April 5, 1861.

XIII

Decision

E VER since December, Fort Sumter had seemed to be the place where war, if it came, would most likely begin. War did begin there, and Major Anderson won accolades for his gallant stand against the attacking Confederates. To Anderson, however, these honors brought no joy. Though Yankees made him the hero of the secession crisis, he had no taste for the role he played. A Kentuckian by birth, he remained loyal to the Federal government but had earnestly hoped to avoid conflict with the South.

Early in January, Anderson had assured the War Department that his position was secure. During the next two months he sent daily reports describing the batteries and fortifications being erected by the secessionists. But he never hinted that he was in danger or in need of reinforcements. Meanwhile the Sumter garrison continued to receive supplies of fresh meats and vegetables from Charleston. And so there was little reason why civil or military officers in Washington should have feared an imminent crisis at Fort Sumter.

What Washington officials did not know, however, was that Anderson's course was controlled by political more than military considerations. Early in April the Major explained in a private letter that he had not asked for reinforcements because he knew he would thereby provoke a Confederate attack "and thus inaugurate civil war." "My policy . . . was to keep still, to preserve peace, to give time for the quieting of the excitement, . . . in the hope of avoiding bloodshed." He concluded: "There is now a prospect . . . that the separation which has been inevitable for months, will be consummated without the shedding of one drop of blood."[1] Peaceful secession, then, was what Anderson desired.

[1] Crawford, *Genesis of the Civil War*, 290–91. See also *Official Records*, Ser. 1, I, 294.

To this end, he finally attempted to convince the Federal government that his garrison ought to be removed from Sumter. In his report to the War Department on February 28, he tried to demonstrate that it was militarily impossible to maintain his position. As soon as the Confederates should discover that reinforcements were approaching they would close every channel in Charleston Harbor. A relief project, he was convinced, would fail without the support of an army numbering at least "twenty thousand good and well disciplined men." To clinch his case he placed narrow time limits upon any attempt to aid him. The garrison would be unable to remain at Sumter much longer because of its "limited supply" of provisions.[2] Anderson then waited expectantly for an order of evacuation.[3]

The Major's letter reached Washington on the morning of Lincoln's inauguration. Secretary of War Holt reported its astonishing contents to Buchanan's cabinet at its last meeting.[4] The next day he sent Anderson's message to the new President. Holt assured Lincoln that Anderson had given no previous information that his supplies were short. A relief expedition had been prepared at New York, but not on a scale "approaching the seemingly extravagant estimates of Major Anderson . . . , for the disclosure of which the Government was wholly unprepared."[5]

The news from Sumter was a severe blow to Lincoln. He had barely moved into the White House; his cabinet nominations had

[2] For alleged evidence that the Sumter garrison was not short of supplies and that Anderson never reported such a shortage see John S. Tilley, Lincoln Takes Command (Chapel Hill, 1941). Tilley bases his argument on two points: first, that Anderson's letter is missing from the Official Records and has never been seen by any historian; second, that Anderson was receiving fresh provisions from Charleston and could not have been short of supplies. What Tilley overlooks was that Anderson was actually running short of staples like pork, flour, beans, coffee, sugar, and salt, and that these staples were not acquired in the Charleston market. Tilley's argument is now destroyed completely, because the "missing" Anderson letter of February 28 is in the Lincoln Papers in the Library of Congress. The Lincoln Papers also contain Anderson's report of March 2 (also missing from the Official Records) in which he made a full statement of his commissary stores and the number of days they would last. This report indicates that Anderson's supplies would be exhausted in approximately six weeks. Copies of the reports of February 28 and March 2 can also be found in a letter book kept by Anderson at Fort Sumter, in the Anderson Papers.

[3] Anderson to Lloyd Tilghman, March 20, 1861, Anderson Papers.

[4] Moore (ed.), Works of Buchanan, XI, 156.   [5] Ibid., 157-58.

just been sent to the Senate; office seekers were hounding him. Lincoln needed time to organize his administration and to become familiar with the details of executive procedure. He must have expected a month or two of continued quiet before having to deal decisively with the secessionists.

Now there was no time at all. Lincoln had to find an immediate solution for a new crisis at the most dangerous point in the South. He had to find that solution while he was still exploring other aspects of the secession problem, while he was still laboring with the patronage, and while he was still getting acquainted with the men in his cabinet. Whom could he trust?

In the end Lincoln decided to trust only himself. Advice he freely sought, but he kept his own counsel as he had done before the inauguration. The Federal government's ultimate response to the crisis at Sumter was largely his work. And Lincoln thereby showed that he had taken hold, that in the new administration his voice would be supreme.

2

A month intervened between the inauguration and the first visible signs that the new administration was ready to act. To Lincoln, suddenly burdened with great responsibilities, that month passed by with painful speed. To the masses of Yankees, however, it seemed like an eternity. Northerners ignored the fact that reorganizing the government and preparing for action took time. After the irksome weeks of crisis deadlock through which they had just passed, another month of seeming inactivity was more than they could bear. And the President soon became deeply conscious of this state of mind.

Even before Lincoln took his presidential oath he had been committed to a "vigorous policy." While the Republican press was attacking Buchanan for his "weakness" and for his "submission to treason" it was also predicting confidently that the new President would quickly demonstrate that "we still have a government." As early as December the New York *Courier and Enquirer* proclaimed: "Mr. Lincoln . . . is not the man to shrink from the performance of any duty. . . . Like Jackson . . . he will not be wanting in the hour of trial." [6] Actually Lincoln had committed himself. In both his Indianapolis speech and his inaugural address he promised to "hold" and "possess" government property and to collect the revenues. In neither instance did he explain that this could only be done after due preparation.

Lincoln, of course, was not idle during the month of March, but most of what he did was concealed in secrecy. Outwardly the government still seemed to be paralyzed. And so within a few weeks the new administration was almost discredited. The disillusionment increased as the country was swept by rumors that Fort Sumter was to be evacuated. Soon Lincoln's political opponents were taunting him for "backing down" and for merely continuing Buchanan's "weak" policy. "This administration," mocked the Democratic Cleveland *Plain Dealer*, "after all its blustering about 'enforcing the laws in all the states,' not only surrenders Sumter but South Carolina and the whole South." Other critics laughed scornfully as they reminded Republicans of their "magnificent flourishes" and "vainglorious boasting" about the expected vigor of the new regime.[7] John A. Dix congratulated Buchanan. The humiliation of Lincoln would make the former President's record "brighten in proportion." [8]

Impatient Republicans bombarded the administration with demands for swift, decisive action and with warnings that they would not tolerate the abandonment of Sumter. The weeks of delay had "almost crushed the spirit" of the party; the intimations that another fort was to be lost were received "with general amazement and sorrow." "I tell you, sir," wrote an angry Republican to Secretary of the Treasury Chase, "if Fort Sumter is evacuated, the new administration is done forever, the Republican party is done. . . ." Before long, predicted another friend of Chase's, the South would proclaim Lincoln "a Damnd fool" and the North

[6] *Morning Courier and New-York Enquirer*, December 14, 1860. See also New York *Evening Post*, January 21, 1861; New York *Daily Tribune*, December 15, 16, 20, 1860; January 19, 1861; Springfield (Mass.) *Daily Republican*, November 15, 1860; January 9, 1861; Indianapolis *Daily Journal*, February 12, 1861.

[7] Cleveland *Daily Plain Dealer*, quoted in New York *World*, March 22, 1861; New York *Herald*, March 12, 16, 25, 1861; New York *Morning Express*, April 1, 1861; Philadelphia *Morning Pennsylvanian*, March 14, 19, 1861; Boston *Daily Courier*, March 16, 1861; Detroit *Free Press*, March 16, 17, 1861.

[8] Moore (ed.), *Works of Buchanan*, XI, 168.

would proclaim him "a Damnd Rascall." [9] Private offers to carry relief to Major Anderson poured in upon the government.[10] Everywhere Republicans agreed that the "terrible suspense" was "past endurance." "We cannot . . . see the necessity which compels it." [11]

Lincoln's party friends did not confine their expressions of discontent to private letters. The Republican press scolded the President openly. At first a few papers tried to pardon the expected surrender of Sumter on the grounds of military necessity or by blaming Buchanan or Major Anderson.[12] But they soon gave it up. The Cincinnati *Commercial*, like most Republican organs, argued: "Difficulties, probably greater than those in the way of relieving Fort Sumter, have been overcome by daring and adventurous men; . . . it seems to us that there will be a few fine chances for immortality thrown away in a meek evacuation. . . ." [13] These papers also joined in the rising clamor for action. By the end of March they were publishing editorials under such sharp titles as "THE DUTY OF THE PRESIDENT," "WHAT WILL BE DONE?" "WANTED—A POLICY!" and "COME TO THE POINT!" The New York *Times* complained: "It is idle to conceal the fact that the Administration thus far has not met public expectations. The country feels no more assurance as to the future . . . than it did on the day Mr. Buchanan left Washington. It sees no indication of an administrative policy adequate to the emergency. . . . We trust this period of indecision, of inaction, of fatal indifference, will have a speedy end. . . . The people want *something* to be

[9] T. J. Young to Chase, March 12, 1861; H. Abram to *id.*, March 25, 1861, Chase Papers. See also S. Austin Allibone to Lincoln, March 29, 1861; J. Watson Webb to *id.*, March 12, 1861; James L. Hill to *id.*, March 14, 1861; O. B. Pierce to *id.*, March 31, 1861, Lincoln Papers. Hundreds of letters of this type are in the papers of Chase, Lincoln, Sherman, Sumner, Trumbull, E. B. Washburne, and Welles.

[10] Henry M. Paine to Welles (misdated February 18), Welles Papers; A. Watson to *id.*, March 9, 1861, Lincoln Papers; J. M. Forbes to Montgomery Blair, March 13, 1861, Blair Papers; Seward, *Seward at Washington*, II, 527.

[11] Harley Wayne to E. B. Washburne, March 15, 1861; E. M. Boring to *id.*, March 16, 1861, E. B. Washburne Papers.

[12] New York *Evening Post*, March 11, 14, 1861; New York *Times*, March 12, 1861; *Morning Courier and New-York Enquirer*, March 14, 1861; Providence *Daily Journal*, March 12, 1861; Boston *Evening Transcript*, March 12, 1861; Chicago *Daily Tribune*, March 13, 1861; L. Anderson to Robert Anderson, March 7, 1861, Anderson Papers.

[13] Cincinnati *Daily Commercial*, March 13, 1861,

decided on—some standard raised—some policy put forward, which shall serve as a rallying point for the abundant but discouraged loyalty of the American heart." [14]

These were not merely the sentiments of war-seeking Republicans. These were the sentiments of nearly the whole North. "Better almost anything than additional suspense," cried a Bell paper.[15] "Lincoln hesitates like an Ass between two stacks of hay," raged a friend of Breckinridge's. "Why if anything is to be done, is it not done or avowed openly, promptly and effectively . . . ?" [16] Even a war policy, thought a Douglas organ, was better than no policy. "Some sort of certainty, be it ever so dismal, may be better than uncertainty." [17]

By March, Yankee businessmen were saying little more about compromise. Like other Northerners, they were filled with anxiety. Only a few Wall Street stock speculators seemed to be pleased with the rumors that Sumter was to be given up.[18] To most merchants and shipowners these rumors were a source of apprehension. Capitalists agreed that it was the lack of "confidence" that was at the root of the commercial depression.[19] Not only the threat of the low southern tariff but the continued uncertainty made them desperate. They had finally reached the point where they believed that war itself was better than indecision. A com-

[14] New York *Times*, April 3, 1861; New York *Daily Tribune*, April 3, 1861; New York *Evening Post*, April 4, 5, 1861; *Morning Courier and New-York Enquirer*, April 4, 1861; New York *Commercial Advertiser*, April 4, 5, 1861; Philadelphia *Daily Evening Bulletin*, March 14, 1861; Philadelphia *Public Ledger*, March 23, 1861; Boston *Evening Transcript*, March 23, 1861; Chicago *Daily Tribune*, March 18, 21, 25, 1861; Madison *Wisconsin Daily State Journal*, March 21, 1861.

[15] New York *Morning Express*, April 5, 1861. See also Boston *Daily Courier*, April 8, 1861.

[16] Boston *Post*, March 23; April 6, 1861. See also New York *Herald*, March 9, 26, 1861; Philadelphia *Morning Pennsylvanian*, March 9, 1861.

[17] Detroit *Free Press*, March 20; April 3, 7, 1861. A Washington newspaper correspondent reported that there was as much pressure for decisive action from Democrats as from Republicans. New York *Daily Tribune*, April 8, 1861.

[18] New York *Herald*, March 12, 1861; *Morning Courier and New-York Enquirer* (Commercial column), March 12, 13, 1861.

[19] Isaac West to Chase, March 9, 1861, Chase Papers; G. W. Mindil to Anderson, March 12, 1861, Anderson Papers; George P. Bissell to Welles, March 15, 1861; Wm. V. Pettit to *id.*, April 2, 6, 1861, Welles Papers; *Morning Courier and New-York Enquirer* (Commercial column), March 12, 1861; New York *Commercial Advertiser*, March 18, 1861; Philadelphia *Public Ledger*, March 13, 1861.

mercial reporter observed: "Commerce, industry, enterprise and speculation are at a standstill throughout the country—no man dares to buy merchandise, or property, or stocks; no man wants to give out any paper; everyone stands nervously waiting for the future, wondering what Mr. Lincoln will do." [20] A New Yorker described the dominant mood of capitalists: "It is a singular fact that merchants who, two months ago, were fiercely shouting 'no coercion,' now ask for anything rather than *inaction*." [21]

Responding to this mass pressure, terrified Republican leaders begged Lincoln to make some decisive move and told him that the loss of Sumter would ruin them all. Francis Preston Blair, Sr., hastened to the White House to inform the President that he was losing public confidence and to insist that Sumter should be yielded only to superior military force.[22] Republican congressmen met secretly in Washington and demanded that reinforcements be sent to Anderson; Wade, Chandler, Trumbull, and other party leaders warned Lincoln that further delay would bring disaster.[23] In the Senate, which was meeting in executive session, Republicans clamored for the immediate enforcement of the laws. Trumbull introduced a resolution that it was the "duty of the President to use all the means in his power to hold and protect public property." [24] Republican governors poured into Washington to exert their influence upon the chief executive. Randall of Wisconsin declared that the Northwest would soon be lost to his party; Morton of Indiana pledged 6,000 troops for a vigorous policy.[25] On April 4 most of these governors conferred with Lincoln and

[20] New York *Herald* (Commercial column), March 26, 1861; New York *Daily Tribune* (Commercial column), March 23, 1861; New York *World*, March 29, 1861; Philadelphia *Press*, March 8, 1861; Boston *Post*, March 19, 1861; S. Churchill to Douglas, March 22, 1861; Charles Upton to *id.*, March 28, 1861, Douglas Papers.

[21] New York *Evening Post* ("Washington Correspondence"), March 29, 1861.

[22] F. P. Blair to Van Buren, May 1, 1861, Van Buren Papers; Crawford, *Genesis of the Civil War*, 364.

[23] New York *Herald* ("Washington Correspondence"), March 11, 12, 1861; New York *Evening Post*, March 11; April 3, 1861; New York *Daily Tribune* ("Washington Correspondence"), March 14, 1861; Springfield (Mass.) *Daily Republican*, March 13, 1861; Cincinnati *Daily Commercial* ("Washington Correspondence"), April 6, 1861; Chicago *Daily Tribune* ("Washington Correspondence"), April 5, 13, 1861.

[24] *Congressional Globe*, 1491–93, 1498–1501, 1512–20; New York *Herald* ("Washington Correspondence"), March 29, 1861.

[25] New York *Times*, March 28, 1861; Foulke, *Morton*, I, 113–14.

assured him that their states were ready for the use of force.[26]

The results of scattered local elections during March and early April confirmed the belief of Republicans that nothing but strong measures could save them. In New Hampshire they maintained their majorities only by giving positive assurances that the forts would be held and the laws enforced.[27] In Connecticut and Rhode Island, Republicans lost strength. These unfavorable returns, local leaders believed, were due to the "fear of a back-down policy on the part of the Administration." [28] In Ohio, Republicans were defeated in various city elections. "Sumter did it," was the usual explanation. "The Republicans, dissatisfied and discouraged, had no heart to work. . . . And if a temporizing policy is to be continued at Washington, this is but the beginning of the end." [29]

Though it was the Sumter crisis that immediately forced Lincoln's hand, that was only a historical accident. Even if the Sumter garrison had been well supplied and entirely secure, the northern people, unwilling to tolerate further suspense, would have given the new President no respite. Neither Anderson's letter nor Yankee impatience changed the strategy that Lincoln had planned to use, but they decidedly increased the speed of its application. The time for delay had passed!

3

Meanwhile reports coming out of the South were removing the last doubts from the northern mind. More and more it appeared that time was not on the side of the Union, that the secession movement was actually gaining in strength. The Confederacy, having perfected a provisional government, went ahead

[26] New York *Herald* ("Washington Correspondence"), April 7, 1861; New York *World* ("Washington Correspondence"), April 5, 1861; Chicago *Daily Tribune* ("Washington Correspondence"), April 13, 1861.

[27] New York *Morning Express* ("Washington Correspondence"), April 2, 1861.

[28] M. Howard to Welles, March 28, 1861, Welles Papers; New York *Evening Post*, April 3, 1861; Springfield (Mass.) *Daily Republican* (letter from "Warrington"), April 6, 1861.

[29] Cincinnati *Daily Gazette*, April 2, 1861; J. H. Jordan to Chase, March 27, 1861; J. W. and J. B. Autram to *id.*, April 2, 1861; Wm. D. Bickham to *id.*, April 2, 1861, Chase Papers; John W. Autram to Lincoln, April 2, 1861, Lincoln Papers.

with its military preparations. In many ways Southerners made it clear that they considered secession a finality. Was it wise to give them still more time to increase their strength? Would not the evacuation of Sumter add to Confederate prestige and bring foreign recognition? Was not Federal inaction reducing the Union government to general contempt? [30]

On March 21, Alexander H. Stephens, provisional Vice-President of the Confederacy, struck another blow at the Union. Northern conservatives had long admired and trusted Stephens as an opponent of secession. But now, in a speech at Savannah, he called disunion an accomplished fact, pledged his loyalty to the Confederacy, and cautioned his listeners to keep their "armor bright" and their "powder dry." [31] Yankees read this speech with dismay. Stephens had "shut the door." He had looked as "calm as a Summer's morning at the fact of war!" [32] The Union had lost its last friend among the influential leaders of the Deep South.

Conditions in the upper South seemed little more promising. The hope of keeping the border states loyal had been a restraining influence upon many Northerners. But by March there were growing signs of dissatisfaction with the kind of qualified Unionism that prevailed in those states. In the Virginia convention, still in session, the Unionists strongly opposed the use of force against the seceders and promised to support the Confederacy if it were attacked. They even defined efforts to collect the revenues or to hold government property as coercion.[33] And now they urged the recognition of Confederate independence and the evacuation of both Sumter and Pickens.[34]

Such "Unionism," Northerners agreed, was worthless. If by enforcing the laws the Federal government lost the support of the border states, "the sooner the better." "Upon an adhesion so quali-

[30] New York *Evening Post*, March 29, 1861; Philadelphia *North American and United States Gazette* (letter from "Independent"), March 13, 1861; Philadelphia *Daily Evening Bulletin*, March 27, 1861.

[31] Frank Moore (ed.), *The Rebellion Record: A Diary of American Events* . . . (New York, 1864), I, 44–49.

[32] Boston *Post*, March 29, 1861; Philadelphia *Press*, March 28, 1861; Cincinnati *Daily Commercial*, March 29, 1861; Providence *Daily Journal*, March 29, 1861.

[33] Henry T. Shanks, *The Secession Movement in Virginia, 1847–1861* (Richmond, 1934), 191.

[34] Geo. W. Summers to Montgomery Blair, March 19, 1861, Blair Papers; Bancroft, *Seward*, II, 120–21.

fied, no government can exist." [35] By holding the forts, many believed, the government would test the loyalty of those states and determine whether their support of the Union was "sound enough to be of any value." [36]

The upper South had lost its power to influence the northern people. By the end of March, Thurlow Weed saw that the program of "voluntary reconstruction" was played out. Nothing, he feared, could now prevent the secession of the border states.[37] Seward's formula of "masterly inactivity" was defeated by the weakness of southern Unionism and by the impatience of northern patriots.

4

But it was not easy for Seward to admit defeat. Certainly Lincoln's February speeches and his inaugural address were not designed to give Seward confidence that his policy would prevail. Yet he entered the cabinet as Secretary of State fully expecting to be the dominant figure.[38] For almost a month he went boldly ahead developing his own program and playing the role of "premier." With incredible blindness he continued to ignore the real situation in the South.[39]

As soon as Seward heard of Anderson's desperate condition he exerted all his influence in favor of evacuation. His aim, he explained to Lincoln, was to save the Union by the "peaceful policy" of waiting until the "blind, unreasoning popular excitement" in the South had subsided. The proper course was to avoid any new irritation and to foster the growth of southern Unionism.[40] Seward readily accepted Anderson's opinion that it was not feasible from a military point of view to provision Fort Sumter, and he held that an attempt to send supplies would not only be futile

[35] New York *Times*, April 9, 1861; New York *World*, April 11, 1861; New York *Daily Tribune*, April 5, 1861; Providence *Daily Journal*, April 8, 1861.

[36] Springfield (Mass.) *Daily Republican*, April 6, 1861.

[37] Bigelow Ms. Diary, entry for March 27, 1861.

[38] Bancroft, *Seward*, II, 95–96; George G. Fogg to Lincoln, February 5, 1861, Lincoln Papers.

[39] Adams, *Autobiography*, 88–89.

[40] Nicolay and Hay (eds.), *Works of Lincoln*, VI, 192–201; Gideon Welles, *Diary of Gideon Welles, Secretary of the Navy under Lincoln and Johnson* (Boston, 1911), I, 8–10,

but would provoke civil war. He strengthened his case by citing the views of other military men who believed that the government lacked the experienced troops needed for a relief expedition. General Scott, still dominated by Seward and serving him faithfully, decidedly favored immediate evacuation.[41] And so the Secretary of State assumed that the fate of Sumter had been settled.

Still confident of his power in the administration, Seward next turned his attention to another problem which challenged his resourcefulness. A few days after the inauguration three Confederate commissioners—Martin J. Crawford, John Forsyth, and A. B. Roman—appeared in Washington to secure recognition for their government. These men were familiar with Seward's hopes for peaceful reunion, and they concluded that he was playing directly into their hands. Since the commissioners were certain that the Confederacy was daily growing stronger, they were quite willing to have Seward "indulge in dreams" which were "not to be realized." [42] The deluded Secretary would unknowingly be their tool.

The commissioners, however, underestimated Seward's talent for intrigue, and they were soon to be themselves victimized. To Seward the presence of these southern agents was not without its value. At a considerable cost to his integrity he negotiated with them for several weeks, and thus he kept the crisis stalemated a little longer. Seward first established indirect contact with them through Senator William M. Gwin of California, and then through Senator Hunter of Virginia. But when the commissioners were unable to get a personal interview, they submitted on March 13 a written demand for recognition. Knowing that this was impossible, yet fearing that a rejection would precipitate an immediate attack upon Fort Sumter, Seward delayed his reply. But, for the moment, the situation must have looked hopeless even to him.

It was then that Seward tried a rash expedient. Perhaps a promise to evacuate Sumter would pacify the commissioners and put off their other business. The Secretary found new intermediaries in Supreme Court Justices Samuel Nelson and John A. Campbell,

[41] Welles, *Diary*, I, 8-10; *Official Records*, Ser. 1, I, 197, 232-35; Crawford, *Genesis of the Civil War*, 346-47; Elliott, *Scott*, 697-707.
[42] Bancroft, *Seward*, II, 118-20.

and through them he gave a pledge that Sumter would be abandoned within a few days. With this assurance the commissioners postponed calling for an answer to their note and notified Confederate leaders that the Charleston fort would soon be theirs.[43]

As the days passed with no sign that evacuation was being prepared, the commissioners grew impatient and Seward had to repeat his pledge. On April 1, however, the Secretary suddenly modified his position. With Lincoln's approval he now told Justice Campbell (Nelson had withdrawn from the negotiations) that no attempt to supply Sumter would be made "without giving notice to Governor Pickens" of South Carolina. This shift was a blow to Campbell, but Seward quickly reassured him by stating his belief that no such attempt would be made. The commissioners, now becoming suspicious, pressed the Justice for an explanation. On April 8 the Secretary wrote slyly to Campbell: "Faith as to Sumter fully kept; wait and see." Technically faith *was* kept, for an agent had been sent to Governor Pickens to give him the notice that Seward had promised. But the pledge to evacuate Sumter, which Seward had made on his own responsibility, was never honored. After keeping the commissioners at bay for a month, the Secretary now sent them his refusal to comply with their demand for recognition.[44] The end of these negotiations and the immediate departure of the angry Confederates meant that war was at hand. It also meant that Seward's game was finished.

Actually the new President and his would-be "premier" had been going in opposite directions. While Seward still trusted in voluntary reconstruction, Lincoln was moving toward an application of the policy outlined in his inaugural address. To be sure, the President hesitated about Sumter until almost the end of March. He hesitated because he at first viewed the problem chiefly in military terms, and Scott and other military experts agreed that the government lacked the military means for a relief attempt that would promise success. Perhaps evacuation *was* a disagreeable military necessity. Lincoln also hesitated because the majority of his cabinet, in opinions submitted on March 15 and 16, revealed that they preferred to give up Sumter rather than be responsible for

[43] *Official Records*, Ser. 1, I, 275, 277.
[44] Crawford, *Genesis of the Civil War*, 314-45; Bancroft, *Seward*, II, 107-42; Potter, *Lincoln and His Party in the Secession Crisis*, 342-49.

DECISION   275

provoking hostilities. (Only Postmaster General Montgomery
Blair demanded, without qualification, that the fort be held.[45])
Besides, if supplies and reinforcements could be thrown into
Sumter only through a major military and naval operation, there
was the danger that some Northerners would accuse the Federal
government of being the aggressor. Such an enterprise would
hardly conform with Lincoln's desire to make the South bear that
burden. And yet, though almost convinced that Sumter would
have to be abandoned, he could never make himself give the order
to withdraw.[46] Instead he waited.

But while he hesitated about Sumter, the President lost no time
in dealing with other matters. Impelled by the Sumter crisis and
by northern unrest, he considered various means of asserting Federal authority in the South. As early as March 9 he ordered General Scott "to exercise all possible vigilance for the maintenance of
all the places within the military department of the United States,
and to promptly call upon all the departments of the government
for the means necessary to that end." [47] Lincoln acted at once to
terminate the armistice that Buchanan had approved at Pensacola.
On March 11, Scott was instructed to order the immediate reinforcement of Fort Pickens with the troops which were still waiting on a warship in the harbor.[48] But on April 6 a messenger arrived from Fort Pickens with the news that the troops had not
disembarked, because a naval officer had denied that Scott's orders
could supersede those of the former Secretary of the Navy. The
President dispatched new instructions the same day, and the reinforcements landed at Pickens on April 12.[49] Meanwhile, when
Lincoln heard that Texas secessionists had deposed Governor
Sam Houston, a Unionist, he offered Houston military and naval

[45] Nicolay and Hay (eds.), *Works of Lincoln*, VI, 192–220.
[46] There is evidence that, in February, Lincoln proposed the evacuation of
Sumter to a delegation of Virginia Unionists if they "would break up their convention, without any row or nonsense." But the offer was rejected. See Potter,
Lincoln and His Party in the Secession Crisis, 353–58. It is obviously impossible
to ascertain positively whether Lincoln seriously expected the Virginians to accept the offer. But his general attitude on the question of holding Federal property makes it highly unlikely that he did.
[47] Nicolay and Hay (eds.), *Works of Lincoln*, VI, 188.
[48] Nicolay and Hay, *Lincoln*, III, 393–94; *Official Records*, Ser. 1, I, 360.
[49] Welles, *Diary*, I, 29–32; Nicolay and Hay, *Lincoln*, IV, 7–9, 11–13; Nicolay,
Outbreak of Rebellion, 53.

support if he would agree to lead the Union forces.[50] Finally, Lincoln began to explore the possibility of either collecting the revenues from naval vessels off southern ports or throwing a blockade around the Confederacy.[51]

All of these projects illustrated the swift unfolding of the President's program to enforce the laws in conformance with his strategy of defense. In every case these measures would have forced the secessionists to retreat, until they found themselves discredited before their own people and, for all practical purposes, back in the Union. Their only alternative was resistance, but always the burden of aggression would be upon them. Lincoln's record would remain clear in the eyes of the northern people.

But before the effects of any of these measures could be realized, the final decision was reached in Charleston Harbor. As the Sumter problem kept revolving in Lincoln's mind, its political aspects, as distinguished from strictly military considerations, became predominant. The President had to weigh northern public opinion; he had to consider the effect evacuation might have upon the prestige of his administration; he had to face the question whether the abandonment of Sumter would really solve anything. Even if Sumter were given up, serious problems would still remain—problems such as the Confederate demand for immediate recognition, the need to maintain the Union's position among foreign powers, the unsolved tariff crisis, and above all, the factor of northern impatience. Assuming that some sort of immediate action was called for, was not Fort Sumter the logical point for a decisive step, provided that he could satisfy Northerners that the step was nonaggressive?

As he thought about these things Lincoln still refused to order the fort's surrender. Instead he showed increasing interest in another plan to send relief. The author of the plan was Captain Gustavus Vasa Fox, brother-in-law of Postmaster General Blair, who had long been eager to direct such a project.[52] On March 13,

[50] For Houston's rejection of this offer see Amelia W. Williams and Eugene C. Barker (eds.), *The Writings of Sam Houston* (Austin, 1938–1943), VIII, 294. See also Nicolay, *Outbreak of Rebellion*, 14; Tarbell, *Lincoln*, II, 20–22.

[51] Nicolay and Hay (eds.), *Works of Lincoln*, VI, 224–25; Gideon Welles to Lincoln, March 20, 1861, Lincoln Papers.

[52] *Official Records*, Ser. 1, I, 203–205; Crawford, *Genesis of the Civil War*, 248–51; Thompson and Wainwright (eds.), *Confidential Correspondence of Gustavus Vasa Fox*, I, 3–5.

Blair took Fox to the White House for an interview with Lincoln. Fox explained his scheme and argued that it was not too late for his relief project to succeed. On March 19 he received permission to go to Fort Sumter to make a personal reconnaissance. There Major Anderson tried hard to dissuade Fox, but when Fox returned to Washington late in March he assured Lincoln that his plan was workable.[53] A few days later the President authorized Seward to tell the Confederate commissioners that Governor Pickens would receive prior notice if relief were to be sent. He gave that pledge, he said, after he had "duly weighed the matter and come to the deliberate conclusion that that would be the best policy." [54] Here was an important sign that the political side of the Sumter crisis had captured Lincoln's mind.

On March 28, General Scott unwittingly provoked Lincoln to make his final decision. Scott, writing another memorandum to urge the evacuation of Sumter, now added a recommendation that Fort Pickens also be abandoned—so as to "soothe and give confidence" to the loyal slave states. This was not military advice; it was a lecture on political strategy! It completely destroyed Lincoln's confidence in the military opinions of the general in chief. That night after a state dinner the President called the members of his cabinet aside and, with considerable agitation, read them Scott's note. Doubtless its contents were no surprise to Seward, but the rest were obviously shocked. Blair exploded angrily that Scott was "playing the part of a politician, not of a general." No one pretended that there was the slightest military necessity for the surrender of Fort Pickens.[55]

[53] Crawford, *Genesis of the Civil War*, 346-47, 369-73; *Official Records*, Ser. 1, I, 208, 211; Welles, *Diary*, I, 14-15; William E. Smith, *The Francis Preston Blair Family in Politics* (New York, 1933), II, 11-13. Lincoln also sent two Illinois friends, Ward H. Lamon and S. A. Hurlbut, on a second mission to Charleston to determine the state of feeling at that point. In Charleston the garrulous Lamon freely stated to Governor Pickens and others that the fort was to be evacuated. Needless to say, Lamon was assuming much, for he had no authority from Lincoln to make such statements. There is evidence, however, that Lamon was close to Seward and had assumed that the Secretary's policy would prevail. See *Official Records*, Ser. 1, I, 281-82; Crawford, *Genesis of the Civil War*, 373-74; Nicolay and Hay, *Lincoln*, III, 391-92; Bancroft, *Seward*, II, 107 n.; Ramsdell, "Lincoln and Fort Sumter," *loc. cit.*, 273-74.
[54] Nicolay and Hay, *Lincoln*, IV, 33-34; Nicolay, *Outbreak of Rebellion*, 55.
[55] Montgomery Blair to Van Buren, April 27, 1861, Van Buren Papers; Welles, *Diary*, I, 13-14; Crawford, *Genesis of the Civil War*, 363, 365-66, 368; Tarbell, *Lincoln*, II, 17-19.

Lincoln acted swiftly. On March 29 he again polled his cabinet on the question of evacuating or supplying Sumter. This time only Seward and Secretary of the Interior Caleb Smith favored evacuation. Secretary of the Navy Gideon Welles argued: "Armed resistance to a peaceable attempt to send provisions to one of our own forts will justify the government in using all the power at its command to reinforce the garrison and furnish the necessary supplies." [56] On that same day the President issued an order "that an expedition to move by sea be got ready to sail as early as the 6th of April next." [57] Captain Fox went to New York to assume command of the enterprise. On April 4, Lincoln gave Fox his final orders to sail and sent notification to Major Anderson that supplies were coming.[58] Two days later he dispatched a messenger to inform Governor Pickens that an attempt would be made "to supply Fort Sumter with provisions only," and that if the attempt were not resisted, there would be "no effort to throw in men, arms, or ammunition . . . without further notice." [59]

At last Lincoln was taking the decisive step. Without exposing himself to a charge of aggression, he now fulfilled the program of his inaugural address. He underscored the defensive nature of his move by his offer merely to send supplies to the "brave and hungry men of the garrison." The Confederates would have to assume the responsibility for initiating military action. Whether they attacked or submitted, Lincoln was sure to triumph.

But Seward had lost. The Sumter expedition, symbol of his defeat, was the source of great personal humiliation. And so at the last minute the Secretary tried frantically to extricate himself and to save face. If there must be a war, he wanted above all to prevent it from starting at the fort whose evacuation he had pledged. In his opinion of March 29 he had argued lamely against provoking "a civil war beginning at Charleston." Instead he urged Lincoln "at once and at every cost" to "prepare for a war at Pensacola and

[56] Nicolay and Hay (eds.), *Works of Lincoln*, VI, 227–31.

[57] *Ibid.*, 226–27.

[58] *Ibid.*, 239–40; Nicolay and Hay, *Lincoln*, IV, 27–29; Crawford, *Genesis of the Civil War*, 404; *Official Records*, Ser. 1, I, 235–36; Kenneth M. Stampp, "Lincoln and the Strategy of Defense in the Crisis of 1861," *Journal of Southern History*, XI (1945), 314.

[59] *Official Records*, Ser. 1, I, 245, 251–52; Nicolay and Hay (eds.), *Works of Lincoln*, VI, 241; Nicolay and Hay, *Lincoln*, IV, 35.

Texas." ⁶⁰ Though he failed in his major purpose, he did get Lincoln's approval for a second expedition, directed by Captain Montgomery C. Meigs, to carry additional supplies and reinforcements to Fort Pickens. Perhaps unknowingly Lincoln even assigned the warship *Powhatan* to Seward's project, though Captain Fox had intended it to be the flagship of his Sumter expedition. The *Powhatan* sailed to Fort Pickens before Lincoln, in response to the angry protest of Gideon Welles, could get his order countermanded. Without his flagship Fox's enterprise was seriously impaired, and Welles later claimed that Seward had deliberately wrecked it in order to vindicate his own proposal for Sumter's evacuation.⁶¹ The validity of Welles's charge is doubtful, but Seward was desperate and evidently ready to try almost anything.

On April 1, Seward made his last bid for power. He submitted to Lincoln a memorandum entitled "Some Thoughts for the President's Consideration." The memorandum was the work of a desperate man. Ignoring all that Lincoln had said and done, the Secretary charged: "We are at the end of a month's administration, and yet without a policy either domestic or foreign." He again urged the abandonment of Sumter, which he justified with some spurious logic. Then, brazenly attempting to seize the initiative in applying Lincoln's own strategy, he proposed to "defend and reinforce all the ports [forts?] in the Gulf" and to prepare a blockade. Someone, he boldly concluded, would have to take control of the administration. And though this was not within his "especial province," he sought neither "to evade nor assume responsibility." ⁶²

Lincoln's brief and courteous reply permanently disposed of Seward's pretensions. The President pointed to his inaugural address and to his instructions to Scott to hold the forts as evidence that the administration did have a policy. The inaugural, he reminded Seward, "comprises the exact domestic policy you now urge, with the single exception that it does not propose to abandon

---

⁶⁰ Nicolay and Hay (eds.), *Works of Lincoln*, VI, 227.

⁶¹ Welles, *Diary*, I, 23–25; Gideon Welles, *Lincoln and Seward* (New York, 1874), 54–71; Nicolay and Hay, *Lincoln*, IV, 3–7; Potter, *Lincoln and His Party in the Secession Crisis*, 363–67. The reinforcements that Meigs brought to Fort Pickens were landed there on April 17. Nicolay and Hay, *Lincoln*, IV, 16–17.

⁶² Nicolay and Hay (eds.), *Works of Lincoln*, VI, 234–36.

Fort Sumter." Moreover, it was the President's duty to direct that policy.[63] Not Seward but Lincoln was "premier"!

5

Lincoln's Sumter maneuver provides a challenging study of human motivation and social causation. What went on in the President's mind while he was reaching his fateful decision? Did he, for sefish political reasons, suddenly decide to provoke a war? Or did he merely blunder into that result? Upon what ethical standards is his action to be judged? How much responsibility can be attributed to one man—even to the President—for the military conflict which grew out of this great national crisis? These are questions which divided Lincoln's contemporaries as much as they have since divided historians.

The Confederates, of course, called the attempt to supply Fort Sumter an act of aggression. A few northern critics, accepting this interpretation, accused Lincoln of acting from altogether sinister motives. Even in March the New York *Herald* had repeatedly predicted that the President would try to prod the Confederacy into an attack upon the Union.[64] Early in April another Democratic paper asserted: "The administration of Mr. Lincoln is disposed to secretly provoke a fight; and . . . it looks to some collision at the South, commenced on that side, to arouse Northern feeling." [65] The critics described the sending of food to the Sumter garrison as a "cunningly contrived plan" designed to afford a "pretext for letting loose the horrors of war." [66] This action, they concluded, was the product of sordid politics. There was to be a civil war "because Abraham Lincoln loves a party better than he loves his country." After the defeats in the spring elections, he had decided: "Nothing but a war can keep together the Re-

---

[63] *Ibid.,* 236–37.

[64] New York *Herald,* March 9, 18, 19, 24, 1861. See also Dubuque *Herald,* March 16, 1861, quoted in Perkins (ed.), *Northern Editorials on Secession,* II, 700–702.

[65] Albany *Atlas and Argus,* quoted in Boston *Post,* April 6, 1861.

[66] Utica *Daily Observer,* quoted in New York *Daily Tribune,* April 13, 1861; New York *Herald,* April 5, 9, 1861; New York *Morning Express,* April 11, 1861; Jersey City *American Standard,* April 12, 1861, quoted in Perkins (ed.), *Northern Editorials on Secession,* II, 706–708.

publican party." [67] Essentially the same explanation of the Sumter incident appears in the writings of several historians.[68]

Even some contemporary Republicans agreed that Lincoln had shrewdly forced the Confederacy to begin hostilities. In March they had expressed the hope that the South would "strike the first blow." [69] Several Republicans suggested the Sumter strategy that Lincoln finally adopted. One of them wrote: "Why not send an unarmed vessel, with provisions simply, to Sumter? We shall see if they attack it, and the feeling that will result." [70] And after the South had reduced the fort, a few of Lincoln's party friends congratulated him upon his masterful stroke. The New York *Times* believed that "the attempt at reinforcement was a *feint*,— that its object was to put upon the rebels the full and clear responsibility of commencing the war. . . ." [71] Jefferson Davis, others exulted, "ran blindly into the trap." The South had captured a "wooden horse" from which would "spring an army." [72]

Most Republicans, however, vigorously asserted that Lincoln's intentions had been peaceful and denounced the Confederate assault as unprovoked aggression. They reviewed the government's patient and forbearing attitude in the face of repeated southern seizures of its property and revenues. "We have done our utmost to avoid strife," they said. "We have given our erring brethren time for reflection, time to retrace their mistaken and destructive footsteps." [73] The expedition to Fort Sumter was "one of peace." [74] The southern attack was "an audacious and insulting

[67] Providence *Daily Post*, April 13, 1861; Boston *Daily Courier* (letter from "K"), April 9, 1861; New York *Journal of Commerce*, quoted in New York *Morning Express*, April 15, 1861.

[68] Scrugham, *Peaceable Americans*, 78–104; Ramsdell, "Lincoln and Fort Sumter," *loc. cit.*; Tilley, *Lincoln Takes Command*.

[69] New York *Times*, March 9, 1861; Milwaukee *Daily Sentinel* (letter from Rufus King), March 16, 1861.

[70] T. D. Lincoln to Chase, March 12, 1861, Chase Papers. See also Philadelphia *North American and United States Gazette*, March 13, 1861; Chicago *Daily Tribune*, March 15, 1861.

[71] New York *Times*, April 17, 1861.

[72] *Daily Pittsburgh Gazette*, April 18, 1861, quoted in Perkins (ed.), *Northern Editorials on Secession*, II, 719–22; Milwaukee *Daily Sentinel*, April 19, 1861; Philadelphia *North American and United States Gazette*, April 8, 1861.

[73] *Morning Courier and New-York Enquirer*, April 12, 1861.

[74] New York *World*, April 8, 1861; Providence *Daily Journal*, April 11, 1861; Springfield (Mass.) *Daily Republican*, April 6, 1861; Indianapolis *Daily Journal*, April 11, 1861; Chicago *Daily Tribune*, April 10, 1861.

aggression upon the authority of the Republic, without provocation or excuse." [75]

In their eagerness to stress the peaceful nature of Lincoln's policy and the reckless belligerency of the Confederates, many administration papers embellished the Sumter story with various distortions. The official secrecy which shrouded the background of the relief expedition made it easy for these fabrications to gain currency. For example, one editor stated that Lincoln had first asked Governor Pickens to furnish supplies for the Sumter garrison, and that only after this request was refused did he attempt to send aid from the North.[76] Actually the President had never carried on such negotiations with the South Carolina governor. Other accounts declared that the Confederates had forced the government to undertake the relief project by cutting off Anderson's local supply of fresh meats and vegetables.[77] This was equally untrue, for the fresh food from Charleston was not withheld until April 7, which was after the Federal ships had been instructed to sail.[78] Still another widely circulated report was that Lincoln had offered to withdraw the garrison from Sumter and leave the fort vacant. But this offer was allegedly rejected by the Confederates, who insisted upon humiliating the government by demanding a formal surrender.[79] Again the facts were quite different, for General P. G. T. Beauregard, who commanded the Confederate troops at Charleston, had promised Major Anderson that no "formal surrender or capitulation" would be required.[80] These myths were the products of heated brains eager to discredit the enemy and vindicate the North.

Lincoln, still seeking to impress the nation with his nonaggressive policy, added his own interpretation of the Sumter expedition. In his message to the special session of Congress which assembled

[75] New Haven *Morning Journal and Courier*, quoted in New York *Daily Tribune*, April 15, 1861.

[76] Providence *Daily Journal*, April 15, 1861.

[77] New York *World*, April 9, 1861; New York *Daily Tribune* (Washington dispatch), April 9, 1861; Rochester *Express*, quoted in New York *Daily Tribune*, April 13, 1861; Worcester (Mass.) *Daily Spy*, April 13, 1861.

[78] *Official Records*, Ser. 1, I, 248.

[79] New York *Daily Tribune*, April 13, 1861; Philadelphia *Press*, April 15, 1861; Boston *Evening Transcript*, April 15, 1861; Worcester (Mass.) *Daily Spy*, April 13, 1861.

[80] *Official Records*, Ser. 1, I, 222.

on July 4, 1861, he noted that reinforcements had first been ordered to land at Fort Pickens. He then suggested that Sumter would have been evacuated if this order had been executed before Anderson's supplies were exhausted. In that way, he said, it would have been clear that he was yielding only to military necessity, and thus the loss of Sumter would not have injured the national cause. But when on April 6 the President learned that the reinforcements had not yet landed at Fort Pickens, it was too late to carry out that plan. Then, he concluded, it became necessary to relieve Sumter in order to prevent "our national destruction." [81]

But Lincoln's assertion that the voluntary surrender of Sumter hinged upon the successful reinforcement of Pickens indicated either that he was confused or that he was deliberately rationalizing. His account is scarcely consistent with the known facts. The President had ordered the reinforcement of Pickens on March 11, and he then had no reason to doubt that his order would be executed at once. Yet the whole debate upon the wisdom of supplying Sumter went on in the cabinet and in his own mind *after* he thought the Pickens question had been settled. Moreover, no member of the cabinet ever revealed that Lincoln had contemplated such a plan. When he polled his Secretaries on March 15 and 29, he asked their advice about supplying Sumter without any reference to the situation at Pickens. Indeed, on April 1, five days before the President received the report that Pickens had not been reinforced, he had informed Seward categorically that he did "not propose to abandon Fort Sumter." [82] It was Seward, not Lincoln, who wanted to reinforce Pickens and give up Sumter.

All the evidence indicates that Lincoln had decided to supply Sumter as early as March 29. It was then that he ordered the expedition prepared in time to sail on April 6. It was on April 4 that Captain Fox received his final instructions and that a letter was sent to Major Anderson informing him that supplies were coming.[83] Finally, even as late as April 6 there was still time to

[81] Nicolay and Hay (eds.), *Works of Lincoln*, VI, 297–325.
[82] *Ibid.*, 236–37.
[83] A copy of the letter of April 4 to Anderson is in the Lincoln Papers in the Library of Congress. On the back of this copy is an endorsement by Lincoln that it was sent by Captain Theodore Talbot on April 6. But Lincoln omitted the fact that the letter was also sent by mail on April 4. The copy carried by Talbot never reached Anderson. But the copy sent by mail arrived at Sumter

send new instructions to Fort Pickens before Anderson's supplies were exhausted. Reinforcements entered Pickens on April 12, which proved that Lincoln not only could but *did* achieve that objective before the Sumter garrison capitulated. Actually the President had dealt with Sumter and Pickens as separate problems, though his action in each case was part of a unified program.

The Sumter expedition, then, was the final culmination of Lincoln's crisis strategy.[84] He had long calculated the risk of hostilities, and he had always intended to make the Confederates be the aggressors. That he anticipated resistance at Charleston is hardly open to doubt. The messengers sent there in March gave him abundant opportunities to know the state of feeling in South Carolina. The whole North assumed in advance that the Sumter expedition meant war; and, on April 4, the state governors returned from their conference with the President to speed their war preparations.[85] Early in April, Lincoln strove to organize the defenses of Washington.[86] On April 9 he warned Pennsylvania's Governor Curtin of "the necessity of being ready" and urged him to prepare for an emergency.[87] John G. Nicolay and John Hay, the President's private secretaries, believed that it was "reasonably certain" that he expected hostilities to ensue. And when the news arrived of the attack upon Sumter, they noted that he was neither surprised nor excited.[88] Indeed, if Lincoln had thought that Sumter could be supplied peacefully, there was no reason why he should ever have considered evacuation as a possible military necessity.

It is equally evident that Lincoln looked upon the results of his Sumter maneuver with satisfaction. Nicolay and Hay were con-

on April 7, and Anderson answered it the next day. See Nicolay, *Outbreak of Rebellion*, 53; Nicolay and Hay, *Lincoln*, IV, 27-29; Stampp, "Lincoln and the Strategy of Defense," *loc. cit.*, 314; Ramsdell, "Lincoln and Fort Sumter," *loc. cit.*, 279.

[84] Stampp, "Lincoln and the Strategy of Defense," *loc. cit.*, 318.

[85] Philadelphia *Daily Evening Bulletin*, April 11, 1861; Philadelphia *Press*, April 9, 1861; Philadelphia *North American and United States Gazette* ("Harrisburg Correspondence"), April 8, 1861; Madison *Wisconsin Daily State Journal*, April 6, 1861.

[86] New York *Evening Post* (Washington dispatch), April 11, 1861; Nicolay and Hay, *Lincoln*, IV, 64-68.

[87] Angle (ed.), *New Letters and Papers of Lincoln*, 266; Nicolay and Hay (eds.), *Works of Lincoln*, VI, 242.

[88] Nicolay and Hay, *Lincoln*, IV, 44-45, 70.

vinced that he regarded the success or failure of the expedition as "a question of minor importance." More significant was his determination that "the rebellion should be put in the wrong," that the Confederates "would not be able to convince the world that he had begun civil war." That, added Nicolay, was his "carefully matured purpose." [89] On April 4, when Captain Fox complained about the limited time for the execution of his relief project, Lincoln replied: "You will best fulfill your duty to your country by making the attempt." [90] Fox later recalled how "anxious" the President had been that the South "should stand before the civilized world as having fired upon bread." [91] After Sumter had fallen, Lincoln wrote Fox a comforting letter: "You and I both anticipated that the cause of the country would be advanced by making the attempt to provision Fort Sumter, even if it should fail; and it is no small consolation now to feel that our anticipation is justified by the result." [92] A few months later he expressed the same opinion to Senator Orville H. Browning of Illinois, and he added that the loss of the fort "did more service" than if it had been held.[93] What Lincoln achieved at Sumter was best described by his private secretaries: "When he finally gave the order that the fleet should sail he was master of the situation; master of his Cabinet; master of the moral attitude and issues of the struggle; master of the public opinion which must arise out of the impending conflict; master if the rebels hesitate or repent, because they would thereby forfeit their prestige with the South; master if they persisted, for he would then command a united North." [94]

In short, the Sumter project was designed to relieve Lincoln from the responsibility for initiating hostilities. It is not in their analysis of his Sumter strategy that Lincoln's contemporary and more recent critics miss the mark. Rather, it is in their failure to place the episode in its proper perspective and in their assumption that he was consciously motivated by sordid purposes. Lincoln did not, on March 29, abruptly determine to provoke a war. He

---

[89] *Ibid.*, 33, 44–45; Nicolay, *Outbreak of Rebellion*, 55, 74.

[90] Crawford, *Genesis of the Civil War*, 404.

[91] Fox to Montgomery Blair, April 17, 1861, in Thompson and Wainwright (eds.), *Confidential Correspondence of Gustavus Vasa Fox*, I, 34–36.

[92] Nicolay and Hay (eds.), *Works of Lincoln*, VI, 261–62.

[93] Pease and Randall (eds.), *Diary of Orville Hickman Browning*, I, 475–76.

[94] Nicolay and Hay, *Lincoln*, IV, 62.

had perceived that possibility ever since December, when he began to assert, first privately and then publicly, his determination to enforce the laws. The Sumter expedition simply fulfilled these earlier promises. If that step precipitated hostilities, one cannot indict Lincoln for taking it unless one challenges the universal standards of "practical" statesmen and the whole concept of "national interest." This was a thing worth fighting for! If Lincoln was no pacifist, neither were his contemporaries, North and South. Southern leaders must share with him the responsibility for a resort to force. They too preferred war to submission.

It would obviously be a gross distortion of history to attribute the Civil War to Lincoln's Sumter maneuver. To do so would be to overlook the real causes that grew out of a generation of sectionalism. To do so would also be to ignore the fact that Lincoln came to power when the secession crisis was in an advanced stage. By the time of his inauguration the North was impatiently calling for action. It could hardly be said that his decision to supply Sumter was displeasing to the majority of Northerners. Quite the contrary. He had responded with remarkable promptness to overwhelming public pressure.

Finally, it may well be true that the outbreak of war saved the Republican party from disintegration, and that a practical politician like Lincoln could not have overlooked that possibility. But the Machiavellian implication that he started the war to achieve that purpose remains unproved. The evidence makes equally valid the conclusion that he thought only in terms of what he understood to be the deep and enduring interests of the whole country. It is also a distinct possibility that he had a comprehensive understanding of what both the country and political expediency demanded. Perhaps it was only Lincoln's good fortune that personal, partisan, and national interests could be served with such favorable coincidence as they were by his Sumter decision.

XIV

"At Last We Have a Government!"

S INCE they will have it so,—in the name of God,—Amen!"
So a Massachusetts radical responded to the Confederate
attack upon Fort Sumter—and expressed the feeling of nearly
every Yankee.[1] The first shot from the Charleston batteries,
thought James Russell Lowell, was destined to become "the most
memorable one ever fired on this continent." How fortunate that
the government had a fort "which it was so profitable to lose!" [2]
The rebel assault, piously remarked a Boston editor, furnished
"precisely the stimulus which . . . a good Providence sends to
arouse the latent patriotism of the people." [3]

War fever actually began to infect the northern people before
they received the news that hostilities had begun. They needed
no greater stimulus than the knowledge that a naval expedition
was being prepared in New York and that the period of painful
inaction was coming to an end. During the first week of April,
as Northerners read reports of impending military and naval
operations in their newspapers, they waited eagerly for the secession crisis to reach its climax. John Sherman wrote from Washington: "The military excitement here is intense. . . . Civil War is
actually upon us, and strange to say, it brings a feeling of relief:
the suspense is over." [4] Lincoln's party friends were overjoyed
that he was carrying out the pledge of his inaugural address. "Republican countenances," wrote one observer, "have been brighter
during the past few days than at any previous time during the

---

[1] S. G. Howe to Andrew, April 13, 1861, Andrew Papers.

[2] [James Russell Lowell], "The Pickens-and-Stealin's Rebellion," *Atlantic
Monthly*, VII (1861), 762.

[3] Boston *Daily Advertiser*, April 15, 1861.

[4] Rachel S. Thorndike (ed.), *The Sherman Letters* . . . (New York, 1894),
110-11. For tenders of troops before the firing upon Sumter see Lincoln Papers.

winter." [5] Many Douglas Democrats also caught the martial spirit when they heard that supplies were en route to Major Anderson.[6] Even Buchanan approved the Sumter expedition and asserted that the Republicans had "delayed too long and talked too much." [7] Businessmen, too, expressed satisfaction that "something was doing by the Government." [8] The North was prepared for war.

The bombardment of Sumter began on April 12, and the Federal garrison surrendered the next day. What followed in the North seemed to promise only a brief existence for the southern Confederacy. The mass hysteria among the Yankees was partly an emotional release from the months of agonizing uncertainty, and partly a nationalistic response to the insult that their government had suffered from "rebel aggressors." Political differences vanished instantly as the people rallied to the defense of the Union. Men of all parties answered Lincoln's call for 75,000 volunteers from the state militias. War meetings assembled in every northern community to pledge support to the President; state legislatures made generous military appropriations; private groups subscribed large funds to aid the families of soldiers. Everywhere Northerners rejoiced, "At last we have a government!" Even an exuberant Republican editor could not exaggerate the true picture: "The seven thousand conspirators who assaulted Fort Sumter have sown the dragon's teeth, which have instantly sprung up armed men. They have made the Free States a unit, and such a unit! . . . Since the landing of the Pilgrims, nothing has occurred on the American Continent equal in grandeur and sublimity to the uprising of the people during the last seven days. . . . In the war of the Revolution there was a powerful minority; in the war of

[5] Cincinnati *Daily Commercial* ("Columbus Correspondence"), April 9, 1861; New York *Daily Tribune* ("Washington Correspondence"), April 9, 1861.

[6] Philadelphia *Press* (Washington dispatch), April 13, 1861; Boston *Herald*, April 8, 1861; New York *Evening Post* (Washington dispatch), April 10, 1861; Pittsburgh *Journal*, quoted in New York *Daily Tribune*, April 13, 1861; Rochester *Daily Union and Advertiser*, quoted in New York *Commercial Advertiser*, April 11, 1861.

[7] Buchanan to Stanton, April 9, 1861, Stanton Papers.

[8] New York *Times*, April 8, 1861; Chicago *Daily Tribune* (Washington dispatch), April 11, 1861; Philadelphia *Press* (letter from "Occasional"), April 10, 1861; James M. Brown to Chase, April 8, 1861; Jas. P. Kilbreth to *id.*, April 11, 1861, Chase Papers.

1812, there was a powerful minority; in the war of 1861 the people are one and indivisible." [9]

Few northern Democrats would let their Republican neighbors exceed them in professions of loyalty and patriotism. Senator Douglas visited Lincoln the day after the fall of Sumter and promised to support a war program. Until his death the following June he spent much of his time addressing Democratic meetings and urging his followers to unite behind the administration.[10] With few exceptions other party leaders and the party press favored military action to preserve the Union.[11] In the state legislatures Democrats united with Republicans in voting war appropriations. The Democratic legislature of New Jersey unanimously resolved, "The most certain and speedy mode of restoring peace is by the most vigorous prosecution of the present war." [12] Devotion to the Union, avowed a pro-Douglas paper, had always been "the moving spirit of the great mass of the Democratic party North." Too long the party had acquiesced in southern "indignities." "The long penance of subserviency and humiliation is at last terminated." [13]

The minority of businessmen who still had opposed war early in April quickly changed their position once the conflict began. The issue was no longer war or peace but victory or defeat, and they believed that defeat would destroy them all. In New York the merchants and financiers met at the Chamber of Commerce and the Stock Exchange, where they adopted patriotic resolutions and subscribed funds for the support of the Union cause. They also sponsored a mammoth public meeting at Union Square on April 20, and many of them served as officers and speakers. At this meeting, the "solid men" of the city agreed to organize a

[9] Boston *Evening Transcript*, April 20, 1861. The mass enthusiasm is reflected in the telegrams and letters which poured in upon Lincoln. See Lincoln Papers.

[10] Welles, *Diary*, I, 32–35; New York *Herald*, April 15, 1861; Milton, *Eve of Conflict*, 559–61; White, *Trumbull*, 153; James N. Slade to Douglas, April 16, 1861, Douglas Papers.

[11] W. S. Holman to Hamilton, April 13, 1861, Hamilton Papers; D. E. Sickles to Cameron, April 17, 1861, Cameron Papers; Moore (ed.), *Works of Buchanan*, XI, 181–86; Brummer, *New York during the Period of the Civil War*, 143–46.

[12] Knapp, *New Jersey during the Civil War and Reconstruction*, 54–57.

[13] New York *Leader*, April 20, 27, 1861; Boston *Herald*, April 17, 1861.

Union Defense Committee to direct local war expenditures.[14] The action of New York's capitalists was duplicated by the merchants, manufacturers, and bankers in every northern city. An observer close to the business interests of Boston shrewdly interpreted their reaction to the war: Capitalists understood "that upon the stability of the Government the security of all property and all the legitimate objects of social life depend." Hence they were contributing generously to the support of the military policy. Idle capital, which had previously clogged the banks, had "at last found a channel into which it could beneficially pour itself." [15]

Two events which occurred shortly after the firing upon Sumter removed any remaining doubts from the minds of the business classes. The first was the Confederate government's offer to commission privateers to prey upon northern commerce. This action spread terror throughout the mercantile communities and converted the last hesitating merchant to the war policy. The conservative Boston *Courier*, for example, did not clearly endorse military action against the South until Jefferson Davis announced that he would issue letters of marque and reprisal. Although the United States had used that weapon during the War of 1812 and had refused to ratify the Declaration of Paris of 1856, which outlawed privateering, northern merchants now unanimously denounced it as "piracy" and a barbarous method of warfare. They flooded the government with demands for an immediate blockade of the South and for naval protection for their shipping.[16] They enthusiastically approved Lincoln's proclamation of a blockade and his threat to punish privateers under the laws against piracy.

[14] *Morning Courier and New-York Enquirer* (Commercial column), April 15, 1861; New York *Herald*, April 16, 18, 21, 22, 24, 1861; New York *Commercial Advertiser*, April 17, 19, 20, 1861; New York *Evening Post*, April 16, 17, 18, 1861; New York *World*, April 16, 18, 22, 1861; New York *Daily Tribune*, April 22, 1861; Union Defense Committee, *The Union Defense Committee of the City of New York: Minutes, Reports, and Correspondence* (New York, 1885), 3-12; Dix (comp.), *Memoirs*, II, 11-13.

[15] Boston *Daily Courier*, April 23, 1861. See also Boston *Daily Advertiser* (letter from Boston merchant), April 25, 1861.

[16] New York *Herald* (Commercial column), April 22, 1861; New York *Daily Tribune*, April 20, 28, 1861; Boston *Daily Courier*, April 19, 26, 30, 1861; Boston *Evening Transcript*, April 19; May 18, 1861; Boston *Daily Advertiser*, April 22, 27, 1861; Boston *Post*, April 19, 20, 24, 1861; New York Chamber of Commerce, *Fourth Annual Report*, 8-10.

The New York *Times* accurately reflected the sentiments of the merchants:

> Jefferson Davis might as well have thrown a lighted match into a powder magazine, as menace the commerce of the North with privateers. The effect of his proclamation upon our community has been only to deepen and make tenfold more intense the hatred and indignation of the public. Our people begin to realize the real character of the foe with whom they have to deal. . . . Those whom they had looked upon as brothers prove to be pirates. . . . They cannot even make war in the spirit of a civilized nation, but go back to the habits and practices of the barbarism of a hundred years ago.[17]

The second event seemed to threaten northern investments in the South. In May, Governor Joseph E. Brown of Georgia proclaimed that money owed to Northerners was to be paid into the state treasury. The same month an act of the Confederate Congress applied this principle to all the seceded states. Angry Yankee capitalists looked upon this policy as the equivalent of debt repudiation. It was "commercial dishonor and robbery," another example of the "perfidiousness of that buccaneering squad who have made Montgomery their headquarters." The northern merchants saw that they had to support the government as the "most efficient means for the recovery of their just debts." They now realized that the conflict was "between honor and infamy, between the rights of property and general confiscation."[18]

Thus in the North at the start of the war an organized opposition was completely lacking. Most of the scattered critics of the Sumter expedition and of Lincoln's call for volunteers were soon either won over or silenced. Throughout the North mobs of enraged patriots threatened to destroy the offices of newspapers which did not immediately endorse the President's action. In New York, James Gordon Bennett saved his *Herald* establishment from the mob by hastily raising the flag and by a sudden switch of editorial policy. Only a handful of newspapers refused to conform.[19]

[17] New York *Times*, April 20, 1861.
[18] New York *Commercial Advertiser*, May 9, 1861; Boston *Post*, May 11, 1861; Philadelphia *Press*, May 10, 1861; Philadelphia *Public Ledger*, May 10, 1861.
[19] New York *Herald*, April 16, 17, 18, 1861; New York *World*, April 18,

Other dissenters were converted with equal speed. Richard Lathers was still touring the South and begging for peace and compromise when the war began. When he returned to New York late in April, he found himself accused of disloyalty. Lathers denied the charge in a public letter and quickly joined his mercantile colleagues in supporting military measures.[20] In Boston, Edward Everett hesitated for a few days and then decided that he "could not hesitate as to the path of duty." The alternatives, he concluded, were "between supporting the government and allowing the country to fall into a state of anarchy." [21] Caleb Cushing soon publicly announced that he too favored the war policy.[22] Not many of the old "doughfaces" held back. One of Cushing's political friends wrote unhappily that even in New York it was no longer safe "for a man to express . . . doubt of the duty of northern men to march in obedience to Lincoln's call." Another friend, who had twice been threatened with violence for criticizing Lincoln, declared that in the future he intended to be "prudent." [23]

William Lloyd Garrison and Wendell Phillips, leaders of the nonpolitical abolitionists, had no trouble in shedding their earlier disunionism and coming out for the war. On April 21, Phillips proclaimed his new course in Boston's Music Hall: "Now for the first time in my antislavery life, I speak under the stars and stripes, and welcome the tread of Massachusetts men marshalled for war. No matter what the past has been or said; to-day the slave asks God for a sight of this banner, and counts it the pledge of his redemption." [24] Garrison urged every abolitionist to support the

1861; Villard, *Memoirs*, I, 161–62; Oliver Carlson, *The Man Who Made the News: James Gordon Bennett* (New York, 1942), 314–20. The most important newspapers which continued to oppose war after the surrender of Sumter were New York *Daily News*, New York *Evening Day Book*, Columbus *Crisis*, and Dayton *Empire*. See also Perkins (ed.), *Northern Editorials on Secession*, I, 765–807.

[20] New York *Morning Express*, April 23, 1861; Alvan F. Sanborn (ed.), *Reminiscences of Richard Lathers* (New York, 1907), 168–73.

[21] Edward Everett Ms. Diary, entry for April 17, 1861; Everett to Crittenden, April 18, 1861, Crittenden Papers.

[22] Fuess, *Cushing*, II, 275–79; Peleg W. Chandler, *Memoir of Governor Andrew, With Personal Reminiscences* (Boston, 1880), 102–105.

[23] Sidney Webster to Cushing, April 17, 19, 20, 1861; Sam De Ford to *id.*, April 18, 1861, Cushing Papers.

[24] Phillips, *Speeches*, 396–414; [Garrison], *Garrison*, IV, 25–27.

national cause. It was no longer wise, he told a friend, to attack Lincoln or the northern political parties, for they were now "instruments in the hands of God to carry forward and help achieve the great object of emancipation. . . ."[25] Before long, Garrison had removed from the *Liberator* his old denunciation of the Constitution as "a covenant with death and an agreement with hell." In its place he inserted: "Proclaim Liberty throughout all the land, and to all the inhabitants thereof."[26]

The American Peace Society was equally incapable of resisting the war spirit. Individual members decided that the present conflict was unlike ordinary wars and pledged their support of the government. Gerrit Smith explained to an officer of the organization that Lincoln was merely acting against "domestic traitors and pirates." "If there are any principles of the Society forbidding this, I am not aware of them."[27] The *Advocate of Peace*, organ of the pacifists, declared that the government's policy was "a simple, rightful enforcement of the laws . . . , a work of justice."[28] Officially the Peace Society held that it was only concerned with the prevention of international wars and that it could not "countenance or tolerate rebellion." The Society suspended its lectures on peace for the duration of the war, and the movement soon collapsed.[29]

And so when the "irrepressible conflict" culminated in war it swept up every element of the Yankee population. At the start of four years of bloody strife Northerners were solidly and resolutely determined to save the Union and vindicate the authority of their government. Any other course, they were convinced, would bring personal ruin, national disaster, and untold evils to future generations. Later, when war lost its glamor amid the sordid realities of death, corruption, and reviving partisanship, this initial ardor and unanimity would pass away. But to the end the great mass of the people would continue to favor the vigorous prosecution of the struggle until final victory. Only then would Yankees pause to consider the results of the choice they had made.

[25] [Garrison], *Garrison*, IV, 14–22.   [26] *Ibid.*, 39.
[27] Harlow, *Smith*, 428–29. See also [Garrison], *Garrison*, IV, 25–27.
[28] *Advocate of Peace*, quoted in Worcester (Mass.) *Daily Spy*, May 8, 1861.
[29] Merle E. Curti, *The American Peace Crusade, 1815–1860* (Durham, 1929), 203; Whitney, *American Peace Society*, 112–13, 115; Cole, *Irrepressible Conflict*, 307–308.

2

But in the spring of 1861 the future still looked propitious. With high hopes, Yankees entered what they expected to be a brief military contest. They knew their cause was just; they were sure the country would be richer and better for the victory they would win.

Northern churches blessed what was "eminently a Christian war, to be defended upon Christian principles." [30] On the Sunday following the fall of Sumter, congregations of every religious denomination listened to sermons which summoned them to fight for the Lord. Church periodicals also called upon the faithful to rally behind the God of battles. Many church buildings became centers for the enlistment of volunteers, and clergymen often served as recruiting agents. A Rhode Island divine asserted that "religion made men loyal to the state, and prepared them to receive a call to arms . . . as they would a voice from heaven." [31] The six bishops of the Methodist Episcopal Church promptly gave their support to the Federal government. Bishop Matthew Simpson of Chicago proclaimed: "We will take our glorious flag —the flag of our country—and nail it just below the cross!" The Reverend Granville Moody of Cincinnati rejoiced that the churches had helped to precipitate the present conflict: "I believe it is true that we did bring it about, and I glory in it, for it is a wreath of glory around our brow." [32]

With the conflict thus sanctified, how could it fail to have a salubrious effect upon the American people? Surely it would bring out and strengthen their finest qualities, for in time of war the things "most noble and god-like in man's nature" would "appear in their most exalted forms." Peace was corrupting—"a na-

[30] Boston *Evening Transcript*, May 10, 1861.

[31] Chester F. Dunham, *The Attitude of the Northern Clergy toward the South, 1860–1865* (Toledo, 1942), 110–15; William W. Sweet, *The Methodist Episcopal Church and the Civil War* (Cincinnati, 1912), 70, 72–73, 76–77, 80–84, 112, 127; Cole, *Irrepressible Conflict*, 306. For sermons preached in New York on Sunday, April 21, see New York *World*, April 22, 1861. See also Cyrus A. Bartol to Bellows, April 16, 1861; Bellows to his son, April 19, 1861, Bellows Papers; Hibben, *Beecher*, 154–55.

[32] Sweet, *Methodist Episcopal Church and the Civil War*, 144, 155–57; Dunham, *Northern Clergy*, 128; Granville Moody to Chase, April 30, 1861, Chase Papers.

tion degenerates when it becomes essentially non-military." Peace "rusts the national character" and causes a country to sink into "demoralization and decay." [33] That was the danger which had threatened the United States because of its long indifference to the military virtues. But now the nation would "come out of the fire like gold purified of its dross, better and brighter than ever." [34] This struggle, said the Philadelphia *Inquirer*, was but a milestone along the road of American progress: "It is by such grand and tragic events that nations are educated and disciplined to their mission. .... Instead, therefore, of beholding in the present state of affairs indications that our glory is departed, and our existence coming to a sudden end, we regard it only as a grand trial through which the nation is passing in the course of its training for its historical mission." [35]

And because the northern people had bravely accepted their "mission," they would receive the material rewards which were their due. Inevitably the conflict would have a beneficial effect upon business. Of course many houses which depended upon the southern trade were failing, some western banks which had invested in southern state bonds were closing their doors, and the stock market was shaken by the first shock of war.[36] But these were exceptions; most Yankees anticipated a swift recovery from the recent economic depression. Western farmers would prosper by providing food for the Union armies. Eastern merchants would monopolize the trade of the West now that the Mississippi River was closed.[37] Manufacturers would benefit from profitable government contracts for military equipment. Only a few weeks after the war began, the most optimistic reports came out of the industrial and commercial cities. Military expenditures had begun to "react on the markets," and the improvement of business had become "quite marked." The war had caused a "brisk demand for goods," and "extraordinary profits" were being made. Blankets for army use had been "cleared off the market"; various New

[33] *Morning Courier and New-York Enquirer*, May 3, 1861; Philadelphia *North American and United States Gazette*, May 6, 1861; Trenton *Daily State Gazette and Republican*, April 20, 1861; Springfield (Mass.) *Daily Republican*, April 20, 1861.
[34] New York *Herald*, April 29, 1861.   [35] Philadelphia *Inquirer*, May 9, 1861.
[36] New York *Herald* (Commercial column), April 15; May 1, 1861.
[37] New York *Independent* (Commercial column), April 18, 1861.

York commercial houses had "entirely sold out" their supplies of goods. Prices were rising "immoderately." A new era of prosperity was dawning.[38] As a New York commercial paper noted, the equipment of an army was no "insignificant matter":

> . . . A great part of the sums required by the federal and state governments will come back to the pockets of our shipbuilders, manufacturers, and merchants. . . . Already we hear of numerous concerns in this city and elsewhere being driven day and night. . . . The clothing required for our troops come from eastern mills, and is made up by New York sewing machines; the leather required for harnesses come from Newark; guns and small arms can be made, if necessary, at hundreds of machine shops all over the North; the mills of Pennsylvania and Delaware will supply us with gunpowder; Wisconsin has an abundance of lead; Pennsylvania and New Jersey will send any number of iron compliments that may be required.[39]

Southerners had miscalculated when they predicted that war would bankrupt the North and that starving workers would be driven to rebellion. Instead, the conflict would "solve" the unemployment problem by providing jobs and by draining off the labor surplus for military service. Men who had no other source of income would "gladly accept the 'bounty' and the pittance per day allowed to soldiers in the American army." Thus they could "live in arms, on the loans of the rich made to the Government."[40]

After the war had been won the national economy would be established upon a firmer basis than ever before. Abolitionists and radical Republicans were determined to "assure the triumph of free labor" by removing the economic canker of slavery.[41] An organ of the Pennsylvania protectionists predicted that the war would stimulate manufacturing, convince the whole nation that

[38] *Morning Courier and New-York Enquirer*, April 27, 1861; New York *Herald*, April 16, 17, 1861; New York *Evening Post*, April 25, 1861; New York *World*, April 16, 1861; *Daily Boston Traveller*, July 10, 1861; Boston *Post*, April 30, 1861; Chicago *Daily Tribune*, April 26, 1861.

[39] New York *Commercial Advertiser*, May 3, 1861.

[40] New York *Morning Express*, April 17, 1861; New York *Herald*, April 14, 1861; Boston *Post*, April 30, 1861.

[41] Dr. Wm. F. Channing to Chase, April 22, 1861, Chase Papers.

a high tariff was sound policy, and demonstrate that a "self-reliant industry" was the "best security for peace." [42] Finally, there would be a New South working harmoniously with the enterprising North and serving as a field for Yankee genius. Eastern Virginia, for example, would emerge from her decadent past when she received "a new influx of ideas and industries, through a new population of Yankees." These migrants from the North would "thread out every inch of her magnificent harbors, and her unrivaled forests, and mark the sites of future cities and towns." They would "explore her soil, and her vast mineral treasures, . . . and teach her the arts of peace." As Virginia's "worn out First Families" gave way to a "sturdier people," a "new and glorious destiny" would open before her. [43]

In the spring of 1861 only the armies of southern rebels stood between the Yankees and these fair promises. These "fiendish murderers" and "lawless assassins" of the South were guilty of a "savage raid upon civilization." Jefferson Davis was a tyrant whose "lust for military glory" drove him to "robbery, arson, [and] piracy." [44] Southerners were "the enemies of all law, of the peace of the world," enemies so "malignant and unscrupulous" as to make decent men "regard them with horror." [45] In behalf of humanity the New York *Tribune* called for a terrible retribution: "We mean to conquer them—not merely to defeat, but to *conquer*, to SUBJUGATE them . . ." Never would traitors be permitted to "return to peaceful and contented homes"; instead they "must find poverty at their firesides, and see privation in the anxious eyes of mothers and the rags of children." [46]

Yankees went to war animated by the highest ideals of the nineteenth-century middle classes, but they waged their war in the usual spirit of vengeance. Perhaps it was that spirit which ultimately tarnished their cause. Perhaps it was the corroding influence of a long war. Perhaps it was the limitations of their social philosophy, which allowed the conflict to end with the rich richer

[42] Philadelphia *North American and United States Gazette*, June 22, 1861.
[43] New York *Times*, June 2, 1861; New York *Daily Tribune*, April 23, 1861.
[44] New York *Times*, April 26, 1861; Philadelphia *North American and United States Gazette*, April 22, 1861; Philadelphia *Press*, May 9, 1861; Providence *Daily Journal*, April 29, 1861; Cincinnati *Daily Commercial*, June 14, 1861.
[45] Philadelphia *North American and United States Gazette*, April 19, 1861.
[46] New York *Daily Tribune*, May 1, 1861.

and the slaves only half free. Nationalists might rejoice that the Union was preserved. But what the Yankees achieved—for their generation at least—was a triumph not of middle-class ideals but of middle-class vices. The most striking products of their crusade were the shoddy aristocracy of the North and the ragged children of the South. Among the masses of Americans there were no victors, only the vanquished.

Bibliography

Manuscript Materials

Robert Anderson Papers, Library of Congress.
John A. Andrew Papers, Massachusetts Historical Society, Boston.
Henry W. Bellows Papers, Massachusetts Historical Society, Boston.
John Bigelow Ms. Diary, New York Public Library.
Jeremiah S. Black Papers, Library of Congress.
Francis Preston Blair Papers, Library of Congress.
Jerome R. Brigham Papers, Historical Society of Wisconsin, Madison.
William Cullen Bryant Papers, New York Public Library.
James Buchanan Papers, Historical Society of Pennsylvania, Philadelphia.
Benjamin F. Butler Papers, Library of Congress.
Simon Cameron Papers, Library of Congress.
Zachariah Chandler Papers, Library of Congress.
Salmon P. Chase Papers, Library of Congress.
Colfax-Orth Papers, Indiana State Library, Indianapolis.
Cooper-Hewitt Papers, Library of Congress.
John J. Crittenden Papers, Library of Congress.
Benjamin R. Curtis Papers, Library of Congress.
Caleb Cushing Papers, Library of Congress.
Dana Papers, Massachusetts Historical Society, Boston.
James R. Doolittle Papers, Historical Society of Wisconsin, Madison.
Stephen A. Douglas Papers, University of Chicago Library.
Edward Everett Papers and Ms. Diary, Massachusetts Historical Society, Boston.
Thomas Ewing Papers, Library of Congress.
William P. Fessenden Papers, Library of Congress.
Hamilton Fish Papers, Library of Congress.
Giddings-Julian Papers, Library of Congress.
Horace Greeley Papers, Library of Congress.

Horace Greeley Papers, New York Public Library.
Greeley-Colfax Papers, New York Public Library.
Allan Hamilton Papers, Indiana State Library, Indianapolis.
Joseph Holt Papers, Library of Congress.
Andrew Johnson Papers, Library of Congress.
Richard Lathers Papers, Library of Congress.
Abraham Lincoln Papers (Robert Todd Lincoln Collection), Library of Congress. (Microfilms in possession of the University of California Library, Berkeley.)
George B. McClellan Papers, Library of Congress.
John McLean Papers, Library of Congress.
Edward McPherson Papers, Library of Congress.
Justin S. Morrill Papers, Library of Congress.
Samuel F. B. Morse Papers, Library of Congress.
Oliver P. Morton Papers, Indiana State Library, Indianapolis.
Godlove S. Orth Papers, Indiana State Library, Indianapolis.
Franklin Pierce Papers (photostats), Library of Congress.
Daniel D. Pratt Papers, Indiana State Library, Indianapolis.
William Schouler Papers, Massachusetts Historical Society, Boston.
Carl Schurz Papers, Library of Congress.
John Sherman Papers, Library of Congress.
Edwin M. Stanton Papers, Library of Congress.
Thaddeus Stevens Papers, Library of Congress.
Charles Sumner Papers, Widener Library, Harvard University.
Samuel J. Tilden Papers, New York Public Library.
Lyman Trumbull Papers, Library of Congress.
Martin Van Buren Papers, Library of Congress.
Benjamin F. Wade Papers, Library of Congress.
Cadwalader C. Washburn Papers, Historical Society of Wisconsin, Madison.
Elihu B. Washburne Papers, Library of Congress.
Thurlow Weed Papers, Library of Congress.
Gideon Welles Papers, Library of Congress.
Henry Wilson Papers, Library of Congress.
Cyrus Woodman Papers, Historical Society of Wisconsin, Madison.

Newspapers

Bangor *Daily Whig and Courier*
Boston *Daily Advertiser*
Boston *Daily Courier*

Boston *Daily Journal*
Boston *Evening Transcript*
Boston *Herald*
Boston *Liberator*
Boston *Post*
Daily Boston Traveller
Centreville *Indiana True Republican*
Daily Chicago Post
Chicago *Daily Tribune*
Cincinnati *Daily Commercial*
Cincinnati *Daily Gazette*
Columbus *Crisis*
Columbus *Daily Ohio Statesman*
Detroit *Free Press*
Indianapolis *Daily Journal*
Indianapolis *Indiana American*
Indianapolis *Indiana Daily State Sentinel*
Jefferson (Ohio) *Ashtabula Sentinel*
Madison *Wisconsin Daily State Journal*
Milwaukee *Daily Sentinel*
Montpelier *Vermont Patriot and State Gazette*
New Albany (Ind.) *Weekly Ledger*
New York *Commercial Advertiser*
New York *Daily Tribune*
New York *Evening Post*
New York *Herald*
New York *Independent*
New York *Journal of Commerce*
New York *Leader*
Morning Courier and New-York Enquirer
New York *Morning Express*
New York *Observer*
New York *Times*
New York *World*
Philadelphia *Daily Evening Bulletin*
Philadelphia *Inquirer*
Philadelphia *Morning Pennsylvanian*
Philadelphia *North American and United States Gazette*
Philadelphia *Press*
Philadelphia *Public Ledger*
Portland (Me.) *Eastern Argus*

Providence *Daily Journal*
Providence *Daily Post*
Springfield (Mass.) *Daily Republican*
Trenton *Daily State Gazette and Republican*
Washington *Daily National Intelligencer*
Washington *Evening Star*
Worcester (Mass.) *Daily Spy*

Contemporary Periodicals

Atlantic Monthly
Harper's New Monthly Magazine
Harper's Weekly
North American Review

Government Documents

Congressional Globe
House Executive Documents, 36 Cong., 2 Sess.
House Miscellaneous Documents, 36 Cong., 2 Sess.
Journal of the House of Representatives, 36 Cong., 2 Sess.
Journal of the Senate, 36 Cong., 2 Sess.
Official Records of the Union and Confederate Navies in the War of the Rebellion, 26 vols. (Washington, 1894–1922).
Reports of Committees of the House of Representatives, 36 Cong., 2 Sess.
Reports of Committees of the Senate, 36 Cong., 2 Sess.
Senate Miscellaneous Documents, 36 Cong., 2 Sess.
War of the Rebellion: A Compilation of the Official Records of the Union and Confederate Armies, 128 vols. (Washington, 1880–1901).

Books and Articles

[Adams, Charles Francis], "The Reign of King Cotton," *Atlantic Monthly*, VII (1861), 451–65.
Adams, Charles Francis, Jr., *Charles Francis Adams*. Boston, 1900.
——, *Charles Francis Adams, 1835–1915, An Autobiography*. Boston, 1916.
Adams, Henry, "The Secession Winter, 1860–61," Massachusetts Historical Society, *Proceedings*, XLIII (1910), 660–87.

Albion, Robert G., *The Rise of New York Port (1815–1860)*. New York, 1939.

Anderson, Frank M., *The Mystery of "A Public Man."* Minneapolis, 1948.

Angle, Paul M., ed., *Herndon's Life of Lincoln: The History and Personal Recollections of Abraham Lincoln as Originally Written by William H. Herndon and Jesse W. Weik*. New York, 1930.

——, *Lincoln, 1854–1861: Being the Day-by-Day Activities of Abraham Lincoln from January 1, 1854 to March 4, 1861*. Springfield, Ill., 1933.

——, ed., *New Letters and Papers of Lincoln*. Boston, 1930.

[Appleton's] *American Annual Cyclopaedia and Register of Important Events*. Vol. I. New York, 1862.

Arnold, Isaac N., *The Life of Abraham Lincoln*. Chicago, 1885.

Auchampaugh, Philip G., *James Buchanan and His Cabinet on the Eve of Secession*. Lancaster, Pa., 1926.

——, *Robert Tyler: Southern Rights Champion, 1847–1866*. Duluth, 1934.

Baker, George E., ed., *The Works of William H. Seward*. 5 vols. New York, 1853–1884.

Bancroft, Frederic, "The Final Efforts at Compromise, 1860–61," *Political Science Quarterly*, VI (1891), 401–23.

——, *Life of William H. Seward*. 2 vols. New York, 1900.

——, ed., *Speeches, Correspondence, and Political Papers of Carl Schurz*. 6 vols. New York, 1913.

——, and Dunning, William A., eds., *The Reminiscences of Carl Schurz*. 3 vols. New York, 1907.

Barbee, David R., and Bonham, Milledge L., Jr., eds., "Fort Sumter Again," *Mississippi Valley Historical Review*, XXVIII (1941), 63–73.

Baringer, William E., *A House Dividing: Lincoln as President Elect*. Springfield, Ill., 1945.

Barnes, Thurlow Weed, ed., *Memoir of Thurlow Weed*. Boston, 1884.

Barrett, Joseph H., *Abraham Lincoln and His Presidency*. 2 vols. Cincinnati, 1904.

Barton, William E., *The Life of Abraham Lincoln*. 2 vols. Indianapolis, 1925.

Beale, Howard K., ed., *The Diary of Edward Bates, 1859–1866*. American Historical Association, *Annual Report*, 1930, IV. Washington, 1933.

Beale, Howard K., "What Historians Have Said About the Causes of the Civil War," in Merle E. Curti, ed., *Theory and Practice in Historical Study: A Report of the Committee on Historiography*, 53–102. New York, 1946.

Beard, Charles A. and Mary R., *The Rise of American Civilization.* 2 vols. New York, 1927.

Belmont, August, *Letters, Speeches, and Addresses of August Belmont.* Privately printed, 1890.

Bigelow, John, *Retrospections of an Active Life.* 5 vols. New York, 1909–1913.

Black, Chauncey F., ed., *Essays and Speeches of Jeremiah S. Black.* New York, 1885.

Blaine, James G., *Twenty Years of Congress: From Lincoln to Garfield.* 2 vols. Norwich, Conn., 1884–1886.

Botts, John M., *The Great Rebellion: Its Secret History, Rise, Progress, and Disastrous Failure.* New York, 1866.

Boutwell, George S., *Reminiscences of Sixty Years in Public Affairs.* 2 vols. New York, 1902.

Brigance, William N., *Jeremiah Sullivan Black.* Philadelphia, 1934.

Brigham, Johnson, *James Harlan.* Iowa City, 1913.

Brummer, Sidney D., *Political History of the State of New York during the Period of the Civil War.* New York, 1911.

[Buchanan, James], *Mr. Buchanan's Administration on the Eve of the Rebellion.* New York, 1866.

Butler, Benjamin F., *Autobiography and Personal Reminiscences of Major-General Benjamin F. Butler: Butler's Book.* Boston, 1892.

Carlson, Oliver, *The Man Who Made the News: James Gordon Bennett.* New York, 1942.

Carman, Harry J., and Luthin, Reinhard H., *Lincoln and the Patronage.* New York, 1943.

Carpenter, Jesse T., *The South as a Conscious Minority, 1789–1861.* New York, 1930.

Chadwick, French E., *Causes of the Civil War.* New York, 1906.

Chandler, Peleg W., *Memoir of Governor Andrew, With Personal Reminiscences.* Boston, 1880.

Channing, Edward, *History of the United States.* 6 vols. New York, 1905–1925.

Chase, Salmon P., *Diary and Correspondence of Salmon P. Chase.* American Historical Association, *Annual Report*, 1902, II. Washington, 1903.

Chittenden, Lucius E., *Personal Reminiscences, 1840–1890*. New York, 1893.

———, *Recollections of President Lincoln and His Administration*. New York, 1891.

———, *A Report of the Debates and Proceedings in the Secret Sessions of the Conference Convention . . . Held at Washington, D.C., in February, A.D. 1861*. New York, 1864.

Clarke, Grace J., *George W. Julian*. Indianapolis, 1923.

Cochrane, William C., "The Dream of a Northwestern Confederacy," Historical Society of Wisconsin, *Proceedings*, 1916, pp. 213–53.

Cole, Arthur C., *The Era of the Civil War, 1848–1870*. Springfield, Ill., 1919.

———, *The Irrepressible Conflict, 1850–1865*. New York, 1934.

———, "Lincoln's Election an Immediate Menace to Slavery in the States?" *American Historical Review*, XXXVI (1931), 740–61.

Coleman, Mrs. Chapman, *Life of John J. Crittenden, with Selections from His Correspondence and Speeches*. 2 vols. Philadelphia, 1871.

Conkling, Alfred R., *Life and Letters of Roscoe Conkling*. New York, 1889.

Coulter, E. Merton, "Effects of Secession upon the Commerce of the Mississippi Valley," *Mississippi Valley Historical Review*, III (1916), 275–300.

Cox, Samuel S., *Three Decades of Federal Legislation, 1855 to 1885*. Providence, 1885.

Craven, Avery O., *The Coming of the Civil War*. New York, 1942.

———, "The Coming of the War between the States," *Journal of Southern History*, II (1936), 303–22.

Crawford, Samuel W., *The Genesis of the Civil War, The Story of Sumter*. New York, 1887.

Crenshaw, Ollinger, *The Slave States in the Presidential Election of 1860*. Baltimore, 1945.

Crippen, Lee F., *Simon Cameron: Ante-Bellum Years*. Oxford, Ohio, 1942.

Current, Richard N., *Old Thad Stevens: A Story of Ambition*. Madison, Wis., 1942.

Curti, Merle E., *The American Peace Crusade, 1815–1860*. Durham, 1929.

———, *The Roots of American Loyalty*. New York, 1946.

Curtis, George T., *Life of James Buchanan*. 2 vols. New York, 1883.

Curtis, George W., ed., *Correspondence of John Lathrop Motley.* 2 vols. New York, 1889.

Dana, Charles A., *Lincoln and His Cabinet.* Cleveland, 1896.

Davis, Stanton L., *Pennsylvania Politics, 1860–1863.* Cleveland, 1935.

Dennett, Tyler, ed., *Lincoln and the Civil War in the Diaries and Letters of John Hay.* New York, 1939.

"The Diary of a Public Man: Unpublished Passages of the Secret History of the American Civil War," *North American Review,* CXXIX (1879), 125–40, 259–73, 375–88, 484–96.

Dix, Morgan, comp., *Memoirs of John Adams Dix.* 2 vols. New York, 1883.

Donald, David, "Billy, You're Too Rampant," *Abraham Lincoln Quarterly,* III (1945), 375–407.

———, *Lincoln's Herndon.* New York, 1948.

Dumond, Dwight L., *Antislavery Origins of the Civil War in the United States.* Ann Arbor, 1939.

———, *The Secession Movement, 1860–1861.* New York, 1931.

———, *Southern Editorials on Secession.* New York, 1931.

Dunham, Chester F., *The Attitude of the Northern Clergy toward the South, 1860–1865.* Toledo, 1942.

Elliott, Charles W., *Winfield Scott, the Soldier and the Man.* New York, 1937.

Fahrney, Ralph R., *Horace Greeley and the Tribune in the Civil War.* Cedar Rapids, 1936.

Fessenden, Francis, *Life and Public Services of William Pitt Fessenden.* 2 vols. Boston, 1907.

Field, Henry M., *Life of David Dudley Field.* New York, 1898.

Fite, Emerson D., *The Presidential Campaign of 1860.* New York, 1911.

———, *Social and Industrial Conditions in the North during the Civil War.* New York, 1910.

Flower, Frank A., *Edwin McMasters Stanton.* Akron, 1905.

Foner, Philip S., *Business & Slavery: The New York Merchants & the Irrepressible Conflict.* Chapel Hill, 1941.

Ford, Worthington C., ed., *Letters of Henry Adams (1858–1891).* Boston, 1930.

Foulke, William D., *Life of Oliver P. Morton.* 2 vols. Indianapolis, 1899.

Freidel, Frank, *Francis Lieber: Nineteenth-Century Liberal.* Baton Rouge, 1947.

Fuess, Claude M., *The Life of Caleb Cushing.* 2 vols. New York, 1923.

[Garrison, Wendell P., and Francis J.], *William Lloyd Garrison, 1805–1879, The Story of His Life Told by His Children.* 4 vols. New York, 1885–1889.

Glover, Gilbert G., *Immediate Pre-Civil War Compromise Efforts.* Nashville, 1934.

Godwin, Parke, *A Biography of William Cullen Bryant.* 2 vols. New York, 1883.

Going, Charles B., *David Wilmot, Freesoiler.* New York, 1924.

Gorham, George C., *Life and Public Services of Edwin M. Stanton.* 2 vols. Boston, 1899.

Greeley, Horace, *The American Conflict.* 2 vols. Hartford, 1864–1866.

———, *Recollections of a Busy Life.* New York, 1868.

Gurowski, Adam, *Diary, March 4, 1861–November 2, 1862.* Boston, 1862.

Hamilton, J. G. de Roulhac, "Lincoln's Election an Immediate menace to Slavery in the States?" *American Historical Review,* XXXVII (1932), 700–11.

Hamlin, Charles E., *Life and Times of Hannibal Hamlin.* Boston, 1899.

Harlow, Ralph V., *Gerrit Smith.* New York, 1939.

Harrington, Fred H., *Fighting Politician: Major General N. P. Banks.* Philadelphia, 1948.

Harris, Wilmer C., *Public Life of Zachariah Chandler, 1851–1875.* Lansing, 1917.

Hart, Albert B., *Salmon Portland Chase.* Boston, 1899.

Hertz, Emanuel, *Abraham Lincoln, A New Portrait.* 2 vols. New York, 1931.

———, *The Hidden Lincoln: From the Letters and Papers of William H. Herndon.* New York, 1938.

Hesseltine, William B., *Civil War Prisons: A Study in War Psychology.* Columbus, 1930.

———, *Lincoln and the War Governors.* New York, 1948.

———, *The South in American History.* New York, 1943.

Hibben, Paxton, *Henry Ward Beecher.* New York, 1927.

Hoar, George F., *Autobiography of Seventy Years.* 2 vols. New York, 1903.

Hofstadter, Richard, *The American Political Tradition.* New York, 1948.

Hollister, Ovando J., *Life of Schuyler Colfax.* New York, 1886.

Howe, M. A. de Wolfe, ed., *Home Letters of General Sherman.* New York, 1909.

Hubbart, Henry C., *The Older Middle West, 1840–1880*. New York, 1936.

Hughes, Sarah F., ed., *Letters and Recollections of John Murray Forbes*. 2 vols. Boston, 1900.

Hunt, Gaillard, ed., "Narrative and Letter of William Henry Trescott, concerning Negotiations between South Carolina and President Buchanan in December, 1860," *American Historical Review*, XIII (1908), 528–56.

Hutchinson, William T., *Cyrus Hall McCormick*. 2 vols. New York, 1935.

Isely, Jeter A., *Horace Greeley and the Republican Party*. Princeton, 1947.

Johnson, Allen, *Stephen A. Douglas: A Study in American Politics*. New York, 1908.

Johnson, Gerald W., *The Secession of the Southern States*. New York, 1933.

Julian, George W., *Life of Joshua R. Giddings*. Chicago, 1892.

———, *Political Recollections, 1840 to 1872*. Chicago, 1884.

———, *Select Speeches of George W. Julian*. Cincinnati, 1867.

———, *Speeches on Political Questions, 1850–1868*. New York, 1872.

King, Horatio, *Turning on the Light: A Dispassionate Survey of President Buchanan's Administration, from 1860 to Its Close*. Philadelphia, 1895.

Klingberg, Frank W., "James Buchanan and the Crisis of the Union," *Journal of Southern History*, IX (1943), 455–74.

Knapp, Charles M., *New Jersey Politics during the Period of the Civil War and Reconstruction*. Geneva, N.Y., 1924.

Knox, Clinton E., "The Possibilities of Compromise in the Senate Committee of Thirteen and the Responsibility for Failure," *Journal of Negro History*, XVII (1932), 437–65.

Lamon, Ward H., *Life of Abraham Lincoln: From his Birth to his Inauguration as President*. Boston, 1872.

———, *Recollections of Abraham Lincoln, 1847–1865*. Washington, 1911.

Larson, Henrietta M., *Jay Cooke, Private Banker*. Cambridge, 1936.

Lippincott, Isaac, *A History of Manufactures in the Ohio Valley to the Year 1860*. Chicago, 1914.

Lothrop, Thornton K., *William Henry Seward*. Boston, 1896.

Lowell, James Russell, *Political Essays*. Boston, 1888.

[Lowell, James Russell], "E Pluribus Unum," *Atlantic Monthly*, VII (1861), 235–46.

[———], "The Pickens-and-Stealin's Rebellion," *Atlantic Monthly*, VII (1861), 757–63.

[———], "The Question of the Hour," *Atlantic Monthly*, VII (1861), 117–21.

Lowery, Lawrence T., *Northern Opinion of Approaching Secession, October, 1859–November, 1860*. Northampton, Mass., 1918.

Luthin, Reinhard H., *The First Lincoln Campaign*. Cambridge, 1944.

McClure, Alexander K., *Abraham Lincoln and Men of War-Times*. Philadelphia, 1892.

———, *Colonel Alexander K. McClure's Recollections of Half a Century*. Salem, Mass., 1902.

———, *Old Times Notes of Pennsylvania*. 2 vols. Philadelphia, 1905.

McCormack, Thomas J., ed., *Memoirs of Gustave Koerner*. 2 vols. Cedar Rapids, 1909.

McLaughlin, Andrew C., *Lewis Cass*. Boston, 1891.

McMaster, John B., *A History of the People of the United States during Lincoln's Administration*. New York, 1927.

Macartney, Clarence E., *Lincoln and His Cabinet*. New York, 1931.

Magruder, Allan B., "A Piece of Secret History: President Lincoln and the Virginia Convention of 1861," *Atlantic Monthly*, XXXV (1875), 438–45.

Marshall, Jessie A., ed., *Private and Official Correspondence of Benjamin F. Butler during the Period of the Civil War*. 5 vols. Norwood, Mass., 1917.

Meigs, Montgomery C., "General M. C. Meigs on the Conduct of the Civil War," *American Historical Review*, XXVI (1921), 285–303.

Merriam, George S., *The Life and Times of Samuel Bowles*. New York, 1885.

Miller, Alphonse B., *Thaddeus Stevens*. New York, 1939.

Milton, George Fort, *The Eve of Conflict: Stephen A. Douglas and the Needless War*. Boston, 1934.

———, "Stephen A. Douglas' Efforts for Peace," *Journal of Southern History*, I (1935), 261–75.

Moore, Frank, ed., *The Rebellion Record: A Diary of American Events, with Documents, Narratives, Illustrative Incidents, Poetry, etc*. 12 vols. New York, 1864–1868.

Moore, John Bassett, ed., *The Works of James Buchanan*. 12 vols. Philadelphia, 1908–1911.

Morehouse, Frances M. I., *The Life of Jesse W. Fell*. Urbana, Ill., 1916.

Morse, John T., Jr., ed., *Diary of Gideon Welles, Secretary of the Navy under Lincoln and Johnson*. 3 vols. Boston, 1911.

Mowry, Duane, "An Appreciation of James Rood Doolittle," Historical Society of Wisconsin, *Proceedings*, 1909, pp. 281–96.

Nevins, Allan, *Hamilton Fish: The Inner History of the Grant Administration*. New York, 1936.

New York Chamber of Commerce, *Fourth Annual Report of the Chamber of Commerce of the State of New York, for the Year 1861–62*. New York, 1862.

Nichols, Roy F., *The Disruption of American Democracy*. New York, 1948.

Nicolay, John G., *The Outbreak of Rebellion*. New York, 1881.

——, and Hay, John, *Abraham Lincoln, A History*. 10 vols. New York, 1890.

——, and ——, eds., *Complete Works of Abraham Lincoln*. 12 vols. New York, 1905.

Oberholtzer, Ellis P., *Jay Cooke: Financier of the Civil War*. 2 vols. Philadelphia, 1907.

Owsley, Frank L., "The Fundamental Cause of the Civil War: Egocentric Sectionalism," *Journal of Southern History*, VII (1941), 3–18.

Parker, William B., *The Life and Public Services of Justin Smith Morrill*. Boston, 1924.

Pearson, Henry G., *Life of John A. Andrew*. 2 vols. Boston, 1904.

——, *James S. Wadsworth of Genesoe*. New York, 1913.

Pease, Theodore C., and Randall, James G., eds., *The Diary of Orville Hickman Browning*. 2 vols. Springfield, Ill., 1927–1933.

Perkins, Howard C., "The Defense of Slavery in the Northern Press on the Eve of the Civil War," *Journal of Southern History*, IX (1943), 501–31.

——, ed., *Northern Editorials on Secession*. 2 vols. New York, 1942.

Phillips, Wendell, *Speeches, Lectures, and Letters*. Boston, 1884.

Piatt, Donn, *Memories of the Men Who Saved the Union*. New York, 1887.

Pierce, Edward L., *Memoir and Letters of Charles Sumner*. 4 vols. Boston, 1878–1893.

Pierce, Franklin, "Some Papers of Franklin Pierce, 1852–1862," *American Historical Review*, X (1905), 356–70.

Poor, Henry V., *History of the Railroads and Canals of the United States of America*. 3 vols. New York, 1860.

Porter, David D., *Incidents and Anecdotes of the Civil War*. New York, 1885.

Porter, George H., *Ohio Politics during the Civil War Period*. New York, 1911.

Potter, David M., "Horace Greeley and Peaceable Secession," *Journal of Southern History*, VII (1941), 145–59.

———, *Lincoln and His Party in the Secession Crisis*. New Haven, 1942.

Ramsdell, Charles W., "The Changing Interpretation of the Civil War," *Journal of Southern History*, III (1937), 1–25.

———, "Lincoln and Fort Sumter," *Journal of Southern History*, III (1937), 259–88.

Randall, James G., "A Blundering Generation," *Mississippi Valley Historical Review*, XXVII (1940), 3–28.

———, *The Civil War and Reconstruction*. New York, 1937.

———, "The Civil War Restudied," *Journal of Southern History*, VI (1940), 439–57.

———, *Lincoln the Liberal Statesman*. New York, 1947.

———, *Lincoln the President*, 2 vols. New York, 1945.

———, "When War Came in 1861," *Abraham Lincoln Quarterly*, I (1940), 3–42.

Rhodes, James Ford, *History of the United States from the Compromise of 1850 to the Final Restoration of Home Rule at the South in 1877*. 7 vols. New York, 1896–1919.

Richards, Laura E., ed., *Letters and Journals of Samuel G. Howe*. 2 vols. Boston, 1909.

Richardson, James D., comp., *A Compilation of the Messages and Papers of the Presidents, 1789–1897*. 10 vols. Washington, 1896–1899.

Riddle, Albert G., *The Life of Benjamin F. Wade*. Cleveland, 1886.

Roseboom, Eugene H., *The Civil War Era, 1850–1873*. Columbus, 1944.

Rusk, Ralph L., *The Letters of Ralph Waldo Emerson*. 6 vols. New York, 1939.

Russel, Robert R., *Economic Aspects of Southern Sectionalism, 1840–1861*. Urbana, Ill., 1924.

Russell, William H., *My Diary, North and South*. Boston, 1863.

Salter, William, *Life of James W. Grimes*. New York, 1876.

Sanborn, Alvan F., ed., *Reminiscences of Richard Lathers*. New York, 1907.

Sandburg, Carl, *Abraham Lincoln, The War Years*. 4 vols. New York, 1939.

Schafer, Joseph, ed., *Intimate Letters of Carl Schurz, 1841–1869*. Madison, Wis., 1928.

Schlesinger, Arthur M., *New Viewpoints in American History*. New York, 1922.

Schuckers, Jacob W., *Life and Public Services of Salmon Portland Chase*. New York, 1874.

Scott, Winfield, *Memoirs of Lieut.-General Scott, LL.D., Written by Himself*. 2 vols. New York, 1864.

Scrugham, Mary, *The Peaceable Americans of 1860–1861*. New York, 1921.

Seward, Frederick W., *Reminiscences of a War-Times Statesman and Diplomat, 1830–1915*. New York, 1916.

——, *Seward at Washington, as Senator and Secretary of State*. 2 vols. New York, 1891.

Shanks, Henry T., *The Secession Movement in Virginia, 1847–1861*. Richmond, 1934.

Sherman, John, *Recollections of Forty Years in the House, Senate and Cabinet*. 2 vols. New York, 1895.

Shryock, Richard H., "The Nationalistic Tradition of the Civil War," *South Atlantic Quarterly*, XXII (1933), 294–305.

Smith, Donnal V., *Chase and Civil War Politics*. Columbus, 1931.

Smith, Edward C., *The Borderland in the Civil War*. New York, 1927.

Smith, Theodore C., *Life and Letters of James Abram Garfield*. 2 vols. New Haven, 1925.

Smith, William E., *The Francis Preston Blair Family in Politics*. 2 vols. New York, 1933.

Stampp, Kenneth M., *Indiana Politics During the Civil War*. Indianapolis, 1949.

——, "Kentucky's Influence Upon Indiana in the Crisis of 1861," *Indiana Magazine of History*, XXXIX (1943), 263–76.

——, ed., "Letters from the Washington Peace Conference of 1861," *Journal of Southern History*, IX (1943), 395–403.

——, "Lincoln and the Strategy of Defense in the Crisis of 1861," *Journal of Southern History*, XI (1945), 297–323.

Stanton, Henry B., *Random Recollections*. New York, 1887.

Stephenson, Nathaniel W., *Lincoln: An Account of His Personal Life Especially of Its Springs of Action as Revealed and Deepened by the Ordeal of War*. Indianapolis, 1922.

Sumner, Charles, *The Works of Charles Sumner.* 15 vols. Boston, 1874–1883.

Sweet, William W., *The Methodist Episcopal Church and the Civil War.* Cincinnati, 1912.

Tarbell, Ida M., *Life of Abraham Lincoln.* 2 vols. New York, 1900.

Taylor, Frank H., *Philadelphia in the Civil War.* Philadelphia, 1913.

Thayer, William R., *Life and Letters of John Hay.* 2 vols. Boston, 1915.

Thompson, Robert M., and Wainwright, Richard, eds., *Confidential Correspondence of Gustavus Vasa Fox.* 2 vols. New York, 1918.

Thorndike, Rachel S., ed., *The Sherman Letters: Correspondence between General and Senator Sherman from 1837 to 1894.* New York, 1894.

Tilberg, W. E., "The Responsibility for the Failure of Compromise in 1860," *Historical Outlook,* XIV (1923), 85–93.

Tilley, John S., *Lincoln Takes Command.* Chapel Hill, 1941.

Tracy, Gilbert A., *Uncollected Letters of Abraham Lincoln.* Boston, 1917.

Tribune Almanac and Political Register for 1861.

Trumbull, Lyman, "Trumbull Correspondence," *Mississippi Valley Historical Review,* I (1914), 101–108.

Union Defense Committee, *The Union Defense Committee of the City of New York: Minutes, Reports, and Correspondence.* New York, 1885.

Villard, Harold G., and Oswold Garrison, eds., *Lincoln on the Eve of '61.* New York, 1941.

Villard, Henry, *Memoirs of Henry Villard.* 2 vols. Boston, 1904.

Warden, Robert B., *An Account of the Private Life and Public Services of Salmon Portland Chase.* Cincinnati, 1874.

Weed, Harriet A., ed., *Autobiography of Thurlow Weed.* Boston, 1883.

Weik, Jesse W., *The Real Lincoln.* Boston, 1922.

Welles, Gideon, "Administration of Abraham Lincoln," *Galaxy,* XXIII (1877), 5–23.

——, "Fort Sumter," *Galaxy,* X (1870), 613–37.

——, *Lincoln and Seward. Remarks upon the Memorial Address of Chas. Francis Adams, on the Late William H. Seward.* New York, 1874.

West, Richard S., *Gideon Welles, Lincoln's Navy Department.* Indianapolis, 1943.

White, Horace, *Life of Lyman Trumbull.* New York, 1913.

White, Laura A., "Charles Sumner and the Crisis of 1860–61," in Avery Craven, ed., *Essays in Honor of William E. Dodd.* Chicago, 1935.

Whitney, Edson L., *The American Peace Society.* Washington, 1928.

Williams, Charles R., ed., *Diary and Letters of Rutherford Birchard Hayes.* 5 vols. Columbus, 1922–1926.

Wilson, James H., *Life of Charles A. Dana.* New York, 1907.

Wittke, Carl, *Against the Current: The Life of Karl Heinzen (1809–80).* Chicago, 1945.

Woodburn, James A., *The Life of Thaddeus Stevens.* Indianapolis, 1913.

Woodley, Thomas F., *Great Leveler: The Life of Thaddeus Stevens.* New York, 1937.

Zorn, Roman J., "Minnesota Public Opinion and the Secession Controversy, December, 1860–April, 1861," *Mississippi Valley Historical Review,* XXXVI (1949), 435–56.

Index

paign of 1860, p. 180; urged to define his policy, 180, 182; views of, on national issues, 181; as a nationalist, 181, 184, 187, 200; belief of, in democracy, 181; and labor, 181; views of, about slavery, 181; clues to views of, about secession, 182-83; and commercial panic, 183; influence of public opinion on, 183, 186-87, 189, 286; and voluntary reconstruction, 184, 190; sees seriousness of crisis, 184, 189-90; rejects peaceful secession, 184, 200; promises to respect rights of South, 185, 194, 200; opposes compromise, 185, 201; reasons for opposing compromise, 185-86; desire to save Republican party, 186, 286; anticompromise pressure on, 186-87; accepts force as means to save Union, 187-89, 190, 200; plans to hold or retake forts, 188, 198-99, 200; advises Curtin, 188; prepares resolutions for Illinois legislature, 188; departure from Springfield, 189; distinguishes coercion from enforcement of laws, 190, 192-93; defensive strategy, 190, 191-92, 194-95, 199, 200-201, 276, 278, 284; "keynote" speech of, in Indianapolis, 192-94, 266; assassination plot in Baltimore against, 195; goes secretly to Washington, 195; meets delegates to Peace Conference, 195-96; embarrasses Seward, 196; alleged resentment of, toward Seward, 196 n.; Seward tries to dominate, 196-97, 272-73, 278-80; inauguration of, 197-98; reaction to inaugural address of, 201-203; effect of inaugural of, on secessionists, 201-202; and impatient demand for action, 236, 266-70, 276, 286; alleged secessionist plots against, 257; informed of crisis at Sumter, 264-65; committed to vigorous action, 265-66; criticism of, for "weak" policy, 266; hesitates about Sumter, 274-75; negotiates with Virginia Unionists, 275 n.; considers ways to enforce laws, 275-76; reinforces Fort Pickens, 275, 279, 283-84; negotiates with Houston, 275-76, 276 n.; seeks way to collect revenues, 276; decides to provision Sumter, 276-78; and Seward's memorandum, 279-80; motives for Sumter expedition, 280-86; expects war, 284; and responsibility for Civil War, 286; calls for volunteers, 288, 291; Douglas promises to support, 289; proclaims blockade, 290

London *Times*, 233

Louisiana, 108, 240; importance to Union, 24, 248

Lovejoy, Rep. Owen, opposes compromise, 137; devotion to antislavery, 149, 252; on importance of radicals in Republican party, 157

Low, A. A., promotes compromise, 126

Lowell, James Russell, defends coercion, 42; on Buchanan's message, 56; on evil and futility of compromise, 149; believes crisis will stimulate nationalism, 243; on significance of Sumter attack, 287

McClelland, revenue cutter, seized by Louisiana, 108

McClernand, Rep. John A., 210; accuses secessionists of coercion, 39-40; and altercation in House, 113; warns secessionists, 211

McKean, Rep. James B., 119

McKenty, Rep. Jacob K., defends Morrill Tariff, 164; ready to accept war, 210

Madison, Wis., 89

Madison *Wisconsin Daily State Journal*, on anticompromise sentiment in West, 145; on Lincoln's inaugural, 202

Maine, 87, 90, 241; amends personal-liberty law, 131

Mallory, Sen. Stephen R., proposes truce at Fort Pickens, 105

Manchester School, English, 148

Manifest Destiny, 239; and slavery expansion, 150, 167-70; menaced by secession, 240-42

Mann, A. Dudley, 229

Manning, Rev. Jacob, 250; war sermon, 89

Manufacturers, northern, injured by secession crisis, 124; work for compromise, 126, 128; aided by Morrill Tariff, 162, 164; and military contracts, 220; and patent rights, 226; fear loss of southern market, 228, 230, 231; and tariff crisis, 231, 237; support war, 290; prosper through war, 295-96

Marshall, John, 32

concessions to, opposed, 142, 147, 148, 149-50, 155, 156, 157, 167, 168-70, 185; expansion of, as "abstraction," 149-50; territories safe from, 175, 206; views of Lincoln on, 181, 185; war as a means of destroying, 247, 249-52, 292-93, 296; southern plot to reopen African slave trade, 254; see also Abolitionists

Slemmer, Lt. A. J., occupies Fort Pickens, 105

Slidell, John, 47, 105, 107, 135 n., 256

Smith, Adam, 148

Smith, Caleb B., favors evacuation of Sumter, 278

Smith, Gerrit, and peaceful secession, 247, 248; supports war, 293

Somes, Rep. Daniel E., on slavery expansion, 150; on need to save Republican party, 156; on cowardice of merchants, 218; predicts war will destroy slavery, 252

South Carolina, 23, 69, 71, 74, 76, 77, 101, 102, 104, 126, 133, 192-93, 199, 210, 228, 266, 284; and nullification, 4, 161; secession movement in, 5, 7, 13, 61, 68, 73, 69-70, 100, 106; congressmen negotiate with Buchanan, 59-61; commissioners negotiate with Buchanan, 69-73, 77-79, 80, 100-102, 113; seizure of Federal property in, 73, 78, 81; resignation of Federal officers in, 73; ready for war, 79; attack on Star of the West, 84-85; accused of starting war, 85, 107; as center of treason, 255; proposal to resettle with Northerners, 258

Spinola, F. B., coercion views of, 92

Sprague, Gov. William, 90, 202

Springfield, Ill., 98; Trumbull's speech in, 17; Lincoln in, 180, 182; Lincoln's departure from, 189

Springfield Daily Illinois State Journal, on secession of South Carolina, 69; on enforcement of the laws, 69, 188-89; equates disunion with treason, 69; relations of, with Lincoln, 69, 183, 188-89; opposes compromise, 147; and Lincoln's inaugural address, 198

Springfield (Mass.) Daily Republican, 22; doubts secession, 15; favors coercion, 41-42; claims North on defensive, 45; on Lincoln's inaugural address, 201

Stanton, Rep. Benjamin, and bill to call volunteers, 111; on enforcement of laws, 112; on defensive policy of government, 117; sponsors "force act," 118-19; proposes closing of southern ports, 119; proposes loyalty test for Washington militia, 121

Stanton, Edwin M., 77, 109; appointed Attorney General, 75-76; dispute of, with Floyd, 76-77; favors reinforcing Sumter, 104-105; urges defense of Washington, 106; supports Black, 109; intrigues with Republicans, 109

Star of the West, and attempted relief of Sumter, 80, 81, 84-85, 92, 97, 99, 100, 170, 221

State rights, inconsistency of politicians on, 3-5; sectional differences on, 32-33, 116-17; see also Secession

Stephens, Alexander H., 16; supports secession, 271

Stevens, Rep. Thaddeus, sponsors bill to close southern ports, 119; opposes compromise, 137, 139; accuses secessionists of rejecting compromise, 153

Stone, James C., 207

Sumner, Sen. Charles, 14, 19, 64, 97, 157, 162, 166, 243; silent in Senate, 65; relations with Stanton, 109; devotion to antislavery, 149; opposes compromise, 153; and peaceful secession, 247, 248

Sumter, Fort, 20, 60, 72, 75, 78, 86, 103, 205, 209, 251, 263, 273, 275 n., 294; Federal occupation of, 71, 73, 76, 78, 100; and problem of supplies, 71, 99, 102-103, 263, 264, 264 n., 272-73, 274-75, 282; demands and proposals for reinforcement, 71, 79, 80, 81, 84-85, 95, 96, 99, 100, 101, 102, 104-105, 199, 221, 222, 264, 266-70, 276-77, 278, 281; Southerners demand evacuation of, 72-73, 76-77, 79, 100-102, 271, 274; symbolic significance of, 96, 98; opposition to surrender of, 96, 97, 98, 112-13, 221, 266-70, 275, 278; proposed armistice at, 101, 102; menaced by Confederate batteries, 102, 104, 263; Anderson favors evacuation of, 264; Lincoln's policy toward, 264-65, 274-75, 276-86; rumors of evacuation of, 266, 267, 268; Seward urges evacuation of, 272-73, 278; Scott favors evacuation of, 273, 277; Seward pledges evacuation of, 273-